GO!
with Microsoft®

Office 2003
Getting Started

GO!
with Microsoft®

Office 2003
Getting Started

John Preston, Sally Preston, Robert L. Ferrett, Linda Foster-Turpen, and Alicia Vargas

Shelley Gaskin, Series Editor

Upper Saddle River, New Jersey

Library of Congress Cataloging-in-Publication Data

Go! with Microsoft Office 2003 : getting started / Shelley Gaskin... [et al.]
    p. cm.
Includes index.
  ISBN 0-13-144421-2 (alk. paper)
  1. Microsoft Office. 2. Business—Computer programs. I. Preston, John M.
HF5548.4.M525G6 2003
005.5—dc22

                                                                    2003021912

Vice President and Publisher: Natalie E. Anderson
Executive Acquisitions Editor: Jodi McPherson
Marketing Manager: Emily Williams Knight
Marketing Assistant: Nicole Beaudry
Associate Director IT Product Development: Melonie Salvati
Senior Project Manager, Editorial: Mike Ruel
Project Manager, Supplements: Melissa Edwards
Senior Media Project Manager: Cathi Profitko
Editorial Assistants: Jasmine Slowik, Jodi Bolognese, Alana Meyers
Manager, Production: Gail Steier de Acevedo
Senior Project Manager, Production: Tim Tate
Manufacturing Buyer: Tim Tate
Design Manager: Maria Lange
Art Director: Pat Smythe
Cover Designer: Brian Salisbury
Cover Photo: Steve Bloom/Getty Images, Inc.
Interior Designer: Quorum Creative Services
Interior Illustrator: Black Dot Group
Full Service Composition: Black Dot Group
Printer/Binder: Von Hoffmann Corporation
Cover Printer: Phoenix Color Corporation

Credits and acknowledgments borrowed from other sources and reproduced, with permission, in this textbook are as follows or on the appropriate page within the text.

Microsoft, Windows, PowerPoint, Outlook, FrontPage, Visual Basic, MSN, The Microsoft Network, and/or other Microsoft products referenced herein are either trademarks or registered trademarks of Microsoft Corporation in the U.S.A. and other countries. Screen shots and icons reprinted with permission from the Microsoft Corporation. This book is not sponsored or endorsed by or affiliated with Microsoft Corporation.

Microsoft and the Microsoft Office Specialist logo are trademarks or registered trademarks of Microsoft Corporation in the United States and/or other countries. Pearson Education is independent from Microsoft Corporation and not affiliated with Microsoft in any manner. This text may be used in assisting students to prepare for a Microsoft Office Specialist Exam. Neither Microsoft, its designated review company, nor Pearson Education warrants that use of this text will ensure passing the relevant exam.

10 9 8 7 6 5 4 3 2 1
ISBN 0-13-144421-2

We dedicate this book to our granddaughters, who bring us great joy and happiness: Clara and Siena & Alexis and Grace.

—John Preston, Sally Preston, and Robert L. Ferrett

I would like to dedicate this book to my awesome family. I want to thank my husband, Dave Alumbaugh, who always lets me be exactly who I am; my kids, Michael, Jordan, and Ceara, who give me hope and my drive for everything that I do; my mom, who never gives up; and my dad, who has been my light, my rock, and one of my best friends every day that I can remember. I love you all and . . . thanks for putting up with me.

—Linda Foster-Turpen

This book is lovingly dedicated to Guadalupe Perez, whose stories enriched the lives of every audience, big or small, young or old, friend or stranger.

—Alicia Vargas

This book is dedicated to my students, who inspire me every day, and to my husband, Fred Gaskin.

—Shelley Gaskin

GO!
Series for Microsoft® Office System 2003

Series Editor: Shelley Gaskin

Office
Getting Started
Brief
Intermediate
Advanced

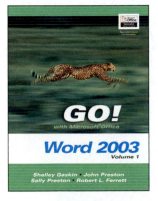

Word
Brief
Volume 1
Volume 2
Comprehensive

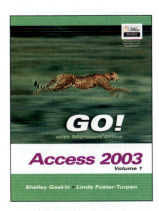

Access
Brief
Volume 1
Volume 2
Comprehensive

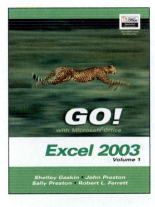

Excel
Brief
Volume 1
Volume 2
Comprehensive

PowerPoint
Brief
Volume 1
Volume 2
Comprehensive

GO! Series Reviewers

We would like to thank the following "Super Reviewers" for both their subject matter expertise and attention to detail from the instructors' perspective. Your time, effort, hard work, and diligence has helped us create the best books in the world. Prentice Hall and your author partners thank you:

Rocky Belcher	Sinclair CC
Judy Cameron	Spokane CC
Gail Cope	Sinclair CC
Larry Farrer	Guilford Tech CC
Janet Enck	Columbus State CC
Susan Fry	Boise State
Lewis Hall	Riverside CC
Jeff Howard	Finger Lakes CC
Jason Hu	Pasadena City College
Michele Hulett	Southwestern Missouri State U.
Donna Madsen	Kirkwood CC
Cheryl Reindl-Johnson	Sinclair CC
Jan Spaar	Spokane CC
Mary Ann Zlotow	College of DuPage

We would also like to thank our valuable student reviewers who bring us vital input from those who will someday study from our books:

Nicholas J. Bene	Southwestern Missouri State U.
Anup Jonathan	Southwestern Missouri State U.
Kimber Miller	Pasadena City College
Kelly Moline	Southwestern Missouri State U.
Adam Morris	Southwestern Missouri State U.
Robert Murphy	Southwestern Missouri State U.
Drucilla Owenby	Southwestern Missouri State U.
Vince Withee	Southwestern Missouri State U.

Finally, we have been lucky to have so many of you respond to review our chapter manuscripts. You have given us tremendous feedback and helped make a fantastic series. We could not have done it without you.

Abraham, Reni	Houston CC
Agatston, Ann	Agatston Consulting
Alejandro, Manuel	Southwest Texas Junior College
Ali, Farha	Lander University
Anik, Mazhar	Tiffin University
Armstrong, Gary	Shippensburg University
Bagui, Sikha	Univ. West Florida
Belton, Linda	Springfield Tech. Com College
Bennett, Judith	Sam Houston State University
Bishop, Frances	DeVry Institute- Alpharetta (ATL)
Branigan, Dave	DeVry University
Bray, Patricia	Allegany College of Maryland
Buehler, Lesley	Ohlone College
Buell, C	Central Oregon CC
Byars, Pat	Brookhaven College
Cacace, Rich	Pensacola Jr. College
Cadenhead, Charles	Brookhaven College
Calhoun, Ric	Gordon College
Carriker, Sandra	North Shore CC

Challa, Chandrashekar	Virginia State University
Chamlou, Afsaneh	NOVA Alexandria
Chapman, Pam	Wabaunsee CC
Christensen, Dan	Iowa Western CC
Conroy-Link, Janet	Holy Family College
Cosgrove, Janet	Northwestern CT Community Technical College
Cox, Rollie	Madison Area Technical College
Crawford, Hiram	Olive Harvey College
Danno, John	DeVry University/ Keller Graduate School
Davis, Phillip Md.	Del Mar College
Doroshow, Mike	Eastfield College
Douglas, Gretchen	SUNY Cortland
Driskel, Loretta	Niagara CC
Duckwiler, Carol	Wabaunsee CC
Duncan, Mimi	University of Missouri-St. Louis
Duvall, Annette	Albuquerque Technical Vocational Institute

Reviewers continues

Reviewers continued

Ecklund, Paula — Duke University
Edmondson, Jeremy — Mount Pisgah School
Erickson, John — University of South Dakota
Falkenstein, Todd — Indiana University East
Fite, Beverly — Amarillo College
Foltz, Brian — East Carolina University
Friedrichsen, Lisa — Johnson County CC
Fustos, Janos — Metro State
Gallup, Jeanette — Blinn College
Gentry, Barb — Parkland College
Gerace, Karin — St. Angela Merici School
Gerace, Tom — Tulane University
Ghajar, Homa — Oklahoma State University
Gifford, Steve — Northwest Iowa CC
Gregoryk, Kerry — Virginia Commonwealth State University

Griggs, Debra — Bellevue CC
Grimm, Carol — Palm Beach CC
Helms, Liz — Columbus State CC
Hernandez, Leticia — TCI College of Technology
Hogan, Pat — Cape Fear CC
Horvath, Carrie — Albertus Magnus College
Howard, Chris — DeVry University
Huckabay, Jamie — Austin CC
Hunt, Laura — Tulsa CC
Jacob, Sherry — Jefferson CC
Jacobs, Duane — Salt Lake CC
Johnson, Kathy — Wright College
Jones, Stacey — Benedict College
Kasai, Susumu — Salt Lake CC
Keen, Debby — Univ. of Kentucky
Kirk, Colleen — Mercy College
Kliston, Linda — Broward CC
Kramer, Ed — Northern Virginia CC
Laird, Jeff — Northeast State CC
Lange, David — Grand Valley State
LaPointe, Deb — Albuquerque TVI
Lenhart, Sheryl — Terra CC
Letavec, Chris — University of Cincinnati
Lightner, Renee — Broward CC
Lindberg, Martha — Minnesota State University
Linge, Richard — Arizona Western College
Loizeaux, Barbara — Westchester CC
Lopez, Don — Clovis- State Center CC District
Low, Willy Hui — Joliet Junior College
Lowe, Rita — Harold Washington College
Lucas, Vickie — Broward CC
Lynam, Linda — Central Missouri State University

Machuca, Wayne — College of the Sequoias
Madison, Dana — Clarion University
Maguire, Trish — Eastern New Mexico University
Malkan, Rajiv — Montgomery College
Manning, David — Northern Kentucky University
Marghitu, Daniela — Auburn University
Marks, Suzanne — Bellevue CC
Marquez, Juanita — El Centro College
Marucco, Toni — Lincoln Land CC
Mason, Lynn — Lubbock Christian University
Matutis, Audrone — Houston CC
McCannon, Melinda (Mindy) — Gordon College
McClure, Darlean — College of Sequoias
McCue, Stacy — Harrisburg Area CC
McEntire-Orbach, Teresa — Middlesex County College
McManus, Illyana — Grossmont College

Menking, Rick — Hardin-Simmons University
Meredith, Mary — U. of Louisiana at Lafayette
Mermelstein, Lisa — Baruch College
Metos, Linda — Salt Lake CC
Meurer, Daniel — University of Cincinnati
Monk, Ellen — University of Delaware
Morris, Nancy — Hudson Valley CC
Nadas, Erika — Wright College
Nadelman, Cindi — New England College
Ncube, Cathy — University of West Florida
Nicholls, Doreen — Mohawk Valley CC
Orr, Claudia — New Mexico State University
Otieno, Derek — DeVry University
Otton, Diana Hill — Chesapeake College
Oxendale, Lucia — West Virginia Institute of Technology

Paiano, Frank — Southwestern College
Proietti, Kathleen — Northern Essex CC
Pusins, Delores — HCCC
Reeves, Karen — High Point University
Rhue, Shelly — DeVry University
Richards, Karen — Maplewoods CC
Ross, Dianne — Univ. of Louisiana in Lafayette
Rousseau, Mary — Broward CC
Sams, Todd — University of Cincinnati
Sandoval, Everett — Reedley College
Sardone, Nancy — Seton Hall University
Scafide, Jean — Mississippi Gulf Coast CC
Scheeren, Judy — Westmoreland County CC
Schneider, Sol — Sam Houston State University
Scroggins, Michael — Southwest Missouri State University

Sever, Suzanne — Northwest Arkansas CC
Sheridan, Rick — California State University-Chico
Sinha, Atin — Albany State University
Smith, T. Michael — Austin CC
Smith, Tammy — Tompkins Cortland CC
Stefanelli, Greg — Carroll CC
Steiner, Ester — New Mexico State University
Sterling, Janet — Houston CC
Stroup, Tracey — Pasadena City College
Sullivan, Angela — Joliet Junior College
Szurek, Joseph — University of Pittsburgh at Greensburg

Taylor, Michael — Seattle Central CC
Thangiah, Sam — Slippery Rock University
Thompson-Sellers, Ingrid — Georgia Perimeter College
Tomasi, Erik — Baruch College
Toreson, Karen — Shoreline CC
Turgeon, Cheryl — Asnuntuck CC
Turpen, Linda — Albuquerque TVI
Upshaw, Susan — Del Mar College
Vargas, Tony — El Paso CC
Vicars, Mitzi — Hampton University
Vitrano, Mary Ellen — Palm Beach CC
Wahila, Lori — Tompkins Cortland CC
Wavle, Sharon — Tompkins Cortland CC
White, Bruce — Quinnipiac University
Willer, Ann — Solano CC
Williams, Mark — Lane CC
Wimberly, Leanne — International Academy of Design and Technology

Worthington, Paula — NOVA Woodbridge
Yauney, Annette — Herkimer CCC
Zavala, Ben — Webster Tech

About the Authors/Acknowledgments

About John Preston, Sally Preston, and Robert L. Ferrett

John Preston is an Associate Professor at Eastern Michigan University in the College of Technology, where he teaches microcomputer application courses at the undergraduate and graduate levels. He has been teaching, writing, and designing computer training courses since the advent of PCs and has authored and co-authored over 60 books on Microsoft Word, Excel, Access, and PowerPoint. He is a series editor for the *Learn 97*, *Learn 2000*, and *Learn XP* books. Two books on Microsoft Access that he co-authored with Robert Ferrett have been translated into Greek and Chinese. He has received grants from the Detroit Edison Institute and the Department of Energy to develop Web sites for energy education and alternative fuels. He has also developed one of the first Internet-based microcomputer applications courses at an accredited university. He has a BS from the University of Michigan in Physics, Mathematics, and Education and an MS from Eastern Michigan University in Physics Education. His doctoral studies were in Instructional Technology at Wayne State University.

Sally Preston is president of Preston & Associates, which provides software consulting and training. She teaches computing in a variety of settings, which provides her with ample opportunity to observe how people learn, what works best, and what challenges are present when learning a new software program. This diverse experience provides a complementary set of skills and knowledge that blends into her writing. Prior to writing for the *GO! series*, Sally was a co-author on the *Learn* series since its inception and has authored books for the *Essentials* and *Microsoft Office User Specialist (MOUS) Essentials* series. Sally has an MBA from Eastern Michigan University. When away from her computer, she is often found planting flowers in her garden.

Robert L. Ferrett recently retired as the director of the Center for Instructional Computing at Eastern Michigan University, where he provided computer training and support to faculty. He has authored or co-authored more than 60 books on Access, PowerPoint, Excel, Publisher, WordPerfect, and Word and was the editor of the *1994 ACM SIGUCCS Conference Proceedings*. He has been designing, developing, and delivering computer workshops for nearly two decades. Before writing for the *GO! series*, Bob was a series editor for the *Learn 97*, *Learn 2000*, and *Learn XP* books. He has a BA in Psychology, an MS in Geography, and an MS in Interdisciplinary Technology from Eastern Michigan University. His doctoral studies were in Instructional Technology at Wayne State University. For fun, Bob teaches a four-week Computers and Genealogy class and has written genealogy and local history books.

Acknowledgments from John Preston, Sally Preston, and Robert L. Ferrett

We would like to acknowledge the efforts of a fine team of editing professionals, with whom we have had the pleasure of working. Jodi McPherson, Jodi Bolognese, Mike Ruel, and Shelley Gaskin did a great job managing and coordinating this effort. We would also like to acknowledge the contributions of Tim Tate, Production Project Manager, and Emily Knight, Marketing Manager, as well as the many reviewers who gave invaluable criticism and suggestions.

About Linda Foster-Turpen

Linda Foster-Turpen is an instructor in Computer Information Systems at Albuquerque TVI in Albuquerque, New Mexico, where she teaches and has developed computer applications courses. Linda received her B.B.A. in Accounting as well as her M.B.A. in MIS and M.B.A. in Accounting from the University of New Mexico. She has developed new courses for her college including courses in Intranets/Extranets, Management Information Systems, and Distance Learning courses in introductory computer applications and Microsoft Access.

In addition to teaching and authoring, Linda likes to hike and backpack with her family. She lives in Corrales, New Mexico, with her husband Dave, her three children, Michael, Jordan, and Ceara, and their animals.

Acknowledgments from Linda Foster-Turpen

I would like to thank everyone at Prentice Hall (and beyond) who was involved with the production of this book. To my reviewers, your input and feedback were appreciated more than you could know. I would not want to write a book without you! To my technical editors, Jan Snyder and Mary Pascarella, thank you for your attention to detail and for your comments and suggestions during the writing of this book. A big thank you to Emily Knight in Marketing, Gail Steier de Acevedo and Tim Tate in Production, and Pat Smythe and Maria Lange in Design for your contributions. To the series editor, Shelley Gaskin, thank you for your wonderful vision for this book and the entire *GO! Series*. Your ideas and inspiration were the basis for this whole project from its inception. To the Editorial Project Manager, Mike Ruel, thanks for making sure all of my ducks were always in a row, and to the Executive Editor, Jodi McPherson, thank you for your faith and confidence in me from the beginning. A huge thanks to my students, you are the reason these books are written! I would also like to thank my colleagues at TVI for giving me a sounding board from which I could bounce ideas or just vent my frustrations. Any book takes a team of people, and I was most fortunate to have all of you on mine. I also want to thank God for . . . everything.

About Alicia Vargas

Alicia Vargas is a faculty member in Business Information Technology at Pasadena City College. She holds a master's and a bachelor's degree in Business Education from California State University, Los Angeles and has authored several textbooks and training manuals on Microsoft Word, Microsoft Excel, and Microsoft PowerPoint.

Acknowledgments from Alicia Vargas

There are many people at Prentice Hall whose dedication and commitment to educational excellence made this book possible. Among those people are Jan Snyder and Mary Pascarella, technical editors extraordinaire, whose work ensured the consistency and credibility of the manuscript; Tim Tate, Production Project Manager, and Emily Knight, Marketing Manager, whose work guaranteed the success of the final product; and Tracey Stroup, whose creative mind made many of the presentations possible. My thanks to all of you and your teams! I would also like to *especially* thank Mike Ruel, Editorial Project Manager, whose humor kept me on task and made the deadlines bearable; Shelley Gaskin, Series Editor, mentor, and friend, whose understanding of college students and their learning is the basis for this series; and Jodie McPherson, Executive Editor, whose energy and intelligence made the *GO! Series* a reality.

On a personal note, I would like to thank my parents, whose commitment to family and education became the foundation for who I am and what I do; and my family and friends whose support makes it all possible. Finally, and most importantly, I would like to thank my husband, Vic, and my three children, Victor, Phil, and Emmy. They keep me busy, they keep me laughing, but most of all, they just keep me! This one's for us!

About Shelley Gaskin

Shelley Gaskin, Series Editor, is a professor of business and computer technology at Pasadena City College in Pasadena, California. She holds a master's degree in business education from Northern Illinois University and a doctorate in adult and community education from Ball State University. Dr. Gaskin has 15 years of experience in the computer industry with several Fortune 500 companies and has developed and written training materials for custom systems applications in both the public and private sector. She is also the author of books on Microsoft Outlook and word processing.

Acknowledgments from Shelley Gaskin

Many talented individuals worked to produce this book, and I thank them for their continuous support. My Executive Acquisitions Editor, Jodi McPherson, gave me much latitude to experiment with new things. Editorial Project Manager Mike Ruel worked with me through each stage of writing and production. Emily Knight and the Prentice Hall Marketing team worked with me throughout this process to make sure both instructors and students are informed about the benefits of using this series. Also, very big thanks and appreciation goes to Prentice Halls' top-notch Production and Design team: Associate Director Product Development Melonie Salvati, Manager of Production Gail Steier de Acevedo, Senior Production Project Manager and Manufacturing Buyer Tim Tate, Design Manager Maria Lange, Art Director Pat Smythe, Interior Designer Quorum Creative Services, and Cover Designer Brian Salisbury.

Thanks to all!
Shelley Gaskin, Series Editor

Why I Wrote This Series

Dear Professor,

If you are like me, you are frantically busy trying to implement new course delivery methods (e.g., online) while also maintaining your regular campus schedule of classes and academic responsibilities. I developed this series for colleagues like you, who are long on commitment and expertise but short on time and assistance.

The primary goal of the **GO! Series**, aside from the obvious one of teaching **Microsoft® Office 2003** concepts and skills, is ease of implementation using any delivery method—traditional, self-paced, or online.

There are no lengthy passages of text; instead, bits of expository text are woven into the steps at the teachable moment. This is the point at which the student has a context within which he or she can understand the concept. A scenario-like approach is used in a manner that makes sense, but it does not attempt to have the student "pretend" to be someone else.

A key feature of this series is the use of Microsoft procedural syntax. That is, steps begin with where the action is to take place, followed by the action itself. This prevents the student from doing the right thing in the wrong place!

The *GO! Series* is written with all of your everyday classroom realities in mind. For example, in each project, the student is instructed to insert his or her name in a footer and to save the document with his or her name. Thus, unidentified printouts do not show up at the printer nor do unidentified documents get stored on the hard drives.

Finally, an overriding consideration is that the student is not always working in a classroom with a teacher. Students frequently work at home or in a lab staffed only with instructional aides. Thus, the instruction must be error-free, clearly written, and logically arranged.

My students enjoy learning the Microsoft Office software. The goal of the instruction in the *GO! Series* is to provide students with the skills to solve business problems using the computer as a tool, for both themselves and the organizations for which they might be employed.

Thank you for using the **GO! Series for Microsoft® Office System 2003** for your students.

Regards,

Shelley Gaskin, Series Editor

Preface

Philosophy

Our overall philosophy is ease of implementation for the instructor, whether instruction is via lecture, lab, online, or partially self-paced. Right from the start, the *GO! Series* was created with constant input from professors just like you. You've told us what works, how you teach, and what we can do to make your classroom time problem free, creative, and smooth running—to allow you to concentrate on not what you are teaching from but who you are teaching to—your students. We feel that we have succeeded with the *GO! Series*. Our aim is to make this instruction high quality in both content and presentation, and the classroom management aids complete—an instructor could begin teaching the course with only 15 minutes advance notice. An instructor could leave the classroom or computer lab; students would know exactly how to proceed in the text, know exactly what to produce to demonstrate mastery of the objectives, and feel that they had achieved success in their learning. Indeed, this philosophy is essential for real-world use in today's diverse educational environment.

How did we do it?

- All steps utilize **Microsoft Procedural Syntax**. The *GO! Series* puts students where they need to be, before instructing them what to do. For example, instead of instructing students to "Save the file," we go a few steps further and phrase the instruction as "On the **Menu** bar, click **File**, then select **Save As**."

- A unique teaching system (packaged together in one easy to use **Instructor's Edition** binder set) that enables you to teach anywhere you have to—online, lab, lecture, self-paced, and so forth. The supplements are designed to save you time:

   - *Expert Demonstration Document*—A new project that mirrors the learning objectives of the in-chapter project, with a full demonstration script for you to give a lecture overview quickly and clearly.

   - *Chapter Assignment Sheets*—A sheet listing all the assignments for the chapter. An instructor can quickly insert his or her name, course information, due dates, and points.

   - *Custom Assignment Tags*—These cutout tags include a brief list of common errors that students could make on each project, with check boxes so instructors don't have to keep writing the same error description over and over! These tags serve a dual purpose: The student can do a final check to make sure all the listed items are correct, and the instructor can check off the items that need to be corrected.

- **Highlighted Overlays**—These are printed and transparent overlays that the instructor lays over the student's assignment paper to see at a glance if the student changed what he or she needed to. Coupled with the Custom Assignment Tags, this creates a "grading and scoring system" that is easy for the instructor to implement.

- **Point Counted Chapter Production Test**—Working hand-in-hand with the Expert Demonstration Document, this is a final test for the student to demonstrate mastery of the objectives.

Goals of the GO! Series

The goals of the *GO! Series* are as follows:

- Make it *easy for the instructor to implement* in any instructional setting through high-quality content and instructional aids and provide the student with a valuable, interesting, important, satisfying, and clearly defined learning experience.

- Enable true diverse delivery for today's diverse audience. The *GO! Series* employs various instructional techniques that address the needs of all types of students in all types of delivery modes.

- Provide *turn-key implementation* in the following instructional settings:

  - Traditional computer classroom—Students experience a mix of lecture and lab.

  - Online instruction—Students complete instruction at a remote location and submit assignments to the instructor electronically—questions answered by instructor through electronic queries.

  - Partially self-paced, individualized instruction—Students meet with an instructor for part of the class, and complete part of the class in a lab setting.

  - Completely self-paced, individualized instruction—Students complete all instruction in an instructor-staffed lab setting.

  - Independent self-paced, individualized instruction—Students complete all instruction in a campus lab staffed with instructional aides.

- Teach—*to maximize the moment*. The *GO! Series* is based on the Teachable Moment Theory. There are no long passages of text; instead, concepts are woven into the steps at the teachable moment. Students always know what they need to do and where to do it.

Pedagogical Approach

The *GO! Series* uses an instructional system approach that incorporates three elements:

- *Steps are written in* **Microsoft Procedural Syntax**, which prevents the student from doing the right thing but in the wrong place. This makes it easy for the instructor to teach instead of untangle. It tells the student where to go first, then what to do. For example—"On the File Menu, click Properties."

- *Instructional strategies* including five new, unique ancillary pieces to support the instructor experience. The foundation of the instructional strategies is performance based instruction that is constructed in a manner that makes it *easy for the instructor* to demonstrate the content with the GO Series Expert Demonstration Document, guide the practice by using our many end-of-chapter projects with varying guidance levels, and assess the level of mastery with tools such as our Point Counted Production Test and Custom Assignment Tags.

- *A physical design* that makes it *easy for the instructor* to answer the question, "What do they have to do?" and makes it easy for the student to answer the question, "What do I have to do?" Most importantly, you told us what was needed in the design. We held several focus groups throughout the country where we showed **you** our design drafts and let you tell us what you thought of them. We revised our design based on your input to be functional and support the classroom experience. For example, you told us that a common problem is students not realizing where a project ends. So, we added an "END. You have completed the Project" at the close of every project.

Microsoft Procedural Syntax

Do you ever do something right but in the wrong place?

That's why we've written the *GO! Series* step text using Microsoft procedural syntax. That is, the student is informed where the action should take place before describing the action to take. For example, "On the menu bar, click File," versus "Click File on the menu bar." This prevents the student from doing the right thing in the wrong place. This means that step text usually begins with a preposition—a locator—rather than a verb. Other texts often misunderstand the theory of performance-based instruction and frequently attempt to begin steps with a verb. In fact, the objectives should begin with a verb, not the steps.

The use of Microsoft procedural syntax is one of the key reasons that the *GO! Series* eases the burden for the instructor. The instructor spends less time untangling students' unnecessary actions and more time assisting students with real questions. No longer will students become frustrated and say "But I did what it said!" only to discover that, indeed, they *did* do "what it said" but in the wrong place!

Chapter Organization—Color-Coded Projects

All of the chapters in every *GO! Series* book are organized around interesting projects. Within each chapter, all of the instructional activities will cluster around these projects without any long passages of text for the student to read. Thus, every instructional activity contributes to the completion of the project to which it is associated. Students learn skills to solve real business problems; they don't waste time learning every feature the software has. The end-of-chapter material consists of additional projects with varying levels of difficulty.

The chapters are based on the following basic hierarchy:

Project Name

Objective Name (begins with a verb)

Activity Name (begins with a gerund)

Numbered Steps (begins with a preposition or a verb using Microsoft Procedural Syntax.)

Project Name ➔ **Project 1A Exploring Outlook 2003**

Objective Name ➔ **Objective 1**
Start Outlook and Identify Outlook Window Elements

Activity Name ➔ **Activity 1.1** Starting Outlook

Numbered Steps ➔ **1** On the Windows taskbar, click the Start button, determine from your instructor or lab coordinator where the Microsoft Office Outlook 2003 program is located on your system, and then click Microsoft Office Outlook 2003.

A project will have a number of objectives associated with it, and the objectives, in turn, will have one or more activities associated with them. Each activity will have a series of numbered steps. To further enhance understanding, each project, and its objectives and numbered steps, is color coded for fast, easy recognition.

In-Chapter Boxes and Elements

Within every chapter there are helpful boxes and in-line notes that aid the students in their mastery of the performance objectives. Plus, each box has a specific title—"Does Your Notes Button Look Different?" or "To Open the New Appointment Window." Our GO! Series Focus Groups told us to add box titles that indicate the information being covered in the box, and we listened!

Alert!

Does Your Notes Button Look Different?
The size of the monitor and screen resolution set on your computer controls the number of larger module buttons that appear at the bottom of the Navigation pane.

Alert! boxes do just that—they alert students to a common pitfall or spot where trouble may be encountered.

Another Way

To Open the New Appointment Window
You can create a new appointment window using one of the following techniques:

• On the menu bar, click File, point to New, and click Appointment.

• On the Calendar Standard toolbar, click the New Appointment button.

Another Way boxes explain simply "another way" of going about a task or shortcuts for saving time.

Note — Server Connection Dialog Box

If a message displays indicating that a connection to the server could not be established, click OK. Even without a mail server connection, you can still use the personal information management features of Outlook.

Notes highlight additional information pertaining to a task.

More Knowledge — Creating New Folders

A module does not have to be active in order to create new folders within it. From the Create New Folder text box, you can change the type of items that the new folder will contain and then select any location in which to place the new folder. Additionally, it is easy to move a folder created in one location to a different location.

More Knowledge is a more detailed look at a topic or task.

Organization of the GO! Series

The *GO! Series for Microsoft® Office System 2003* includes several different combinations of texts to best suit your needs.

- **Word, Excel, Access, and PowerPoint 2003** are available in the following editions:

  - **Brief:** Chapters 1–3 (1–4 for Word 2003)

  - **Volume 1:** Chapters 1–6
    ~ Microsoft Office Specialist Certification

  - **Volume 2:** Chapters 7–12 (7–8 for PowerPoint 2003)

  - **Comprehensive:** Chapters 1–12 (1–8 for PowerPoint 2003)
    ~ Microsoft Office Expert Certification for Word and Excel 2003.

- Additionally, the *GO! Series* is available in four combined **Office 2003** texts:

  - **Microsoft® Office 2003 Getting Started** contains the Windows XP Introduction and first chapter from each application (Word, Excel, Access, and PowerPoint).

  - **Microsoft® Office 2003 Brief** contains Chapters 1–3 of Excel, Access, and PowerPoint, and Chapters 1–4 of Word. Four additional supplementary "Getting Started" books are included (Internet Explorer, Computer Concepts, Windows XP, and Outlook 2003).

  - **Microsoft® Office 2003 Intermediate** contains Chapters 4–8 of Excel, Access, and PowerPoint, and Chapters 5–8 of Word.

  - **Microsoft® Office 2003 Advanced** version picks up where the Intermediate leaves off, covering advanced topics for the individual applications. This version contains Chapters 9–12 of Word, Excel, and Access.

Microsoft Office Specialist Certification

The *GO! Series* has been approved by Microsoft for use in preparing for the Microsoft Office Specialist exams. The Microsoft Office Specialist program is globally recognized as the standard for demonstrating desktop skills with the Microsoft Office System of business productivity applications (Microsoft Word, Microsoft Excel, Microsoft Access, Microsoft PowerPoint, and Microsoft Outlook). With Microsoft Office Specialist certification, thousands of people have demonstrated increased productivity and have proved their ability to utilize the advanced functionality of these Microsoft applications.

Instructor and Student Resources

Instructor's Resource Center and Instructor's Edition

The *GO! Series* was designed for you—instructors who are long on commitment and short on time. *We asked you how you use our books and supplements and how we can make it easier for you and save you valuable time.* We listened to what you told us and created this Instructor's Resource Center for you—different from anything you have ever had access to from other texts and publishers.

What is the Instructor's Edition?

1) Instructor's Edition

New from Prentice Hall, exclusively for the *GO! Series*, the Instructor's Edition contains the entire book, wrapped with vital margin notes—things like objectives, a list of the files needed for the chapter, teaching tips, Microsoft Office Specialist objectives covered, and MORE! Below is a sample of the many helpful elements in the Instructor's Edition.

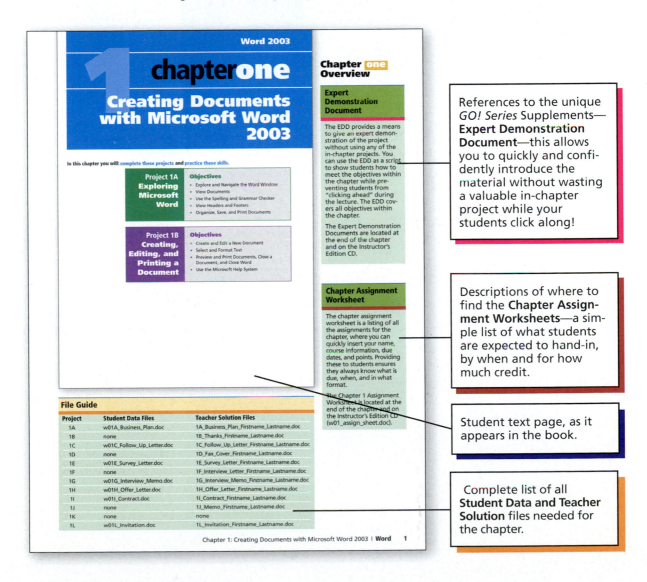

References to the unique *GO! Series* Supplements—**Expert Demonstration Document**—this allows you to quickly and confidently introduce the material without wasting a valuable in-chapter project while your students click along!

Descriptions of where to find the **Chapter Assignment Worksheets**—a simple list of what students are expected to hand-in, by when and for how much credit.

Student text page, as it appears in the book.

Complete list of all **Student Data and Teacher Solution** files needed for the chapter.

Reference to Prentice Hall's Companion Website for the *GO! Series*: **www.prenhall.com/go**

Each chapter also tells you where to find another unique *GO! Series* Supplement—the **Custom Assignment Tags**—use these in combination with the highlighted overlays to save you time! Simply check off what the students missed or if they completed all the tasks correctly.

Companion Website

CW

www.prenhall.com/go

The Companion Website is an online training tool that includes personalization features for registered instructors. Data files are available here for download as well as access to additional quizzing exercises.

Custom Assignment Tags

Custom Assignment Tags, which are meant to be cut out and attached to assignments, serve a dual purpose: the student can do a final check to make sure all the listed items are correct, and the instructor can quickly check off the items that need to be corrected and simply return the assignment.

The Chapter 1 Custom Assignment Tags are located at the end of the chapter and on the Instructor's Edition CD (w01_assign_tags.doc).

The Perfect Party

The Perfect Party store, owned by two partners, provides a wide variety of party accessories including invitations, favors, banners and flags, balloons, piñatas, etc. Party-planning services include both custom parties with pre-filled custom "goodie bags" and "parties in a box" that include everything needed to throw a theme party. Big sellers in this category are the Football and Luau themes. The owners are planning to open a second store and expand their party-planning services to include catering.

© Getty Images, Inc.

Getting Started with Microsoft Office Word 2003

Word processing is the most common program found on personal computers and one that almost everyone has a reason to use. When you learn word processing you are also learning skills and techniques that you need to work efficiently on a personal computer. Use Microsoft Word to do basic word processing tasks such as writing a memo, a report, or a letter. You can also use Word to do complex word processing tasks, including sophisticated tables, embedded graphics, and links to other documents and the Internet. Word is a program that you can learn gradually, adding more advanced skills one at a time.

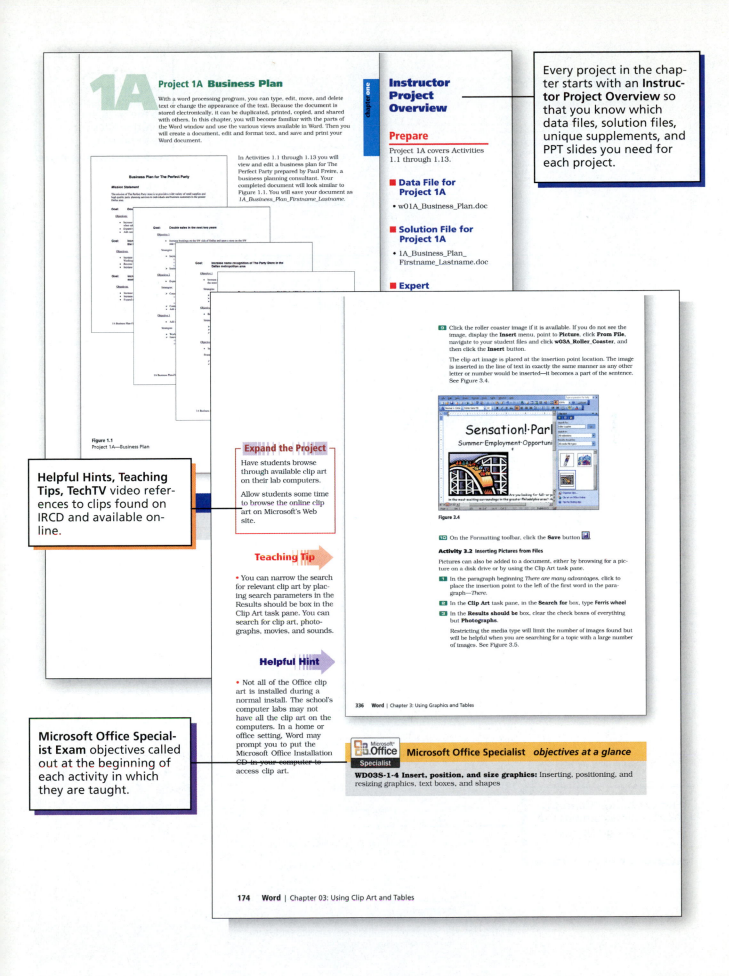

Every project in the chapter starts with an **Instructor Project Overview** so that you know which data files, solution files, unique supplements, and PPT slides you need for each project.

Helpful Hints, Teaching Tips, TechTV video references to clips found on IRCD and available online.

Microsoft Office Specialist Exam objectives called out at the beginning of each activity in which they are taught.

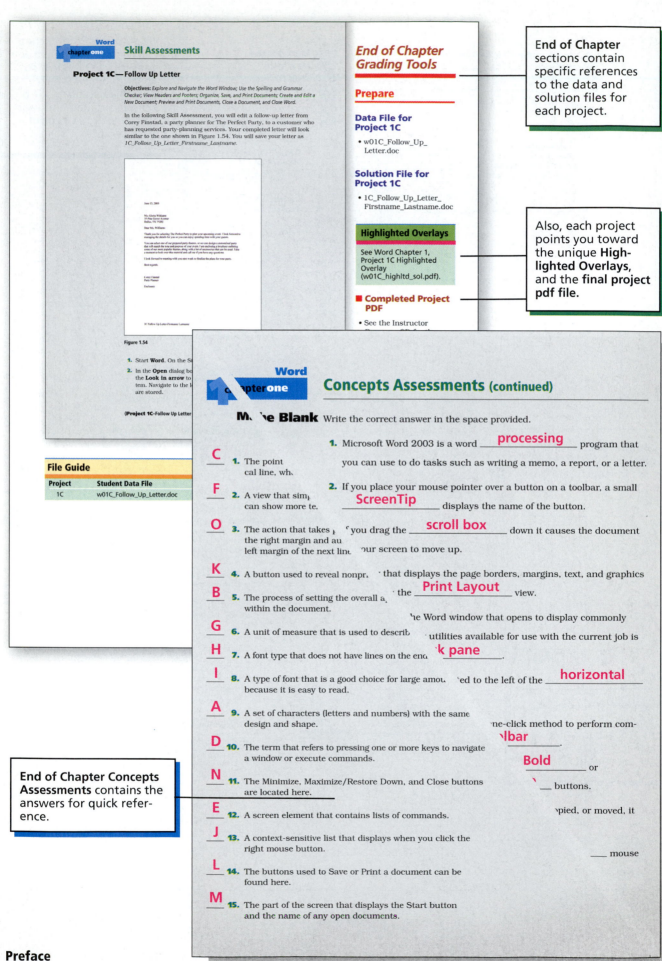

End of Chapter sections contain specific references to the data and solution files for each project.

Also, each project points you toward the unique **Highlighted Overlays**, and the **final project pdf file.**

End of Chapter Concepts Assessments contains the answers for quick reference.

Word

chapter one

Skill Assessments

Project 1C—Follow Up Letter

Objectives: Explore and Navigate the Word Window; Use the Spelling and Grammar Checker; View Headers and Footers; Organize, Save, and Print Documents; Create and Edit a New Document; Preview and Print Documents, Close a Document, and Close Word.

In the following Skill Assessment, you will edit a follow-up letter from Corey Finstad, a party planner for The Perfect Party, to a customer who has requested party-planning services. Your completed letter will look similar to the one shown in Figure 1.54. You will save your letter as *1C_Follow_Up_Letter_Firstname_Lastname.*

Figure 1.54

1. Start **Word**. On the S...
2. In the **Open** dialog bo... the **Look in arrow** to... tem. Navigate to the l... are stored.

(Project 1C–Follow Up Letter...

File Guide

Project	Student Data File
1C	w01C_Follow_Up_Letter.doc

End of Chapter Grading Tools

Prepare

Data File for Project 1C
- w01C_Follow_Up_ Letter.doc

Solution File for Project 1C
- 1C_Follow_Up_Letter_ Firstname_Lastname.doc

Highlighted Overlays

See Word Chapter 1, Project 1C Highlighted Overlay (w01C_highltd_sol.pdf).

■ **Completed Project PDF**
- See the Instructor...

Word

chapter one

Concepts Assessments (continued)

Fill the Blank Write the correct answer in the space provided.

C ____ 1. The point... cal line, wh...

F ____ 2. A view that simp... can show more te...

O ____ 3. The action that takes... you drag the ____ **scroll box** ____ down it causes the document the right margin and au... left margin of the next line... ur screen to move up.

K ____ 4. A button used to reveal nonpr... that displays the page borders, margins, text, and graphics ____ the **Print Layout** ____ view.

B ____ 5. The process of setting the overall a... within the document.

G ____ 6. A unit of measure that is used to describ... utilities available for use with the current job is

H ____ 7. A font type that does not have lines on the end... k pane ____ .

I ____ 8. A type of font that is a good choice for large amou... 'ed to the left of the ____ **horizontal** because it is easy to read.

A ____ 9. A set of characters (letters and numbers) with the same design and shape. ne-click method to perform com-

D ____ 10. The term that refers to pressing one or more keys to navigate a window or execute commands. lbar

N ____ 11. The Minimize, Maximize/Restore Down, and Close buttons are located here. **Bold** ____ or ____ buttons.

E ____ 12. A screen element that contains lists of commands. ...pied, or moved, it

J ____ 13. A context-sensitive list that displays when you click the right mouse button.

L ____ 14. The buttons used to Save or Print a document can be found here. ____ mouse

M ____ 15. The part of the screen that displays the Start button and the name of any open documents.

1. Microsoft Word 2003 is a word ____ **processing** ____ program that you can use to do tasks such as writing a memo, a report, or a letter.

2. If you place your mouse pointer over a button on a toolbar, a small ____ **ScreenTip** ____ displays the name of the button.

Chapter summary pages contain links to Glossary and Key Terms, as well as information about Online Courses and Prentice Hall's Train and Assess Generation IT—online training and assessment.

Another supplement exclusive to the *GO! Series* is the **Point Counted Production Test.** Reminders are put on each chapter summary page, the printed documents are provided in the back of each chapter, and we also provide electronic versions in Word format on the IE CD-ROM for easy customization.

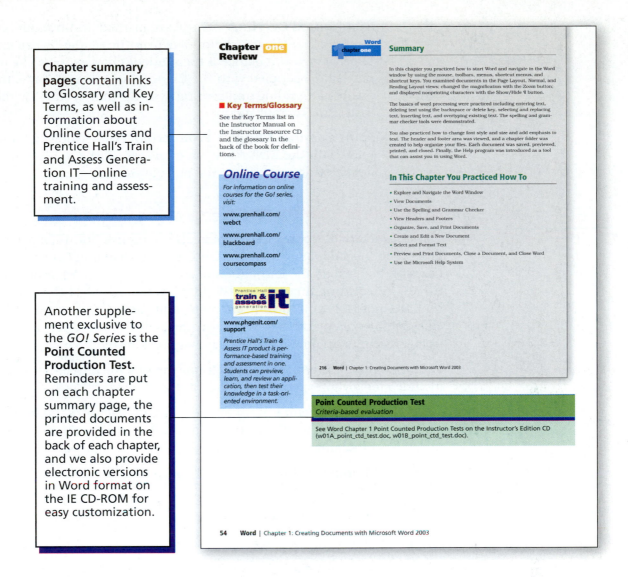

The Instructor's Edition also contains printed copies of these supplement materials *unique* to the *GO! Series*:

- *Expert Demonstration Document (EDD)*—A mirror image of each in-chapter project, accompanied by a brief script. The instructor can use it to give an expert demonstration of each objective that will be covered in the chapter, without having to use one of the chapter's projects. This EDD also prevents students from "working ahead during the presentation," as they do not have access to this document/project.

- *Chapter Assignment Sheets*—With a sheet listing all the assignments for the chapter, the instructor can quickly insert his or her name, course information, due dates, and points.

- *Custom Assignment Tags*—These cutout tags include a brief list of common errors that students could make on each project, with check boxes so instructors don't have to keep writing the same error description over and over! These tags serve a dual purpose: The student can do a final check to make sure all the listed items are correct, and the instructor can check off the items that need to be corrected.

- *Highlighted Overlays*—These are printed and transparent overlays that the instructor lays over the student's assignment paper to see at a glance if the student changed what he or she needed to. Coupled with the Custom Assignment Tags, this creates a "grading and scoring system" that is easy for the instructor to implement.

- *Point Counted Chapter Production Test*—Working hand-in-hand with the EDD, this is a final test for the student to demonstrate mastery of the objectives.

2) Enhanced Instructor's Resource CD-ROM

The Instructor's Resource CD-ROM is an interactive library of assets and links. The Instructor's Resource CD-ROM writes custom "index" pages that can be used as the foundation of a class presentation or online lecture. By navigating through the CD-ROM, you can collect the materials that are most relevant to your interests, edit them to create powerful class lectures, copy them to your own computer's hard drive, and/or upload them to an online course management system.

The new and improved Prentice Hall Instructor's Resource CD-ROM includes tools you expect from a Prentice Hall text:

- The Instructor's Manual in Word and PDF formats—includes solutions to all questions and exercises from the book and Companion Website

- Multiple, customizable PowerPoint slide presentations for each chapter

- Data and Solution Files

- Complete Test Bank

- Image library of all figures from the text

- TestGen Software with QuizMaster

  - TestGen is a test generator that lets you view and easily edit test bank questions, transfer them to tests, and print in a variety of formats suitable to your teaching situation. The program also offers many options for organizing and displaying test banks and tests. A built-in random number and text generator makes it ideal for creating multiple versions of tests that involve calculations and provides more possible test items than test bank questions. Powerful search and sort functions let you easily locate questions and arrange them in the order you prefer.

  - QuizMaster allows students to take tests created with TestGen on a local area network. The QuizMaster utility built into TestGen lets instructors view student records and print a variety of reports. Building tests is easy with TestGen, and exams can be easily uploaded into WebCT, Blackboard, and CourseCompass.

3) Instructor's Edition CD-ROM

The Instructor's Edition CD-ROM contains PDF versions of the Instructor's Edition as well as Word versions of the *GO! Series* unique supplements for easy instructor customization.

Training and Assessment— www2.phgenit.com/support

 Prentice Hall offers performance-based training and assessment in one product— Train&Assess IT. The training component offers computer-based training that a student can use to preview, learn, and review Microsoft Office application skills. Web or CD-ROM delivered, Train IT offers interactive, multimedia, computer-based training to augment classroom learning. Built-in prescriptive testing suggests a study path based not only on student test results but also on the specific textbook chosen for the course.

The assessment component offers computer-based testing that shares the same user interface as Train IT and is used to evaluate a student's knowledge about specific topics in Word, Excel, Access, PowerPoint, Outlook, the Internet, and Computing Concepts. It does this in a task-oriented environment to demonstrate proficiency as well as comprehension of the topics by the students. More extensive than the testing in Train IT, Assess IT offers more administrative features for the instructor and additional questions for the student.

Assess IT also allows professors to test students out of a course, place students in appropriate courses, and evaluate skill sets.

Companion Website @ www.prenhall.com/go

This text is accompanied by a Companion Website at www.prenhall.com/go. Features of this new site include an interactive study guide, downloadable supplements, online end-of-chapter materials, additional practice projects, Web resource links, and technology updates and bonus chapters on the latest trends and hottest topics in information technology. All links to Web exercises will be constantly updated to ensure accuracy for students.

CourseCompass— www.coursecompass.com

 CourseCompass is a dynamic, interactive online course-management tool powered exclusively for Pearson Education by Blackboard. This exciting product allows you to teach market-leading Pearson Education content in an easy-to-use, customizable format.

Blackboard— www.prenhall.com/blackboard

 Prentice Hall's abundant online content, combined with Blackboard's popular tools and interface, result in robust Web-based courses that are easy to implement, manage, and use—taking your courses to new heights in student interaction and learning.

WebCT—www.prenhall.com/webct

Course-management tools within WebCT include page tracking, progress tracking, class and student management, gradebook, communication, calendar, reporting tools, and more. Gold Level Customer Support, available exclusively to adopters of Prentice Hall courses, is provided free-of-charge on adoption and provides you with priority assistance, training discounts, and dedicated technical support.

TechTV—www.techtv.com

TechTV is the San Francisco-based cable network that showcases the smart, edgy, and unexpected side of technology. By telling stories through the prism of technology, TechTV provides programming that celebrates its viewers' passion, creativity, and lifestyle.

TechTV's programming falls into three categories:

1. **Help and Information**, with shows like *The Screen Savers*, TechTV's daily live variety show featuring everything from guest interviews and celebrities to product advice and demos; *Tech Live*, featuring the latest news on the industry's most important people, companies, products, and issues; and *Call for Help*, a live help and how-to show providing computing tips and live viewer questions.

2. **Cool Docs**, with shows like *The Tech Of...*, a series that goes behind the scenes of modern life and shows you the technology that makes things tick; *Performance*, an investigation into how technology and science are molding the perfect athlete; and *Future Fighting Machines*, a fascinating look at the technology and tactics of warfare.

3. **Outrageous Fun**, with shows like *X-Play*, exploring the latest and greatest in videogaming; and *Unscrewed* with Martin Sargent, a new late-night series showcasing the darker, funnier world of technology.

For more information, log onto www.techtv.com or contact your local cable or satellite provider to get TechTV in your area.

Visual Walk-Through

Project-based Instruction

Students do not practice features of the application; they create real projects that they will need in the real world. Projects are color coded for easy reference.

Projects are named to reflect skills the student will be practicing, not vague project names.

Word 2003

chapter**one**

Creating Documents with Microsoft Word 2003

In this chapter you will: complete these projects and practice these skills.

Project 1A
Exploring Microsoft Word

Objectives
- Explore and Navigate the Word Window
- View Documents
- Use the Spelling and Grammar Checker
- View Headers and Footers
- Organize, Save, and Print Documents

Project 1B
Creating, Editing, and Printing a Document

Objectives
- Create and Edit a New Document
- Select and Format Text
- Preview and Print Documents, Close a Document, and Close Word
- Use the Microsoft Help System

Learning Objectives

Objectives are clustered around projects. They help students to learn how to solve problems, not just learn software features.

The Greater Atlanta Job Fair

The Greater Atlanta Job Fair is a nonprofit organization that holds targeted job fairs in and around the greater Atlanta area several times each year. The fairs are widely marketed to companies nationwide and locally. The organization also presents an annual Atlanta Job Fair that draws over 2,000 employers in more than 70 industries and generally registers more than 5,000 candidates.

©Getty Images, Inc.

Getting Started with Outlook 2003

Do you sometimes find it a challenge to manage and complete all the tasks related to your job, family, and class work? Microsoft Office Outlook 2003 can help. Outlook 2003 is a personal information management program (also known as a PIM) that does two things: (1) it helps you get organized, and (2) it helps you communicate with others efficiently. Successful people know that good organizational and communication skills are important. Outlook 2003 electronically stores and organizes appointments and due dates; names, addresses, and phone numbers; to do lists; and notes. Another major use of Outlook 2003 is its e-mail and fax capabilities, along with features with which you can manage group work such as the tasks assigned to a group of coworkers. In this introduction to Microsoft Office Outlook 2003, you will explore the modules available in Outlook and enter data into each module.

Each chapter opens with a story that sets the stage for the projects the student will create, not force them to pretend to be someone or make up a scenario themselves.

Each chapter has an introductory paragraph that briefs students on what is important.

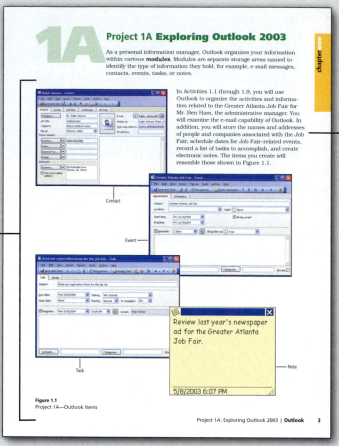

1A Project 1A Exploring Outlook 2003

As a personal information manager, Outlook organizes your information within various **modules**. Modules are separate storage areas named to identify the type of information they hold, for example, e-mail messages, contacts, events, tasks, or notes.

In Activities 1.1 through 1.9, you will use Outlook to organize the activities and information related to the Greater Atlanta Job Fair for Mr. Ben Ham, the administrative manager. You will examine the e-mail capability of Outlook. In addition, you will store the names and addresses of people and companies associated with the Job Fair, schedule dates for Job Fair–related events, record a list of tasks to accomplish, and create electronic notes. The items you create will resemble those shown in Figure 1.1.

Contact

Event

Task

Review last year's newspaper ad for the Greater Atlanta Job Fair.

5/8/2003 6:07 PM

Note

Figure 1.1
Project 1A—Outlook Items

Project 1A: Exploring Outlook 2003 | **Outlook** 3

Objective 1
Start Outlook and Identify Outlook Window Elements

Activity 1.1 Starting Outlook

1 Find out from your instructor or lab coordinator where the microsoft office 2003 program is located on your system. On the Windows taskbar, click the **Start** button, then click **Microsoft Office Outlook 2003**.

Organizations and individuals store computer programs in a variety of ways. In organizations where Outlook is used as the standard e-mail program, it may display at the top of the Start menu along with Internet Explorer. Or it may display on the All Programs list, either by itself or on a submenu associated with the Microsoft Office suite. Refer to Figure 1.2 for an example.

Microsoft Office Outlook 2003 on the Start menu

Start button

Microsoft Office Outlook 2003 on the All Programs menu

Figure 1.2

Alert! **Server Connection Dialog Box**

If a message displays indicating that a connection to the server could not be established, click OK. Even without a mail server connection, you can still use the personal information management features of Outlook.

2 If the Outlook window is not already maximized, on the Microsoft Office Outlook 2003 title bar, click the **Maximize** button.

The default and most common Outlook setup is for the Mail module to open when you start Outlook 2003. The Mail module organizes your e-mail messages into various folders.

4 **Outlook** | Chapter 1: Getting Started with Outlook 2003

Steps

Color coded to the current project, easy to read, and not too many to confuse the student or too few to be meaningless.

Sequential Page Numbering

No more confusing letters and abbreviations.

End of Project Icon

All projects in the *GO! Series* have clearly identifiable end points, useful in self-paced or on-line environments.

Microsoft Procedural Syntax

All steps are written in Microsoft Procedural Syntax in order to put the student in the right place at the right time.

Objective 5
Organize, Save, and Print Documents

In the same way that you use file folders to organize your paper documents, Windows uses a hierarchy of electronic folders to keep your electronic files organized. Check with your instructor or lab coordinator to see where you will be storing your documents (for example, on your own disk or on a network drive) and whether there is any suggested file folder arrangement. Throughout this textbook, you will be instructed to save your files using the file name followed by your first and last name. Check with your instructor to see if there is some other file naming arrangement for your course.

Activity 1.12 Creating Folders for Document Storage and Saving a Document

When you save a document file, the Windows operating system stores your document permanently on a storage medium—either a disk that you have inserted into the computer, the hard drive of your computer, or a network drive connected to your computer system. Changes that you make to existing documents, such as changing text or typing in new text, are not permanently saved until you perform a Save operation.

1. On the menu bar, click **File**, and then click **Save As**.

   The Save As dialog box displays.

2. In the **Save As** dialog box, at the right edge of the **Save in** box, click the **Save in arrow** to view a list of the drives available to you as shown in Figure 1.30. The list of drives and folders will differ from the one shown.

Figure 1.30

Activity 1.13 Printing a Document From the Toolbar

In Activity 1.13, you will print your document from the toolbar.

1. On the Standard toolbar, click the **Print** button .

   One copy of your document prints on the default printer. A total of four pages will print, and your name and file name will print in the footer area of each page.

2. On your printed copy, notice that the formatting marks designating spaces, paragraphs, and tabs, do not print.

3. From the **File** menu, click **Exit**, saving any changes if prompted to do so.

   Both the document and the Word program close.

Another Way

Printing a Document

There are two ways to print a document:

- On the Standard or Print Preview toolbar, click the Print button, which will print a single copy of the entire document on the default printer.
- From the File menu, click Print to display the Print dialog box, from which you can select a variety of different options, such as printing multiple copies, printing on a different printer, and printing some but not all pages.

End You have completed Project 1A

chapter one

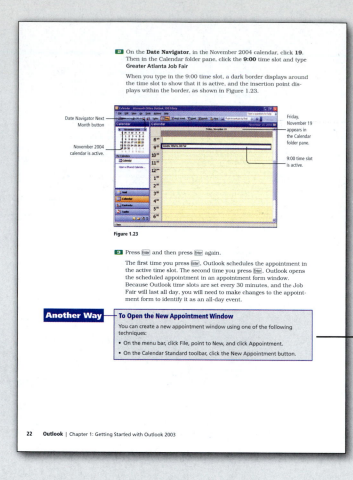

Alert box
Draws students' attention to make sure they aren't getting too far off course.

Another Way box
Shows students other ways of doing tasks.

More Knowledge box
Expands on a topic by going deeper into the material.

Note box
Points out important items to remember.

End-of-Chapter Material
Take your pick... Skills Assessment, Performance Assessment, or Mastery Assessment. Real-world projects with high, medium, or low guidance levels.

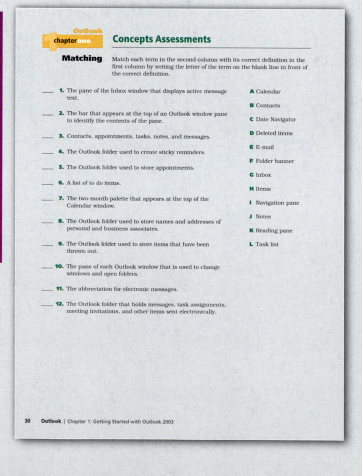

Objectives List

Each project in the GO! Series end-of-chapter section starts with a list of the objectives covered, in order to easily find the exercises you need to hone your skills.

Performance Assessments

Project 1D — Creating Folders for College Fairs

Objectives: *Start Outlook and Create Outlook Folders.*

The fairs for Mercer College and Georgia Tech have been set for April 2005. As a result, you need to create folders to hold vendor information for the fairs. When you have created the contact folders for these two fairs, your Contacts list will appear as in Figure 1.35.

Figure 1.35

1. Start Outlook, open the **Contacts** module, open the main **Contacts** folder, and on the menu bar, click **File**, point to **Folder**, and click **New Folder** to open the **Create New Folder** dialog box.

2. In the **Name** text box, type **Mercer College Fair 2005** ensure that **Contact Items** appears in the **Folder contains** text box, and click **OK**.

3. Repeat the procedures in Steps 1 and 2 to create another contacts folder named **Georgia Tech Fair 2005**

End You have completed Project 1D

End of Each Project Clearly Marked

Groups of steps that the student performs; the guided practice in order to master the learning objective.

On the Internet

In this section, students are directed to go out to the Internet for independent study.

On the Internet

Locating Friends on the Web

The World Wide Web not only stores information about companies, Web sites for bidding on items, and so forth, but it also contains telephone book information as well as e-mail addresses for many people—especially those who are students at universities! Search the Web for the colleges that three of your friends attend. After you locate the sites, search each university's e-mail directory for one of your friends. Then record these friends and their university e-mail addresses in your contacts list. Print a copy of each contact form as you create it.

GO! with Help

Training on Outlook

Microsoft Online has set up a series of training lessons at its online Web site. You can access Microsoft.com and review these training sessions directly from the Help menu in Outlook. In this project, you will work your way through the links on the Microsoft Web site to see what training topics they currently offer for Outlook. Log onto the required networks, connect to the Internet, and then follow these steps to complete the exercise.

1. If necessary, start Outlook. On the menu bar, click **Help** and then click **Office on Microsoft.com**.

   The Microsoft Office Online Web page opens in the default browser window.

2. On the left side of the Microsoft Office Online Web page, click the **Training** link.

   The Training Home Web page opens.

3. On the Training Home page, under Browse Training Courses, click **Outlook**.

   The Outlook Courses Web page opens.

4. On the Outlook Courses Web page list, click **Address your e-mail: Get it on the To line fast**.

   The Overview Web page displays information about the training session, identifies the goals of the session, and displays links for continuing the session. Navigation buttons appear in a grey bar toward the top of the Overview page for playing, pausing, and stopping the session. Yellow arrows appear above the navigation bar to advance to the next session page.

5. In the upper right side of the Overview page, on the gray navigation bar, click **Play**.

GO! with Help

A special section where students practice using the HELP feature of the Office application.

Contents in Brief

Table of Contents

Excel 2003

Chapter 1 Getting Started with Excel 2003 ... 131

Access 2003

Chapter 1 Getting Started with Access Databases and Tables 219

PowerPoint 2003

Chapter 1   Getting Started with PowerPoint 2003 299

1 chapterone

Getting Started with Windows XP

In this chapter, you will: practice these skills.

Project 1A
Working with Windows XP and Managing Files

Objectives

- Get Started with Windows
- Resize, Move, and Scroll Windows
- Maximize, Restore, Minimize, and Close a Window
- Create a New Folder
- Copy, Move, Rename, and Delete Files
- Find Files and Folders
- Compress Files

Getting Started with Windows XP

Windows is an **operating system** that coordinates the activities of your computer. It controls how your screen is displayed, how you open and close programs, the startup and shutdown procedures for your computer, and general navigation.

Before you can use Microsoft Office effectively, you need to have at least a basic familiarity with the Microsoft Windows operating system. You need to know how to work with the Start button and taskbar and how to open, close, move, and resize windows.

Introduction

It is important that you understand the difference between Windows (with a capital "W") and windows (with a lowercase "w"). When you see the word *Windows*, it will often be accompanied by the version, such as Windows 98, Windows NT, Windows 2000, or Windows XP (the version introduced in this chapter). These operating systems are similar and use what is known as a ***graphical user interface (GUI)***. A graphic user interface uses graphics or pictures to represent commands and actions. It also enables you to see document formatting as it looks when printed. When you see the word *Windows* with a capital *W*, it always refers to the operating system that runs the computer.

A ***window*** (lowercase "w"), on the other hand, refers to a rectangular area on the screen, sometimes the whole screen, that is used to display files or documents. A window can be opened and closed. It can also be resized and moved around the screen. You can have more than one window open at a time on the screen. These windows can overlap one another, or one window can take up the whole screen, with other windows hidden behind it. You can also reduce a window to the size of a button, to be opened and closed using only a click of the mouse.

1A

Project 1A **Working with Windows XP and Managing Files**

Using Office 2003 effectively requires a good working knowledge of the Windows XP operating system. You will need to know how to open, close, and resize a window; how to keep more than one window open at a time, and how to manage files.

In completing the exercises for Objectives 1.1 through 1.7, you will practice navigating Windows XP. You will also work with files and folders and compress and decompress files for easy file transfer. See Figure 1.1.

Files copied to the A: drive

Folders created on the A: drive

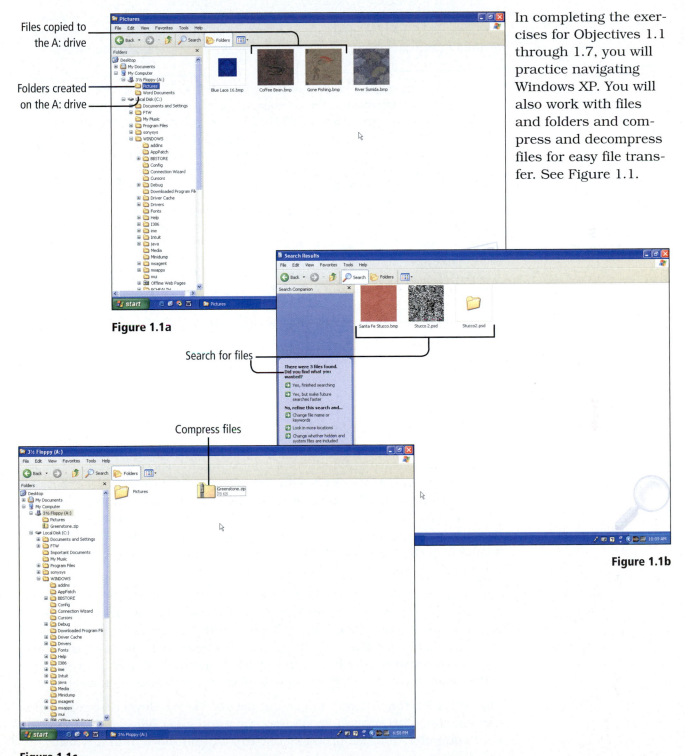

Search for files

Compress files

Figure 1.1a

Figure 1.1b

Figure 1.1c
a) Windows XP My Computer view, b) Searching for files, c) compressing ("zipping") files

chapter one

Note — **What You Need to Know First**

Much of the work you will do on a computer involves creating files. After you create a document, you need to save it before you turn off the computer. After the power is turned off, any work is lost unless it has been saved to a storage device. When you save your work, it is saved as a *file* and is usually stored on a disk drive or a network drive. Most of the time you store files on the **hard disk drive**, a **floppy disk drive**, or similar type of storage device. If you are going to become a regular computer user, you need to know how to effectively use disks to store files. You also need to know how to compress one or more files into a single file. This enables you to copy files more quickly and saves a great deal of time when you are sending files as attachments to e-mails.

Your computer's hard disk drive is the main storage device on your computer. It stores the programs that run on your computer in addition to the files that you create. A hard drive is usually identified on your computer by the notation C:\ (and sometimes D:\, E:\, and so on for additional drives). A floppy disk drive provides storage on a floppy disk and is generally identified on your computer by the notation 3½ Floppy (A:). The advantage of using a floppy disk is the ability to take the disk with you and use it in other computers.

You may also have access to files on another type of storage device, a **CD-ROM**. CD-ROM stands for Compact Disc-Read Only Memory. This is a storage device from which you can read and open files. If you are using files stored on a CD-ROM, you will need to open a file from the disc and then save it to a writable disk or copy a file from the CD-ROM to another disk and then open it. Many computers now have writable CD drives built in. They can store information on one of two types of CDs—a CD that can be written to but not erased (**CD-R**) or a CD that can be written to and erased many times (**CD-RW**).

Objective 1
Get Started with Windows

In most cases, starting Windows is an automatic procedure. You turn on your computer, and Windows (whichever version you are using) eventually appears. Some versions require that you log in, and some do not. If you are using a different version of Windows, some of the procedures used in this lesson will work differently. Also, note that Windows XP is available in two versions—a Professional Edition and a Home Edition. They are very similar, especially for basic tasks.

One of the strengths of Windows XP is its flexibility. It can be customized in endless ways. If you are working in a lab, security measures will be added to the operating system, and some of the most common Windows features may be disabled. The look of your screen will also vary, depending on the software that has been installed. Because of this, your screen will look different from the screens displayed throughout this lesson.

The **Start button** is a very important part of the Windows desktop. You can use it to start programs, set up your printer, get help, and shut down your computer. You will probably use this button more than any other.

In the following steps, you learn how to start Windows, use the mouse, and use the Start button to open a built-in calculator application.

1 Turn on your computer.

After a few seconds, a Welcome screen, also known as a Logon screen, is displayed, as shown in Figure 1.2. The exact look of the screen depends on the version of Windows being used and the number of users that have been identified. If you are working in a lab, you will probably have special instructions on how to log on to the computer.

Different users can log onto the same computer ———

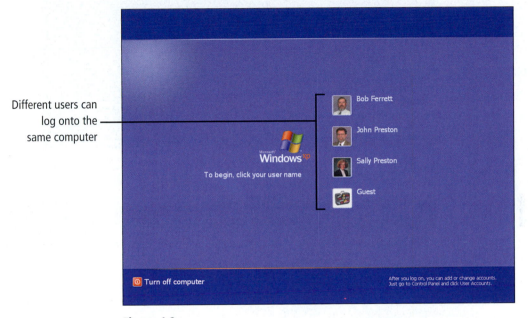

Figure 1.2

Note — If You Do Not See This Screen

If your computer is set up with only one user, you will not see this screen. Rather, the first screen will be the desktop.

2 On the **Welcome** screen, click the appropriate picture or name. If you are working in a computer lab, log on according to your instructor's directions.

The Windows desktop displays, as shown in Figure 1.3. The look of the screen will vary, depending on which version of Windows you are using. The figures in this chapter show Windows XP Home Edition. Common Windows elements are identified in the table in Figure 1.4.

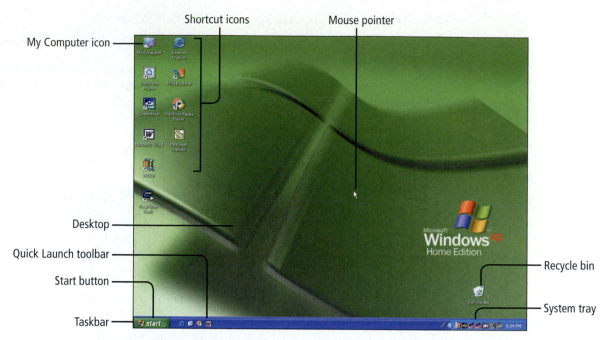

Shortcut icons
Mouse pointer
My Computer icon
Desktop
Quick Launch toolbar
Start button
Taskbar
Recycle bin
System tray

Figure 1.3

Windows Screen Elements

Element	Function
Desktop	The basic screen from which Windows and applications are run. The desktop consists of program icons, a taskbar, a Start button, and a mouse pointer.
Icon	Graphic representation; often a small image on a button that enables you to run a program or program function.
Mouse pointer	The arrow, I-beam, or other symbol that indicates a location or position on your screen. It is also called the pointer.
My Computer icon	An icon that gives you access to the files and folders on your computer.
Quick Launch toolbar	An area to the right of the Start button that contains shortcut icons for commonly used programs.
Recycle bin	A storage area for files that have been deleted. Files can be either recovered from the Recycle bin or permanently removed.
System tray	A notification area on the right side of the taskbar that keeps you informed about processes that are occurring in the background, such as antivirus software, network connections, and other utility programs. The system tray often displays the time.
Taskbar	A bar, usually at the bottom of the screen, that contains the Start button, buttons representing open programs, and other buttons that will activate programs.

Figure 1.4

Alert!

What If Your Computer Asks for a Password?

If you are using a computer in a lab or on a network, a box, called a *dialog box*, may open and ask for a username and password. In some cases, you can press Esc, press Enter, or click the Cancel button, which will bypass the security. If this doesn't work, ask your instructor or network administrator how to proceed.

More Knowledge — Taskbar Location

The taskbar may not appear at the bottom of the desktop. If you cannot see the taskbar, it may have been hidden. To see it, move the mouse pointer to the bottom of the screen. The taskbar should pop up. The taskbar also may not appear at the location shown in the figure. It may have been moved to the top or to the left or right side of the desktop.

3 Move the mouse across a flat surface such as a mouse pad to control the pointer on your screen. On the desktop, position the tip of the pointer in the center of the **My Computer** icon and click once, using the left mouse button. (If the **My Computer** icon is not visible, click the **My Documents** icon or other appropriate icon.)

The My Computer window is displayed, as shown in Figure 1.5. A window is a box that displays information or a program. Common window elements are identified in the table in Figure 1.6. When a window is open, the name of the window is displayed in the title bar and in a button on the taskbar, at the bottom of the desktop.

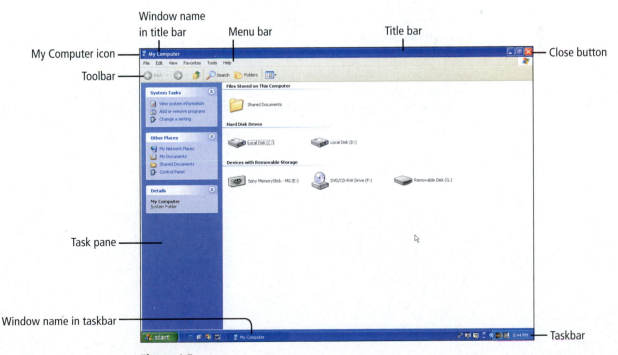

Figure 1.5

Parts of a Window

Part	Function
Menu	A list of associated commands available from a command in a menu bar or from a list opened by right-clicking an object.
Menu bar	The bar, directly beneath the title bar, that contains commands. These commands are words, not icons.
ScreenTip	A small box containing the name of a button that pops up when you pause the mouse pointer over it.
Status bar	The bar at the bottom of a window that gives additional information about the window.
Task pane	A pane that opens on the side of a window and that is used to display commonly used tools.
Title bar	The line at the top of a window that contains the name of the application and document, along with the Minimize, Maximize/Restore Down, and Close buttons.
Toolbar	The bar, usually directly beneath the menu bar, that contains commands. These commands are buttons with icons, not words.

Figure 1.6

Alert!

Did the Window Open?

If the My Computer window did not open, the single-click selected the icon. This means that Windows has been set to require a double-click to open the window. If necessary, quickly double-click the left mouse button while holding the mouse pointer steady over the icon. If this does not work, it may be that you moved the mouse while you were double-clicking the button. It may also mean that you did not click the mouse button fast enough. In either case, try again. If you are unfamiliar with a mouse, it may take a while to become proficient.

Another possible reason the My Computer window may not open is that your computer is in a lab with security installed. Some levels of security will not allow you to open the My Computer window. If this is the case, ask your instructor how to proceed.

4 In the upper right corner of the **My Computer** window title bar, click the **Close** button ![X].

The My Computer window closes. If you have difficulty identifying buttons on a window, move the mouse pointer slowly over the buttons until you can see the ScreenTip that identifies each button.

5 On the **My Computer** icon, click the right mouse button.

A *shortcut menu* displays. Shortcut menus are context-sensitive menus used to perform operations quickly without having to use a menu bar or a toolbar. A context-sensitive menu provides quick access to commands that are appropriate to the window area clicked on. On this shortcut menu, the Open command is displayed in bold because it is the default action that occurs when you double-click this icon. See Figure 1.7.

The command in bold is the default action ⟶

Shortcut menu ⟶

Figure 1.7

More Knowledge — Using Shortcut Menus

The shortcut menu you activated by clicking the right mouse button on the My Computer icon displays commands that are appropriate for the selected object. Right-clicking displays a context-sensitive menu for most objects in Windows and in Microsoft Office applications. Try right-clicking an object first instead of using a toolbar or menu. You will find shortcut menus can be great timesavers.

6 In the shortcut menu, move the mouse pointer over the word **Open**.

The Open command is highlighted, which means it is selected.

7 Click the left mouse button once. Click the disk drive that is labeled **Local Disk (C:)**.

The My Computer window displays. This action performs exactly the same task as single-clicking (or double-clicking) the icon. In both Microsoft Windows and Microsoft Office, nearly every procedure and task can be performed several ways! The specifications of the hard drive are displayed in the Details area of the task pane. If the Details area does not display any information, click the expand/collapse arrow next to Details to expand this section of the task pane. See Figure 1.8.

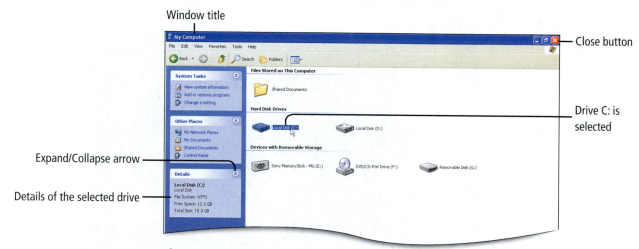

Figure 1.8

Note — Clicking the Mouse Buttons

The first five steps of this lesson demonstrate three basic techniques for using the mouse. The most common is to click once using the left mouse button. Throughout the rest of this book, when you are instructed to click the mouse, it means click the left mouse button once. To double-click the mouse means to click the left mouse button twice in rapid succession. This action is used to open programs, open files, or initiate other default actions. The third technique—right-click—uses a single click of the right mouse button. This action is used to open shortcut menus. Later you will learn how to use the mouse to click and drag.

chapter one

8 In the **My Computer** window title bar, click the **Close** button ✕.
Move the pointer to the **Start** button 🟢 **start** and click it once
using the left mouse button.

The Start menu displays. Notice that some of the commands have
arrows on the right, as shown in Figure 1.9. These arrows indicate
that a **submenu** is available for a command. A submenu is a second-
level menu. The items on the left side of the Start menu in the figure
will be different from those on your screen, and the right side will be
somewhat different. You can customize the Start menu to include
shortcuts to programs and files you use often.

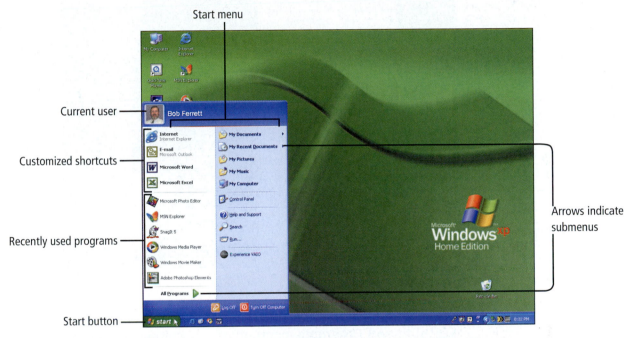

Figure 1.9

More Knowledge — Keeping Recently Used Documents Handy

The My Recent Documents menu displays files you have used recently. It is
shown by default in Windows XP Professional Edition but is not displayed in
the Home Edition. If you are using the Home Edition on your own computer,
you can turn on this useful feature using the following procedure. Right-click
the Start button and click Properties from the shortcut menu. Click the Start
Menu tab at the top of the dialog box (you will learn more about dialog
boxes later in this chapter). Click the Customize button, click the Advanced
tab at the top of the dialog box, and then click the *List my most recently
opened documents* box. Click OK twice to close both dialog boxes. If you do
not feel comfortable doing this yet, wait until you finish this chapter, and
then come back and try it!

9 In the **Start** menu, move the pointer to the **All Programs** command, but do not click the mouse button.

The All Programs menu displays. Your menu will look somewhat different from Figure 1.10 because your computer will have different programs installed. Folders in the menu contain more programs, or more folders, or some of each. Programs that were recently installed are shown with a light shaded background.

Figure 1.10

10 In the **All Programs** menu, move the pointer up to the **Accessories** command, but do not click the mouse button.

The Accessories submenu displays.

11 In the **Accessories** submenu, move the pointer down to the **Calculator** command.

The Calculator command is highlighted, as shown in Figure 1.11.

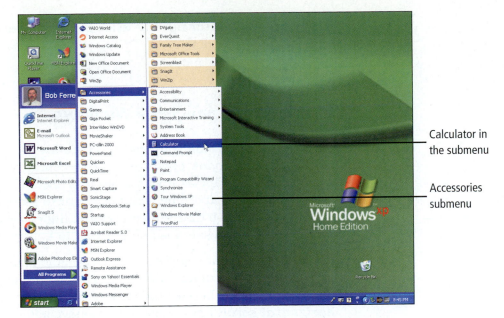

Figure 1.11

Calculator in the submenu

Accessories submenu

More Knowledge — **Using Accessories While Other Programs Are Open**

You can use the Accessories programs from the Start menu while you are using other Office programs. For example, you might want to make a quick calculation while you are typing a document in Microsoft Word. You can go to the Start button and open the calculator, make the calculation, and then place the answer in your Word document without ever closing Word.

12 Using the left mouse button, click the **Calculator** command.

The Start menu closes, and the Calculator window displays.

13 Try using the calculator. Point and click numbers and keys exactly as you would press keys on a calculator. See Figure 1.12.

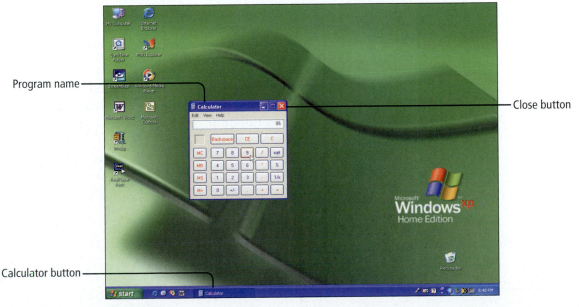

Program name

Close button

Calculator button

Figure 1.12

14 In the **Calculator** title bar, click the **Close** button ⊠ to close the calculator window.

Objective 2
Resize, Move, and Scroll Windows

Another Windows skill you need is the ability to resize and move windows. When a window opens on your screen, it generally opens in the same size and shape as it was when last used. If you are using more than one window at a time, you may want to increase or decrease the size of a window so that you can see the information you need. Moving a window on your desktop is another way to help you see what you need.

In many cases, your computer will not be able to display all the information contained in a document. Scroll bars are included if the information in a window extends beyond the right or lower edges of the window. The *horizontal scroll bar* enables you to move left and right to view information that extends beyond the left or right edge of the screen. The *vertical scroll bar* enables you to move up and down to view information that extends beyond the top or bottom of the screen.

In the following steps, you open, resize, and move the My Computer window. You also use the scroll bars in the My Computer window to look at information that does not fit on the screen.

1 On the desktop, click (or double-click) the **My Computer** icon.

The My Computer window opens.

Note — If the My Computer Window Fills the Screen

The My Computer window may open in a view that fills the screen. If this is the case, click the Restore Down button, which is the middle of three buttons on the right end of the title bar, to return the window to a smaller size.

---

2 Move the pointer to the lower right corner of the window. (You can use any of the corners for this example.)

The pointer changes to a diagonal two-headed arrow, as shown in Figure 1.13. When the mouse pointer is in this shape, you can use it to change the size and shape of the window.

Two-headed
resize pointer

Figure 1.13

3 Hold down the left mouse button, drag diagonally up and to the left, and then release the mouse button. If you are using a different corner, drag toward the opposite corner of the window.

Compare your screen with Figure 1.14. Notice that a scroll bar displays on the right side of the window. A scroll bar appears whenever the window contains more than it can display.

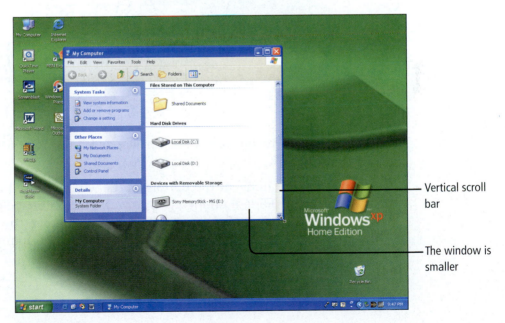

Vertical scroll
bar

The window is
smaller

Figure 1.14

4 On the **My Computer** title bar, move the pointer to a blank area.
Click and hold down the left mouse button, drag down and to the
right, and release the mouse button.

When you release the mouse button, the window drops into the new
location. See Figure 1.15.

Title bar ——— 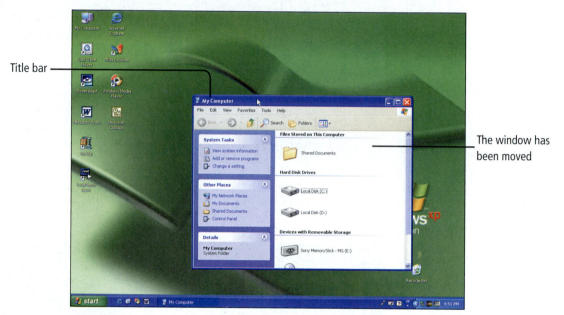 ——— The window has
been moved

Figure 1.15

5 At the bottom of the vertical scroll bar, point to the **down arrow** and
click.

The items at the bottom of the window scroll up so that you can see
the folders and icons that were not visible before, as shown in
Figure 1.16. You can click and hold down the left mouse button on
the down arrow to scroll rapidly through many items.

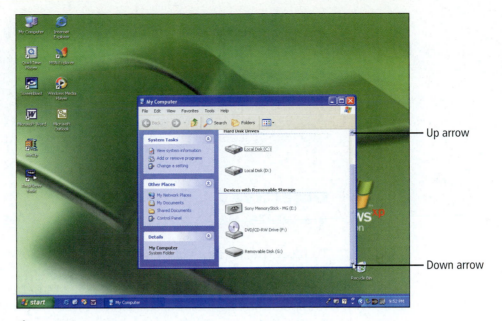

Up arrow

Down arrow

Figure 1.16

6 On the **up arrow** on the same scroll bar, click and hold down the left mouse button.

The list scrolls up until the first item is displayed.

7 In the vertical scroll bar, using the left mouse button, click the scroll box and drag down.

The ***scroll box*** enables you to move quickly up or down a window. The location of the scroll box indicates your relative location in the window. It also gives you more control as you scroll because you can see the information as it moves up or down the window. See Figure 1.17.

Scroll box

Figure 1.17

Objective 3
Maximize, Restore, Minimize, and Close a Window

To meet the previous objective, you resized the My Computer window. You can **maximize** the window, which enables the window to take up the whole screen, and **restore** the window, which takes it back to the size it was before being maximized. You can also **minimize** a window, removing it from the screen and representing it as a button on the taskbar until it is needed again.

In the following steps, you maximize, restore, minimize, and close the My Computer window.

1 In the upper right corner of the **My Computer** window, on the **My Computer** title bar, place the pointer on the **Maximize** button 🔲.

The Maximize button is the middle button in the group of three. When you point to it, a ScreenTip displays, as shown in Figure 1.18. ScreenTips tell you the name and function of a button.

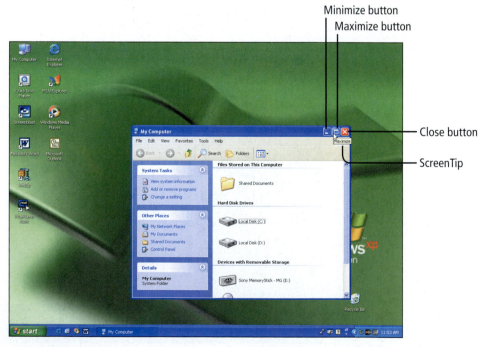

Figure 1.18

2 Using the left mouse button, click the **Maximize** button ☐.
Alternatively, you can maximize or restore a window by double-
clicking anywhere in the window's title bar.

The My Computer window now occupies the entire screen, as shown
in Figure 1.19. The Maximize button is replaced by the Restore
Down button, which has a different icon.

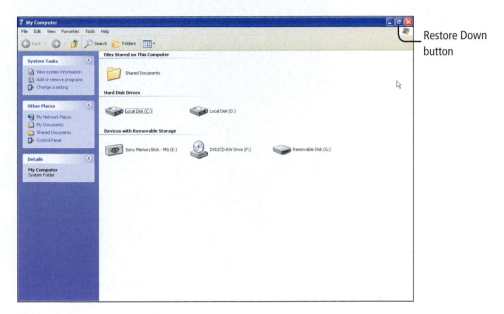

Restore Down
button

Figure 1.19

3 On the **My Computer** title bar, click the **Restore Down** button ☐.

The window returns to the size it was before you clicked the
Maximize button. See Figure 1.20.

Window restored to previous size

Minimize
button

Figure 1.20

4 On the **My Computer** title bar, click the **Minimize** button ▬.

The My Computer program is still running but the window is minimized. It is represented by a button on the taskbar at the bottom of the screen, as shown in Figure 1.21. The window has not been closed, only temporarily hidden.

Minimized window ——

Taskbar ——

Figure 1.21

5 On the taskbar, click the **My Computer** button.

The window reappears in the same location as it occupied when you clicked the Minimize button.

6 On the **My Computer** title bar, click the **Maximize** button ▢ to maximize the **My Computer** window.

The window now takes up the whole screen, as shown in Figure 1.22.

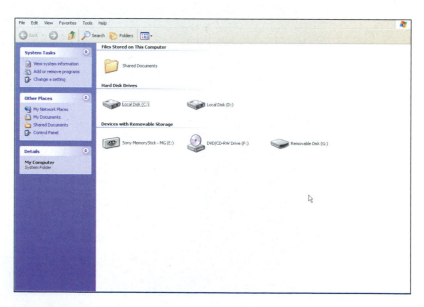

Figure 1.22

7 On the taskbar, click the **Start** button 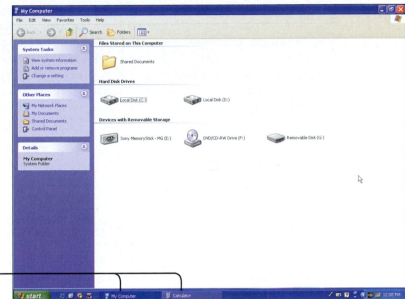, click **All Programs**, click **Accessories**, and then click **Calculator**.

The calculator program opens.

8 Click anywhere on the **My Computer** window.

Notice that the My Computer window is brought to the front. The calculator is still open, but you cannot see the calculator window. This means that you cannot click it to bring the window to the front, but you can use the taskbar. See Figure 1.23.

Two programs are running at the same time

Figure 1.23

9 On the taskbar, click the **Calculator** button.

The calculator window moves to the front and is now ready to use, as shown in Figure 1.24.

Calculator button in the taskbar

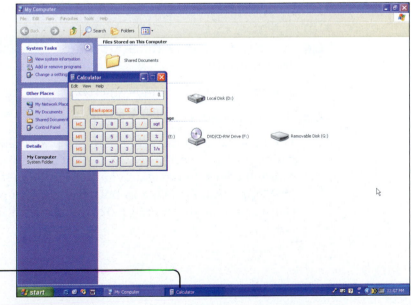

Figure 1.24

10 On the **Calculator** title bar, click the **Close** button ☒. In the **My Computer** window title bar, click the **Close** button ☒.

> **More Knowledge** — **Keeping More Than One Application Window Open at a Time**
>
> The ability to keep more than one window open at a time will become more and more important as you become more familiar with Microsoft Office. If you want to take information from two word processing documents to create a third document, you can open all three documents and use the taskbar to move back and forth among them, copying and pasting text from one document to another. You can also copy a chart from Excel and paste it into Word or take a table of data and paste it into PowerPoint. You can even have the same document open in two windows. Having multiple documents open greatly reduces the amount of time it takes to do many everyday computer tasks.

Objective 4
Create a New Folder

Folders are used to organize files or other folders. As you use the computer more and more, you will accumulate files that you want to save. If you put all the files in one place, searching for the right one might be difficult. Folders enable you to store your important files by type or by subject and make handling them more manageable. In most cases, you will use folders on hard drives or other drives that have large capacities. You can also create folders on floppy disks.

In the following steps, you will create your folders on a floppy disk. You will need to have a floppy disk available. If you are using your own computer, you might want to create the folders in the My Documents folder. If you are using a computer in a lab, you may have space assigned to you on a shared drive. You can create these folders on another drive if you wish.

1 In the taskbar, click the **Start** button ⊞ start and click **My Computer**.

The My Computer window opens.

2 On the toolbar, click the **Folders** button ▭ Folders.

The task pane changes to a Folders pane, displaying the drives and folders on your computer, as shown in Figure 1.25. This view makes it much easier to navigate your computer. The floppy drive, labeled 3½ Floppy (A:), is visible in both the Folders pane on the left and the Contents pane on the right. You can open it using either icon.

Toolbar   Folders button

The task pane becomes
a Folders pane
My Documents folder

Floppy disk drive

Contents pane

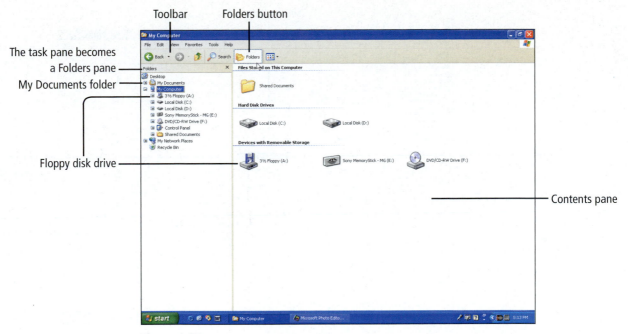

Figure 1.25

More Knowledge — Formatting a Floppy Disk

Floppy disks sometimes need to be formatted which prepares them to be used for the first time. If you want to use a disk that has previously been used in a Macintosh or you are using a disk that has been heavily used and you want to clean it up, you can reformat it by going to My Computer, right-clicking on the 3½ Floppy (A:) drive, and choosing Format from the shortcut menu.

---

3 Insert a floppy disk into drive A on your computer. In the **Folders** pane, click the **3½ Floppy (A:)** choice.

The contents of the disk in the A: drive are displayed in the Contents pane—in this case, the disk is empty.

4 In the **Contents** pane, right-click in a blank area. In the shortcut menu, move the pointer over the **New** command.

A submenu displays, showing the various items that can be created using the New command. See Figure 1.26.

Shortcut menu

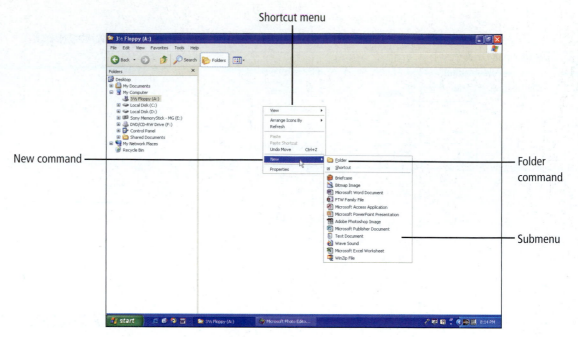

New command

Folder command

Submenu

Figure 1.26

5 Move the pointer to the **Folder** command and click it using the left mouse button.

A new folder is created with the name of the folder displayed in the edit mode, as shown in Figure 1.27.

Box around folder name indicates it is ready to be edited

New folder

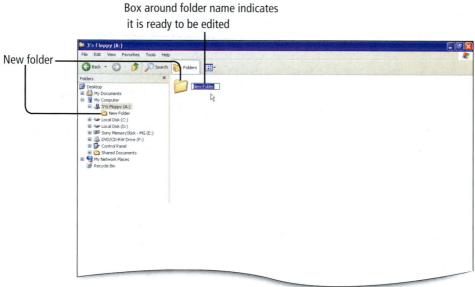

Figure 1.27

6 Over the default **New Folder** name, type **Word Documents** and press Enter.

The folder now has a meaningful name. See Figure 1.28.

Renamed folder

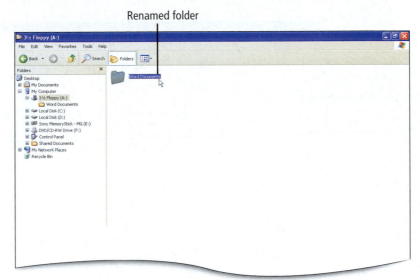

Figure 1.28

Another Way ── **Rename a Folder**

If you accidentally press Enter before you have a chance to name the folder, you can still rename it. Right-click the folder, click Rename from the shortcut menu, type a new name, and then press Enter. Alternatively, you can click the folder once, pause, and then click the folder again.

7 From the **File** menu, click **New**.

A different submenu is displayed, but it also contains the Folder command, as shown in Figure 1.29.

File command

Drop-down menu

New command

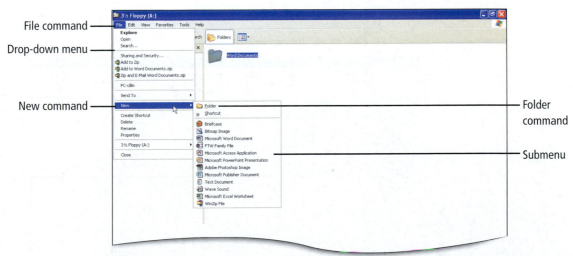

Folder command

Submenu

Figure 1.29

8 In the submenu, click **Folder**. Type **Pictures** and press ⟨Enter⟩.

You have now added two folders on your floppy disk. The folders are currently in the Icons view, but several other views are available. See Figure 1.30.

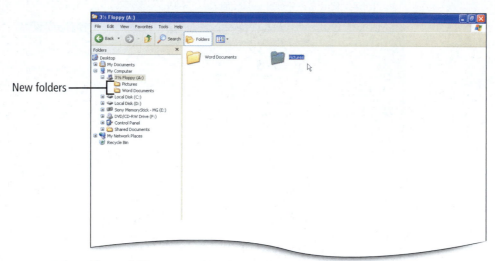

New folders

Figure 1.30

9 From the My Computer toolbar, click the **Views** button ⊞▾ and then click **Details**.

The folders display in a list format, with more information, including the date they were last modified. Notice the order in which the folders appear.

10 At the top of the Name column, click the **Name** heading, which is called a *column selector* when clicked. Click the **Name** column selector again.

The folders are sorted in alphabetical order, from *a* to *z*, as shown in Figure 1.31. Clicking the column selector again would switch the order, from *z* to *a*.

Name column selector

Views button

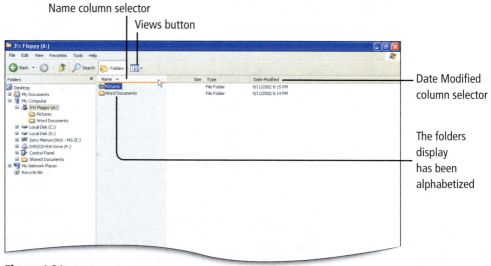

Date Modified column selector

The folders display has been alphabetized

Figure 1.31

More Knowledge — Sorting Files by Size, Date Modified, or File Type

When you sort from smallest to largest file size, the folders within the folder being sorted are listed first in alphabetical order. If you sort by size from largest to smallest, the folder names are listed last in reverse alphabetical order. To see the cumulative size of the files within a folder, right-click on the folder and click Properties.

Objective 5
Copy, Move, Rename, and Delete Files

You will often need to copy files from one location to another. As you work through this book, you will want to make copies of your files to have them as backups. You can copy a file from a hard disk to a floppy disk, a network drive, or even a recordable CD. You may also want to copy files that you have worked on in a lab so that you can put them on the hard drive on your own computer. Knowing how to copy files is an important skill when using a computer.

As you use the Office applications more frequently, you will begin to accumulate a large number of documents. At some point, you will want to remove unnecessary files to reduce clutter on your hard drive, and you might also want to move documents into other folders to archive them. Finally, there are times when you would like to make the file names more descriptive. Windows makes it easy to change the name of a file.

In the following steps, you copy files into the folders you created in Objective 4. You also move and rename files and delete files and folders.

1 With the **My Computer** window still open, click the **plus (+)** to the left of the C: drive in the **Folders** pane to expand the folder.

The folders in the C: hard drive display, and the plus changes to a minus.

2 In the **Folders** pane, click the **WINDOWS** folder.

The folders in the WINDOWS folder display in the Folders pane on the left, and the folders and files in the WINDOWS folder display in the Contents pane on the right, as shown in Figure 1.32.

Figure 1.32

Shows that there are subfolders in this folder

Shows that the folder has been expanded

Subfolders in the WINDOWS folder

Files in the WINDOWS folder

Note — **If You Do Not See the Windows Folder**

If you do not see the WINDOWS folder, open the WINNT folder instead. Substitute the WINNT folder for the WINDOWS folder for the rest of this lesson.

Alert!

Can't Get into the Windows Folder?

In some instances, because of lab security you will not be able to open the WINDOWS folder. If this is the case, find some other files in the My Documents folder or your shared network drive and substitute them for the ones used in the rest of this task. If you can get to the bitmap images but your images differ from the ones used, choose a different set of files.

---

3 In the My Computer toolbar, click the **Views** button and then click **Details**.

The subfolders in the WINDOWS folder display. The files in the folder extend below the bottom of the screen.

4 At the top of the **Type** column in the **Contents** pane, click the **Type** column selector twice, and then scroll down until you can see some of the bitmap images.

When you click the Type column selector, the folders are moved to the bottom, and the individual files appear at the top in reverse alphabetical order. Clicking it a second time changes the list to *a*-to-*z* order. Bitmap images are small graphics included with Windows XP. See Figure 1.33.

The Type column selector

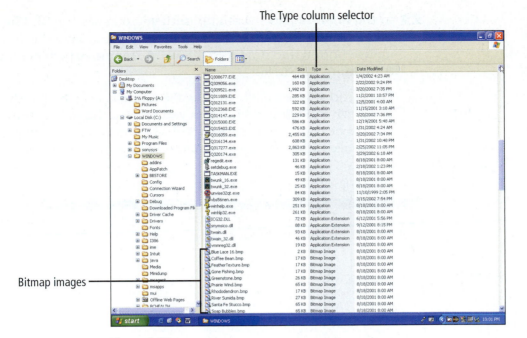

Bitmap images

Figure 1.33

More Knowledge — Understanding and Displaying File Extensions

The files you see may display three letters following the file name, such as *.doc*. These are known as *file extensions*, and nearly all files have these extensions. Files created by Microsoft Office programs have a standard set of extensions that identify the type of program used to create the file. For example, Microsoft Word documents end in *.doc*, Excel spreadsheets end in *.xls*, PowerPoint presentations end with *.ppt*, and so on.

In this chapter, it is assumed that the file extensions are turned on. To turn the file extensions on or off, from the Tools menu click Folder Options, and then click the View tab if necessary. Click the check box to the left of the phrase *Hide extensions for known file types* and then click OK.

5 In the **Name** column in the **Contents** pane, click the **Blue Lace 16.bmp** file.

The file is selected.

6 In the **Folders** pane, scroll up until you can see the **3½ Floppy (A:)** drive. On the **Blue Lace 16.bmp** file, click and hold down the left mouse button and drag it to the **Word Documents** folder on the **3½ Floppy (A:)** drive.

The A: drive is selected, and the file name is attached to the pointer, as shown in Figure 1.34. When you release the mouse button, the file will be copied. Files are copied when dragged to a different drive, and moved when dragged to a different location in the same drive.

File being copied

Selected folder

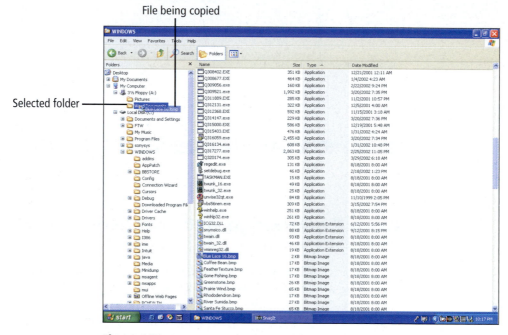

Figure 1.34

7 Release the mouse button.

A dialog box shows that the file is being copied. See Figure 1.35.

Copying dialog box

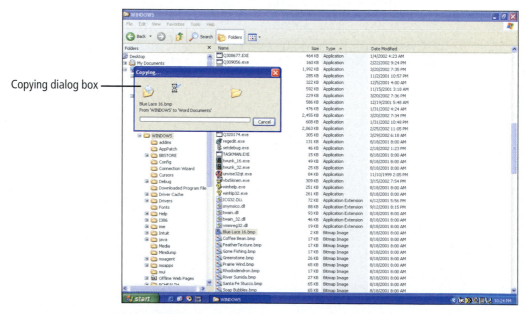

Figure 1.35

Note — Using the Shortcut Menu to Send Files to the Floppy Drive

You can also copy files to a floppy drive by right-clicking on the file, clicking Send To, and then clicking 3½ Floppy (A:).

8 In the **Name** column in the **Contents** pane, click the **Coffee Bean.bmp** file. Hold down Ctrl and click the **Gone Fishing.bmp** file and the **River Sumida.bmp** file.

The Ctrl key enables you to select multiple files that are not next to each other. Compare your screen with Figure 1.36.

Multiple files are selected ⟶

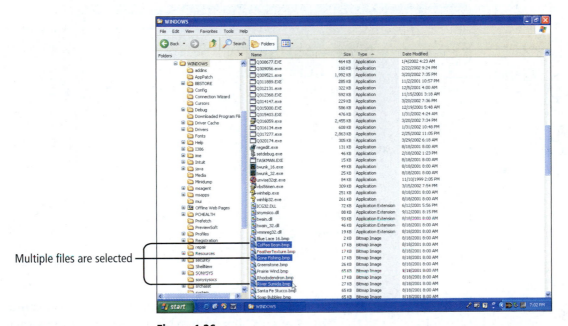

Figure 1.36

More Knowledge — Selecting Multiple Files

If the files are all next to one another, you can click the first one, hold down Shift, and then click the last file. The first and last file and all the files in between are selected. You can then right-click any one of the selected files and send them all to the floppy disk, or you can left-click any one of the files and drag them all to another location.

9 In the **Contents** pane, click any one of the selected files, hold down the mouse button, and then drag the files to the **Pictures** folder on the **3½ Floppy (A:)** drive.

The files display lightly as you drag them to the Pictures folder.

10 In the **Folders** pane, when the **Pictures** folder is highlighted, release the mouse button. Click the **Pictures** folder. Click the **Views button arrow** and then click **Thumbnails**.

Small thumbnail images display in the Contents pane, as shown in Figure 1.37.

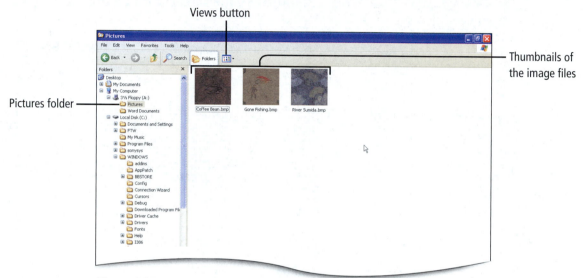

Views button

Pictures folder

Thumbnails of the image files

Figure 1.37

11 In the **Folders** pane, on the floppy drive, click the **Word Documents** folder. Drag the **Blue Lace 16.bmp** file from the **Word Documents** folder to the **Pictures** folder in drive A.

When you drag a file between two folders on the same disk, the file is moved instead of copied.

12 In the **Folders** pane, click the **Pictures** folder in drive A to be sure the fourth file was copied. If necessary, from the toolbar click the **Views** button and then click **Thumbnails**. See Figure 1.38.

The file has been moved

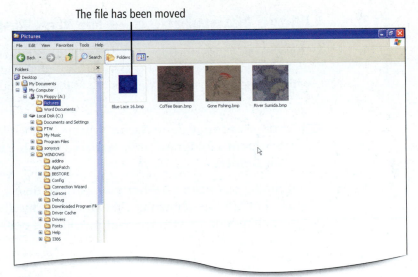

Figure 1.38

More Knowledge — Using Cut and Paste to Move Files

You can also move a file using the cut-and-paste method. To do this, right-click the file and click Cut from the shortcut menu. Click the new drive or folder to which you want to move the file, right-click in an open area, and then click Paste from the shortcut menu.

13 In the **Name** column in the **Contents** pane, right-click the **Blue Lace 16.bmp** file.

A shortcut menu displays, including a Rename command.

14 From the shortcut menu, click the **Rename** command. Type **Blue.bmp** and press Enter.

When the file extensions are displayed, you need to include the extension when you rename the file. See Figure 1.39.

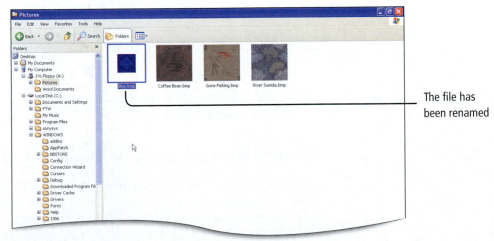

The file has been renamed

Figure 1.39

More Knowledge — File Name Restrictions

There are several restrictions for naming files or folders. A file name can contain up to 255 characters, including spaces, although the file name cannot begin with a space. It also cannot contain the following characters: \ / : * ? " < > |

15 In the **Contents** pane **Name** column, right-click the **Word Documents** folder on drive A. From the shortcut menu, click **Delete**.

A dialog box asks whether you want to delete the folder and all its contents, as shown in Figure 1.40. Any files in the folder will be deleted along with the folder. You can delete files using this same method.

Note — If You Can't Delete a File

Sometimes you will try to delete a file and Windows Explorer will display a dialog box saying that the file cannot be deleted. This usually means that the file is open. You must close a document before you can delete it.

Word Documents folder —

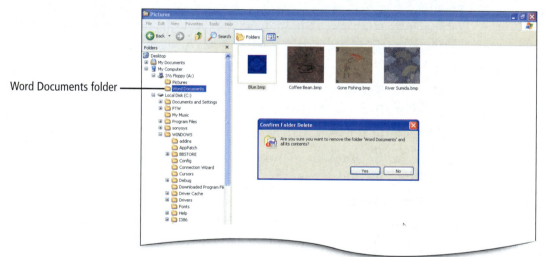

Figure 1.40

16 In the **Confirm Folder Delete** dialog box, click **Yes**.

The folder is deleted.

17 In the title bar, click the **Close** button ☒ to close the **My Computer** window.

More Knowledge — Recovering Deleted Files

If you accidentally delete a file from a hard disk drive that you want to keep, there is a good chance you can recover it. Windows temporarily stores files deleted from your hard drive in a Recycle bin, which you can find on the desktop or in the My Computer Folders pane. You can open the Recycle bin in the same way as you open a file folder. If the discarded files have not been permanently removed, you can right-click the file name in the Contents pane and click Restore in the shortcut menu.

Alert!

Removing Read-Only Status from a File

Each file has certain properties that are established when the file is created. These include the date and time the file was created, the last time it was modified, the last time it was accessed, the type of file, and the file location. If you are using an earlier version of Windows, three file attributes—read-only, archive, and hidden—are also set and may need to be changed. For most files, the attribute is set as archive. However, files copied from a CD-ROM and some network drives using older versions of Windows may be read-only. You need to change this attribute in order to edit the file.

To change the attribute of a file that has been copied from a CD, right-click the file name and click Properties from the shortcut menu. Click the Read-only check box to deselect it and then click OK. If you have copied a number of files, you can select them all and use this method once to remove the read-only status from all the files.

Objective 6
Find Files and Folders

If you use a computer long enough, you will accumulate a large number of files and folders. You will also occasionally forget where you put a file, or what you called it. Windows XP provides a way to search the computer for files and folders, and even for text within a document. You can also specify the type of file or the date it was last modified.

In the following steps, you use several different methods to search for files and folders.

1 In the taskbar, click the **Start** button ![start] and then click **My Computer**.

The My Computer window opens.

2 On the toolbar, click the **Search** button ![Search].

The options in the task pane change, showing the search options for your computer. Notice that you can search for specific file types or you can search through all the files and folders. See Figure 1.41.

Search button

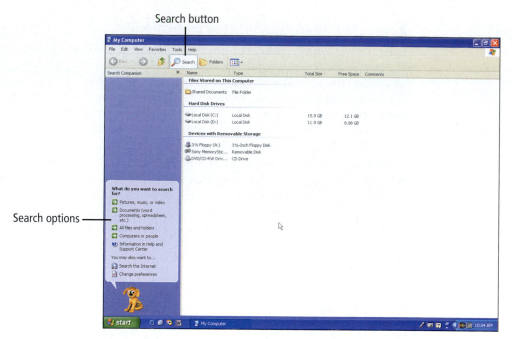

Search options —

Figure 1.41

3 In the task pane, click the **All files and folders** option.

A search dialog box displays. This enables you to specify the file name (or part of a file name) or text contained in the file. It also enables you to narrow the search by specifying the search location. By default, the program is set to check all available drives.

4 In the **All or part of the file name** box, type **zapotec**

The actual file name is capitalized, but this search option is not case sensitive. See Figure 1.42.

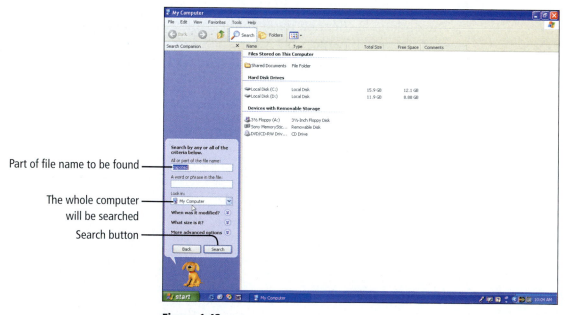

Part of file name to be found —

The whole computer will be searched —

Search button —

Figure 1.42

Note — **Narrowing Your Search**

To narrow your search, open the drive you wish to search. When you click the Search button, the default location will be the open drive.

5 At the bottom of the task pane, click the **Search** button 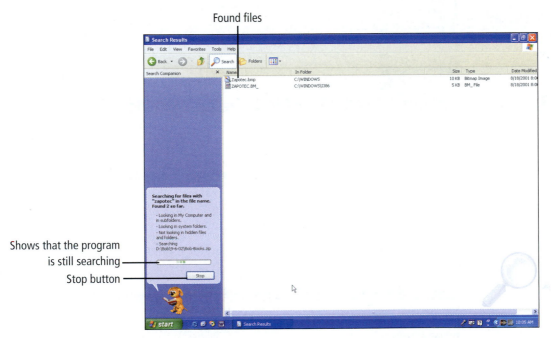.

The search begins. Notice that a couple of files appear rather quickly, but the search program goes on and on. See Figure 1.43. (You may see only one file, depending on the way your computer has been set up.) This is because you did not specify a location, so the program is checking all storage locations on the computer. You can click the Stop button at any time if the procedure seems to be taking too long.

Found files

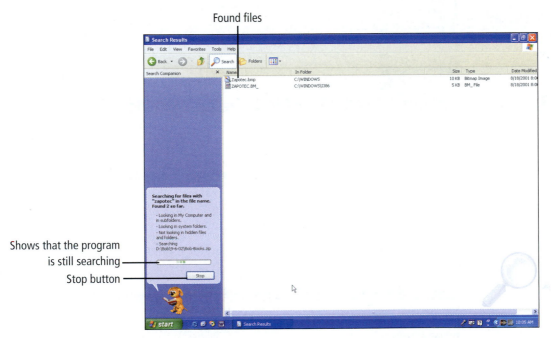

Shows that the program is still searching

Stop button

Figure 1.43

6 If necessary, at the bottom of the task pane, click **Stop** to stop the current search. Click the **Start a new search** option. Click the **Pictures**, **music**, or **video** option.

A new dialog box displays, showing the options for finding this type of file.

7 At the bottom of the task pane, click the **Pictures and Photos** check box. In the **All or part of the file name** box, type **stucco**

This is part of the Santa Fe Stucco.bmp file name. See Figure 1.44.

The program will search for pictures and photos only

Partial file name

Advanced search options

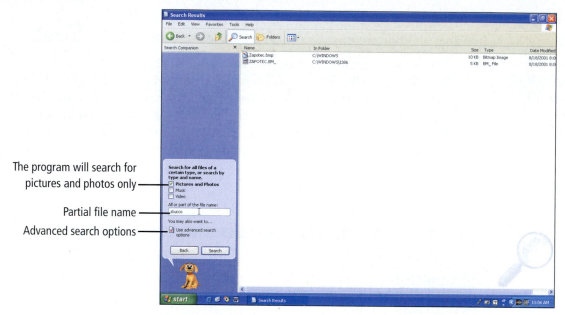

Figure 1.44

8 In the task pane, click the **Use advanced search options** check box.

An expanded dialog box displays.

9 At the right of the **Look in** box, click the arrow.

A menu of possible file locations is displayed, as shown in Figure 1.45.

Possible file locations

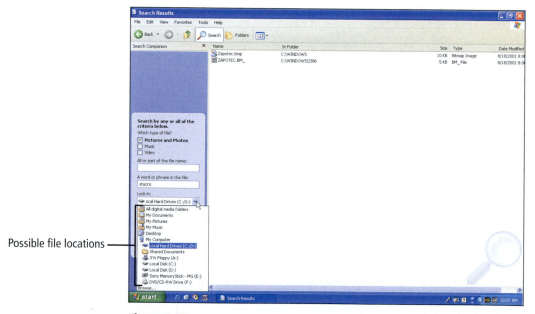

Figure 1.45

10 From the location list, click **Local Disk (C:)**.

This will greatly speed up your search.

11 At the bottom of the task pane, click the **Search** button ⌕ Search .

The Santa Fe Stucco.bmp file is found, along with another file and a file folder, as shown in Figure 1.46. Again, your search results may show only one file. The search may still take several minutes, but it is much faster than a search of all files in all storage locations.

Results of the search —
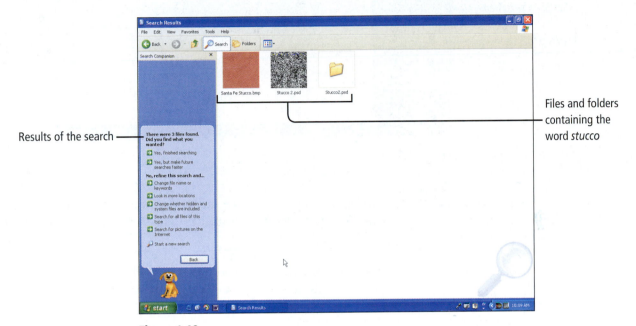
— Files and folders containing the word *stucco*

Figure 1.46

12 Scroll down, if necessary, and click the **Start a new search** option. Click the **Documents (word processing, spreadsheet, etc.)** option.

This dialog box gives you greater control over the search. You can search for documents that have specified file extensions, or you can search for documents last modified during a certain time period. You can even combine the two.

13 In the task pane, click **Within the last week**, and type ***.doc** in the **All or part of the document name box**. If your computer is not used often, click **Past month** instead.

This restricts the search to Word documents (that have the .doc extension) modified in the past week. The asterisk is called a ***wild-card*** and means that you will be searching for anything that has the .doc extension. This is very helpful if you can't remember the file name or where you put it. See Figure 1.47.

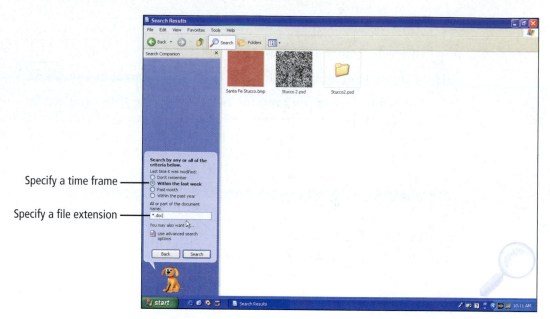

Specify a time frame ────

Specify a file extension ────

Figure 1.47

14 In the task pane, click the **Use advanced search options** check box, click the arrow to the right of the **Look in** box, and then click **Local Disk (C:)**. Click the **Search** button [🔍 Search].

The Contents pane displays the files modified in the past week that have the .doc extension. The files found on your computer will be different from the ones shown in Figure 1.48.

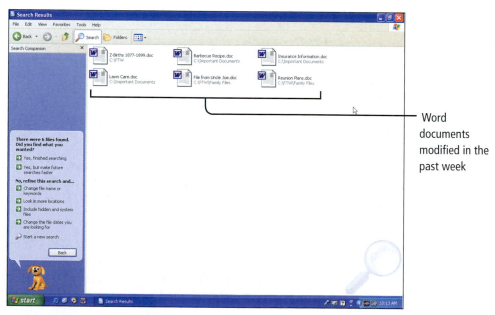

Word documents modified in the past week

Figure 1.48

Objective 7
Compress Files

Circumstances may arise when you would like your file sizes to be smaller. For example, some files containing graphics can be larger than the capacity of a floppy disk. Also, when you send files as e-mail attachments, the smaller they are, the faster you can send them. In fact, if you are using a computer that has a modem, reducing the file size may mean the difference between successfully transmitting the file or having the system time out—end the online session—before the transfer is complete.

Windows XP includes a built-in compression feature. This enables you to quickly compress (zip) one or more files into a single file that uses a *.zip* file extension. These files can then be unzipped for editing on any other computer running Windows XP or any earlier version of Windows that has a third-party zip program installed. If you are using a third-party zip program, such as WinZip® or PKZIP®, you will need to use that program to complete this task—the procedure listed below will not work.

In the following steps, you compress a single file and then compress several files at the same time.

1 With the **My Computer** window open, click the **Folders** button [Folders] to activate the **Folders** pane. In the toolbar, click the **Views** button [⊞▾] and then click **Details**.

The search results are kept in a special temporary storage area, as shown in Figure 1.49.

Folders button

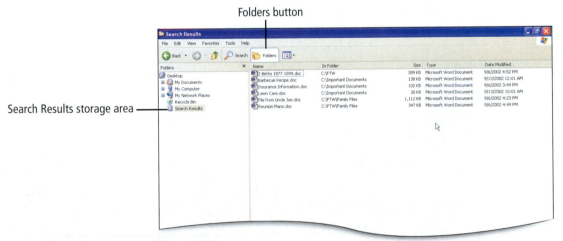

Search Results storage area

Figure 1.49

2 Click **My Computer**, open the **C:** drive, and open the **WINDOWS** (or **WINNT**) folder.

The Windows system files display in the Contents pane.

3 Click the **Type** column selector and scroll down, if necessary, so that you can see the text document files (files that have a *.txt* extension if you have extensions turned on). Move the pointer over the **setuplog.txt** file. If you do not have this file, choose any other file that is listed as a text document.

A ScreenTip displays, providing information about the file, as shown in Figure 1.50. The setuplog.txt file is automatically created during setup. The size of this file will be different on each computer.

Setuplog.txt file   Type column selector

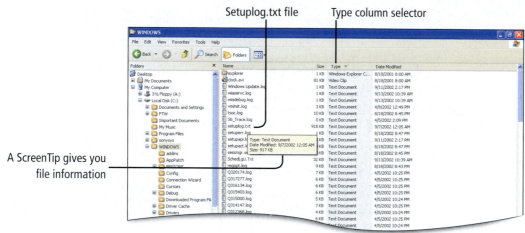

A ScreenTip gives you file information

Figure 1.50

4 Right-click **setuplog.txt**, and move the pointer to **Send To**.

The Send To submenu is displayed, as shown in Figure 1.51. Your submenu will probably look somewhat different.

Send To command

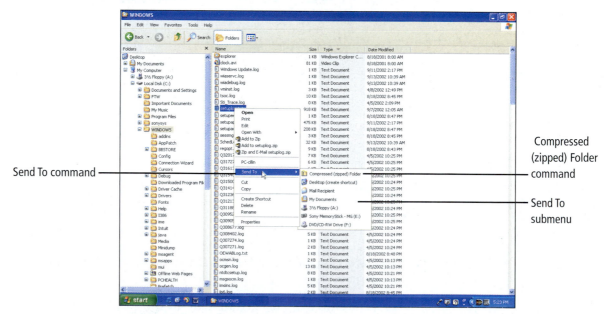

Compressed (zipped) Folder command

Send To submenu

Figure 1.51

5 From the shortcut menu, click the **Compressed (zipped) Folder** command.

A new file, called setuplog.zip (or the name of whichever text file you selected), is created. The file displays at the bottom of the Contents pane.

6 In the **Contents** pane, click the **Date Modified** column selector twice to show the recent documents first. If necessary, scroll to the top of the **Contents** pane.

In Figure 1.52, you can see that the file size has been reduced from 918 KB to 64 KB (your numbers will be different). Files created by different applications will compress at different rates. Some, like this text file, will compress by about 90 percent. Excel files often compress by about 75 percent, but PowerPoint files compress only by 10 percent or so.

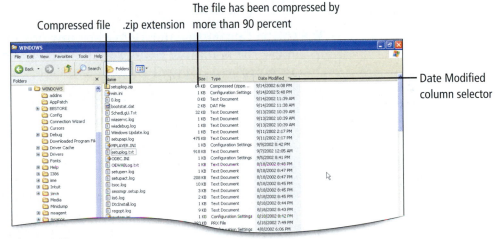

Compressed file   .zip extension   The file has been compressed by
more than 90 percent

Date Modified
column selector

Figure 1.52

More Knowledge — File Associations and Compression Programs

You may see a dialog box when you click the Compressed (zipped) Folder command. Because every file type needs to be associated with a program, your computer may already associate files that have the *.zip* extension with a third-party program such as WinZip. The dialog box will ask whether you want to designate Compressed (zipped) Folders as the application for handling ZIP files (compressed files that have a *.zip* extension). If you are working in a lab, ask the lab manager how to answer this question. If you are working at home, click Yes unless you want to use another program to compress your files.

7 In the **Contents** pane, click the **Type** column selector twice, and scroll down so that you can see the bitmap files. Click the **Soap Bubbles.bmp** file, hold down Ctrl, and click the **Prairie Wind.bmp** and **Greenstone.bmp** files.

You should have three files selected, as shown in Figure 1.53.

Three bitmap files
are selected

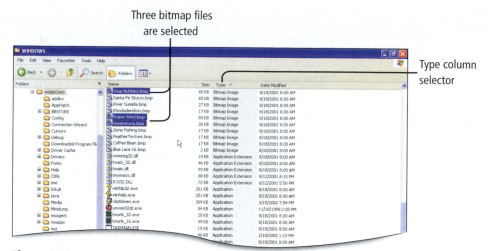

Type column
selector

Figure 1.53

8 In the **Contents** pane, right-click any one of the selected files, and move the pointer to **Send To**. From the **Send To** submenu, click the **Compressed (zipped) Folder** command.

The files are all placed in a single zipped folder.

9 Scroll to the bottom of the **Contents** pane.

A new folder displays, as shown in Figure 1.54. The icon is a folder, unlike the icon that is displayed when you compress a single file. The folder means that multiple files have been compressed. The folder name is the name of whichever file you right-clicked, although it contains all three files. Notice that the files have been compressed to 78 KB from an original 156 KB, a size reduction of 50 percent.

Zipped folder icon

Compressed file size

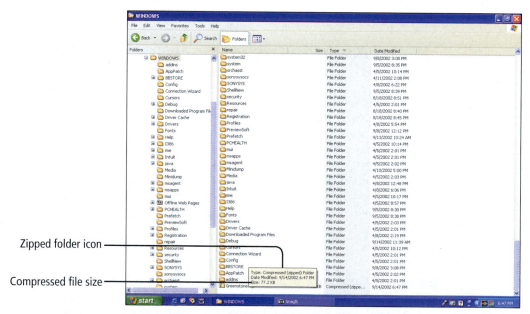

Figure 1.54

10 In the **Folders** pane, scroll up until you can see the **3½ Floppy (A:)** icon. Drag the zipped folder, in this example the **Greenstone.zip** folder, to the floppy drive.

The zipped folder is copied to the floppy disk.

11 In the **Folders** pane, click the **3½ Floppy (A:)** drive.

The zipped folder appears next to the Pictures folder you created in Objective 5, as shown in Figure 1.55.

New zipped folder

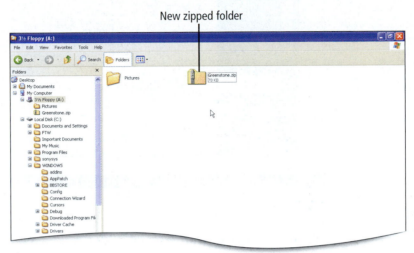

Figure 1.55

12 In the **Contents** pane, double-click the **Greenstone.zip** folder.

All the compressed files are displayed in a new window, as shown in Figure 1.56.

Extract all files option

Contents of the zipped folder

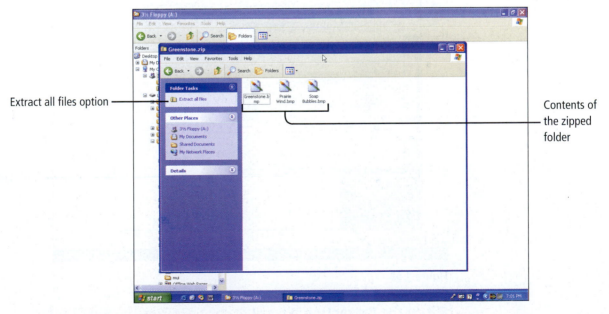

Figure 1.56

13 In the **Greenstone.zip** window, click the **Extract all files** option.

The first Extraction Wizard dialog box displays. See Figure 1.57.

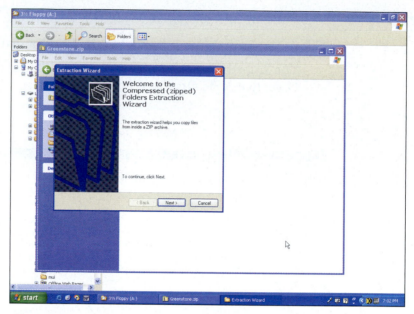

Figure 1.57

14 In the **Extraction Wizard** dialog box, click the **Next** button.

A second Extraction Wizard dialog box displays, as shown in Figure 1.58. You can designate the destination location of the extracted files. For this task, you will accept the default location, which is the floppy drive.

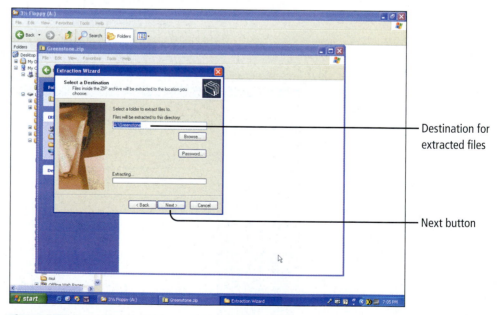

Destination for extracted files

Next button

Figure 1.58

15 In the **Extraction Wizard** dialog box, click the **Next** button.

The files are extracted, and a third Extraction Wizard dialog box displays.

16 In the **Extraction Wizard** dialog box, click the **Finish** button. Close all windows except the My Computer window.

The extracted files are stored in a new folder. The name of the folder is the same as the name of the zipped folder file name without the *.zip* extension, as shown in Figure 1.59.

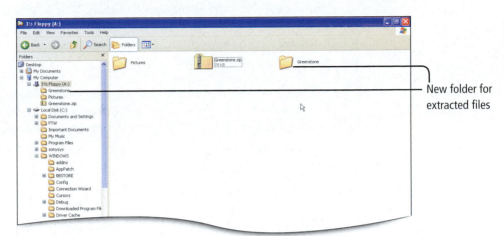

New folder for extracted files

Figure 1.59

17 Under **Folders**, under drive A, double-click the **Greenstone** folder (not the zipped folder). From the toolbar, click the **Views** button, and then click **Details**.

The files have been restored to their original size, as shown in Figure 1.60.

Extracted files

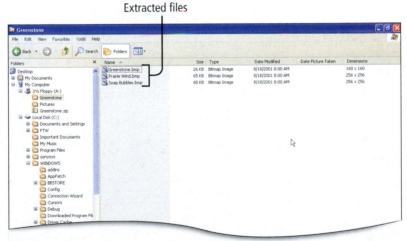

Figure 1.60

18 Submit the files as directed by your instructor. Delete the two *.zip* files you created in this task, and then close the **My Computer** window.

Another Way

Zipping a Folder

If you want to zip all of the files in a folder, it is easier to zip the folder than to select and zip the individual files. This method also has the advantage of giving the zip file the same name as the folder.

Summary

A working knowledge of Windows is necessary in order to use Microsoft Office effectively. In this chapter, you practiced setting up, organizing, and navigating the Windows desktop. You learned how to maximize, minimize, and restore windows and how to move windows on the desktop. You learned how to use the Windows taskbar, how to find files, and how to use the Start button.

Another Windows feature you worked with was managing your files. You created folders to store your documents and then moved files between folders. You copied, renamed, and deleted files and then learned how to compress one or more documents to save space and facilitate sending files over the Internet.

In This Chapter You Practiced How To

- Get Started with Windows
- Resize, Move, and Scroll Windows
- Maximize, Restore, Minimize, and Close a Window
- Create a New Folder
- Copy, Move, Rename, and Delete Files
- Find Files and Folders
- Compress Files

Concepts Assessments

Matching   Match each term in the second column with its correct definition in the first column by writing the letter of the term on the blank line in front of the correct definition.

_____ **1.** A bar that contains the Start button, buttons representing open programs, and other buttons that will activate programs.

_____ **2.** The moving arrow (or other object) on the screen that is used to select or activate objects and programs.

_____ **3.** Enables you to view text that extends beyond the edges of the screen.

_____ **4.** A box that displays information and usually consists of a title bar, menu bar, status bar, and toolbars, and always has a Minimize button.

_____ **5.** Used to keep related files stored together in one location.

_____ **6.** Character used to substitute for several characters in a file search.

_____ **7.** Three-letter ending to a file name that identifies the file type but that may or may not be displayed.

_____ **8.** Used to find files or folders.

_____ **9.** Area at the top of the window that displays the file name and also contains the Minimize, Maximize/Restore Down, and Close buttons.

_____ **10.** Lets you see your document in its final format.

A. A window

B. Title bar

C. Mouse pointer

D. Graphical User Interface (GUI)

E. Taskbar

F. Wildcard

G. Folder

H. Search button

I. Scroll bar

J. Extension

Fill in the Blank Write the correct answer in the space provided.

1. A(n) _____, which consists of the last three characters of a file name, indicates which program was used to create the
file.

2. A(n) _____ is a graphic representation that enables
you to run a program or use a program function.

3. Windows XP is an example of a(n) _____, which
coordinates the activities of a computer.

4. The _____ button on the left end of the taskbar is
used to run programs, change system settings, or find help.

5. To make a window fill the screen, use the _____
button from the title bar.

6. When more than one document or program is open at the same
time, you can switch back and forth between them by clicking the
appropriate button in the _____.

7. A(n) _____ is a second-level menu that is accessed
using a menu command.

8. When you delete a file, it is stored in a temporary area called the
_____, from which it can often be recovered.

9. You can hide a program or document without closing it by clicking
the _____ button.

10. In My Computer, you can sort file names alphabetically by clicking
the _____ column selector.

chapterone

Creating Documents with Microsoft Word 2003

In this chapter you will: complete these projects and practice these skills.

Project 1A **Exploring Microsoft Word**	**Objectives** • Explore and Navigate the Word Window • View Documents • Use the Spelling and Grammar Checker • View Headers and Footers • Organize, Save, and Print Documents
Project 1B **Creating, Editing, and Printing a Document**	**Objectives** • Create and Edit a New Document • Select and Format Text • Preview and Print Documents, Close a Document, and Close Word • Use the Microsoft Help System

The Perfect Party

The Perfect Party store, owned by two partners, provides a wide variety of party accessories including invitations, favors, banners and flags, balloons, piñatas, etc. Party-planning services include both custom parties with pre-filled custom "goodie bags" and "parties in a box" that include everything needed to throw a theme party. Big sellers in this category are the Football and Luau themes. The owners are planning to open a second store and expand their party-planning services to include catering.

© Getty Images, Inc.

Getting Started with Microsoft Office Word 2003

Word processing is the most common program found on personal computers and one that almost everyone has a reason to use. When you learn word processing you are also learning skills and techniques that you need to work efficiently on a personal computer. Use Microsoft Word to do basic word processing tasks such as writing a memo, a report, or a letter. You can also use Word to do complex word processing tasks, including sophisticated tables, embedded graphics, and links to other documents and the Internet. Word is a program that you can learn gradually, adding more advanced skills one at a time.

Project 1A Business Plan

With a word processing program, you can type, edit, move, and delete text or change the appearance of the text. Because the document is stored electronically, it can be duplicated, printed, copied, and shared with others. In this chapter, you will become familiar with the parts of the Word window and use the various views available in Word. Then you will create a document, edit and format text, and save and print your Word document.

In Activities 1.1 through 1.13 you will view and edit a business plan for The Perfect Party prepared by Paul Freire, a business planning consultant. Your completed document will look similar to Figure 1.1. You will save your document as *1A_Business_Plan_Firstname_Lastname.*

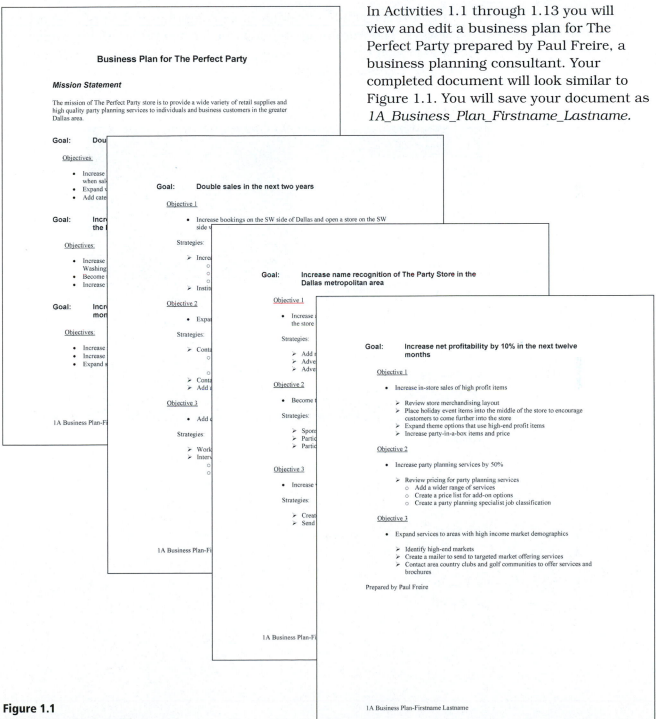

Figure 1.1
Project 1A—Business Plan

Objective 1
Explore and Navigate the Word Window

Activity 1.1 Starting Word and Identifying Parts of the Word Window

1 On the left side of the Windows taskbar, point to and then click the **Start** button ![start].

The Start menu displays.

2 On the computer you are using, locate the Word program and then click **Microsoft Office Word 2003**.

Organizations and individuals store computer programs in a variety of ways. The Word program might be located under All Programs or Microsoft Office or at the top of the main Start menu. Refer to Figure 1.2 as an example.

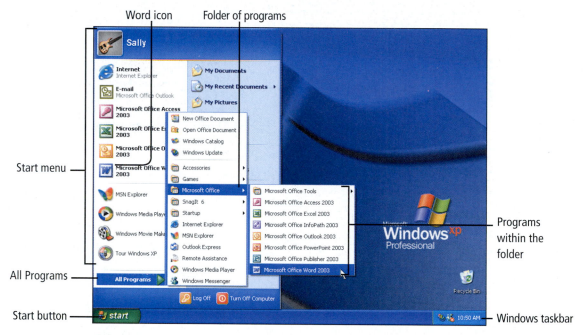

Figure 1.2

3 Look at the opening Word screen, and then take a moment to study the main parts of the screen as shown in Figure 1.3 and described in the table in Figure 1.4.

Alert!

Does your screen differ?

There are several ways to look at a document in the Word window. The appearance of the screen depends on various settings that your system administrator established when the program was installed and how the program has been modified since installation. In many cases, whether a screen element displays depends on how the program was last used.

4 On the Formatting toolbar, click the **Toolbar Options** button. If the Standard and Formatting toolbars are on two separate rows as shown in Figure 1.3, move the pointer into the Word document window and click to close the list without making any changes. If the toolbars are sharing a single row, click **Show Buttons on Two Rows**.

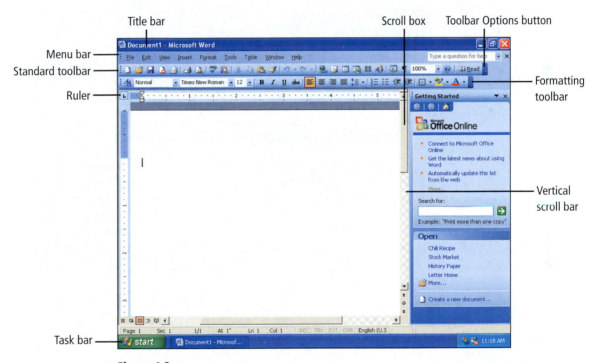

Title bar   Scroll box   Toolbar Options button

Menu bar
Standard toolbar
Ruler

Formatting toolbar

Vertical scroll bar

Task bar

Figure 1.3a

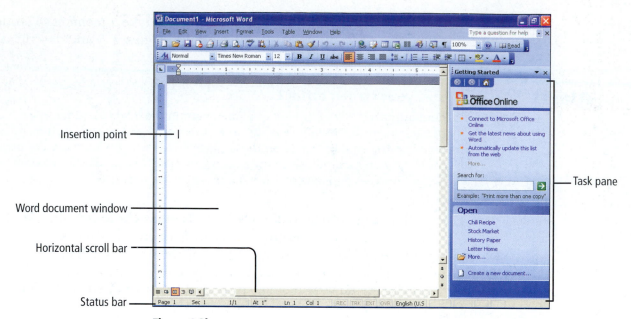

Insertion point ——— |

Word document window ———

Horizontal scroll bar ———

Status bar ———

Figure 1.3b

It is easier to use the toolbars if all of the most commonly used buttons are displayed. Most Word users keep the Standard and Formatting toolbars displayed on separate rows.

More Knowledge — Turning on Toolbars

If a toolbar is missing entirely, point to an existing toolbar or to the menu bar and click the right mouse button (also known as right-clicking). On the shortcut menu that displays, point to the name of the toolbar you want to display and click the left mouse button. A shortcut menu is a context-sensitive menu of commands relevant to the particular item. Alternatively, display the View menu, click Toolbars, and then click the name of the toolbar you want to display. If a toolbar is open, a check mark displays to the left of the toolbar name.

Microsoft Word Screen Elements

Screen Element	Description
Title bar	Displays the program icon, the name of the document, and the name of the program. The Minimize, Maximize/Restore Down, and Close buttons are grouped on the right side of the title bar.
Menu bar	Contains a list of commands. To display a menu, click on the menu name.
Standard toolbar	Contains buttons for some of the most common commands in Word. It may occupy an entire row or share a row with the Formatting toolbar.
Formatting toolbar	Contains buttons for some of the most common formatting options in Word. It may occupy an entire row or share a row with the Standard toolbar.
Ruler	Displays the location of margins, indents, columns, and tab stops.
Vertical scroll bar	Enables you to move up and down in a document to display text that is not visible.
Horizontal scroll bar	Enables you to move left and right in a document to display text that is not visible.
Scroll box	Provides a visual indication of your location in a document. It can also be used with the mouse to drag a document up and down.
Toolbar Options button	Displays a list of all of the buttons associated with a toolbar. It also enables you to place the Standard and Formatting toolbars on separate rows or on the same row.
Word document window	Displays the active document.
Insertion point	Indicates, with a blinking vertical line, where text or graphics will be inserted.
Task pane	Displays commonly used commands related to the current task.
Taskbar	Displays the Start button and the name of any open documents. The taskbar may also display shortcut buttons for other programs.
Status bar	Displays the page and section number and other Word settings.

Figure 1.4

Activity 1.2 Opening an Existing Document

1 On the Standard toolbar, click the **Open** button .

The Open dialog box displays.

2 In the **Open** dialog box, click the **Look in arrow** at the right edge of the **Look in** box to view a list of the drives available on your system. See Figure 1.5 as an example—the drives and folders displayed on your screen will differ.

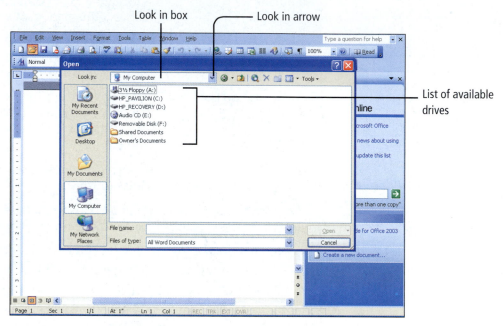

Look in box — Look in arrow — List of available drives

Figure 1.5

3 Navigate to the location where the student files for this textbook are stored.

4 Locate **w01A_Business_Plan** and click once to select it. Then, in the lower right corner of the **Open** dialog box, click the **Open** button. Alternatively, *double-click* the file name to open it—click the left mouse button twice in rapid succession.

The document displays in the Word window. See Figure 1.6.

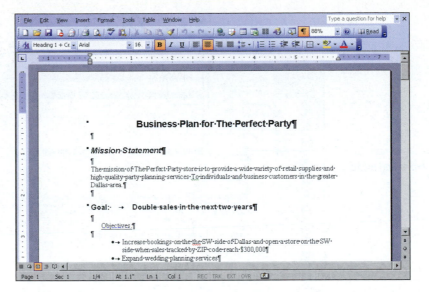

Figure 1.6

Note — Turning Off the Office Assistant

One of Word's Help features is an animated object called the Office Assistant. Many people like to turn this feature off. To hide the Office Assistant, click the right mouse button on the Office Assistant. In the menu that displays, click Hide with the left mouse button. The instruction in this textbook assumes that the Office Assistant is turned off.

Activity 1.3 Accessing Menu Commands and Displaying the Task Pane

Word commands are organized in **menus**—lists of commands within a category. The **menu bar** at the top of the screen provides access to the Word commands. The buttons on the toolbars provide one-click short-cuts to menu commands.

1 On the menu bar, click **View**.

The View menu displays in either the short format as shown in Figure 1.7, or in the full format, which displays all of the menu commands. If the full menu does not display, you can do one of three things:

- Wait a moment and the full menu will display if your system is set to do so.

- At the bottom of the menu, click the double arrows to expand the menu to display all commands.

- Before opening a menu, point to the menu name in the menu bar, and then double-click. This ensures that the full menu displays.

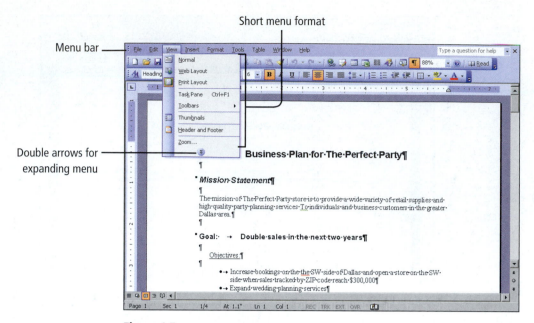

Figure 1.7

Note — Turning On Full Menus

The instruction in this textbook assumes that the full menus display when you click a menu command. To turn on full menus, go to the menu bar, click Tools, and then click Customize. In the Customize dialog box, click the Options tab, and then click the *Always show full menus* check box. Click the Close button to close the dialog box.

2 Be sure that the full menu is displayed as shown in Figure 1.8, and notice to the right of some commands there is a ***keyboard shortcut***; for example, *Ctrl+F1* for the task pane.

A keyboard shortcut enables you to perform commands using a combination of keys from your keyboard. For example, if you press and hold down Ctrl and then press F1, the result is the same as clicking View on the menu bar and then clicking Task Pane. Many commands in Word can be accomplished in more than one way.

Keyboard shortcut

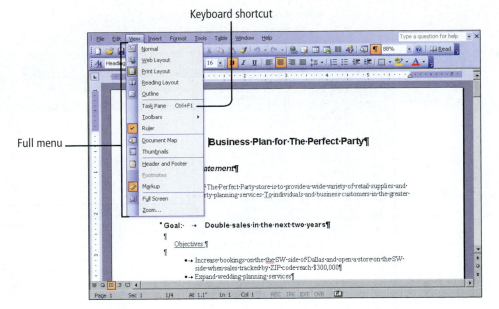

Full menu

Figure 1.8

3 On the displayed **View** menu, to the left of some command names, notice the image of the button that represents this command on a toolbar.

This is a reminder that you can initiate the command with one click from a toolbar, rather than initiating the command with multiple clicks from the menu.

4 On the displayed **View** menu, pause the mouse pointer over **Toolbars** but do not click.

An arrow to the right of a command name indicates that a submenu is available. When you point to this type of menu command, a submenu displays. See Figure 1.9.

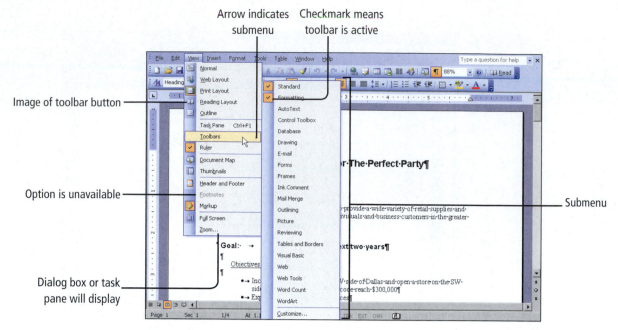

Arrow indicates submenu   Checkmark means toolbar is active

Image of toolbar button

Option is unavailable

Submenu

Dialog box or task pane will display

Figure 1.9

5 Look at the full **View** menu on your screen, and notice the various symbols and characters. These are standard across all Microsoft products. Take a moment to study the table in Figure 1.10 for a description of these elements.

Word Menu Characteristics

Characteristic	Description	Example
... (ellipsis)	Indicates that either a dialog box requesting more information or a task pane will display.	Zoom...
▶ (right arrow)	Indicates that a submenu—another menu of choices—will display.	Toolbars ▶
No symbol	Indicates that the command will perform immediately.	Web Layout
✔ (check mark)	Indicates that a command is turned on or active.	✔ Ruler
Gray option name	Indicates that the command is currently unavailable.	Footnotes

Figure 1.10

6 With the **View** menu still displayed, click **Task Pane**.

The Getting Started task pane displays as shown in Figure 1.11. If the task pane was already displayed, it will close. If the task pane was not visible, it will display on the right side of the screen. As you progress in your study of Word, you will see various task panes to assist you in accomplishing Word tasks.

Task Pane

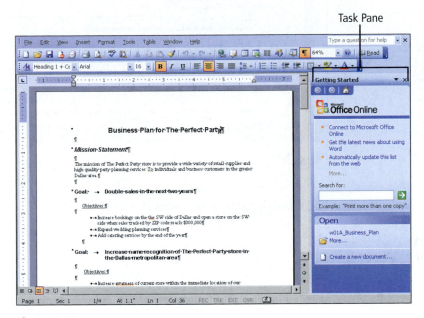

Figure 1.11

7 On the menu bar, click **View**, and then click **Task Pane** again to close the task pane.

For the remainder of this book the task pane should be closed, except when otherwise instructed.

Activity 1.4 Navigating a Document Using the Vertical Scroll Bar

Most Word documents are larger than the Word window. Therefore, there are several ways to ***navigate*** (move) in a document.

1 At the right of your screen, in the vertical scroll bar, locate the down arrow at the bottom of the bar as shown in Figure 1.12. Then, click the **down scroll arrow** five times.

Notice that the document scrolls up a line at a time. In this document, Word has flagged some spelling and grammar errors (red and green wavy lines), which you will correct in Activity 1.9.

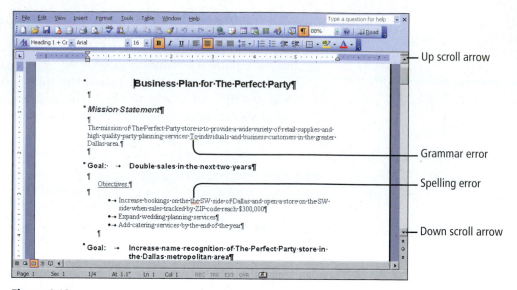

Figure 1.12

2 Point to the **down scroll arrow** again, and then click and hold down the mouse button for several seconds.

The document text scrolls up continuously, a line at a time.

3 At the top of the vertical scroll bar, point to the **up scroll arrow**, and then click and hold down the mouse button until you have scrolled back to the top of the document. As you do so, notice that the scroll box moves up in the scroll bar.

4 At the top of the vertical scroll bar point to the scroll box, and then press and hold down the left mouse button.

A **ScreenTip**—a small box that displays information about, or the name of, a screen element—displays. In this instance, the ScreenTip indicates the page number and the first line of text at the top of the page. See Figure 1.13.

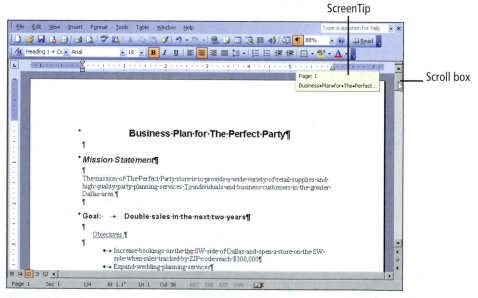

Figure 1.13

5 ***Drag*** (hold down the left mouse button while moving your mouse) the scroll box down to the bottom of the scroll bar. As you do so, watch the ScreenTip.

The ScreenTip changes as each new page reaches the top of the screen. See Figure 1.14.

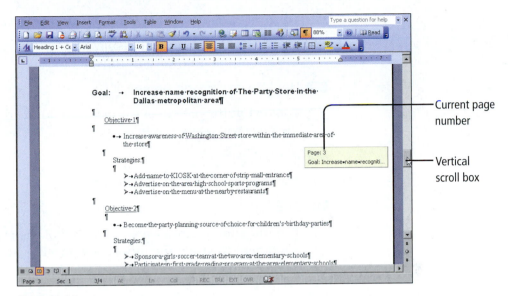

Current page number

Vertical scroll box

Figure 1.14

6 Release the mouse button, and then click in the gray area above the scroll box.

The document scrolls up one screen.

7 Practice clicking in the area above and below the scroll box.

This is a quick way to scan a document.

Another Way

Using the Wheel Button on the Mouse

If your mouse has a small wheel button between the left and right mouse buttons, you can scroll up and down in the document by rotating the wheel.

Activity 1.5 Navigating a Document Using the Keyboard

Keyboard shortcuts are another way to navigate your document quickly. Keyboard shortcuts provide additional navigation techniques that you cannot accomplish with the vertical scroll bar. For example, using keyboard shortcuts, you can move the insertion point to the beginning or end of a word or line.

1 On your keyboard, hold down Ctrl and press Home.

The top of the document displays, and the insertion point moves to the left of the first word in the document.

2 Hold down Ctrl and press End.

The text at the bottom of the last page in the document displays, and the insertion point moves to the right of the last word in the document.

3 Press Page Up.

The document scrolls up one screen.

4 Press End.

The insertion point moves to the end of the current line of text. Take a moment to study the table shown in Figure 1.15, which lists the most commonly used keyboard shortcuts.

Navigating a Document Using Keyboard Shortcuts

To Move	Press
To the beginning of a document	Ctrl + Home
To the end of a document	Ctrl + End
To the beginning of a line	Home
To the end of a line	End
To the beginning of the previous word	Ctrl + ←
To the beginning of the next word	Ctrl + →
To the beginning of the current word (if insertion point is in the middle of a word)	Ctrl + ←
To the beginning of the previous paragraph	Ctrl + ↑
To the end of the next paragraph	Ctrl + ↓
To the beginning of the current paragraph (if insertion point is in the middle of a paragraph)	Ctrl + ↑
Up one screen	Page Up
Down one screen	PageDown

Figure 1.15

5 Hold down Ctrl and press Home to position the insertion point at the beginning of the document.

Objective 2
View Documents

In addition to different document views, there is a method to view characters on your screen that do not print on paper. Examples of these characters include paragraph marks, tabs, and spaces.

Activity 1.6 Displaying Formatting Marks

When you press Enter, Spacebar, or Tab on your keyboard, characters are placed in your document to represent these keystrokes. These characters do not print, and are referred to as ***formatting marks*** or ***nonprinting characters***. Because formatting marks guide your eye in a document like a map and road signs guide you along a highway, these marks will be displayed throughout this instruction.

1 In the displayed document, look at the document title *Business Plan for The Perfect Party* and determine if a paragraph symbol (¶) displays at the end of the title as shown in Figure 1.16. If you do *not* see the paragraph symbol, on the Standard toolbar, click the **Show/Hide ¶** button ¶ to display the formatting marks.

Paragraph marks display at the end of every paragraph. Every time you press Enter, a new paragraph is created, and a paragraph mark is inserted. Paragraph marks are especially helpful in showing the number of blank lines inserted in a document. Spaces are indicated by dots, and tabs are indicated by arrows as shown in Figure 1.16.

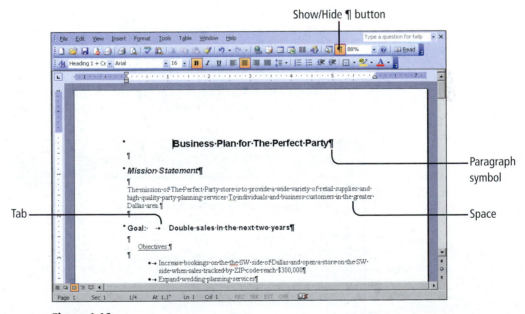

Figure 1.16

2 Click the **Show/Hide ¶** button ¶. This turns off the display of non-printing characters. Then, click the **Show/Hide ¶** button ¶ once more to turn it on again.

Viewing Documents

There are five ways to view your document on the screen. Each view is useful in different situations.

- The Print Layout view displays the page borders, margins, text, and graphics as they will look when you print the document. Most Word users prefer this view for most tasks, and it is the default view.

- The Normal view simplifies the page layout for quick typing, and shows a little more text on the screen than the Print Layout view. Graphics, headers, and footers do not display.

- The Web Layout view shows how the document will look when saved as a Web page and viewed in a Web browser.

- The Reading Layout view creates easy-to-read pages that fit on the screen to increase legibility. This view does not represent the pages as they would print. Each screen page is labeled with a screen number, rather than a page number.

- The Outline view shows the organizational structure of your document by headings and subheadings and can be collapsed and expanded to look at individual sections of a document.

Activity 1.7 Changing Views

1 To the left of the horizontal scroll bar, locate the **View buttons**.

These buttons are used to switch to different document views. Alternatively, you can switch views using the commands on the View menu.

2 Click the **Normal View** button ▤.

The work area covers the entire width of the screen. See Figure 1.17. Page margins are not displayed, and any inserted graphics, ***headers***, or ***footers*** do not display. A header is information at the top of every page, and a footer is information at the bottom of every printed page.

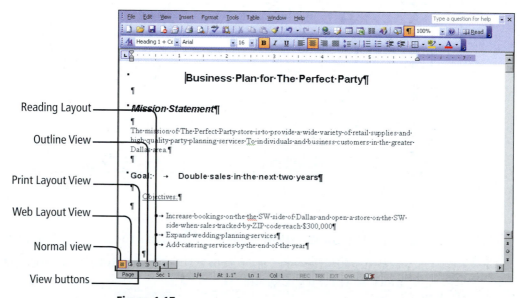

Figure 1.17

3 Click the **Reading Layout** button [image].

An entire page is displayed, and the text reaches nearly to the bottom. However, this is only about half of the text that is actually on the page as it is formatted and if it were printed. This view has its own toolbars and is optimized for easy reading. You can display side-by-side pages in longer documents, and you can *edit*—make changes to—the document in this view.

Note — Opening the Reading Layout view

The Reading Layout view is also accessible by clicking the Read button [image] on the Standard toolbar.

---

4 At the top of the screen, in the Reading Layout toolbar, click **Close** button [image].

Closing the Reading Layout view returns you to the previous view, which was Normal view.

5 At the left of the horizontal scroll bar, click the **Print Layout View** button [image].

In this view you can see all of the elements that will display on paper when you print the document. The instruction in this textbook will use the Print Layout View for most documents.

Activity 1.8 Using the Zoom Button

To **zoom** means to increase or to decrease the viewing area of the screen. You can zoom in to look closely at a particular section of a document, and then zoom out to see a whole page on the screen. It is also possible to view multiple pages on the screen.

1 On the Standard toolbar, click the **Zoom button arrow** [image].

The Zoom list displays as shown in Figure 1.18.

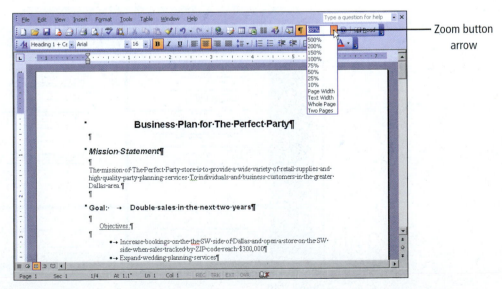

Zoom button arrow

Figure 1.18

2 On the displayed list, click **150%**.

The view of the text is magnified. See Figure 1.19.

Zoom changed to 150%

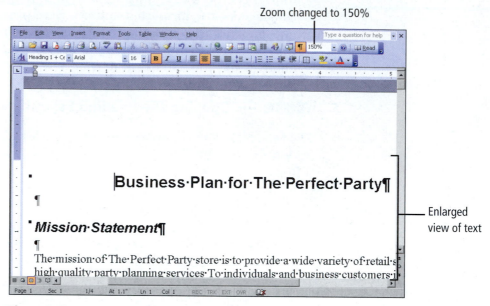

Enlarged
view of text

Figure 1.19

3 On the Standard toolbar, click the **Zoom button arrow** [100% ▾] again and then click **Two Pages**.

Two full pages display on the screen. This magnification enables you to see how the text is laid out on the page and to check the location of other document elements, such as graphics.

4 On the vertical scroll bar, click the down scroll arrow five times.

Notice that you can now see parts of four pages, and you can see how the text flows from one page to another. See Figure 1.20.

Two page view

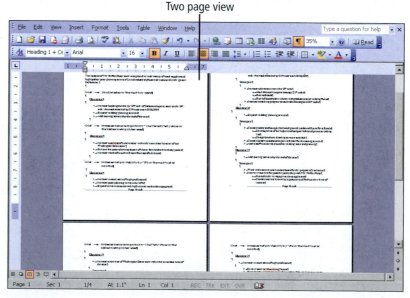

Figure 1.20

5 On the Standard toolbar, click the **Zoom button arrow** `100%` and from the displayed list click **Page Width**.

This is a flexible magnification, displaying the maximum page width, regardless of the size of your screen. The size shown in the Zoom box will vary depending on screen size and resolution.

6 On the Standard toolbar, click on the number in the Zoom box to highlight the number currently displayed. Type **100** and then press `Enter`.

Typing a number directly into the Zoom box is another method of changing the zoom level.

Objective 3
Use the Spelling and Grammar Checker

As you type, Word compares your words to those in the Word dictionary and compares your phrases and punctuation to a list of grammar rules. Words that are not in the Word dictionary are marked with a wavy red underline. Phrases and punctuation that differ from the grammar rules are marked with a wavy green underline. Because a list of grammar rules applied by a computer program can never be exact, and because a computer dictionary cannot contain all known words and proper names, you will need to check any words flagged by Word as misspellings or grammar errors.

Finally, Word does not check for usage. For example, Word will not flag the word *sign* as misspelled, even though you intended to type *sing a song* rather than *sign a song*, because both are legitimate words contained within Word's dictionary.

Activity 1.9 Checking Individual Spelling and Grammar Errors

One way to check spelling and grammar errors flagged by Word is to right-click the flagged word or phrase and, from the displayed shortcut menu, select a suitable correction or instruction.

1 Hold down `Ctrl` and press `Home` to move the insertion point to the top of the document. Scan the text on the screen to locate green and red wavy underlines.

> ## Note — Activating Spelling and Grammar Checking
>
> If you do not see any wavy red or green lines under words, the automatic spelling and/or grammar checking has been turned off on your system. To activate the spelling and grammar checking, display the Tools menu, click Options, and then click the Spelling & Grammar tab. Under Spelling, click the *Check spelling as you type* check box. Under Grammar, click the *Check grammar as you type* check box. There are also check boxes for hiding spelling and grammar errors. These should not be checked. Close the dialog box.

2 In the second line of the *Mission Statement,* locate the word *To* with the wavy green underline. Position your mouse pointer over the word and right-click.

A shortcut menu displays as shown in Figure 1.21. A suggested replacement is shown in the top section of the shortcut menu. In this instance, Word has identified an incorrectly capitalized word in the middle of a sentence.

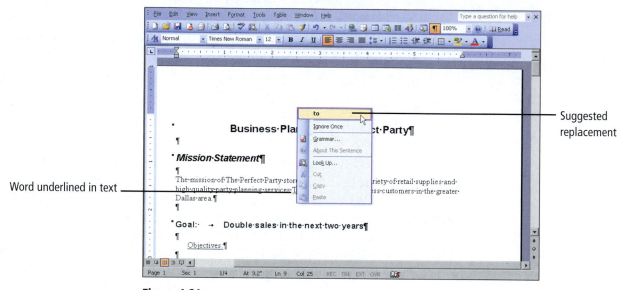

Figure 1.21

3 On the shortcut menu, click **to**.

The incorrect word is replaced.

4 In the first bullet point, find the word *the* with a wavy red underline. Position the mouse pointer over the word and right-click.

Word identified a duplicate word, and provides two suggestions—*Delete Repeated Word* or *Ignore*. See Figure 1.22. The second option is included because sometimes the same word will be used twice in succession.

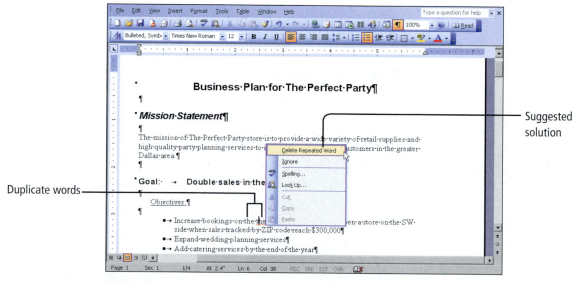

Figure 1.22

5 On the displayed shortcut menu, click **Delete Repeated Word**.

The repeated word is deleted.

Activity 1.10 Checking Spelling and Grammar in an Entire Document

Initiating the spelling and grammar checking feature from the menu or toolbar displays the Spelling and Grammar dialog box, which provides more options than the shortcut menus.

1 On the Standard toolbar, click the **Spelling and Grammar** button to begin a check of the document. If necessary, move your mouse pointer to the title bar of the dialog box, and drag the dialog box out of the way so you can see the misspelled word *awarness*.

The Spelling and Grammar dialog box displays. Under Not in Dictionary, a misspelled word is highlighted, and under Suggestions, two suggestions are presented. See Figure 1.23.

2 Take moment to study the spelling and grammar options available in the **Spelling and Grammar** dialog box as shown in the table in Figure 1.24.

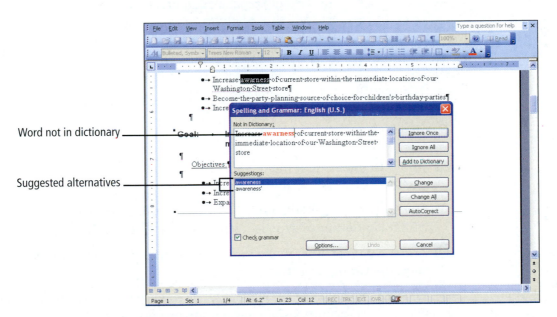

Word not in dictionary

Suggested alternatives

Figure 1.23

Spelling and Grammar Dialog Box Buttons

Button	Action
Ignore Once	Ignores the identified word one time, but flags it in other locations in the document.
Ignore All	Discontinues flagging any instance of the word anywhere in the document.
Add to Dictionary	Adds the word to a custom dictionary, which can be edited. This option does not change the built-in Microsoft Office dictionary.
Change	Changes the identified word to the word highlighted under Suggestions.
Change All	Changes every instance of the word in the document to the word highlighted under Suggestions.
AutoCorrect	Adds the flagged word to the AutoCorrect list, which will subsequently correct the word automatically if misspelled in any documents typed in the future.
Ignore Rule (Grammar)	Ignores the specific rule used to determine a grammar error and removes the green wavy line.
Next Sentence (Grammar)	Moves to the next identified error.
Explain (Grammar)	Displays the rule used to identify a grammar error.
Options	Displays the Spelling and Grammar tab of the Options dialog box.

Figure 1.24

3 Under **Suggestions**, make sure *awareness* is selected, and then click the **Change** button.

The correction is made and the next identified error is highlighted, which is another misspelled word, *merchandixing*.

4 Under **Suggestions**, make sure *merchandising* is selected, and then click the **Change** button.

The misspelled word is corrected, the next identified error is highlighted, and a number of suggestions are provided. This time the word is a proper noun, and it is spelled correctly. You could add this word to your dictionary, or choose to ignore it. See Figure 1.25.

Proper noun

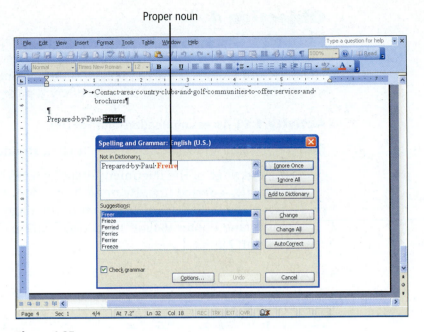

Figure 1.25

5 Click the **Ignore Once** button.

A dialog box displays indicating that the spelling and grammar check is complete. See Figure 1.26.

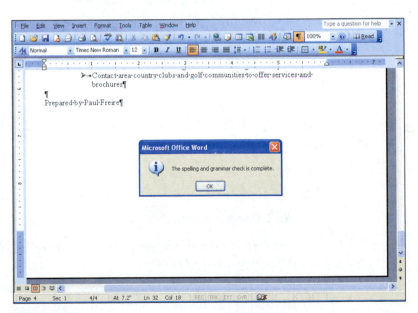

Figure 1.26

6 Click **OK** to close the dialog box.

Objective 4
View Headers and Footers

Headers and footers are areas reserved for text and graphics that repeat at the top (header) or bottom (footer) of each page in a document.

Activity 1.11 Accessing Headers and Footers

1 Display the **View** menu, and then click **Header and Footer**.

The first page of the document displays with the Header area outlined with a dotted line. By default, headers and footers are placed 0.5 inch from the top and bottom of the page, respectively. The Header and Footer toolbar displays, floating on your screen as shown in Figure 1.27.

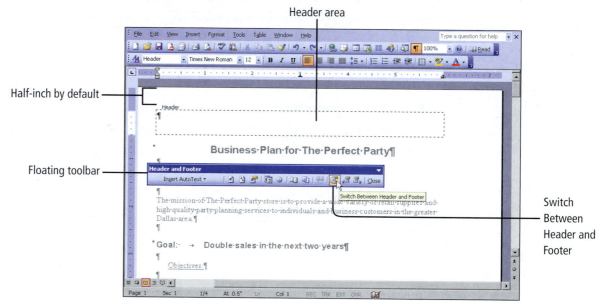

Figure 1.27

2 On the Header and Footer toolbar, click the **Switch Between Header and Footer** button.

The footer area displays with the insertion point blinking at the left edge of the footer area.

3 In the footer area, using your own name, type **1A Business Plan-Firstname Lastname** as shown in Figure 1.28.

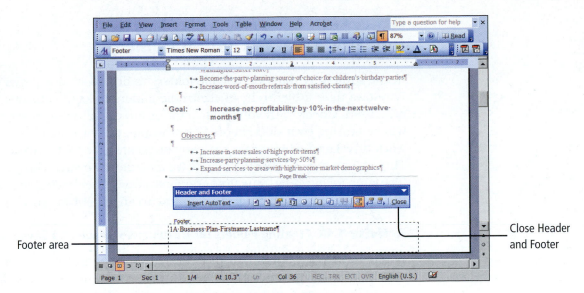

Footer area

Close Header and Footer

Figure 1.28

4 On the Header and Footer toolbar, click the **Close** button Close. Alternatively, double-click anywhere in the text area of the document to close the Header and Footer toolbar.

5 Scroll down until you can see the footer on the first page.

The footer displays in light gray as shown in Figure 1.29. Because it is a proper name, your name in the footer may display with wavy red lines.

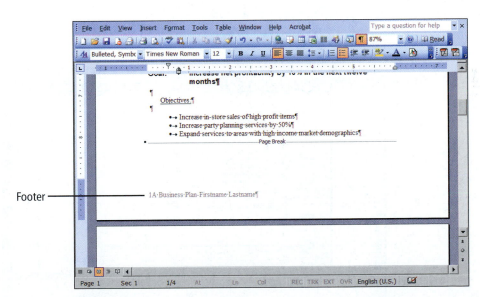

Footer

Figure 1.29

More Knowledge — Moving to the Header or Footer

A quick way to edit an existing header or footer is to double-click in the header or footer area. This will display the Header and Footer toolbar, and also place the insertion point at the beginning of the header or footer.

Objective 5
Organize, Save, and Print Documents

In the same way that you use file folders to organize your paper documents, Windows uses a hierarchy of electronic folders to keep your electronic files organized. Check with your instructor or lab coordinator to see where you will be storing your documents (for example, on your own disk or on a network drive) and whether there is any suggested file folder arrangement. Throughout this textbook, you will be instructed to save your files using the file name followed by your first and last name. Check with your instructor to see if there is some other file naming arrangement for your course.

Activity 1.12 Creating Folders for Document Storage and Saving a Document

When you save a document file, the Windows operating system stores your document permanently on a storage medium—either a disk that you have inserted into the computer, the hard drive of your computer, or a network drive connected to your computer system. Changes that you make to existing documents, such as changing text or typing in new text, are not permanently saved until you perform a Save operation.

1 On the menu bar, click **File**, and then click **Save As**.

The Save As dialog box displays.

2 In the **Save As** dialog box, at the right edge of the **Save in** box, click the **Save in arrow** to view a list of the drives available to you as shown in Figure 1.30. Your list of drives and folders will differ from the one shown.

Save in box

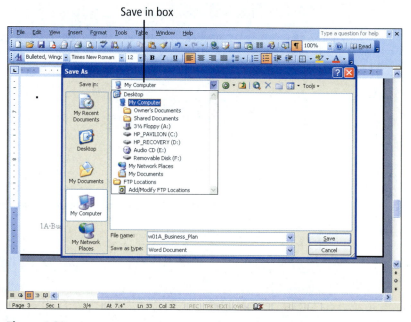

Figure 1.30

3 Navigate to the drive on which you will be storing your folders and projects for this chapter—for example, 3½ Floppy (A:) or the drive designated by your instructor or lab coordinator.

4 In the **Save As** dialog box toolbar, click the **Create New Folder** button.

The New Folder dialog box displays.

5 In the **Name** box, type **Chapter 1** as shown in Figure 1.31, and then click **OK**.

The new folder name displays in the Save in box, indicating that the folder is open and ready to store your document.

Create New Folder button

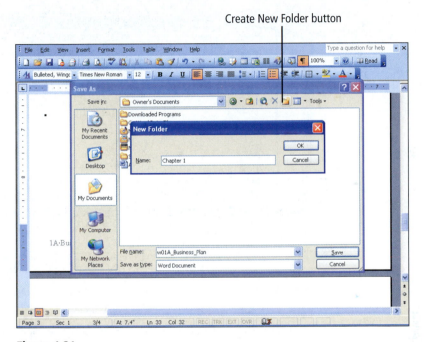

Figure 1.31

6 In the lower portion of the **Save As** dialog box, locate the **File name** box.

The file name *w01A_Business_Plan* may be highlighted in blue, in which case your new typing will delete the existing text.

More Knowledge — Renaming a Folder

You can rename folders as well as files. To rename a folder, right-click the folder in the Save As dialog box, click Rename from the shortcut menu, and then type a new folder name. This procedure also works in My Computer or Windows Explorer.

7 If necessary, select or delete the existing text, and then in the **File name** box, using your own first and last name, type **1A_Business_Plan_Firstname_Lastname** as shown in Figure 1.32.

The Microsoft Windows operating system recognizes file names with spaces. However, some Internet file transfer programs do not. To facilitate sending your files over the Internet using a course management system such as Blackboard, eCollege, or WebCT, in this textbook you will be instructed to save files using an underscore instead of a space. The underscore key is the shift of the ⎯ key, located two keys to the left of ⎡← Bksp⎤.

Underscore
characters
in file name
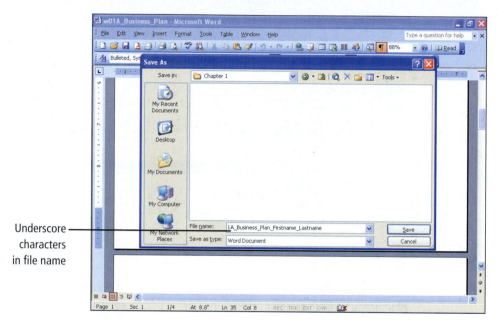

Figure 1.32

8 In the lower portion of the **Save As** dialog box, click the **Save** button, or press ⎡Enter⎤.

Your file is saved in the new folder with the new file name.

More Knowledge — Saving Your Document Often

Save your documents frequently to avoid losing the information you have created in a new document or the changes you have made to an existing document. In rare instances, problems arise with your computer system or your electrical power source. After a document is saved, hardware or electrical problems will not harm your document. However, you could lose any new editing that you performed on the document after the last save operation.

Activity 1.13 Printing a Document from the Toolbar

In Activity 1.13, you will print your document from the toolbar.

1 On the Standard toolbar, click the **Print** button 🖨.

One copy of your document prints on the default printer. A total of four pages will print, and your name will print in the footer area of each page.

2 On your printed copy, notice that the formatting marks designating spaces, paragraphs, and tabs do not print.

3 From the **File** menu, click **Exit**, saving any changes if prompted to do so.

Both the document and the Word program close.

Another Way ── **Printing a Document**

There are two ways to print a document:

- On the Standard or Print Preview toolbar, click the Print button, which will print a single copy of the entire document on the default printer.

- From the File menu, click Print to display the Print dialog box, from which you can select a variety of different options, such as printing multiple copies, printing on a different printer, and printing some but not all pages.

End **You have completed Project 1A** ────────────────

Project 1B **Thank You Letter**

In Project 1A you opened and edited an existing document. In Project 1B you will create and edit a new document.

In Activities 1.14 through 1.22 you will create a letter from Gabriela Quinones, a co-owner of The Perfect Party, to Paul Freire, a business consultant who was involved in preparing the business plan. Your completed document will look similar to Figure 1.33. You will save your document as *1B_ Thanks_Firstname_Lastname*.

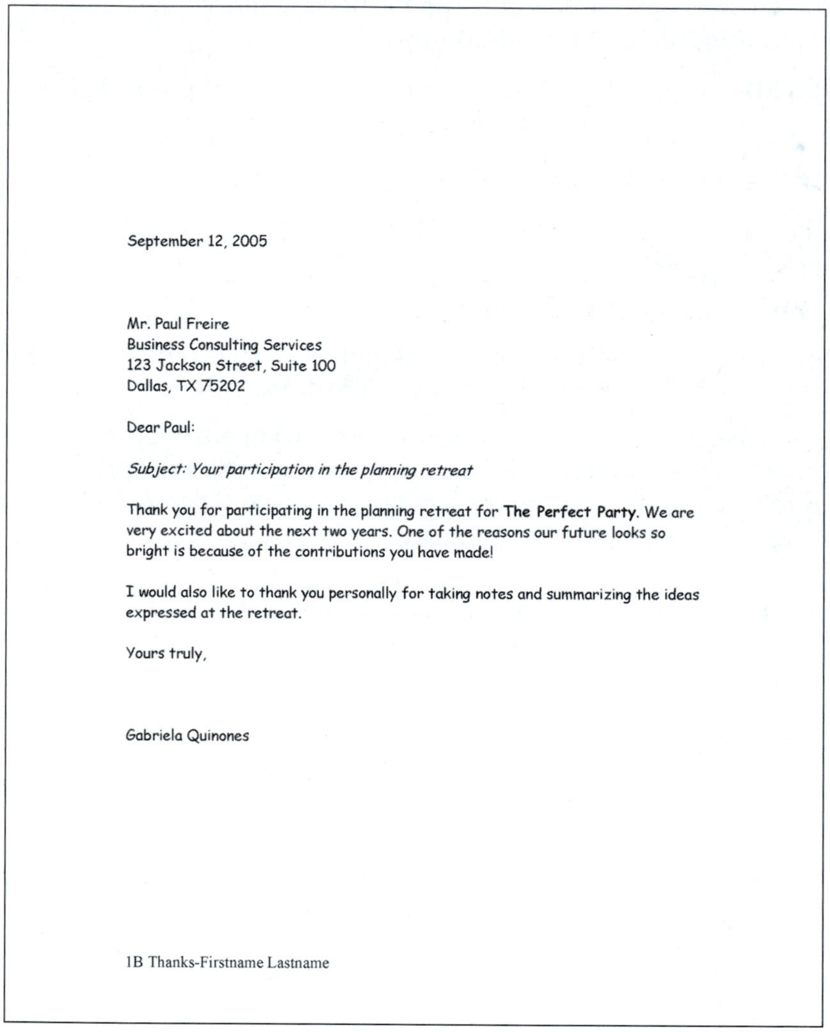

September 12, 2005

Mr. Paul Freire
Business Consulting Services
123 Jackson Street, Suite 100
Dallas, TX 75202

Dear Paul:

Subject: Your participation in the planning retreat

Thank you for participating in the planning retreat for **The Perfect Party**. We are very excited about the next two years. One of the reasons our future looks so bright is because of the contributions you have made!

I would also like to thank you personally for taking notes and summarizing the ideas expressed at the retreat.

Yours truly,

Gabriela Quinones

1B Thanks-Firstname Lastname

Figure 1.33
Project 1B—Thank you letter

Objective 6
Create and Edit a New Document

In Activities 1.14 through 1.17, you will practice the basic skills needed to create a new document, insert and delete text, and edit text.

Activity 1.14 Creating a New Document

1 Start Word. If necessary, close the Getting Started task pane by clicking the small Close button ☒ in the upper right corner of the task pane.

When Word is started, a new blank document displays.

2 In the blue title bar, notice that *Document1* displays.

Word displays the file name of a document in both the blue title bar at the top of the screen and on a button in the taskbar at the lower edge of the screen—including new unsaved documents. The new unsaved document displays *Document1* or *Document2* depending on how many times you have started a new document during your current Word session. See Figure 1.34.

Default document name ——

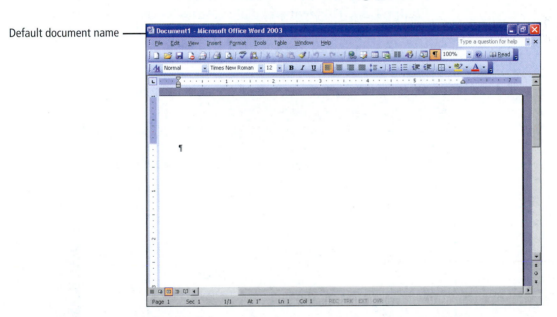

Figure 1.34

Opening a New Document

There are five ways to begin a new document in Word:

- Start the Word program; a new blank document displays.

- On the Standard toolbar, click the New Blank Document button.

- From the menu bar, click File, and then click New.

- From the Getting Started task pane, under Open, click *Create a new document.*

- From the New Document task pane, under New, click *Blank document.*

Activity 1.15 Entering Text and Inserting Blank Lines

1 Verify that formatting marks are displayed. If necessary, click the Show/Hide ¶ button to display them. With the insertion point blinking in the upper left corner of the document to the left of the default first paragraph mark, type **Sept**

A ScreenTip displays *September (Press ENTER to Insert)* as shown in Figure 1.35. This feature, called ***AutoComplete***, assists in your typing by suggesting commonly used words and phrases after you type the first few characters.

Show/Hide button

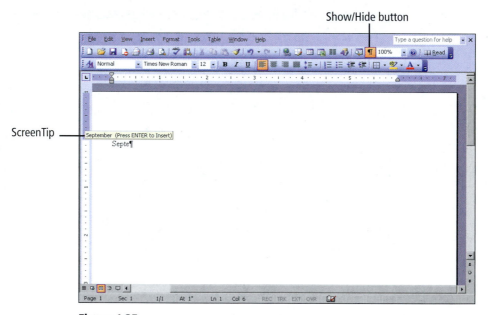

ScreenTip

Figure 1.35

2 To finish the word *September*, press [Enter]. Press [Spacebar] once and then type **12, 2005** and press [Enter]. (If you are completing this activity during the month of September, AutoComplete may offer to fill in the current date. To ignore the suggestion, type as indicated.)

The first paragraph is complete and the insertion point is positioned at the beginning of the next line. A paragraph is created when you press [Enter]. Thus, a paragraph can be a single line like the date line, or a blank line.

A purple dotted underscore beneath the date indicates that Word has flagged this as a *recognizer*. A recognizer indicates that Word recognizes this as a date. As you progress in your study of Microsoft Office, you will discover how dates such as this one can be added to other Office programs like Microsoft Outlook.

3 Press [Enter] three more times.

Three empty paragraphs, which function as blank lines, display below the typed date.

4 Type **Mr. Paul Freire** and then press [Enter].

5 On three lines, type the following address:

Business Consulting Services

123 Jackson Street, Suite 100

Dallas, TX 75202

6 Press [Enter] twice. Type **Dear Paul:** and then press [Enter] twice.

7 Type **Subject: Your participation in the planning retreat** and press [Enter] twice.

Compare your screen to Figure 1.36. The purple dotted line under the street address is another recognizer, indicating that you could add the address to your Microsoft Outlook address book or perform other useful tasks with the address. Additionally, the proper name *Freire* is flagged as misspelled because it is a proper name not contained in the Word dictionary.

Recognizers —

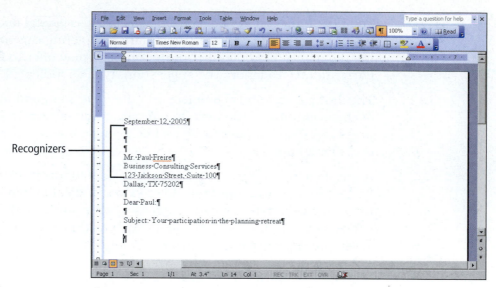

Figure 1.36

8 As you type the following text, press the Spacebar only once at the end of a sentence: **Thank you for participating in the retreat for The Perfect Party. We are really very excited about the next two years. One of the reasons our future looks so bright is because of the contributions you have made!** Press Enter twice.

As you type, the insertion point moves to the right, and when it reaches the right margin, Word determines whether or not the next word in the line will fit within the established right margin. If the word does not fit, Word will move the whole word down to the next line. This feature is **_wordwrap_**.

Note — Spacing at the End of Sentences

Although you may have learned to press Spacebar twice at the end of a sentence, it is common practice now to space only once at the end of a sentence.

9 Type **I would also like to thank you personally for taking notes and also for summarizing the ideas expressed at the retreat.**

10 Press ⏎ two times. Type **Your** and when the ScreenTip *Yours truly,* *(Press ENTER to Insert)* displays, press ⏎ to have AutoComplete complete the closing of the letter.

11 Press ⏎ four times, and then type **Angie Nguyen**

Compare your screen to Figure 1.37.

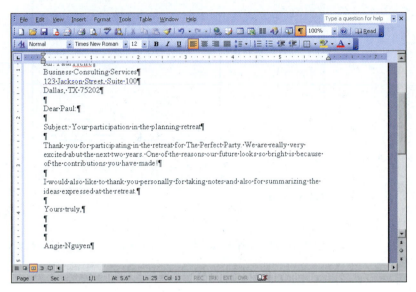

Figure 1.37

12 On the Standard toolbar, click the **Print Preview** button 🔍. If necessary, change the Zoom setting on the Print Preview toolbar to Whole Page to see the entire page as it will print.

Your document displays as it will print on paper. Notice that there is a large amount of blank space at the bottom of this short letter.

13 On the Print Preview toolbar, click **Close**. Display the **File** menu, and then click **Page Setup**.

14 On the displayed **Page Setup** dialog box, click the **Layout tab**. Under **Page**, click the **Vertical alignment arrow**. From the displayed list, click **Center** as shown in Figure 1.38.

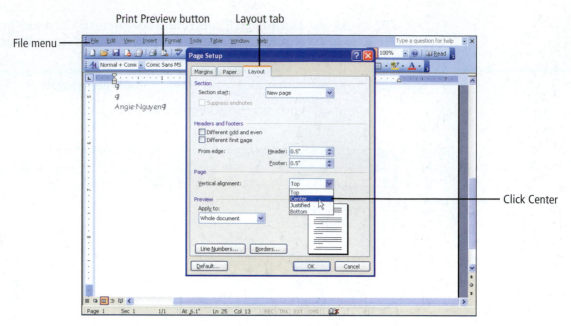

Print Preview button   Layout tab

File menu

Click Center

Figure 1.38

15 In the lower right corner of the **Page Setup** dialog box, click **OK**. On the Standard toolbar, click the **Print Preview** button.

Your document displays as it will print on paper. The text is centered on the page between the top and bottom margin. You can see that vertically centering one-page letters results in a more attractive and professional looking document.

16 On the Print Preview toolbar, click the **Close** button. On the Standard toolbar, click the **Save** button.

Because this document has never been saved, the Save As dialog box displays.

17 Use the **Save in arrow** to navigate to the **Chapter 1 folder** that you created in your storage location. In the lower portion of the **Save As** dialog box, in the **File name** box, delete any existing text and then type **1B_Thanks_Firstname_Lastname**

Make sure you type your own first name and last name as the last two parts of the new file name.

18 In the lower right portion of the **Save As** dialog box, click the **Save** button or press Enter.

Your file is saved in your Chapter 1 folder with the new file name.

Activity 1.16 Editing Text with the Delete and Backspace Keys

1 Scroll as necessary to view the upper portion of your document. In the paragraph beginning *Thank you,* at the end of the first line, click to position your insertion point to the left of the word *very.*

The insertion point is blinking to the left of the word *very.*

2 Press ⎡←Bksp⎤ once.

The space between the words *really* and *very* is removed. See Figure 1.39.

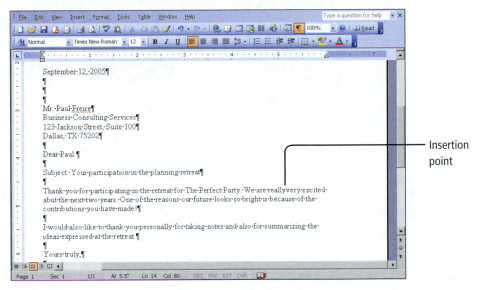

Insertion point

Figure 1.39

3 With the insertion point between the two words, press ⎡←Bksp⎤ six times.

The word *really* is removed. Make sure there is only one dot (dots are the formatting marks that indicate spaces) between *are* and *very.* You can see that when editing text, it is useful to display formatting marks.

4 In the paragraph beginning *I would,* in the first line, locate the phrase *for summarizing* and then click to position the insertion point to the left of the word *for.*

5 Press ⎡←Bksp⎤ five times.

The word *also* and the space between the words is removed.

6 Press ⎡Delete⎤ four times.

The word *for* to the right of the insertion point is removed, along with the space following the word. Make sure there is only one dot (space) between *and* and *summarizing.* See Figure 1.40.

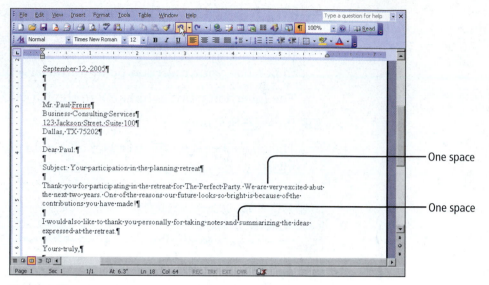

One space

One space

Figure 1.40

7 On the Standard toolbar, click the **Save** button ![save] to save the changes you have made to your document since your last save operation.

Activity 1.17 Inserting New Text and Overtyping Existing Text

When you place the insertion point in the middle of a word or sentence and start typing, the existing text moves to the right to make space for your new keystrokes. This is called ***insert mode*** and is the default setting in Word. If you press the [Insert] key once, ***overtype mode*** is turned on. In overtype mode, existing text is replaced as you type. When overtype mode is active, the letters *OVR* display in black in the status bar. When insert mode is active, the letters *OVR* are light gray.

1 In the paragraph beginning *Thank you,* in the first line, click to place the insertion point to the left of the word *retreat.*

The space should be to the left of the insertion point.

2 Type **planning** and then press Spacebar.

As you type, the existing text moves to the right to make space for your new keystrokes, and the overtype indicator (OVR) in the status bar is gray. See Figure 1.41.

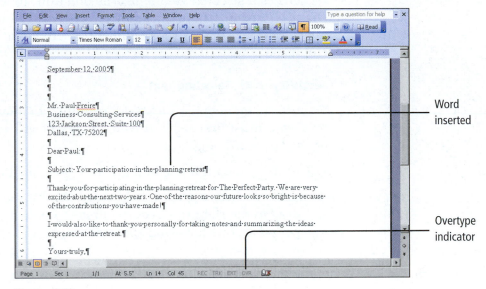

Figure 1.41

3 In the last line of the document, click to place the insertion point to the left of *Angie Nguyen*.

4 Press Insert, and notice that in the status bar, the OVR indicator is black, indicating that overtype mode is active.

When you begin to type, the new text will replace the old text, rather than move it to the right.

5 Type **Gabriela Quinones**

Notice that as you type, the characters replace the existing text.

6 Press Insert to turn off overtype mode. Alternatively, double-click the overtype indicator in the status bar.

7 On the Standard toolbar, click the **Save** button 🖫 to save the changes you have made to your document.

Objective 7
Select and Format Text

Selecting text refers to highlighting, by dragging with your mouse, areas of text so that the text can be edited, formatted, copied, or moved. Word recognizes a selected area of text as one unit, to which you can make changes. ***Formatting text*** is the process of setting the overall appearance of the text within the document by changing the color, shading, or emphasis of text.

Activity 1.18 Selecting Text

To perform an action on text—for example, to move, delete, or emphasize text—you must first select it. You can select text using either the mouse or the keyboard.

1 In the paragraph beginning *Thank you,* position the I-beam pointer to the left of *Thank*, hold down the left mouse button, and then drag to the right to select the first sentence including the ending period and its following space as shown in Figure 1.42. Release the mouse button.

The first sentence of the paragraph is selected. Dragging is the technique of holding down the left mouse button and moving over an area of text. Selected text is indicated when the background and color of the characters are reversed—the characters are white and the background is black as shown in Figure 1.42. Selecting takes a steady hand. If you are not satisfied with your result, click anywhere in a blank area of the document and begin again.

Period and space included in the selection

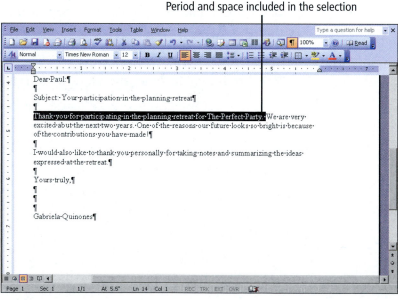

Figure 1.42

2 Click anywhere in the document to deselect the sentence. Then, in the same sentence, move the pointer over the word *Perfect* and double-click the mouse button.

The entire word is selected. Double-clicking takes a steady hand. The speed of the two clicks is not difficult (although you only have about a second between clicks), but you must hold the mouse perfectly still between the two clicks. If you are not satisfied with your result, try again.

3 Click anywhere to deselect the word *Perfect*. Then, move the pointer over the word *Perfect* and triple-click the mouse button.

The entire paragraph is selected. Recall that keeping the mouse perfectly still between the clicks is critical.

4 Hold down Ctrl and press A.

The entire document is selected. See Figure 1.43. There are many shortcuts for selecting text. Take a moment to study the shortcuts shown in the table in Figure 1.44.

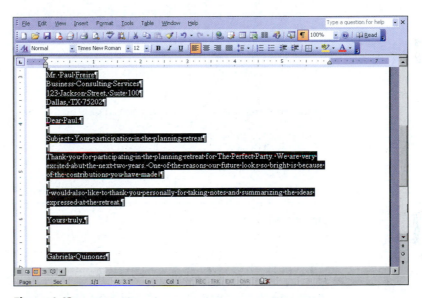

Figure 1.43

Selecting Text in a Document

To Select	Do This
A portion of text	Click to position the insertion point at the beginning of the text you want to select, hold down [Shift], and then click at the end of the text you want to select. Alternatively, hold down the left mouse button and drag from the beginning to the end of the text you want to select.
A word	Double-click the word.
A sentence	Hold down [Ctrl] and click anywhere in the sentence.
A paragraph	Triple-click anywhere in the paragraph; or, move the pointer to the left of the line, into the margin area. When the pointer changes to a right-pointing white arrow, double-click.
A line	Move the pointer to the left of the line. When the pointer turns to a right-pointing white arrow, click once.
One character at a time	Position the insertion point at the left of the first character, hold down [Shift] and press [→] or [←] as many times as desired.
A string of words	Position the insertion point to the left of the first word, hold down [Shift] and [Ctrl], and then press [→] or [←].
Consecutive lines	Hold down [Shift] and press [↑] or [↓].
Consecutive paragraphs	Hold down [Shift] and [Ctrl] and press [↑] or [↓].
The entire document	Hold down [Ctrl] and press [A] or move the pointer to the left of the line. When it turns to a right-pointing white arrow, triple-click.

Figure 1.44

5 Click anywhere in the document to cancel the text selection.

Activity 1.19 Changing Font and Font Size

A *font* is a set of characters with the same design and shape. There are two basic types of fonts—serif and sans serif. **Serif fonts** contain extensions or lines on the ends of the characters and are good choices for large amounts of text because they are easy to read. Examples of serif fonts include Times New Roman, Garamond, and Century Schoolbook. **Sans serif fonts** do not have lines on the ends of characters. Sans serif fonts are good choices for headings and titles. Examples of sans serif fonts include Arial, Verdana, and Comic Sans MS. The table in Figure 1.45 shows examples of Serif and Sans Serif fonts.

Examples of Serif and Sans Serif Fonts

Serif Fonts	Sans Serif Fonts
Times New Roman	Arial
Garamond	Verdana
Century Schoolbook	Comic Sans MS

Figure 1.45

1 Move the mouse pointer anywhere over the subject line in the letter and triple-click.

The entire paragraph is selected. Recall that a paragraph is defined as one paragraph mark and anything in front of it, which could be one or more lines of text or no text at all in the case of a blank line.

2 On the Formatting toolbar, locate the **Font Size button arrow** and click the arrow. On the displayed list, click **14** as shown in Figure 1.46.

Font size

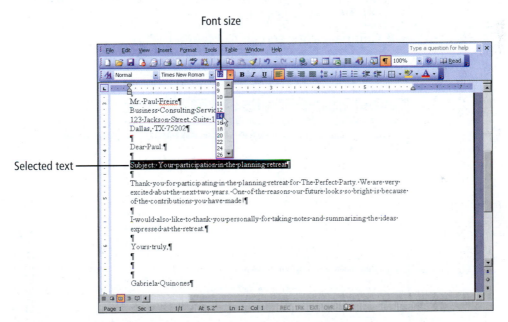

Selected text

Figure 1.46

Fonts are measured in **points**, with one point equal to 1/72 of an inch. A higher point size indicates a larger font size. For large amounts of text, font sizes between 10 point and 12 point are good choices. Headings and titles are often formatted using a larger font size. The word *point* is abbreviated as **pt**.

3 On the Formatting toolbar, locate the **Font button arrow** `Times New Roman ▾` and click the arrow.

On the displayed list, the fonts are displayed in alphabetical order. Word assists in your font selection by placing fonts recently used on this computer at the top of the list.

4 Scroll the displayed list as necessary and then click **Arial**. Click anywhere in the document to cancel the selection.

5 Hold down `Ctrl` and press `A` to select the document.

6 With the document selected, click the **Font button arrow** `Times New Roman ▾`. On the displayed list, scroll as necessary and then click **Comic Sans MS**.

The selected text changes to the Comic Sans MS font. In a letter, it is good practice to use only one font for the entire letter. This font is less formal than the default font of Times New Roman.

7 With the entire document selected, click the **Font Size button arrow** `12 ▾` and change the font size to **11**. Alternatively, you can type **11** in the Font Size box. Click anywhere in the document to cancel the text selection.

8 Compare your screen to Figure 1.47.

Font name ——————————   Font Size

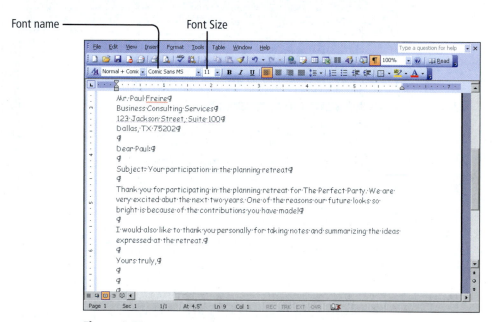

Figure 1.47

9 On the Standard toolbar, click the **Save** button 🖫 to save the changes you have made to your document. Leave the document open for Activity 1.20.

Activity 1.20 Adding Emphasis to Text

Font styles emphasize text and are a visual cue to draw the reader's eye to important text. Font styles include bold, italic, and underline, although underline is not commonly used for emphasis. You can add emphasis to existing text, or you can turn the emphasis on before you start typing the word or phrase and then turn it off.

1 Move the pointer over the subject line and triple-click to select the paragraph.

2 On the Formatting toolbar, click the **Italic** button 𝐼.

Italic is applied to the paragraph that forms the Subject line.

3 In the paragraph beginning *Thank you*, use any method to select the text *The Perfect Party*.

Another Way ── **Applying Font Styles**

There are three methods to apply font styles:

- On the Standard toolbar, click the Bold, Italic, or Underline button.

- From the menu bar, click Format, click Font, and apply styles from the Font dialog box.

- From the keyboard, use the keyboard shortcuts of Ctrl + B for bold, Ctrl + I for italic, or Ctrl + U for underline.

---

4 On the Formatting toolbar, click the **Bold** button **B**. Click anywhere in the document to cancel the selection.

5 On the Standard toolbar, click the **Print Preview** button and compare your screen to Figure 1.48.

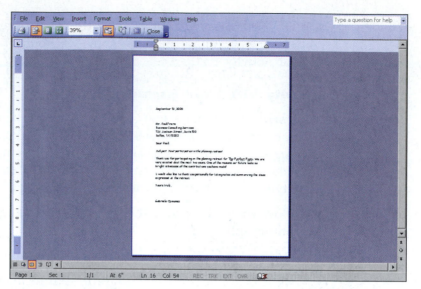

Figure 1.48

6 On the Print Preview toolbar, click **Close**.

7 In the inside address, right-click *Freire* and then click **Ignore All**. Correct any other spelling or grammar errors in your document.

8 On the Standard toolbar, click the **Save** button 📘 to save your changes.

More Knowledge — Using Toggle Buttons

The bold, italic, and underline buttons are toggle buttons; that is, you can click the button once to turn it on and again to turn it off.

Objective 8
Preview and Print Documents, Close a Document, and Close Word

While creating your document, it is helpful to check the print preview to make sure you are getting the result you want. Before printing, make a final check with print preview to make sure the document layout is exactly what you want.

Activity 1.21 Previewing and Printing a Document and Closing Word

1 From the **View** menu, click **Header and Footer**. (The large header area at the top is a result of vertically centering the document on the page.) On the displayed Header and Footer toolbar, click the **Switch Between Header and Footer** button 🔲.

The footer area displays. The insertion point is at the left edge of the footer area.

2 In the footer area, using your own name, type **1B Thanks-Firstname Lastname** as shown in Figure 1.49.

File name ⟶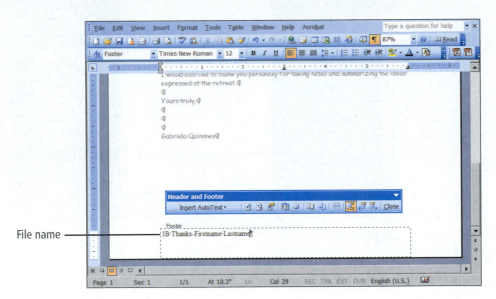

Figure 1.49

3 Double-click anywhere in the text area of the document to close the Header and Footer toolbar. Alternatively, on the Header and Footer toolbar, click the Close button Close .

4 On the Standard toolbar, click the **Print Preview** button .

Your document displays exactly as it will print. The formatting marks, which do not print, are not displayed.

5 In the **Print Preview** window, move the mouse pointer anywhere over the document.

The pointer becomes a magnifying glass with a plus in it, indicating that you can magnify the view. See Figure 1.50.

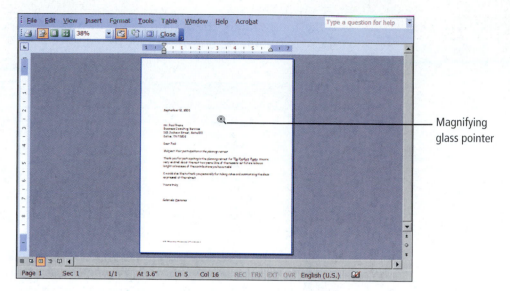

Magnifying glass pointer

Figure 1.50

6 Move the pointer over the upper portion of the document and click once.

The top portion of the document is magnified, and is easier to read. The pointer changes to a magnifying glass with a minus sign.

7 Click anywhere on the document.

The full page displays again.

8 On the Print Preview toolbar, click **Close**. On the Standard toolbar, click the **Save** button to save your changes.

9 Display the **File** menu, and then click **Print**.

The Print dialog box displays. See Figure 1.51. Here you can specify which pages to print and how many copies you want. Additional command buttons for Options and Properties provide additional printing choices. The printer that displays will be the printer that is selected for your computer.

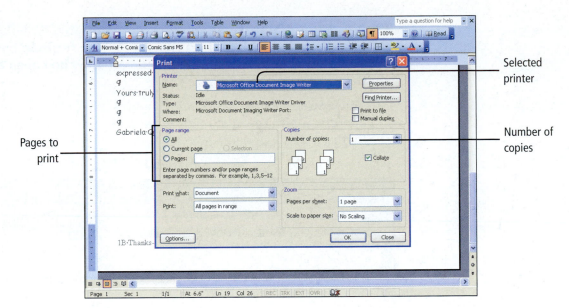

Pages to print

Selected printer

Number of copies

Figure 1.51

10 In the displayed **Print** dialog box, under **Copies**, change the number of copies to 2 by either typing **2** in the text box or clicking the **up arrow** in the spin box. See Figure 1.51. At the bottom of the **Print** dialog box, click **OK**.

Two copies will print.

11 From the **File** menu, click **Close**, saving any changes if prompted to do so. At the far right edge of the blue title bar, click the **Close** button ☒.

The Word program is closed.

Objective 9
Use the Microsoft Help System

As you work with Word, you can get assistance by using the Help feature. You can ask questions and Help will provide you with information and step-by-step instructions for performing tasks.

Activity 1.22 Typing a Question for Help

The easiest way to use Help is to type a question in the *Type a question for help* box, located at the right side of the menu bar.

1 If necessary, start Word. Move your pointer to the right side of the menu bar and click in the **Type a question for help** box. With the insertion point blinking in the box, type **How do I open a file?** and then press [Enter].

The Search Results task pane displays a list of topics related to opening a file. Your list may be quite different than the one shown in Figure 1.52.

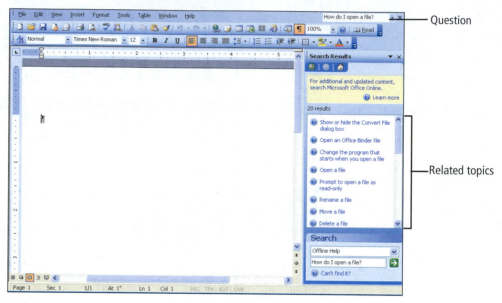

Figure 1.52

2 On the displayed list in the task pane, point to and then click **Open a file**.

The Microsoft Word Help window opens at listing instructions for opening a file. Text in blue at the bottom of the Help window indicates links to related instructions or related information.

3 At the bottom of the **Microsoft Office Word Help** window, click **Tips** to display additional information about opening files.

4 In the second bulleted item, point to and then click the blue highlighted words **task pane** to display a green definition of a task pane as shown in Figure 1.53.

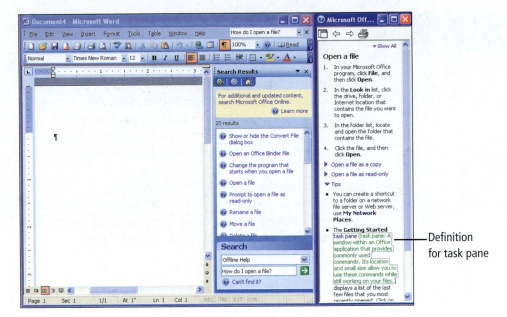

Definition for task pane

Figure 1.53

5 Click **task pane** again to close the definition.

6 In the **Microsoft Office Word Help** window, click the **Close** button ☒.

On the **Search Results** task pane, click the **Close** button ☒.

7 From the **File** menu, click **Exit** to close the Word program.

Another Way ── **Getting Help Using the Task Pane and the Office Assistant**

You can access Help by clicking the Microsoft Word Help button on the Standard toolbar. This action opens the Help task pane. In the Search box, type a topic that you want to learn more about and then press Enter. Results are displayed in the Search Results task pane. The Office Assistant, an animated character that provides tips as you work, can be displayed from the Help menu by clicking Show the Office Assistant.

End **You have completed Project 1B** ───────────────────────

Summary

In this chapter you practiced how to start Word and navigate in the Word window by using the mouse, toolbars, menus, shortcut menus, and shortcut keys. You examined documents in the Page Layout, Normal, and Reading Layout views; changed the magnification with the Zoom button; and displayed nonprinting characters with the Show/Hide ¶ button.

The basics of word processing were practiced including entering text, deleting text using the backspace or delete key, selecting and replacing text, inserting text, and overtyping existing text. The spelling and grammar checker tools were demonstrated.

You also practiced how to change font style and size and add emphasis to text. The header and footer area was viewed, and a chapter folder was created to help organize your files. Each document was saved, previewed, printed, and closed. Finally, the Help program was introduced as a tool that can assist you in using Word.

In This Chapter You Practiced How To

- Explore and Navigate the Word Window
- View Documents
- Use the Spelling and Grammar Checker
- View Headers and Footers
- Organize, Save, and Print Documents
- Create and Edit a New Document
- Select and Format Text
- Preview and Print Documents, Close a Document, and Close Word
- Use the Microsoft Help System

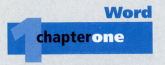

Concepts Assessments

Matching   Match each term in the second column with its correct definition in the first column by writing the letter of the term on the blank line in front of the correct definition.

_____ **1.** The point in the Word window, indicated by a blinking vertical line, where text will be inserted when you start to type.

_____ **2.** A view that simplifies the page layout for quick typing and can show more text on a smaller screen.

_____ **3.** The action that takes place when the insertion point reaches the right margin and automatically moves down and to the left margin of the next line.

_____ **4.** A button used to reveal nonprinting characters.

_____ **5.** The process of setting the overall appearance of the text within the document.

_____ **6.** A unit of measure that is used to describe the size of a font.

_____ **7.** A font type that does not have lines on the ends of characters.

_____ **8.** A type of font that is a good choice for large amounts of text because it is easy to read.

_____ **9.** A set of characters (letters and numbers) with the same design and shape.

_____ **10.** The term that refers to pressing one or more keys to navigate a window or execute commands.

_____ **11.** The Minimize, Maximize/Restore Down, and Close buttons are located here.

_____ **12.** A screen element that contains lists of commands.

_____ **13.** A context-sensitive list that displays when you click the right mouse button.

_____ **14.** The buttons used to Save or Print a document can be found here.

_____ **15.** The part of the screen that displays the Start button and the name of any open documents.

A Font

B Formatting

C Insertion point

D Keyboard shortcuts

E Menu bar

F Normal

G Point

H Sans serif

I Serif

J Shortcut menu

K Show/Hide ¶

L Standard toolbar

M Taskbar

N Title bar

O Wordwrap

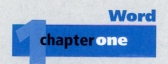

Fill in the Blank Write the correct answer in the space provided.

1. Microsoft Word 2003 is a word _____ program that you can use to do tasks such as writing a memo, a report, or a letter.

2. If you place your mouse pointer over a button on a toolbar, a small _____ displays the name of the button.

3. If you drag the _____ down it causes the document on your screen to move up.

4. The view that displays the page borders, margins, text, and graphics is known as the _____ view.

5. The portion of the Word window that opens to display commonly used commands or utilities available for use with the current job is known as the _____.

6. The View buttons are located to the left of the _____ scroll bar.

7. A row of buttons that provides a one-click method to perform common commands is called a _____.

8. To add emphasis to text, use the _____ or _____ or _____ buttons.

9. Before text can be edited, changed, formatted, copied, or moved, it must first be _____.

10. To display a shortcut menu, click the _____ mouse button.

Project 1C—Follow Up Letter

Objectives: *Explore and Navigate the Word Window; Use the Spelling and Grammar Checker; View Headers and Footers; Organize, Save, and Print Documents; Create and Edit a New Document; Preview and Print Documents, Close a Document, and Close Word.*

In the following Skill Assessment, you will edit a follow-up letter from Corey Finstad, a party planner for The Perfect Party, to a customer who has requested party-planning services. Your completed letter will look similar to the one shown in Figure 1.54. You will save your letter as *1C_Follow_Up_Letter_Firstname_Lastname.*

Figure 1.54

1. Start **Word**. On the Standard toolbar, click the **Open** button.

2. In the **Open** dialog box, at the right edge of the **Look in** box, click the **Look in arrow** to view a list of the drives available on your system. Navigate to the location where the student files for this textbook are stored.

(Project 1C–Follow Up Letter continues on the next page)

(Project 1C–Follow Up Letter continued)

3. Locate and click the file **w01C_Follow_Up_Letter**. In the lower portion of the **Open** dialog box, click the **Open** button.

4. If necessary, on the Standard toolbar click the **Show/Hide ¶** button to display formatting marks.

5. On the menu bar, click **File**, and then click **Save As**. In the **Save As** dialog box, click the **Save in arrow**, and then navigate to the location where you are saving your projects for this chapter. Recall that you created a Chapter 1 folder for this purpose.

6. In the **File name** box, using your own first and last name, type **1C_Follow_Up_Letter_Firstname_Lastname**

7. In the lower portion of the **Save As** dialog box click the **Save** button.

8. Be sure the insertion point is positioned to the left of the blank line at the top of the document. If necessary, hold down ⌃Ctrl and press ⌂Home to move the insertion point to the top of the document.

9. Begin typing today's date and let AutoComplete assist in your typing by pressing ⏎Enter when the ScreenTip displays. Press ⏎Enter four times. Notice the purple dotted line under the date, which is the recognizer that could add this date to your Outlook calendar. Type the following on three lines:

   Ms. Gloria Williams

   35 Pine Grove Avenue

   Dallas, TX 75202

10. Press ⏎Enter twice, type **Dear Ms. Williams:** and then press ⏎Enter once.

11. Hold down ⌃Ctrl and press ⏎End to move the insertion point to the end of the document. Press ⏎Enter twice, type **Best regards,** and then press ⏎Enter four times.

12. Finish the letter by typing the following on two lines:

   Corey Finstad

   Party Planner

13. Press ⏎Enter twice and type **Enclosure**

14. On the Standard toolbar, click the **Spelling and Grammar** button. The first error—a duplicated word—is highlighted, unless you made a typing error earlier in the document.

15. In the **Spelling and Grammar** dialog box, click the **Delete** button to delete the second occurrence of *the*. The next error is highlighted.

(Project 1C–Follow Up Letter continues on the next page)

(Project 1C–Follow Up Letter continued)

16. Under **Suggestions**, the first suggestion is correct. Click the **Change** button to change the misspelled word to the highlighted suggestion of *brochure*. The next error is highlighted.

17. Be sure *themes* is highlighted under **Suggestions**, and then click the **Change** button. Correct the next two errors, and then click **Ignore Once** to ignore the name *Finstad*. Click **OK** to close the box indicating the check is complete.

18. Drag the vertical scroll box to the top of the scroll bar to display the top of the document. In the paragraph beginning *Thank you*, double-click the word *handle* to select it and type **plan**

    Notice that your typing replaces the selected word.

19. In the paragraph beginning *You can select*, locate the first occurrence of the word *party*, click to the left of the word, type **prepared** and then press once.

20. On the menu bar, click **View**, and then click **Header and Footer**. Click the **Switch Between Header and Footer** button. In the footer area, using your own name, type **1C Follow Up Letter-Firstname Lastname**

21. On the Header and Footer toolbar, click the **Close** button.

22. Display the **File** menu, click **Page Setup**, and then in the displayed **Page Setup** dialog box, click the **Layout tab**. Under **Page**, click the **Vertical alignment arrow**, and from the displayed list, click **Center**. Recall that vertically centering one-page letters results in a more attractive letter. In the lower right corner of the dialog box, click **OK**.

23. On the Standard toolbar, click the **Save** button to save the changes you have made to your document.

24. On the Standard toolbar, click the **Print Preview** button to make a final check of your letter before printing. On the Print Preview toolbar, click the **Print** button, and then on the same toolbar, click the **Close** button.

25. From the **File** menu, click **Close** to close the document, saving any changes if prompted to do so. Display the **File** menu again and click **Exit** to close Word. Alternatively, you can close Word by clicking the **Close** button at the extreme right end of the blue title bar.

End **You have completed Project 1C**

Project 1D—Fax Cover

Objectives: *Explore and Navigate the Word Window; Create and Edit a New Document; View Documents; View Headers and Footers; Select and Format Text; Preview and Print Documents, Close a Document, and Close Word.*

In the following Skill Assessment, you will create a cover sheet for a facsimile (fax) transmission. When sending a fax, it is common practice to include a cover sheet with a note describing the pages that will follow. Your completed document will look similar to Figure 1.55. You will save your document as *1D_Fax_Cover_Firstname_Lastname.*

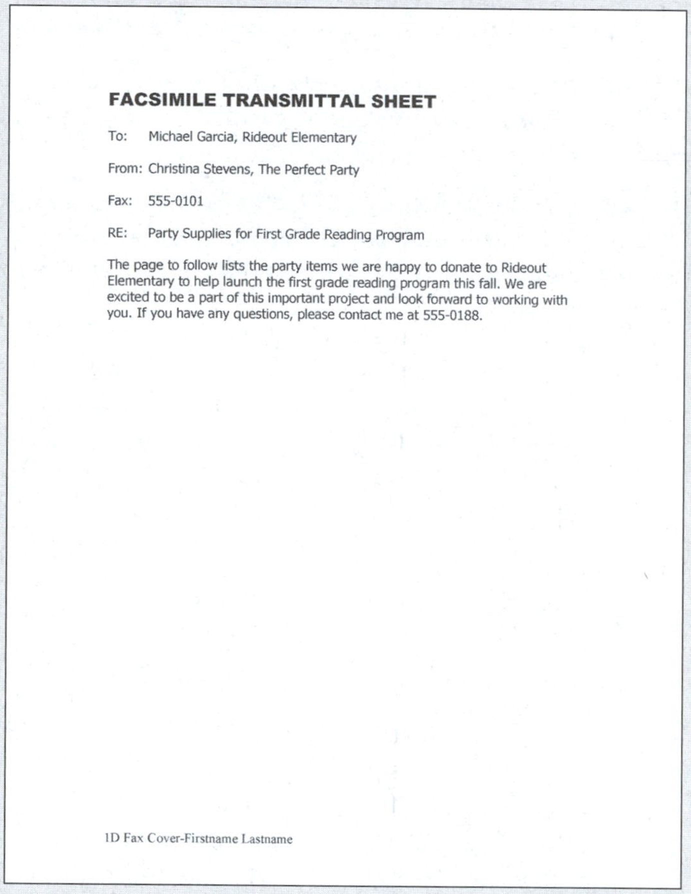

FACSIMILE TRANSMITTAL SHEET

To: Michael Garcia, Rideout Elementary

From: Christina Stevens, The Perfect Party

Fax: 555-0101

RE: Party Supplies for First Grade Reading Program

The page to follow lists the party items we are happy to donate to Rideout Elementary to help launch the first grade reading program this fall. We are excited to be a part of this important project and look forward to working with you. If you have any questions, please contact me at 555-0188.

1D Fax Cover-Firstname Lastname

Figure 1.55

1. Start **Word** and make sure the **Show/Hide ¶** button is active so you can view formatting marks. If necessary, close the task pane.

2. On your keyboard, press CapsLock. With the insertion point at the top of the document, type **FACSIMILE TRANSMITTAL SHEET** and then press Enter twice. Press CapsLock again to turn the feature off.

(Project 1D–Fax Cover continues on the next page)

Skill Assessments (continued)

(Project 1D–Fax Cover continued)

3. On the Standard toolbar click the **Save** button. Because this new document has never been saved, the **Save As** dialog box displays. Click the **Save in arrow**, and then navigate to the location where you are saving your projects for this chapter. In the **File name** box type **1D_Fax_Cover_Firstname_Lastname** and in the lower portion of the **Save As** dialog box, click the **Save** button.

4. Type **To:** press ⸤Tab⸥, type **Michael Garcia, Rideout Elementary** and then press ⸤Enter⸥ twice. Type the remainder of the fax headings as follows, pressing ⸤Tab⸥ after each colon (:) and pressing ⸤Enter⸥ twice at the end of each line. Refer to Figure 1.55.

   From: Christina Stevens, The Perfect Party

   Fax: 555-0101

   RE: Party Supplies for First Grade Reading Program

5. Type the following, and as you do so, remember to let wordwrap end the lines for you and to press the ⸤Spacebar⸥ only once at the end of a sentence:

   The page to follow lists the party items we are happy to donate to Rideout Elementary to help launch the first grade reading program this fall. We are excited to be a part of this important project and look forward to working with you. If you have any questions, please contact me at 555-0188.

6. On the Standard toolbar click the **Save** button to save your work.

7. Press ⸤Ctrl⸥ + ⸤A⸥ to select the entire document. On the Formatting toolbar, click the **Font arrow**, scroll as necessary, and then click **Tahoma**. Click anywhere in the document to cancel the selection.

8. Move the mouse pointer into the margin area to the left of *FACSIMILE TRANSMITTAL SHEET* until the pointer displays as a white arrow. Click to select the title line only. On the Formatting toolbar, click the **Font arrow**, scroll as necessary, and then click **Arial Black**. You can also type the first letter of the font to move quickly in the Font box. With the text still selected, click the **Font Size arrow**, and then click **16**. Click anywhere to cancel the text selection.

(Project 1D–Fax Cover continues on the next page)

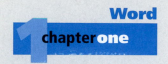
(Project 1D–Fax Cover continued)

9. On the menu bar, click **View**, and then click **Header and Footer**. On the Header and Footer toolbar, click the **Switch Between Header and Footer** button. In the footer area, type **1D Fax Cover-Firstname Lastname** using your own name. On the Header and Footer toolbar, click the **Close** button.

10. On your screen, notice that the word *Rideout*, which appears twice, is flagged as misspelled, and *The* is flagged as a grammar error. On the Standard toolbar, click the **Spelling and Grammar** button.

11. At the first occurrence of *Rideout*, click **Ignore All**. This action will remove the red flag from the second occurrence of the word. For the grammar error *The*, click **Ignore Once**. Because the word *The* is part of the proper name of the company, it is correct as written. If the Spelling and Grammar checker stops on your name, click **Ignore Once**. Click **OK** when the check is complete or, if necessary, click the **Close** button on the title bar of the **Spelling and Grammar** dialog box.

12. On the Standard toolbar, click the **Save** button to save your changes.

13. On the Standard toolbar, click the **Print Preview** button. On the Print Preview toolbar, click the **Print** button, and then click the **Close** button. From the **File** menu, click **Close**.

14. At right end of the title bar, click the **Close** button to close Word.

 You have completed Project 1D ————————————————

Project 1E—Survey Letter

Objectives: *Explore and Navigate the Word Window; View Documents; Create and Edit a New Document; Use the Spelling and Grammar Checker; Select and Format Text; View Headers and Footers; Organize, Save, and Print Documents; Preview and Print Documents, Close a Document, and Close Word.*

In the following Skill Assessment, you will edit a cover letter that will be sent with a survey to clients. Your completed document will look similar to Figure 1.56. You will save your document as *1E_Survey_Letter_Firstname_Lastname.*

November 23, 2005

Dear Customer:

Subject: We want to hear your opinion!

Thank you for using The Perfect Party services for your recent event. We hope that the party exceeded your expectations and that you will recommend us to your friends and associates.

As a new business, we are always looking for ways to expand our services. We know that our customers are our best advertising, and often they provide excellent suggestions that can help us develop our services. Please take a few moments to complete the short survey that is enclosed. Your candid comments and feedback are welcomed.

We look forward to working with you again when you want to throw another *Perfect Party.*

Best regards,

Angie Nguyen
Owner

Enclosure

1E Survey Letter-Firstname Lastname

Figure 1.56

1. Start **Word**. On the Standard toolbar, click the **Open** button.

2. In the **Open** dialog box, at the right edge of the **Look in** box, click the **Look in arrow** to view a list of the drives available on your system. Navigate to the location where the student files for this textbook are stored.

(Project 1E–Survey Letter continues on the next page)

(Project 1E–Survey Letter continued)

3. Locate and click the file **w01E_Survey_Letter**. In the lower portion of the **Open** dialog box, click the **Open** button.

4. If necessary, on the Standard toolbar, click the **Show/Hide ¶** button to display formatting marks.

5. On the menu bar, click **File**, and then click **Save As**. In the **Save As** dialog box, click the **Save in arrow**, and then navigate to the location where you are saving your projects for this chapter.

6. In the **File name** box, using your own first and last name, type **1E_Survey_Letter_Firstname_Lastname** and then click the **Save** button.

7. Move the pointer into the left margin to the left of the subject line until the pointer takes the shape of a white arrow. Click once to select the subject line. On the Formatting toolbar, click the **Font arrow**, and then click **Arial Black**.

8. In the sentence beginning *We once again*, drag to select the phrase *We once again want to* and then press ⌈Delete⌉ to remove this phrase. Press ⌈Delete⌉ to delete the *t* in *thank*, and then type **T**

9. In the same paragraph, select the phrase *hopes and dreams* and then type **expectations** and adjust spacing if necessary.

10. In the same paragraph, click to place your insertion point to the left of the word *recommend* and type **will** and then press ⌈Spacebar⌉.

11. In the paragraph beginning *As a new*, right-click *adverticing*, which is flagged as a spelling error. On the displayed shortcut menu, click *advertising*. In the same sentence double-click *ideas* to select it, and then type **suggestions** to replace it. In the same sentence replace the word *expand* with **develop**

12. In the same paragraph, right-click *moment*, which is flagged as a grammar error. From the displayed shortcut menu, click *moments*.

13. In the paragraph beginning *We look*, click to position the insertion point to the left of *Perfect Party*. Hold down ⌈Shift⌉ and ⌈Ctrl⌉ and then press ⌈→⌉ twice to select *Perfect* and then *Party*. Recall that this is a keyboard shortcut for selecting a string of words. On the Formatting toolbar, click the **Italic** button to apply the Italic font style to this phrase.

(Project 1E–Survey Letter continues on the next page)

(Project 1E–Survey Letter continued)

14. In the closing of the letter, click to position the insertion point to the left of *Sincerely* and then press ⌨Insert on your keyboard to activate Overtype mode. The OVR indicator on the status bar displays in black. Type **Best regards,** and then press ⌨Delete three times to delete the remaining unnecessary characters. Press ⌨Insert again to turn off Overtype mode and dim the OVR indicator.

15. Hold down ⌨Ctrl and press ⌨End to position the insertion point at the end of the document. Press ⌨Enter twice and then type **Enclosure**

16. On the menu bar, click **View**, and then click **Header and Footer**. On the Header and Footer toolbar, click the **Switch Between Header and Footer** button. In the footer area, type **1E Survey Letter-Firstname Lastname** and then on the Header and Footer toolbar, click the **Close** button.

17. From the **File** menu, click **Page Setup**, and then on the displayed **Page Setup** dialog box, click the **Layout tab**. Under **Page**, click the **Vertical alignment arrow**, and then click **Center**. In the lower right corner of the dialog box, click **OK**. Recall that one-page letters are commonly centered vertically on the page to give a more professional appearance.

18. On the Standard toolbar, click the **Save** button to save the changes you have made to your document. On the Standard toolbar, click the **Print Preview** button to view your document as it will print. On the Print Preview toolbar, click the **Print** button to print the letter, and then on the same toolbar, click the **Close** button.

19. From the **File** menu, click **Close** to close the document. At the right edge of the blue title bar, click the **Close** button to close Word.

End **You have completed Project 1E**

Project 1F—Interview Letter

Objectives: *View Headers and Footers; Create and Edit a New Document; Organize, Save, and Print Documents; and Preview and Print Documents, Close a Document, and Close Word.*

In the following Performance Assessment, you will create a letter to schedule an interview for Gabriela Quinones with a catering service. Your completed document will look similar to Figure 1.57. You will save your document as *1F_Interview_Letter_Firstname_Lastname.*

Figure 1.57

(Project 1F–Interview Letter continues on the next page)

(Project 1F–Interview Letter continued)

1. Start **Word** and, if necessary, close the task pane. Beginning at the top of the page type the address on three lines as shown:

   The Perfect Party
   700 Washington Street
   Dallas, TX 75202

2. Press Enter four times. Type **September 22, 2005** and press Enter twice. Type the following on three lines:

   Louise's Catering
   2302 Boardwalk
   Dallas, TX 75202

3. Press Enter two times and then type **RE: Catering Services**
   Press Enter two times and type the salutation **Dear Ms. Gomez:**

4. Press Enter twice and type the body of the letter as follows, pressing Enter two times at the end of each paragraph:

   We have received a tremendous response to our ad for catering services. Your resume and sample menus are outstanding and seem to fit with the vision for our business. We would like to interview you and give you a chance to ask us questions. We will be conducting interviews the week of October 10. My assistant, Ms. Finstad, will call to schedule a time that will be convenient for you.

   For the interview, we would invite you to bring a sample of your favorite dishes so we can have an opportunity to taste your creations. There will be only two people conducting the interview so a small sample would be appropriate.

   We are looking forward to meeting with you.

5. Press Enter twice and type **Cordially,** create three blank lines (press Enter four times), and then type the following on two lines:

   Gabriela Quinones
   Owner

(Project 1F–Interview Letter continues on the next page)

(Project 1F–Interview Letter continued)

6. On the Standard toolbar, click the **Save** button. In the **Save As** dialog box, navigate to the location where you are saving your projects for this chapter. In the **File name** box, using your own name, type **1F_Interview_Letter_Firstname_Lastname** and then click the **Save** button.

7. Display the **View** menu, and then click **Header and Footer**. Click the **Switch Between Header and Footer** button. In the footer area, using your own information, type **1F Interview Letter-Firstname Lastname**

8. Double-click in the body of the document to close the Header and Footer toolbar and return to the document.

9. Display the **File** menu, click **Page Setup**, and then click the **Layout tab**. Under **Page**, click the **Vertical alignment arrow**, and then click **Center**. Click **OK** to center the letter on the page.

10. Proofread the letter to make sure it does not contain any typographical or spelling errors. Use the Spelling and Grammar checker to correct any errors.

11. On the Standard toolbar, click the **Print Preview** button to see how the letter will print on paper. On the Print Preview toolbar, click the **Print** button to print the letter. Close Print Preview and then click the **Save** button to save your changes. Close the document and close Word.

 You have completed Project 1F ———————————

Project 1G — Interview Memo

Objectives: *Create and Edit a New Document; Select and Format Text; View Headers and Footers; and Organize, Save, and Print Documents.*

In the following Performance Assessment, you will edit a memo for Corey Finstad to Gabriela Quinones listing interviews that The Perfect Party has scheduled with catering firms. Your completed document will look similar to Figure 1.58. You will save your document as *1G_Interview_Memo_Firstname_Lastname.*

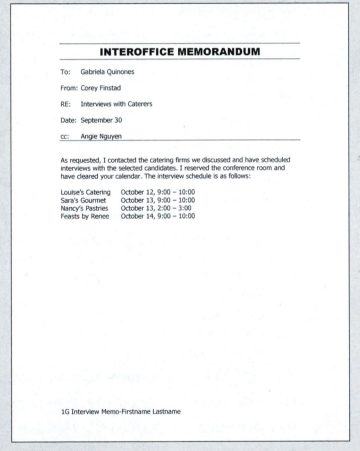

INTEROFFICE MEMORANDUM

To: Gabriela Quinones

From: Corey Finstad

RE: Interviews with Caterers

Date: September 30

cc: Angie Nguyen

As requested, I contacted the catering firms we discussed and have scheduled interviews with the selected candidates. I reserved the conference room and have cleared your calendar. The interview schedule is as follows:

Louise's Catering   October 12, 9:00 – 10:00
Sara's Gourmet   October 13, 9:00 – 10:00
Nancy's Pastries   October 13, 2:00 – 3:00
Feasts by Renee   October 14, 9:00 – 10:00

1G Interview Memo-Firstname Lastname

Figure 1.58

(Project 1G–Interview Memo continues on the next page)

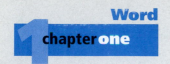

(Project 1G–Interview Memo continued)

1. Start **Word**. On the Standard toolbar, click the **Open** button. Navigate to the location where the student files for this textbook are stored. Locate and open the file *w01G_Interview_Memo*.

2. From the **File** menu, click **Save As**. In the **Save As** dialog box, navigate to the location where you are saving your projects for this chapter. In the **File name** box, type **1G_Interview_Memo_Firstname_Lastname** and then click the **Save** button.

3. Click after the colon in the word *To:* then press ⟨Tab⟩ and type **Gabriela Quinones**

   Press ⟨↓⟩ twice to move to right of *From:* then press ⟨Tab⟩ and type **Corey Finstad**

4. Use the same keystroke technique to complete the heading portion of the memo as shown:

   RE: Interviews with Caterers

   Date: September 30

   CC: Angie Nguyen

5. Click to position the insertion point at the beginning of the third empty line in the body of the memo, and then type the following:

   As requested, I contacted the catering firms we discussed and have scheduled interviews with the selected candidates. I reserved the conference room and have cleared your calendar. The interview schedule is as follows:

6. Press ⟨Enter⟩ twice. Type **Louise's Catering** Press ⟨Tab⟩ and type **October 12, 9:00 –10:00** and then press ⟨Enter⟩. Repeat this pattern to enter the remainder of the interview dates.

Sara's Gourmet	**October 12, 9:00–10:00**
Chef Michelangelo	**October 13, 9:00–10:00**
Nancy's Pastries	**October 13, 2:00–3:00**
Feasts by Renee	**October 14, 9:00–10:00**

(Project 1G–Interview Memo continues on the next page)

(Project 1G–Interview Memo continued)

7. On the Standard toolbar, click the **Spelling and Grammar** button. Click **Ignore Once** to ignore the any proper names that are flagged and correct any other errors that may be identified.

8. Beginning with the paragraph *As requested*, select all of the text of the memo and change the font to **Tahoma**, which is the same font used in the top portion of the memo.

9. Navigate to the top of the document and select the text *INTEROFFICE MEMORANDUM*. Change the font to **Arial Black** and the font size to **18** point.

10. Display the **View** menu and click **Header and Footer**. Click the **Switch Between Header and Footer** button. In the footer area, using your own information, type **1G Interview Memo-Firstname Lastname**

Select the text you just typed in the footer and change the font to **Tahoma**, **12** point. Double-click the body of the document to close the Header and Footer toolbar and return to the document.

11. On the Standard toolbar, click the **Save** button to save your changes. On the Standard toolbar, click the **Print Preview** button to preview the document before it is printed. Print the document. Close the file and close Word.

 End **You have completed Project 1G**

Project 1H—Offer Letter

Objectives: *Explore and Navigate the Word Window; View Documents; Use the Spelling and Grammar Checker; View Headers and Footers; Create and Edit a New Document; Select and Format Text; and Preview and Print Documents, Close a Document, and Close Word.*

In the following Performance Assessment, you will edit a letter for Gabriela Quinones to Sara's Gourmet requesting a follow-up meeting to discuss a possible business partnership. Your completed document will look similar to Figure 1.59. You will save your letter as *1H_Offer_Letter_Firstname_Lastname.*

The Perfect Party
700 Washington Street
Dallas, TX 75202

October 20, 2005

Sara's Gourmet
3200 Penny Lane
Dallas, TX 75202

Dear Sara:

We enjoyed meeting with you last week and were absolutely delighted with the appetizers you brought to the interview. You presented some unique ideas for party food, and demonstrated skill in the art of food presentation.

We would like to meet with you again before the end of the month to explore some possible business arrangements that would be mutually satisfying. As we stated in the interview, we are interested in working with someone on a contract basis initially, with a view to a longer term relationship that could include becoming a partner in *The Perfect Party*. We would like to discuss how your plans to grow your business might intersect with our need to add a catering component to our party planning business.

Please call my office at (214)-555-0188 to set up a time when you could meet with us. My partner, Angie Nguyen, is looking forward to meeting you.

Yours truly,

Gabriela Quinones
Owner

1H Offer Letter-Firstname Lastname

Figure 1.59

1. Start **Word**. On the Standard toolbar, click the **Open** button. Navigate to the location where the student files for this textbook are stored. Locate and open the file *w01H_Offer_Letter.*

2. Display the **File** menu, click **Save As**, and then use the **Save in arrow** to navigate to the location where you are storing your projects for this chapter. In the **File name** box, using your own information, type **1H_Offer_Letter_Firstname_Lastname**

(Project 1H–Offer Letter continues on the next page)

(Project 1H–Offer Letter continued)

3. In the paragraph that begins *We enjoyed meeting*, select *liked* and type **were absolutely delighted with** and then adjust the spacing if necessary.

4. In the same paragraph, select *interesting* and replace it with **unique** In the same sentence delete the word *alternatives.* In the same sentence, select the phrase *are very skillful* and replace it with **demonstrated skill**

5. In the paragraph that begins *We would like*, delete the word *once.* In the same sentence, replace the word *consider* with **explore** In the same sentence, place the insertion point at the end of the word *mutual* and type **ly**

6. There are some grammar and spelling errors that need to be corrected. Right-click on the duplicate or misspelled words and correct as necessary.

7. In the paragraph that begins with *We would like*, use the technique of Ctrl + Shift + → to select the three words *The Perfect Party* and then change the font to **Lucida Calligraphy**. If you do not have that font, choose a similar font from the list. Change the font size to **11** point. With the name still selected, click the **Bold** button.

8. Click in the blank line following *Yours truly* and add two more blank lines by pressing Enter two times. Three blank lines is the standard space allotted for a signature in a letter. Display the Page Setup dialog box and center the letter vertically on the page.

9. Display the **View** menu and then click **Header and Footer**. Click the **Switch Between Header and Footer** button. In the footer area, using your own information, type **1H Offer Letter-Firstname Lastname** Double-click in the body of the document to close the Header and Footer toolbar and return to the document.

10. Use Ctrl + Home to navigate to the top of the letter. On the Standard toolbar, click the **Read** button to display the document in Reading Layout view. Proofread the letter to make sure it is correct. In this format, two pages display to make the reading easier, but recall that this is not the page preview. When printed, the document will print on one page.

11. On the Reading Layout toolbar, click the **Close** button to return to the Page Layout view. Click the **Save** button to save your changes. Preview the letter in Print Preview and then print the document. Close the file and then close Word.

End You have completed Project 1H

Project 1I — Contract

Objectives: *Explore and Navigate the Word Window; View Documents; View Headers and Footers; Create and Edit a New Document; Use the Spelling and Grammar Checker; Select and Format Text; Organize, Save, and Print Documents; and Preview and Print Documents, Close a Document, and Close Word.*

In the following Mastery Assessment, you will complete a contract that is given to clients of The Perfect Party. Your completed document will look similar to Figure 1.60. You will save your document as *1I_Contract_Firstname_Lastname*.

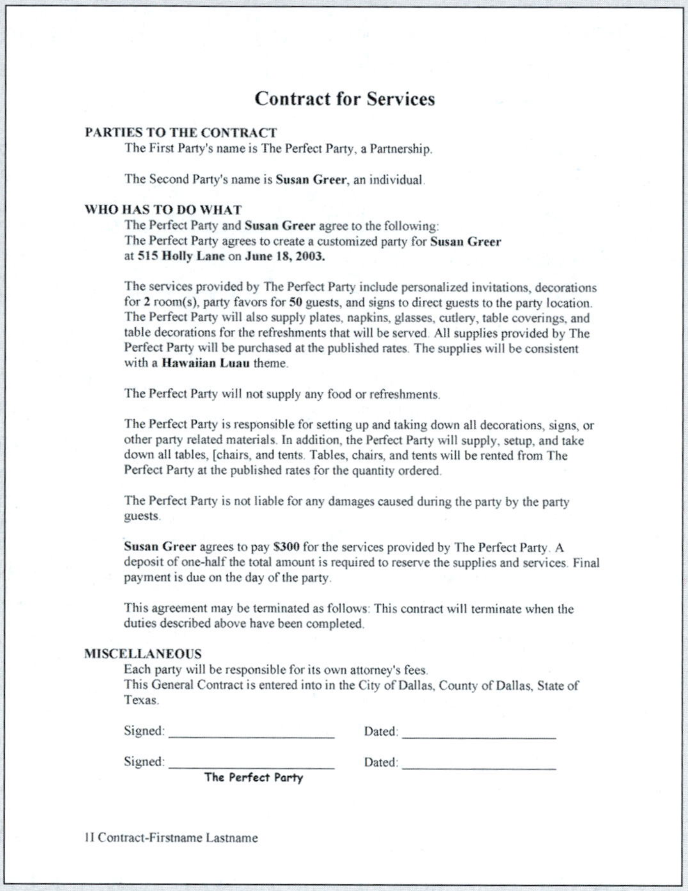

Contract for Services

PARTIES TO THE CONTRACT
The First Party's name is The Perfect Party, a Partnership.

The Second Party's name is **Susan Greer**, an individual.

WHO HAS TO DO WHAT
The Perfect Party and **Susan Greer** agree to the following:
The Perfect Party agrees to create a customized party for **Susan Greer**
at **515 Holly Lane** on **June 18, 2003.**

The services provided by The Perfect Party include personalized invitations, decorations for **2** room(s), party favors for **50** guests, and signs to direct guests to the party location. The Perfect Party will also supply plates, napkins, glasses, cutlery, table coverings, and table decorations for the refreshments that will be served. All supplies provided by The Perfect Party will be purchased at the published rates. The supplies will be consistent with a **Hawaiian Luau** theme.

The Perfect Party will not supply any food or refreshments.

The Perfect Party is responsible for setting up and taking down all decorations, signs, or other party related materials. In addition, the Perfect Party will supply, setup, and take down all tables, [chairs, and tents. Tables, chairs, and tents will be rented from The Perfect Party at the published rates for the quantity ordered.

The Perfect Party is not liable for any damages caused during the party by the party guests.

Susan Greer agrees to pay **$300** for the services provided by The Perfect Party. A deposit of one-half the total amount is required to reserve the supplies and services. Final payment is due on the day of the party.

This agreement may be terminated as follows: This contract will terminate when the duties described above have been completed.

MISCELLANEOUS
Each party will be responsible for its own attorney's fees.
This General Contract is entered into in the City of Dallas, County of Dallas, State of Texas.

Signed: _____   Dated: _____

Signed: _____   Dated: _____
          The Perfect Party

1I Contract-Firstname Lastname

Figure 1.60

1. Display the **Open** dialog box. Navigate to the student files, and then locate and open the file *w01I_Contract*. Display the **File** menu, click **Save As**, and then use the **Save in arrow** to navigate to the location where you are storing your projects for this chapter. In the **File name** box, type **1I_Contract_Firstname_Lastname**

2. Click the **Read** button to view this document and read through the contents of the contract. In the reading view, text size is increased to ease your reading of the document on the screen. Notice that there are three headings that are shown in all uppercase letters.

(Project 1I–Contract continues on the next page)

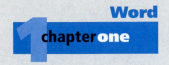
(Project 1I–Contract continued)

3. On the Reading View toolbar, click the **Close** button to return to the Print Layout view. Use the **Spelling and Grammar** checker to correct the errors in the document. The last error flagged shows *State*, and suggests that this needs to be changed to *and State*. Click **Ignore Once** to ignore this occurrence.

4. Locate the three headings in uppercase letters. Select each one and add bold emphasis.

5. Locate the black lines in the document that represent blanks to be filled in. Press [Insert] on your keyboard to turn on the overtype feature. Alternatively, double-click the **OVR** button displayed in the Status bar at the bottom of the Word Window.

6. In the line beginning *The Second Party's name*, click to position your insertion point after the space following *is*. Type **Susan Greer** and notice that as you type, your typing will be displayed in bold. Make sure you do not type over any of the words in the contract. Then, use [Delete] or [←Bksp] to remove the unused portion of the black line. On the next two black lines, type **Susan Greer** again and delete the rest of both black lines. On the fourth black line, following the word *at*, type **515 Holly Lane** and delete the rest of the black line. At the beginning of the next black line, type the current date followed by a period and delete the rest of the black line. Delete unused portions of the black lines using [Delete] or [←Bksp] as needed in the remaining steps.

7. In the paragraph that begins with *The services provided*, type **2** for the number of rooms to be decorated, and type **50** for the number of guests. On the last black line in this paragraph, type **Hawaiian Luau** as the theme for the party.

8. Locate the next black line, and type **Susan Greer** and in the next black line type **300** following the dollar sign.

9. At the end of the contract, under *Signed*, select *The Perfect Party* and change the font size to **10**, change the font to **Comic Sans MS**, and add bold emphasis.

10. Display the footer area, and then, using your own information, type **1I Contract-Firstname Lastname**

11. Save the changes. Preview the document and then print it. Close the file. On the Status bar, double-click the **OVR** button to turn off the overtype feature. Close Word.

End **You have completed Project 1I** ——————————————————

Project 1J — Memo

Objectives: *Create and Edit a New Document; View Documents; View Headers and Footers; Organize, Save, and Print Documents; Select and Format Text; Preview and Print Documents, Close a Document, and Close Word.*

In the following Mastery Assessment, you will create a memo for Christina Stevens requesting a copy of a contract from another Perfect Party employee and asking him to work at an upcoming event. Your completed memo will look similar to Figure 1.61. You will save your document as *1J_Memo_Firstname_Lastname.*

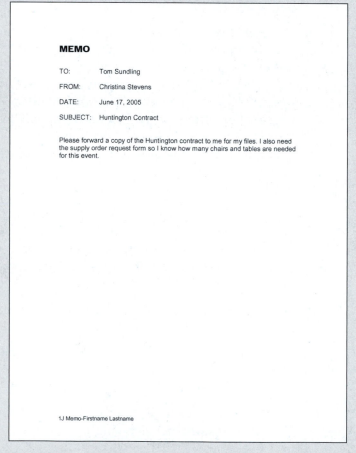

MEMO

TO: Tom Sundling

FROM: Christina Stevens

DATE: June 17, 2005

SUBJECT: Huntington Contract

Please forward a copy of the Huntington contract to me for my files. I also need the supply order request form so I know how many chairs and tables are needed for this event.

1J Memo-Firstname Lastname

Figure 1.61

1. Open **Word** and begin with a new document. Change the font to **Arial Black**, and the font size to **16**. Press CapsLock, type **MEMO** and press Enter twice. Change the font to **12-point Arial**.

2. Save the project in your storage location as **1J_Memo_Firstname_Lastname**

(Project 1J–Memo continues on the next page)

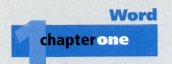

(Project 1J–Memo continued)

3. Change the font to **12-point Arial**. Type **TO:** and press Tab twice. Type **Tom Sundling** and press Enter twice. Follow the same pattern to enter the remainder of the heading, pressing Enter twice to create a blank line between each heading line. You will need to press Tab twice after *DATE* and then type the current date for the date line. Use the appropriate number of tabs to line up the text. Press CapsLock to turn it off.

   FROM: **Christina Stevens**

   DATE:

   SUBJECT: Huntington Contract Party

4. Make sure the information entered in the memo heading aligns as shown in Figure 1.61. Save your document.

5. At the end of the Subject line, press Enter three times and type the body of the memo as follows:

   Please forward a copy of the Huntington contract to me for my files. I also need the supply order request form so I know how many chairs and tables are needed for this event.

6. Save your document. Create a footer and type **1J Memo-Firstname Lastname** and then format the text in the footer to **10-point Arial** font.

7. Proofread the document and use the Spelling and Grammar checker to correct any errors if necessary.

8. Print the memo, save your changes, and close the file.

End **You have completed Project 1J** ——————————

Project 1K — Party

Objectives: *Create and Edit a New Document; View Headers and Footers; Organize, Save, and Print Documents; Select and Format Text; Preview and Print Documents, Close a Document, and Close Word.*

Using the information provided, draft a letter for the owners of The Perfect Party describing the services available to potential customers. Save your document as *1K_Party_Firstname_Lastname*.

1. Open **Word**. Type the current date and press Enter four times to create two blank lines. Type **Dear** and then create a blank line.

2. Compose a letter that explains the services offered by The Perfect Party. The tone of the letter should be positive and sales oriented. The letter should answer the question "why do I need this service?" As you write the letter, use your own imagination along with the information in the beginning of the chapter that describes the company. The letter should contain three paragraphs—an introductory paragraph, a second paragraph describing the services offered, and a closing paragraph.

3. Add an appropriate closing, such as **Sincerely**
   Create three blank lines and then type:

   Angie Nguyen

   Owner

4. Proofread the letter and correct any spelling or grammar errors.

5. Change the font of the letter to a font and font size of your choosing.

6. Create a footer and, using your own information, type **1K Party-Firstname Lastname**

7. Preview the letter. Use the **Page Setup** dialog box to center the letter vertically on the page.

8. Save the letter in your storage location as **1K_Party_Firstname_Lastname** Print the letter. Close the file and close Word.

 End **You have completed Project 1K**

Project 1L — Invitation

Objectives: *Create and Edit a New Document; View Headers and Footers; Organize, Save, and Print Documents; Select and Format Text; Preview and Print Documents, Close a Document, and Close Word.*

Create a sample invitation for The Perfect Party that could be used for birthday parties. Save your invitation as *1L_Invitation_Firstname_Lastname.*

1. From your student files, open the file *w01L_Invitation* and save it in your storage location as **1L_Invitation_Firstname_Lastname**. This document contains only a title. On separate lines add labels for information that is typically found on an invitation, such as who the party is for; when, where, and why it is being held; any party theme; refreshments provided; and an R.S.V.P line. Place a blank line between each line of information.

2. Change the font of the title to **Batang** and increase the font size so the title is large and easy to read. Add bold emphasis to the title. If Batang is not available on your computer, choose another font.

3. Format the labels to **12-point Batang**. Add bold emphasis to the labels.

4. Next to each label, add a statement in brackets that describes the information to enter in each empty space; for example, **[Enter address of party]**

5. Change the font of the instructions on each line to a font of your choice in an appropriate font size.

6. View the footer area and, using your own information, type **1L Invitation-Firstname Lastname**

7. Save your changes and print the invitation. Close the file and close Word.

End **You have completed Project 1L** ━━━━━━━━━━━━━━━

On the Internet

Microsoft Word Specialist Certification

As you progress through this textbook, you will practice skills necessary to complete the Microsoft certification test for Word 2003. Access your Internet connection and go to the Microsoft certification Web site at **www.microsoft.com/traincert/mcp/officespecialist/requirements.asp**. Navigate to the Microsoft Word objectives for the certification exam. Print the Core (Specialist) objectives for the Microsoft Word user certification and any other information about taking the test.

GO! with Help

Getting Help While You Work

The Word Help system is extensive and can help you as you work. In this exercise, you will view information about getting help as you work in Word.

1. Start **Word**. On the Standard toolbar, click the **Microsoft Office Word Help** button. In the **Search for** box, on the **Microsoft Word Help** task pane type **help**. Click the green **Start searching** button to the right of the *Search for* box.

2. In the displayed **Search Results** task pane, click *About getting help while you work*. Maximize the displayed window, and at the top of the window, click the **Show All** link. Scroll through and read all the various ways you can get help while working in Word.

3. If you want, print a copy of the information by clicking the printer button at the top of Microsoft Office Word Help task pane.

4. Close the Help window, and then close Word.

chapterone

Getting Started with Excel 2003

In this chapter, you will: complete these projects and practice these skills.

Project 1A
Navigating a Workbook

Objectives

- Start Excel and Navigate a Workbook
- Create Headers and Footers
- Preview and Print a Workbook
- Save and Close a Workbook and Exit Excel

Project 1B
Creating a New Workbook

Objectives

- Create a New Workbook
- Enter and Edit Data in a Worksheet
- Create Formulas
- Use Zoom and the Spelling Checker Tool
- Print a Worksheet Using the Print Dialog Box
- Use Excel Help

The City of Desert Park

Desert Park, Arizona, is a thriving city with a population of just under 1 million in an ideal location serving major markets in the western United States and Mexico. Desert Park's temperate year-round climate attracts both visitors and businesses, and it is one of the most popular vacation destinations in the world. The city expects and has plenty of space for long-term growth, and most of the undeveloped land already has a modern infrastructure and assured water supply in place.

© Getty Images, Inc.

Working with Spreadsheets

Using Microsoft Office Excel 2003, you can create and analyze data organized into columns and rows. After the data is in place, you can perform calculations, analyze the data to make logical decisions, and create a visual representation of the data in the form of charts. In addition to its spreadsheet capability, Excel can manage your data, sort your data, and search for specific pieces of information within your data.

In this chapter you will learn to create and use an Excel workbook. You will learn the basics of spreadsheet design, how to create a footer, how to enter and edit data in a worksheet, how to navigate within a workbook, and how to save, preview, and print your work. You will create formulas to add and multiply numbers. You will use AutoComplete, Excel's spelling checker tool, and access Excel's Help feature.

Project 1A **Gas Usage**

In this project, you will start the Excel program and practice moving around in a workbook. You will also create a footer with your name and print the four worksheets in the workbook.

In Activities 1.1 through 1.12, you will *edit* (update and make changes to) an existing Excel workbook for Dennis Johnson, Police Chief of Desert Park. The Desert Park Police Department has three 12-passenger vans—one at each of the three police stations in the city. Chief Johnson has asked all station captains to track the amount of gasoline and mileage for the vans by recording the number of miles traveled each time gasoline is purchased. The four worksheets of your completed workbook will look similar to Figure 1.1. You will save your workbook as *1A_Gas_Usage_Firstname_Lastname*.

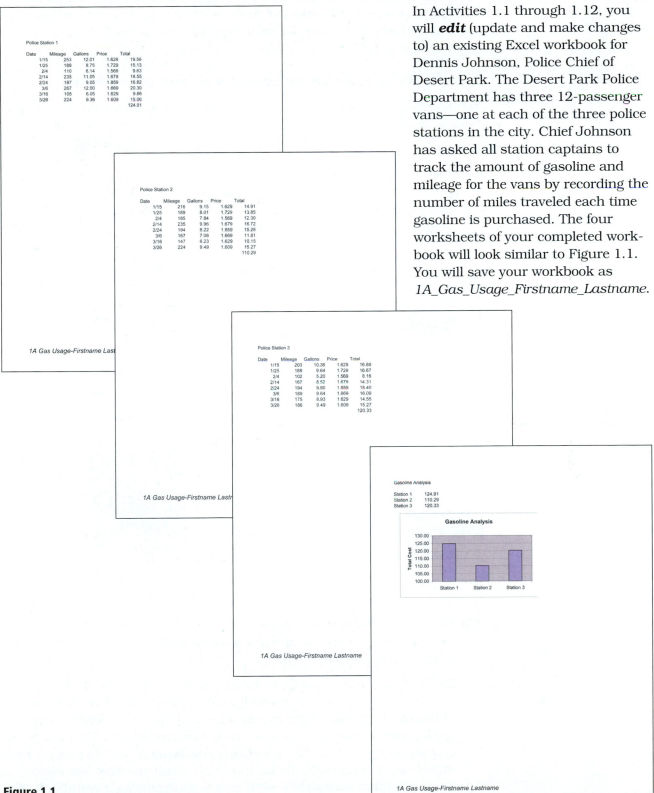

Police Station 1

Date	Mileage	Gallons	Price	Total
1/15	253	12.01	1.629	19.56
1/25	189	8.75	1.729	15.13
2/4	110	6.14	1.569	9.63
2/14	235	11.05	1.679	18.55
2/24	187	9.05	1.859	16.82
3/6	267	12.00	1.669	20.30
3/16	105	6.05	1.629	9.86
3/26	224	9.36	1.609	15.06
				124.91

Police Station 2

Date	Mileage	Gallons	Price	Total
1/15	216	9.15	1.629	14.91
1/25	189	8.01	1.729	13.85
2/4	185	7.84	1.569	12.30
2/14	235	9.96	1.679	16.72
2/24	194	8.22	1.859	15.28
3/6	167	7.08	1.669	11.81
3/16	147	6.23	1.629	10.15
3/26	224	9.49	1.609	15.27
				110.29

Police Station 3

Date	Mileage	Gallons	Price	Total
1/15	203	10.36	1.629	16.88
1/25	189	9.64	1.729	16.67
2/4	102	5.20	1.569	8.16
2/14	167	8.52	1.679	14.31
2/24	194	9.90	1.859	18.40
3/6	189	9.64	1.669	16.09
3/16	175	8.93	1.629	14.55
3/26	186	9.49	1.609	15.27
				120.33

Gasoline Analysis

Station 1	124.91
Station 2	110.29
Station 3	120.33

1A Gas Usage-Firstname Lastname

Figure 1.1
Project 1A—Gas Usage

Objective 1
Start Excel and Navigate a Workbook

When you start the Excel program, a new blank **workbook** displays. Within a workbook are one or more pages called **worksheets**. A worksheet is formatted as a pattern of uniformly spaced horizontal and vertical lines. This grid pattern of the worksheet forms vertical columns and horizontal rows. The intersection of a column and a row forms a small rectangular box referred to as a **cell**.

Activity 1.1 Starting Excel and Identifying the Parts of the Window

You start Excel in the same manner as you start other Microsoft Office System 2003 programs.

1 On the Windows taskbar, click the **Start** button ![start] .

The Start menu displays. Organizations and individuals store computer programs in a variety of ways. The Excel program might be installed under "All Programs" or "Microsoft Office" or some other arrangement. See Figure 1.2 for an example.

All Programs

Start button

Microsoft Excel Office 2003

Figure 1.2

2 Point to **All Programs**, determine where the Excel program is located, point to **Microsoft Office Excel 2003**, and then click once to start the program.

Excel opens, and a blank workbook displays. The default Excel working environment consists of a menu bar, toolbars across the top of the window, and a main window divided into two sections—the **task pane** on the right and the worksheet on the left. The task pane is a window within a Microsoft Office application that displays commonly used commands. Its location and small size give you easy access to these commands while still working on your workbook. See Figure 1.3.

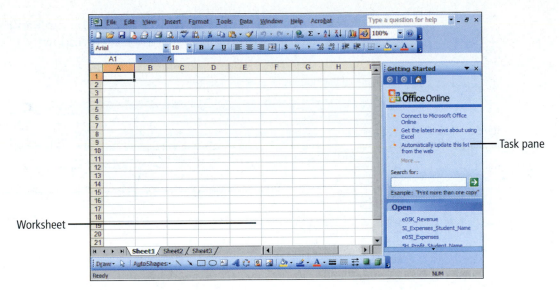

Worksheet

Task pane

Figure 1.3

3 In the upper right corner of the task pane, click the **Close** button ☒ to close the task pane.

The task pane closes. When not in use, you can close the task pane in this manner to allow the maximum amount of screen space for your worksheet. See Figure 1.4.

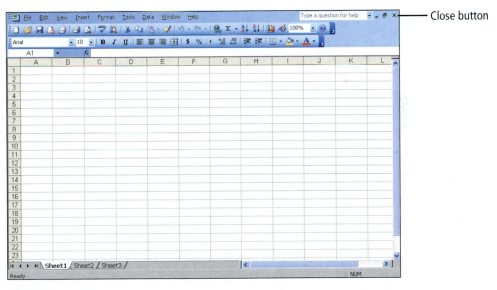

Close button

Figure 1.4

4 Take a moment to study Figure 1.5a-b and the table in Figure 1.6 to become familiar with the parts of the Excel window.

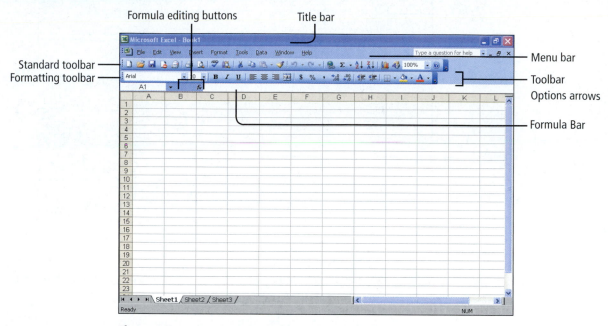

Formula editing buttons   Title bar

Standard toolbar
Formatting toolbar

Menu bar

Toolbar
Options arrows

Formula Bar

Figure 1.5a

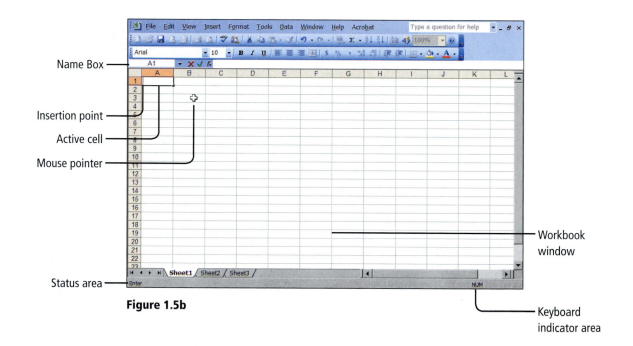

Name Box

Insertion point

Active cell

Mouse pointer

Workbook
window

Status area

Figure 1.5b

Keyboard
indicator area

Parts of the Excel Window

Excel Window Element	Description
Title bar	Displays the program icon, the program name, and the workbook name. The Minimize, Maximize or Restore, and Close buttons are at the extreme right edge of the title bar.
Menu bar	Contains the menus of commands. Display a menu by clicking on its name in the menu bar or by pressing Alt and pressing the underlined letter in the menu name.
Standard toolbar	Contains buttons for some of the most common commands in Excel, for example, Print and Save. It may occupy an entire row or share a row with the Formatting toolbar.
Formatting toolbar	Contains buttons for some of the most common formatting commands in Excel. It may occupy an entire row or share a row with the Standard toolbar.
Toolbar Options arrow	Displays additional buttons on the Formatting and Standard toolbars and also permits moving the toolbar to a separate or shared row.
Name Box	Identifies the selected cell, chart item, or drawing object. Also used to type a name for a cell or range of cells.
Formula editing buttons	Display when you are entering or editing data in a cell and assist in editing. The X button cancels the entry; the check mark button functions in the same manner as pressing Enter—it locks in your information; and the *fx* button displays the Insert Function dialog box to assist you in building a formula.
Formula Bar	Displays the value or formula contained in the active cell. Also permits entry or editing of values or formulas in cells or charts.
Insertion point	A blinking vertical bar that indicates where typed text or numbers will be inserted.
Active cell	The cell in which the next keystroke or command will take place. A black border surrounds the cell when it is active.
Mouse pointer	A graphic screen image controlled by your movement of the mouse.
Workbook window	The area of the Excel window containing the worksheets and the rows, columns, and cells of the active worksheet. The area of the workbook window ruled with horizontal and vertical lines makes up the worksheet's cells.
Status area	Displays information about the active cell.
Keyboard indicator area	Displays the current status of various keyboard functions such as the on or off status of NumLock.

Figure 1.6

Activity 1.2 Using the Menu Bar, ScreenTips, and the Toolbars

1 On the menu bar, click **File**.

The File menu displays in either the full format, as shown in Figure 1.7, or in a short format, as shown in Figure 1.8. Excel's commands are organized in *menus*—lists of commands within a category. A short menu will display fully after a few seconds, or you can click the double arrows at the bottom to display the full menu. The File menu, when displayed in full, lists the last four to nine workbooks used on your computer. Whether your full menu displays immediately or is delayed by a few seconds depends on the options that are set for this software. Likewise, the number of previous workbook names displayed depends on how the software was set up. These default settings can be changed in the Options dialog box (displayed from the Tools menu) on systems where it is permissible to do so.

Full format ———
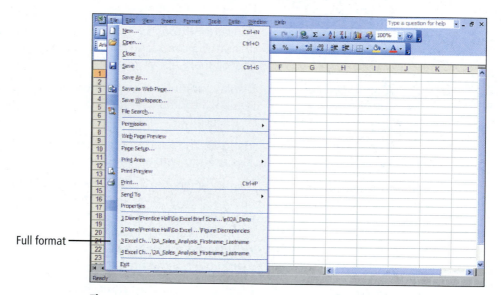

Figure 1.7

Short format ———
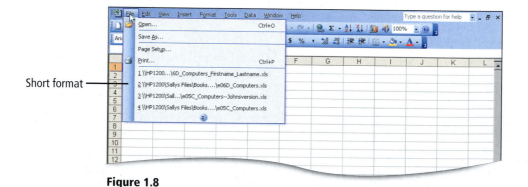

Figure 1.8

Note — Displaying Full Menus

Many Excel users prefer the automatic full menu display. To set a system to always display full menus, display the Tools menu, click Customize, and then click the Options tab. Under Personalized Menus and Toolbars, select the Always show full menus check box. Click the Reset menu and toolbar usage data button, click Yes, and then click Close.

2 If the full menu is not displayed, pause your mouse pointer over the **Expand arrows** to expand the **File** menu. See Figure 1.9.

On the left side of some command names is an image of the button that represents this command on a toolbar. This is a reminder that you can use the toolbar button to start the command with only one click. Likewise, to the right of some commands is a reminder that you can use a keyboard shortcut (holding down a combination of keys) to start the command.

Expand arrow

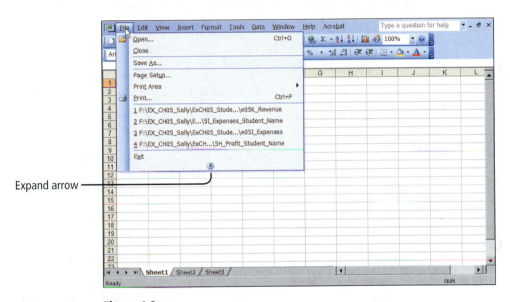

Figure 1.9

3 Look at the full **File** menu on your screen.

Following or to the right of some menu commands, you will see various symbols, characters, or formatting, which are standard across all Microsoft products. The table in Figure 1.10 lists these characteristics and describes what will happen when you select the command.

Microsoft Menu Characteristics

Characteristic	Description	Example
... (ellipsis)	Indicates that a dialog box requesting more information will display.	Print...
▶ (triangle)	Indicates that a submenu—another menu of choices—will display.	Send to ▶
No symbol	Indicates that the command will perform immediately.	Exit
✓ (check mark)	Indicates that a command is turned on or active.	✓ Standard
Gray option name	Indicates that the command is currently unavailable (grayed out).	Properties

Figure 1.10

4 On the menu bar, click **File** again to close the menu.

If you decide not to select a command from a displayed menu, close the menu either by clicking its name, clicking outside the menu, or by pressing (Esc).

5 On the menu bar, click **View**, and then point to **Toolbars**.

A list of available toolbars displays. A check mark indicates that the toolbar is displayed.

6 On the displayed list of toolbars, be sure that **Standard** and **Formatting** are both checked. Clear any other checked toolbar on the list by clicking its check mark to clear it, and then, if the list is still displayed, click outside the menu to close it.

7 Below the menu bar, be sure two rows of toolbars display, as shown in Figure 1.11. If, instead, your toolbars are sharing one row, as shown in Figure 1.12, at the end of the toolbar click the **Toolbar Options** button ▐, and then click **Show Buttons on Two Rows**.

The toolbars will display on two rows, as shown in Figure 1.11. Alternatively, from the Tools menu, click Customize, click the Options tab, and then select the Show Standard and Formatting toolbars on two rows check box.

Toolbars on two rows —

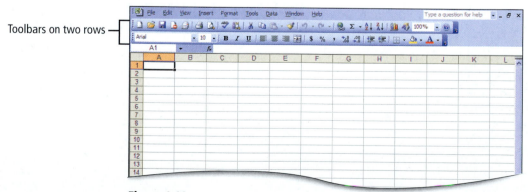

Figure 1.11

Toolbars on one row ———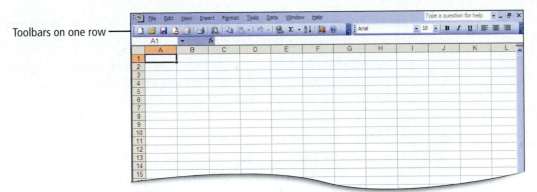

Figure 1.12

8 On the Standard toolbar, locate and pause your mouse pointer over the **New** button .

When you position the mouse pointer over a button, Excel displays the button's name in a **_ScreenTip_**. The ScreenTip _New_ displays, indicating that clicking this button will activate the command to create a new workbook. See Figure 1.13.

New button ———
ScreenTip ———

Figure 1.13

9 Pause your pointer over several buttons on both the Standard and Formatting toolbars to become familiar with the commands available to you. A toolbar button is a one-click method to activate frequently used commands that are also available from the menus. The ScreenTip describes the command that will be activated when you click the toolbar button.

Activity 1.3 Opening an Existing Workbook

1 From the menu bar, display the **File** menu, and then click **Open**. Alternatively, click the Open button 📂 on the Standard toolbar.

The Open dialog box displays.

2 At the right side of the **Look in** box, click the **Look in arrow**, and then navigate to the student files that accompany this textbook.

3 Click to select the file **e01A_Gas_Usage**, and then, in the lower right corner of the dialog box, click **Open**.

The workbook e01A_Gas_Usage displays. Alternatively, you can double-click a file name to open it. The workbook includes data already captured from gas slips, including the number of gallons purchased and the total amounts printed on the actual slips. Excel calculates the total of all slips by using a formula.

4 Take a moment to study Figures 1.14a and 1.14b and the table in Figure 1.15 to become familiar with the Excel workbook window.

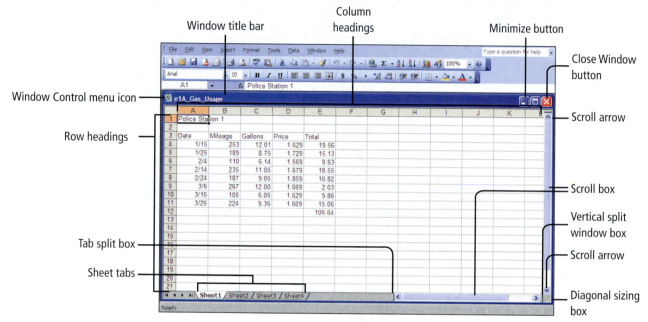

Figure 1.14a

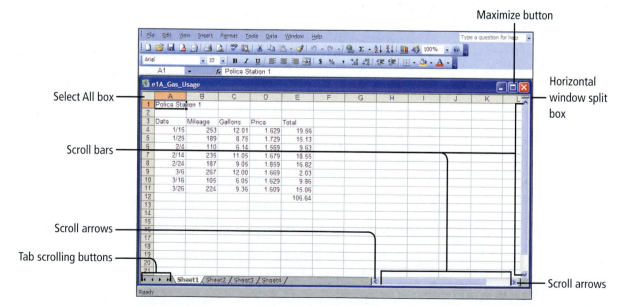

Figure 1.14b

Excel Workbook Elements

Workbook Element	Description
Close Window button	Closes the workbook.
Column headings	Indicate the column letter.
Diagonal sizing box	Indicates that the window can be resized; dragging this box changes the window size.
Horizontal window split box	Splits the worksheet into two vertical views of the same worksheet.
Maximize button	Displays the active window in its full size in the Excel workspace.
Minimize button	Collapses the active window to a button on the taskbar.
Row headings	Indicates the row number.
Scroll arrows	Scroll one column or row at a time.
Scroll bars	Scroll the Excel window up and down or left and right.
Scroll boxes	Used with the mouse to drag the position of a window up and down or left and right.
Select All box	Selects all cells in a worksheet.
Sheet tabs	Changes the active worksheet in a workbook.
Tab scrolling buttons	Display sheet tabs that are not in view; used when there are more sheet tabs than will display in the space provided.
Tab split box	Adjusts the space available for sheet tabs.
Vertical split window box	Splits the worksheet into two horizontal views of the same worksheet.
Window Control menu icon	Also known as the control program box. Allows keyboard access to move, resize, minimize, maximize, and close the worksheet window.
Window title bar	Displays the application name along with the name of the current workbook.

Figure 1.15

Activity 1.4 Selecting Columns, Rows, Cells, Ranges, and Worksheets

Recall that a *cell* is the rectangular box formed by the intersection of a column and a row. *Selecting* refers to highlighting, by clicking or dragging with your mouse, one or more cells so that the selected range of cells can be edited, formatted, copied, or moved. Excel treats the selected range of cells as a single unit; thus, you can make the same change, or combination of changes, to more than one cell at a time.

1 In the upper left corner of the displayed worksheet, position your mouse pointer over the letter **A** until the pointer ⬇ displays, as shown in Figure 1.16, and then click once.

Column A is selected (highlighted). A *column* is a vertical group of cells in a worksheet. Beginning with the first letter of the alphabet, A, a unique letter identifies each column—this is called the *column heading*. After using the entire alphabet from A to Z, Excel begins naming the columns AA, AB, AC, and so on.

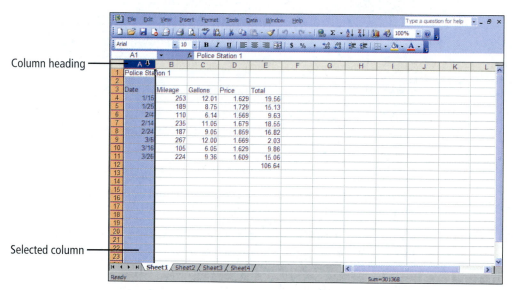

Column heading

Selected column

Figure 1.16

2 At the left edge of the workbook, position your mouse pointer over the number **3** until the pointer ➡ displays, as shown in Figure 1.17, and then click once.

Row 3 is selected. A *row* is a horizontal group of cells in a worksheet. Beginning with number 1, a unique number identifies each row—this is the *row heading*, located at the left side of the worksheet.

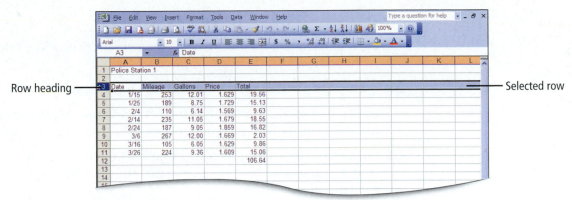

Row heading ——————— Selected row

Figure 1.17

3 In the displayed worksheet, click the word **Date**. See Figure 1.18.

A black border surrounds the cell, indicating that it is the *active cell*. The active cell in a worksheet is the cell ready to receive data or be affected by the next Excel command. A cell is identified by the intersecting column letter and row number, which forms the *cell address*. A cell address is also referred to as a *cell reference*.

4 At the left end of the Formula Bar, look at the **Name Box**.

The cell address of the active cell, A3, displays.

5 Look at the Formula Bar.

The value of the cell—the word *Date*—displays. See Figure 1.18.

Intersecting row   Value displayed in
and column   Formula Bar

Cell reference (cell address)
displayed in Name box

Intersecting row and column

Active cell

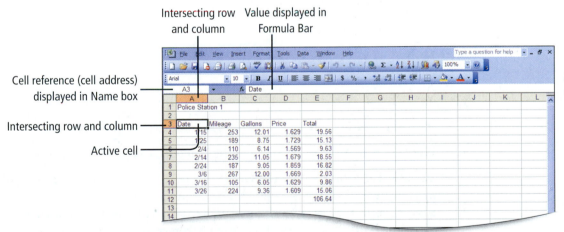

Figure 1.18

6 On the keyboard, press ↓ three times.

Cell A6 becomes the active cell. Pressing an arrow key relocates the active cell.

7 With your mouse, point to and then click cell **B4**.

In the Name Box, notice that the cell address, *B4*, is indicated, and in the Formula Bar, the value of the cell, *253*, is indicated.

8 With the mouse pointer 🕂 over cell **B4**, hold down the left mouse button, drag down to select cells **B5**, **B6**, and **B7**, and then release the left mouse button.

The four cells, B4 through B7, are selected. This *range* (group) of cells is referred to as *B4:B7*. When you see a colon (:) between two cell references, the range includes all the cells between the two cell addresses—in this instance, all the cells from B4 through B7. Use this technique to select a range of cells adjacent (next) to one another in a worksheet. See Figure 1.19.

Selected range B4:B7 ──

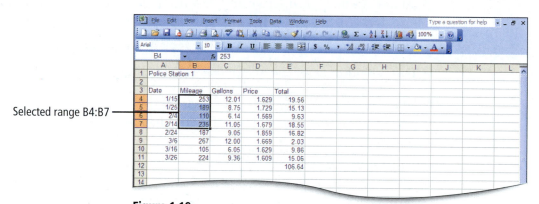

Figure 1.19

9 Point to and then click cell **B4** to make it the active cell.

10 Press and hold down Ctrl, click cell **B7**, and then click cell **C6**.

Cells B4, B7, and C6 are all selected. See Figure 1.20.

Use this technique to select cells that are nonadjacent (not next to one another). A range of cells can be adjacent or nonadjacent. A range of cells that is nonadjacent is separated with commas instead of a colon. In this instance, the range is referred to as *B4, B7, C6*.

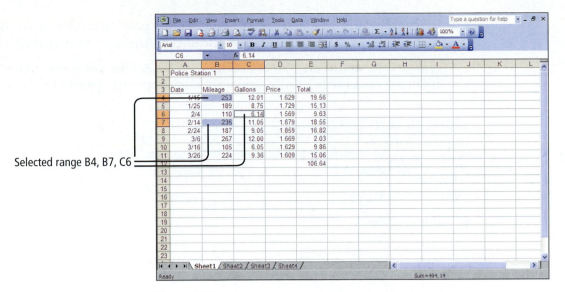

Figure 1.20

Selected range B4, B7, C6

11 Select **column C**.

Notice that when you select an entire column, the address of the first cell in the column displays in the Name Box. See Figure 1.21.

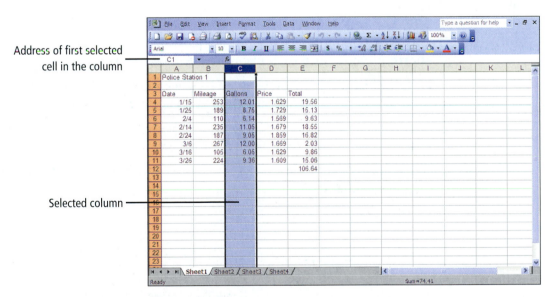

Address of first selected cell in the column

Selected column

Figure 1.21

12 With **column C** selected, pause your mouse pointer anywhere in the highlighted area, and then ***right-click*** (click the right mouse button).

A ***shortcut menu*** displays. See Figure 1.22. A shortcut menu offers the most commonly used commands relevant to the selected area.

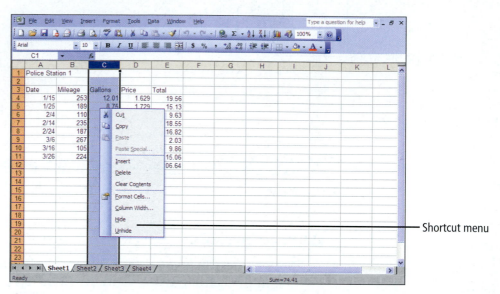

Figure 1.22

13 Move the pointer anywhere outside **column C** and away from the shortcut menu, and then click the left mouse button.

You have canceled the selection of—***deselected***—column C. The column is no longer highlighted, and the shortcut menu is closed.

14 At the left edge of the worksheet, move your mouse pointer over the **row 4** heading, and click to select the row.

When you select an entire row, the address of the first cell in the row displays in the Name Box. See Figure 1.23.

Address of first selected cell in the row

Selected row

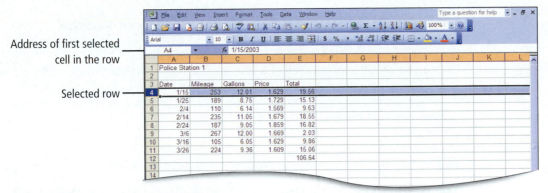

Figure 1.23

15 With **row 4** selected, move the mouse pointer anywhere over the highlighted area, and right-click.

A shortcut menu displays the most commonly used row commands, as shown in Figure 1.24.

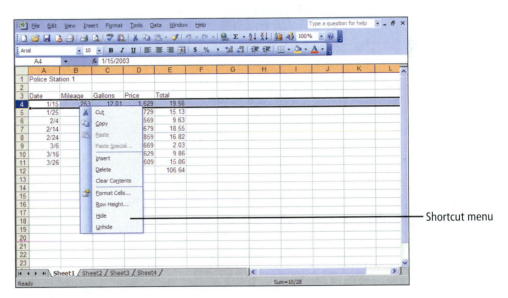

Shortcut menu

Figure 1.24

16 Click anywhere outside **row 4** to cancel the selection.

17 At the upper left corner of your worksheet, locate the **Select All** button—the small gray box above row heading 1 and to the left of column heading A—as shown in Figure 1.25.

Select All button ————

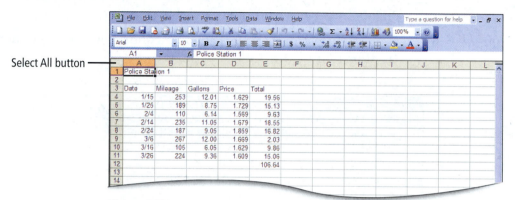

Figure 1.25

18 Click the **Select All** button.

All the cells in the worksheet are selected.

19 Move your pointer anywhere in the worksheet and click once.

The selection is canceled.

Activity 1.5 Navigating Using the Scroll Bars

An Excel worksheet contains 256 columns and 65,536 rows. Of course, you cannot see that many rows and columns on your computer's screen all at the same time, so Excel provides scroll bars for you to display and view different parts of your worksheet. A scroll bar has a scroll box and two scroll arrows. *Scroll* is the action of moving the workbook window either vertically (up and down) or horizontally (side to side) to bring different areas of the worksheet into view on your screen. See Figure 1.26.

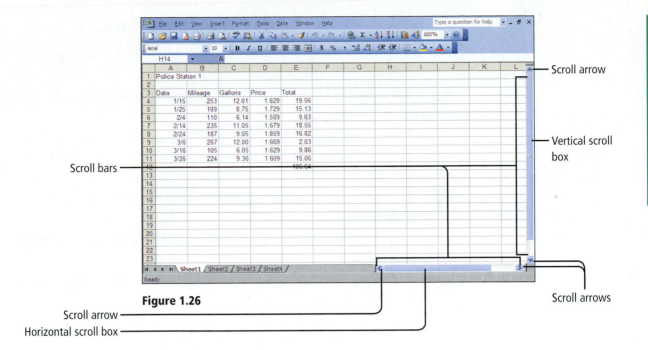

Figure 1.26

Scroll arrow — (to vertical scroll bar, top right)

Vertical scroll box

Scroll bars —

Scroll arrows —

Scroll arrow —

Horizontal scroll box —

1 In the horizontal scroll bar, point to and then click the **right scroll arrow**.

The workbook window moves one column to the right so that column A moves out of view, as shown in Figure 1.27. The number of times you click the arrows on the horizontal scroll bar determines the number of columns by which the window shifts—either to the left or to the right.

Column A scrolled out of view —

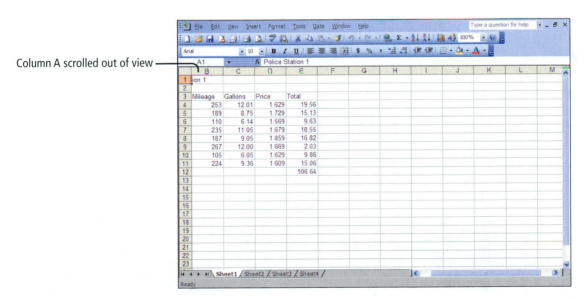

Figure 1.27

2 In the horizontal scroll bar, click the **left scroll arrow**.

The workbook window shifts one column to the left, moving column A back into view.

3 Click in the space between the **horizontal scroll box** and the **right scroll arrow**.

An entire group of columns, equivalent to the number visible on your screen, scrolls to the left and out of view; in fact, the data has moved out of view.

4 Click in the space between the **horizontal scroll box** and the **left scroll arrow**.

The first group of columns, beginning with column A, moves back into view.

5 In the vertical scroll bar, point to and then click the **down scroll arrow**.

Row 1 is no longer in view. The number of times you click the arrows on the vertical scroll bar determines the number of rows shifted either up or down.

6 In the vertical scroll bar, point to and then click the **up scroll arrow**.

Row 1 comes back into view.

Activity 1.6 Navigating Using the Name Box

1 To the left of the Formula Bar, point to the **Name Box** to display the **I-beam** pointer ⬚, as shown in Figure 1.28, and then click once.

Name Box with I-beam pointer displayed

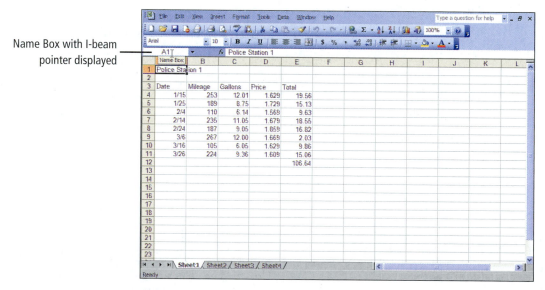

Figure 1.28

The cell reference that was displayed is highlighted in blue and aligned at the left. In Microsoft products, when text is highlighted in blue within a box, it is an indication that when you begin to type, the existing text will be deleted and replaced with your new keystrokes.

2 Using the keyboard, type **b6** and then press [Enter].

Cell B6 becomes the active cell. Typing a cell address in the Name Box is another way to select a cell and cause it to become the active cell. Notice that you do not have to use the capital letter B—typing in either uppercase or lowercase will result in *B6* displaying in the Name Box.

3 Selecting a cell to make it the active cell can also be accomplished using the keys on the keyboard. Take a moment to study the table shown in Figure 1.29 to become familiar with these keyboard commands.

Keyboard Commands

To Move the Location of the Active Cell:	Press:
Left, right, up, or down one cell	[←], [→], [↑], or [↓]
Down one cell	[Enter]
Up one cell	[Shift] + [Enter]
Up one full screen	[Page Up]
Down one full screen	[PageDown]
Left one full screen	[Alt] + [Page Up]
Right one full screen	[Alt] + [PageDown]
To column A of the current row	[Home]
To the last cell in the last column of the *active area* (the rectangle formed by all the rows and columns in a worksheet that contain or contained entries.)	[Ctrl] + [End]
To cell A1	[Ctrl] + [Home]
Right one cell	[Tab]
Left one cell	[Shift] + [Tab]

Figure 1.29

Activity 1.7 Navigating Among the Worksheets in a Workbook

The default setting for the number of worksheets in a workbook is three. You can add worksheets or delete worksheets. Each worksheet has a total of 16,777,216 cells (256 columns × 65,536 rows). Sometimes a project may require that you enter data into more than one worksheet.

When you have more than one worksheet in a workbook, you can **navigate** (move) among worksheets by clicking the **sheet tab**. Sheet tabs identify each worksheet in a workbook. Sheet tabs are located along the lower border of the worksheet window. When you have more worksheets in the workbook than can be displayed in the sheet tab area, use the four tab scrolling buttons to move sheet tabs into and out of view. See Figure 1.30.

Notice that the background color for the Sheet1 tab displays in the same color as the background color for the worksheet and also displays as bold characters. See Figure 1.30. This indicates that *Sheet1* is the active worksheet within the current workbook.

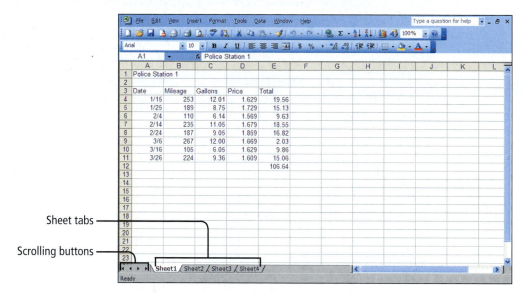

Figure 1.30

1 Point to and then click the **Sheet2 tab**.

The second worksheet in the workbook displays and becomes the active worksheet. Notice that cell A1 displays the text *Police Station 2* because the second worksheet of this workbook contains data for the 12-passenger van at Police Station 2.

2 Click the **Sheet1 tab**.

The first worksheet in the workbook becomes the active worksheet, and cell A1 displays *Police Station 1*.

Activity 1.8 Viewing a Chart

Excel can produce a graphical representation of your data. Data presented as a graph is easier to understand than rows and columns of numbers. Within Excel, a visual representation of your data using graphics is called a ***chart***.

1 In the row of sheet tabs, click the **Sheet4 tab**.

A worksheet containing a chart displays. See Figure 1.31. The chart represents the total gasoline expenses for the 12-passenger vans at each of the three police stations—graphically displaying the differences. The chart uses data gathered from the other three worksheets to generate the graphical representation. If you change the numbers in any of the worksheets, Excel automatically redraws the chart to reflect those changes.

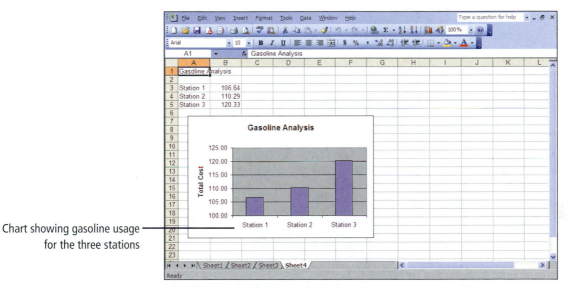

Chart showing gasoline usage for the three stations

Figure 1.31

2 Notice the height of the bar for Station 1. Then, click the **Sheet1 tab**, and click to select cell **E9**.

3 Notice the column total of 106.64 in cell **E12**. In cell **E9**, replace the current value of *2.03* by typing **20.30** and then press Enter.

When you type a value into a cell that already contains a value, the new value replaces the old. It is not necessary to delete the original contents of the cell first. With a new value in cell E9, pressing Enter caused Excel to recalculate the column total and display the new total, 124.91, in cell E12.

4 Click the **Sheet4 tab**.

The size of the bar representing Station 1 in the chart has changed to reflect the new total from the Station 1 worksheet as shown in Figure 1.32. This is an example of Excel's powerful ability to perform calculations and then update the visual representations of the data.

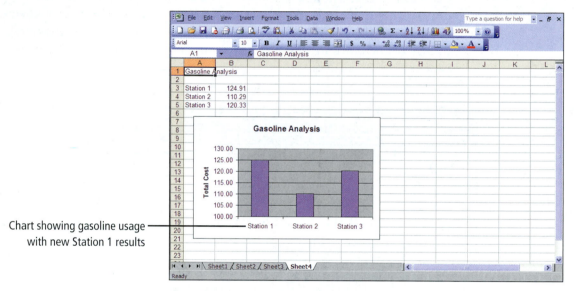

Chart showing gasoline usage with new Station 1 results

Figure 1.32

Activity 1.9 Renaming a Sheet Tab

Excel names the first worksheet in a workbook Sheet1 and each additional worksheet in order—Sheet2, Sheet3, and so on. Usually you will want to assign names to your worksheets that are more meaningful to you. Use either of two methods to rename a worksheet within a workbook:

• Right-click the sheet tab to display the shortcut menu, and then click the Rename command.

• Double-click the sheet tab, and then type a new name directly on the tab.

In this activity, you will rename the worksheets so that they are more descriptive.

1 Point to the **Sheet4 tab** and right-click. On the displayed shortcut menu, click **Rename**.

The Sheet tab name is selected.

2 Type **Chart** and then press Enter.

3 *Double-click* (click the left mouse button twice in rapid succession, keeping the mouse still between the clicks) the **Sheet1 tab** to select its name, and then type **Station 1**

4 Using either method, rename **Sheet2** to **Station 2** and **Sheet3** to **Station 3**

Objective 2
Create Headers and Footers

Headers and *footers* are text, page numbers, graphics, and formatting that print at the top (header) or bottom (footer) of every page.

Throughout this textbook, you will type the project name and your name on each of your worksheets by placing them in a footer. This will make it easier for you to identify your printed documents in a shared printer environment such as a lab or classroom.

Activity 1.10 Creating Headers and Footers

1 Point to the **Station 1 tab** and right-click. On the displayed shortcut menu, click **Select All Sheets**.

When a group of worksheets is selected, the word *Group* displays in the title bar to the right of the file name, as shown in Figure 1.33. By selecting all sheets, you will cause the Header and Footer information that you create to print on each worksheet in this workbook—not only on the active sheet.

Alert!

What Is "Read-Only"?

In addition to [Group], your title may display [Read-Only]. Workbook files provided by the textbook publisher frequently have this designation. It means that you cannot make permanent changes to the workbook. To make permanent changes, you will have to save the workbook with a new name, which you will be instructed to do.

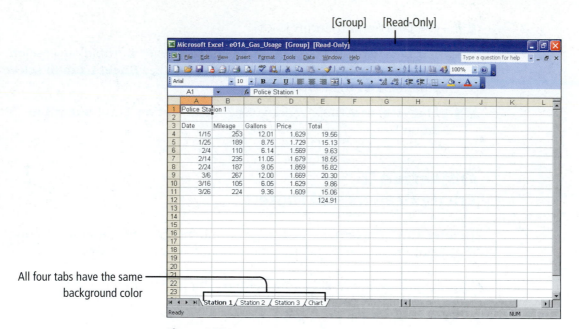

[Group]   [Read-Only]

All four tabs have the same
background color

Figure 1.33

2 On the menu bar, click **View**, and then click **Header and Footer**.

The Page Setup dialog box displays, as shown in Figure 1.34.

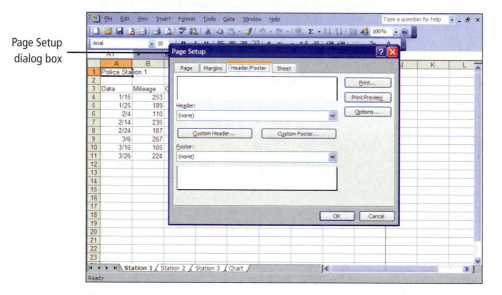

Page Setup
dialog box

Figure 1.34

3 In the top portion of the **Page Setup** dialog box, click the **Header/Footer tab** once if necessary.

4 In the center of the dialog box, click the **Custom Footer** button.

The Footer dialog box displays, as shown in Figure 1.35. A flashing vertical line displays at the left edge of the *Left section* box. This is the ***insertion point***, the point at which anything you type will be inserted. The insertion point in this box is left-aligned—text you enter will begin at the left.

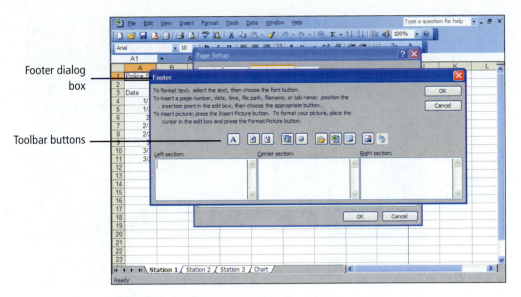

Footer dialog box

Toolbar buttons

Figure 1.35

5 In the center of the **Footer** dialog box, locate the toolbar buttons shown in Figure 1.35, and then click the **Font** button [A]. These toolbar buttons do not display ScreenTips.

The Font dialog box displays, as shown in Figure 1.36.

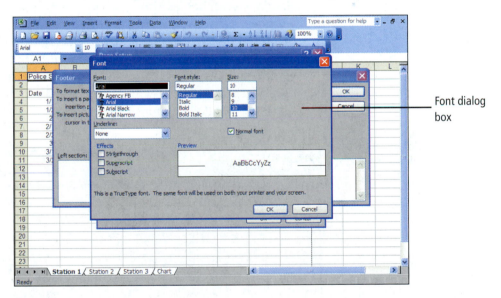

Font dialog box

Figure 1.36

6 Under **Font**, click the **scroll bar arrows** as necessary, and then click **Arial**. Under **Font style**, scroll as necessary, and then click **Italic**. Under **Size**, scroll as necessary, and then click **14**. Then, in the lower right corner, click the **OK** button.

7 Using your own first and last name, type **1A Gas Usage-Firstname Lastname** and notice that as you type, Excel wraps the text to the next line in the box. When you print your workbook, the footer will print on one line.

Compare your screen with Figure 1.37.

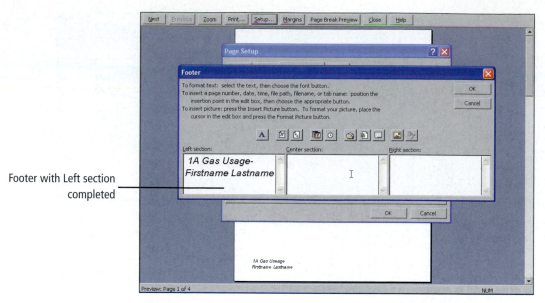

Footer with Left section
completed

1A Gas Usage-
Firstname Lastname

Figure 1.37

8 In the upper right of the **Footer** dialog box, click **OK**, and then at the lower right of the **Page Setup** dialog box, click **OK** to return to the workbook.

Headers and footers that you create do not display in the worksheet window; they display only on the page preview screen and on the printed page. The vertical dotted line between columns indicates that as currently arranged, only the columns to the left of the dotted line will print on the first page, as shown in Figure 1.38. The exact position of the dotted line will depend on the default printer settings. Yours may fall elsewhere.

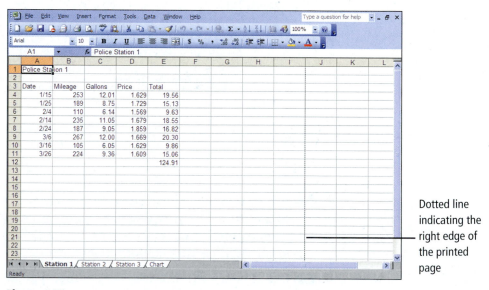

Dotted line
indicating the
right edge of
the printed
page

Figure 1.38

9 Right-click the **Station 1 tab**, and then click **Ungroup Sheets** to ungroup the sheets.

The word *Group* no longer displays in the worksheet title bar, indicating that the worksheet grouping has been removed.

More Knowledge — Removing the [Group] Indicator on the Title Bar

If sheets in a workbook are grouped, clicking any sheet tab other than that of the active sheet ungroups the sheets and removes the [Group] indicator from the title bar.

Objective 3
Preview and Print a Workbook

Before you print your worksheet or an entire workbook, you will want to check the formatting, placement, and layout. Excel's Print Preview feature lets you do this before printing your worksheets on paper.

From your instructor or lab coordinator, determine the default printer for the computer at which you are working, and check to see whether it is available for you to use.

Activity 1.11 Previewing and Printing a Workbook

1 Point to the **Station 1 tab** and right-click. On the displayed shortcut menu, click **Select All Sheets**.

The title bar shows [Group] indicating that multiple worksheets in the workbook are selected.

2 On the Standard toolbar, click the **Print Preview** button .

Your worksheet displays as an image of a piece of paper so that you can see how your worksheet will be placed on the page, including the footer. See Figure 1.39. Because more than one worksheet is being previewed, in the lower left of the preview window *Page 1 of 4* displays.

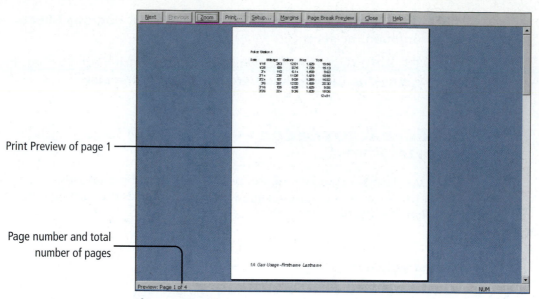

Print Preview of page 1

Page number and total number of pages

Figure 1.39

3 On the Print Preview toolbar, click the **Next** button to view page 2. Then, click the **Next** button two more times to view pages 3 and 4.

As you scroll forward and backward using the Next and Previous buttons, the words in the lower left of the Preview window change to indicate the page you are currently viewing—*Page 3 of 4* and so forth.

4 On the Print Preview toolbar, click the **Close** button to exit Print Preview.

5 On the Standard toolbar, click the **Print** button .

One copy of each worksheet in the workbook prints—a total of four sheets.

6 Right-click the **Station 1 tab**, and then click **Ungroup Sheets**.

The [Group] indication in the title bar is removed and the worksheets are no longer grouped together.

Objective 4
Save and Close a Workbook and Exit Excel

In the same way you use file folders to organize your paper documents, Windows uses a hierarchy of electronic folders to store and organize your electronic files (workbooks). In the following activities you will save the workbook with a name and in a location that will be easy for you to find.

Activity 1.12 Creating a New Folder and Saving a Workbook with a New Name

Creating a new folder in which to save your work will make finding the workbooks you create easier. Before saving, you will need to determine where you will be storing your workbooks, for example, on your own disk or on a network drive.

1 On the menu bar, click **File** to display the File menu, and then click **Save As**.

The Save As dialog box displays, as shown in Figure 1.40.

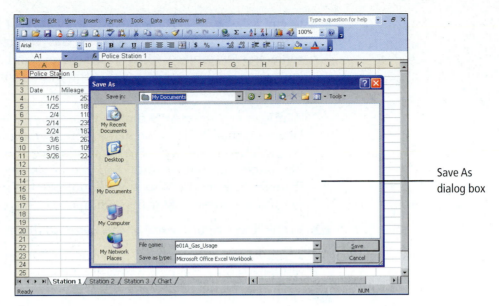

Save As
dialog box

Figure 1.40

2 Click the **Save in arrow** to view a list of the drives available to you, and then navigate to the drive on which you will be storing your folders and documents; for example, 3½ Floppy (A:).

3 In the upper right of the dialog box, click the **Create New Folder** button .

The New Folder dialog box displays.

4 In the displayed **New Folder** dialog box, in the **Name** box, type **Excel Chapter 1** as shown in Figure 1.41 and then click **OK**.

Windows creates the *Excel Chapter 1* folder and makes it the active folder in the Save As dialog box.

New Folder dialog box with
folder name typed

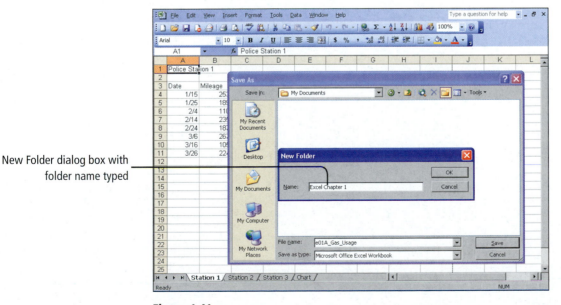

Figure 1.41

5 In the **File name** box, delete any existing text by selecting it and pressing the ⌈Delete⌉ key, and type **1A_Gas_Usage_Firstname_Lastname** replacing *Firstname* with your first name and *Lastname* with your last name, being sure to include the underscore (⌈Shift⌉ + ⌈-⌉) instead of spaces between words.

Windows recognizes file names that use spaces between words. However, many electronic file transfer programs do not. In this text, you will use underscores instead of spaces between words for your file names. In that manner, you can be assured that if you need to transfer files on the Web, for example, using Blackboard or WebCT for online courses, your files will move easily on the Internet.

6 In the lower right corner of the **Save As** dialog box, click **Save**.

The file is saved in the new folder with the new name. The workbook redisplays, and the new name displays in the title bar.

7 On the menu bar, click **File**, and then click **Close**.

Your workbook closes. The Excel program remains open, even when no workbooks are open.

8 At the extreme right of the title bar, click the **Close** button ⊠ to close Excel.

Note — Renaming Folders

You can rename folders by right-clicking a folder and selecting Rename from the shortcut menu. The folder name will display in an edit mode and you can type to rename the folder. You can also click once on the folder name, and then click a second time to invoke the edit mode, and then type a new folder name.

End **You have completed Project 1A** ───────────────

Project 1B **Salary Analysis**

In this project, you will create a new workbook and enter data into it. Then you will create formulas to perform mathematical calculations and use the spelling checker to check for misspelled words in your spreadsheet.

In Activities 1.13 through 1.29, you will create a new workbook for Police Chief Johnson that contains an employee list showing the name, shift, date of hire, and current weekly salary of the police officers assigned to each police station. You will enter the data for Police Station 1. The resulting workbook will look similar to Figure 1.42. You will save your workbook as *1B_Salary_Analysis_Firstname_Lastname.*

Police Station 1 Weekly Salaries

Emp	Shift	Hired on	Salary	Annual
J Bryon	Day	5/13/1996	460	23920
T Cassidy	Day	6/11/1998	685	35620
L Shasta	Night	7/30/1998	550	28600
G Adams	Day	3/15/1999	526	27352
S Front	Day	4/17/2001	767	39884
M Pong	Night	5/17/2002	389	20228
Total			3377	175604

1B Salary Analysis-Firstname Lastname

Figure 1.42
Project 1B—Salary Analysis

Objective 5
Create a New Workbook

When you save a file, the Windows operating system stores your workbook permanently on a storage medium—either a disk that you have inserted into the computer, the hard drive of your computer, or a network drive to which your computer system is connected. Changes that you make to existing workbooks, such as changing data or typing in new data, are not permanently saved until you perform a Save operation.

Save your workbooks frequently to avoid losing the data you have created in a new workbook or the changes you have made to an existing workbook. In rare instances, problems arise with your computer system or your electrical power source.

Activity 1.13 Creating a New Workbook

In the following activity, you will begin a new workbook and then save it in your Excel Chapter 1 folder.

1 If the Excel program is open, close it now.

2 **Start** the Excel program. If the **Getting Started** task pane is open, click its **Close** button ☒. Notice that *Book1* displays in both the title bar and the taskbar. See Figure 1.43.

Excel displays the file name of a workbook in both the blue title bar at the top of the screen and on a button in the taskbar at the bottom of the screen—including new, unsaved workbooks. The unsaved workbook displays as *Book1* or *Book2*, depending on the number of times you have started a new workbook during your current Excel session.

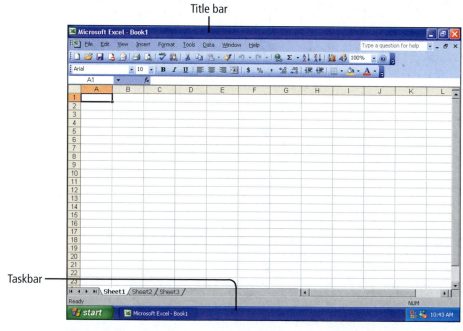

Figure 1.43

The complete file name is not visible in the taskbar?

The size of taskbar buttons varies, depending on your computer setup. To view the full file name in the taskbar, pause the mouse pointer over the button to display a ScreenTip containing the complete workbook name.

3 Display the **File** menu, and then click **Close**. Click **No** if you are prompted to save any changes to the workbook.

When all Excel workbooks are closed, most of the toolbar buttons display in gray, indicating that they are unavailable, and the workbook area displays in a darker shade. See Figure 1.44. Your screen will look like this when the Excel program is running but no workbooks are open.

Unavailable (grayed) toolbar buttons

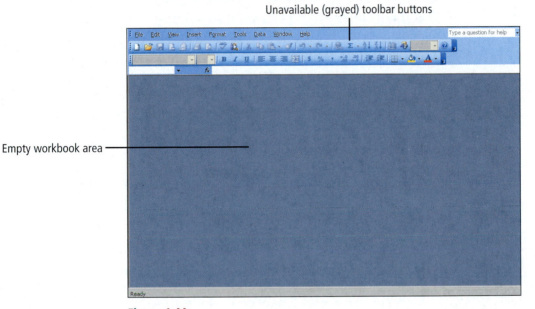

Empty workbook area

Figure 1.44

4 On the Standard toolbar, click the **New** button.

Recall that a toolbar button is a one-click method of performing a command. Alternatively, you could display the File menu and then click New, but this would require more than one click.

A new blank workbook displays, the toolbar buttons are reactivated, and *Book2* displays in the title bar and in the taskbar. Each time you open a new workbook during an Excel session, the number will increase by one. There is no limit to the number of blank workbooks. Each time you exit and then restart Excel, the numbering of blank workbooks begins again with the number 1.

Begin a New Workbook

You can begin a new workbook in any of the following ways:

- Start Excel. The program opens with a new workbook displayed.
- From the File menu, click New.
- On the keyboard, press [Ctrl] + [N].
- From the Getting Started task pane, click *Create a new workbook*.
- From the New Workbook task pane, click *Blank workbook*.

Activity 1.14 Saving and Naming a New Workbook

When Excel displays *Book* followed by a number, for example, *Book1*, *Book2*, and so forth, it indicates that this workbook has never been saved. To save the workbook, perform a Save As to specify a file name and the location where you want to store the workbook.

Your computer's memory stores changes you make to your workbook until you perform another Save operation. Get in the habit of saving changes you have made to an existing workbook by clicking the Save button on the Standard toolbar. The Save button saves any changes you have made to the file—without changing the file name or storage location.

1 On the Standard toolbar, click the **Save** button.

Because this workbook has never been saved with a name, the Save As dialog box displays. Alternatively, you can display the File menu and then click Save As.

2 In the **Save As** dialog box, click the **Save in arrow** to view a list of the drives available to you.

3 Navigate to the drive and folder in which you are storing your projects for this chapter; for example, 3½ Floppy (A:). Recall that you created an **Excel Chapter 1** folder previously for this purpose.

4 In the **File name** box, delete any existing text and type **1B_Salary_Analysis_Firstname_Lastname** as shown in Figure 1.45.

Recall that in this textbook, you will use underscores instead of spaces in your file names. This will make it easier to send files over the Internet if you need to do so.

Save As dialog box

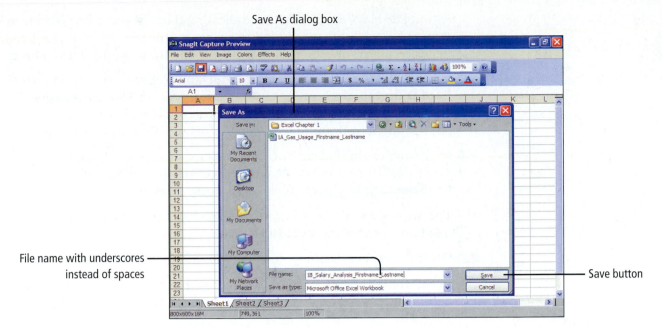

File name with underscores
instead of spaces

Save button

Figure 1.45

5 In the lower right corner of the **Save As** dialog box, click **Save**, or press Enter. The new workbook name displays in the title bar and on the taskbar.

Objective 6
Enter and Edit Data in a Worksheet

Every cell in a worksheet contains *formatting* information—information about how data typed into the cell will look. Formatting is easily changed, and as you progress in your study of Excel, you will practice applying various formats that will make your worksheets visually appealing.

Anything typed into a cell is referred to as *cell content*. Cell content can be one of only two things: a *constant value* or a *formula*. A constant value, also referred to simply as a *value*, can be numbers, text, dates, or times of day that you type into a cell. A formula, on the other hand, is an equation that you type into a cell. A formula acts as an instruction for Excel to perform mathematical calculations (such as adding and subtracting) on values in other cells.

In the next group of activities, you will enter various types of constant values. After you enter values into a cell, they can be edited (changed) or cleared from the cell.

Activity 1.15 Entering Text

Words (text) typed in a worksheet usually provide information about numbers in other worksheet cells. For example, *Police Station 1* gives the reader an indication that the data in this worksheet relates to information about Police Station 1. To enter text into a cell, activate the cell and type. Before entering text in this activity, you will create the footer with your name.

1 Point to the **Sheet1 tab** and right-click. On the displayed shortcut menu, click **Select All Sheets**.

[Group] displays in the title bar, indicating that the three worksheets are grouped. Recall that grouping the sheets in this manner will place your footer on all the sheets in the workbook—not only on the active sheet.

2 Display the **View** menu, click **Header and Footer**, click the **Custom Footer** button, and under **Left section**, type **1B Salary Analysis-Firstname Lastname** using your own first and last name. Do not change the font or font size—use the default font and font size.

3 In the upper right corner of the **Footer** dialog box, click **OK**. In the lower right corner of the **Page Setup** dialog box, click **OK**. Right-click the **Sheet2 tab**, and then click **Ungroup Sheets**.

The sheets are no longer grouped together, and [Group] no longer displays in the worksheet title bar.

4 On the Standard toolbar, click the **Save** button 🖫.

Recall that adding the footer causes the dotted line to display, indicating where the page would end if printed on the default printer. This may vary among printers.

5 Click the **Sheet1 tab** so that Sheet 1 is the active sheet. In cell **A1** type **Police Station 1 Weekly Salaries** and then press Enter.

After you type data into a cell, you must lock in the entry to store it in the cell. One way to do this is to press the Enter key, which makes another cell active and locks in the entry. You can use other keyboard movements, such as Tab, or one of the arrow keys on your keyboard to make another cell active and lock in the entry.

6 Look at the text you typed in cell **A1**.

Notice that the text is aligned at the left edge of the cell. Left alignment is the default for text entries and is an example of the formatting information stored in a cell. Cell A2 is the active cell, as indicated by the black border surrounding it.

7 Look at the **row 2 heading** and **column A heading**, as shown in Figure 1.46.

The shading indicates that the active cell is at the intersection of column A and row 2. In addition, the Name Box displays the cell reference, *A2*.

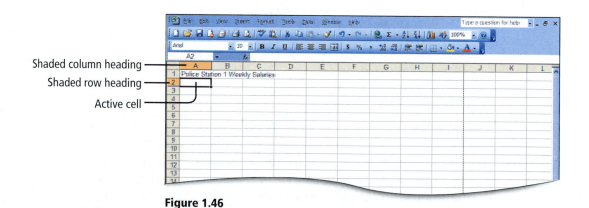

Shaded column heading
Shaded row heading
Active cell

Figure 1.46

8 Press and hold down Ctrl and then press Home to make cell **A1** the active cell.

Recall that this keyboard shortcut is a quick way to move to cell A1 and make it the active cell.

9 Press Enter two times to move to cell **A3**. Type **Emp** and if you make a typing error press Bksp. Notice that as you type, a vertical line called the *insertion point* blinks, indicating where your keystrokes will be inserted. Press Enter.

10 Click cell **A1** to make it the active cell, look at the Formula Bar, and notice that the words *Police Station 1 Weekly Salaries* display.

11 Click cell **B1** and look at the Formula Bar.

No text displays in the Formula Bar. Although the display of the value in cell A1 overlaps into cell B1, the value itself is contained within cell A1. When a value is too wide for its cell, Excel will display the value in the adjacent cell—if the adjacent cell is empty. If the adjacent cell is *not* empty, Excel displays only as much of the value as there is space to do so.

12 Click cell **A4**, and then type the remaining text into **column A** as shown in Figure 1.47. Press Enter after you type the text for each cell to lock in the entry and move down to the next cell. While typing in a cell, press Bksp to correct any errors.

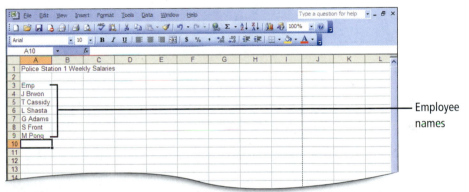

Figure 1.47

13 Click cell **B3** to make it the active cell, type **Shift** and then press Tab to move to cell **C3**.

More Knowledge — More Ways to Use the Enter Key

Pressing the [Tab] key makes the cell to the right the active cell. Pressing the [Enter] key makes the cell in the next row the active cell. If you prefer to have the [Enter] key make the cell to the right the active cell, select a group of horizontal cells, and then begin typing in the first cell. Then press [Enter]—the cell to the right will become the active cell. This is useful if you are entering data from the numeric keypad, where [Enter] is the only key available on the keypad to lock in the entry.

14 In cell **C3** type **Date** and then press [Tab].

15 In cell **D3** type **Salary** and then press [Enter].

B4 becomes the active cell. Because you used [Tab] to move the active cell to column C and then to column D, pressing [Enter] causes the active cell to return to the column in which you first pressed [Tab].

16 Compare your screen with Figure 1.48.

Column headings

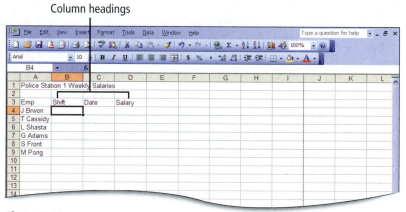

Figure 1.48

Activity 1.16 Using AutoComplete to Enter Data

Excel assists you in typing. If the first few characters you type in a cell match an existing entry in the column, Excel fills in the remaining characters for you. This feature, called *AutoComplete*, speeds your typing. It is useful because, in a spreadsheet, you frequently type the same information over and over. AutoComplete assists only with alphabetic values; it does not assist with numeric values.

1 To check that the AutoComplete feature is available on your system, display the **Tools** menu, click **Options,** and then in the displayed **Options** dialog box, click the **Edit tab**. Under **Settings**, determine whether *Enable AutoComplete for cell values* is selected (checked) as shown in Figure 1.49. If a check mark appears, click **OK** to close the dialog box. If no check mark appears, click to select the option, and then click **OK**.

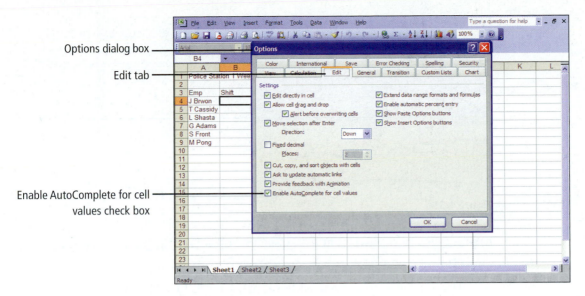

Options dialog box ⎯⎯

Edit tab ⎯⎯

Enable AutoComplete for cell ⎯⎯
values check box

Figure 1.49

2 Be sure that cell **B4** is the active cell. Type **Day** and then press Enter.

3 In cell **B5**, type **D**

Excel completes the word *Day* because the first character matches an existing text entry in column B. See Figure 1.50.

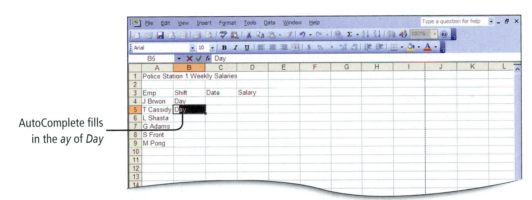

AutoComplete fills ⎯⎯
in the *ay* of *Day*

Figure 1.50

4 Press Enter to accept the entry.

Day is automatically entered in the cell, saving you from typing the entire word. The completed entry will match the pattern of upper-case and lowercase letters of the existing entry. If you do not want to accept an AutoComplete suggestion, press Bksp to delete the characters, or continue typing to replace the characters with your own typing.

5 Enter the remaining data in **column B** as shown in Figure 1.51, using **AutoComplete** when it is useful to complete the cell entry.

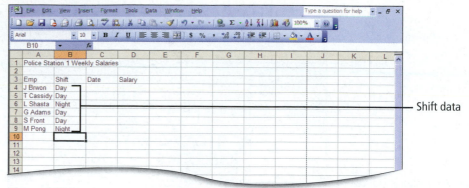

Figure 1.51

Shift data

---

6 On the Standard toolbar, click the **Save** button to save the changes you have made to your worksheet.

The changes to your workbook are saved. Recall the importance of saving your work periodically.

Activity 1.17 Entering Numbers

When typing numbers, you can use either the number keys across the top of your keyboard or the number keys and Enter key on the numeric keypad. Try to develop some proficiency in touch control of the numeric keypad. On a desktop computer, the Num Lock light indicates that the numeric keypad is active. If necessary, press the Num Lock key to activate the numeric keypad.

1 In **column D**, under *Salary*, click cell **D4**, type **500** and then press Esc (located in the upper left corner of your keyboard).

Your typing is canceled, and D4 remains the active cell. If you change your mind about an entry while typing in a cell, press Esc or click the Cancel [X] button on the Formula Bar.

2 With **D4** as the active cell, type **460** and then press Enter.

The weekly salary of 460 is locked into cell D4, as shown in Figure 1.52. Notice that after you lock in the entry, the numbers align at the right edge of the cell. This is called *right alignment*. When you type a value consisting of numbers in a cell, the default alignment is right. Right alignment of numbers is another example of formatting information that is stored in a cell.

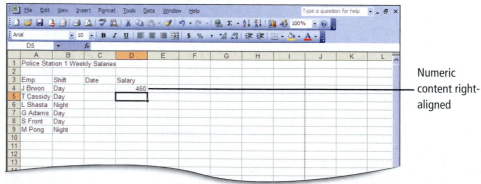

Numeric content right-aligned

Figure 1.52

3 Click cell **D5**, type **685** and then press Enter. Continue entering the weekly salary amounts for **column D,** as shown in Figure 1.53.

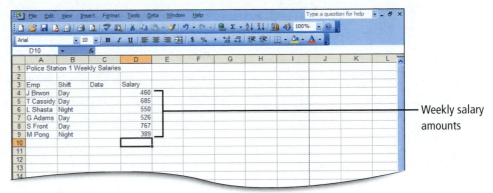

Figure 1.53

4 These numbers will affect your final worksheet, so take a moment to check that you have typed accurately. To correct a cell, click it and type the data again. There is no need to delete the old value—typing a new value replaces any existing cell values.

5 On the Standard toolbar, click the **Save** button 💾.

Activity 1.18 Typing Dates into a Worksheet

Date values are a type of content frequently typed into a worksheet. Date values entered in any of the following formats will be recognized by Excel as a date:

- m/d/yy   For example, 7/4/05

- d-mmm   For example, 4-Jul

- d-mmm-yy   For example, 4-Jul-05

- mmm-yy   For example, Jul-05

On your keyboard, [-] (the hyphen key) and [/] (the forward slash key) function identically in any of these formats and can be used interchangeably. You may abbreviate the month name to three characters or spell it out. You may enter the year as two digits, four digits, or even leave it off. When left off, the current year is assumed but does not display in the cell.

A two-digit year value of 30 through 99 is interpreted by the Windows operating system as the four-digit years of 1930 through 1999. All other two-digit year values are assumed to be in the 21st century. Get in the habit of typing year values as four digits, even though only two digits may display in the cell. In that manner, you can be sure that Excel interprets the year value as you intended. See the table in Figure 1.54 for examples.

How Excel Interprets Dates

Date Typed As:	Completed by Excel As:
7/4/05	7/4/2005
7-4-96	7/4/1996
7/4	4-Jul (current year assumed)
7-4	4-Jul (current year assumed)
July 4	4-Jul (current year assumed)
Jul 4	4-Jul (current year assumed)
Jul/4	4-Jul (current year assumed)
Jul-4	4-Jul (current year assumed)
July 4, 1996	4-Jul-96
July 2005	Jul-05
July 1996	Jul-96

Figure 1.54

1 In **column C**, under *Date*, click cell **C4** to make it the active cell, type **5/13/2004** and then press Enter.

The date right-aligns in the cell and displays as 5/13/2004, using the m/d/yyyy format.

Alert!

The date does not display as 5/13/2004?

The Windows setting in the Control Panel under Regional and Language Options determines the default format for dates. If your result is different, it is likely that the formatting of the default date was adjusted on the computer at which you are working.

2 Click cell **C4** again to make it the active cell, press and hold down Ctrl, and then press ; (the semicolon key) on your keyboard. Press Enter to lock in the entry.

Excel enters the current date, obtained from your computer's internal calendar, into the selected cell using the m/d/yyyy formatting that was previously created in that cell. This is a convenient keyboard shortcut for entering the current date.

3 Click cell **C4** again, type **5/13/96** and press Enter. Then, enter the remaining dates as shown in Figure 1.55.

Because the year was between 30 and 99, Excel assumed a 20th century date and changed *96* to *1996* to complete the four-digit year.

4 On the Standard toolbar, click the **Save** button 🖫.

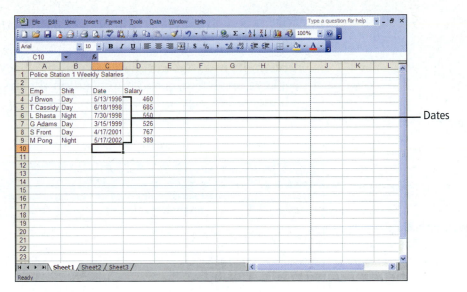

Dates

Figure 1.55

Activity 1.19 Editing Data in Cells

Before you lock in a cell entry by pressing Enter or by making another cell the active cell, you can correct typing errors in one of three ways:

- Press Bksp to delete characters to the left of the insertion point, one character at a time.

- Press Esc to cancel the entire entry.

- On the Formula Bar, click the Cancel button to cancel the entire entry.

Corrections can also be made after locking in the entry by either making the cell active and typing in new data, in which case the existing data will be replaced by your new keystrokes, or by activating Edit mode and editing a portion of the data in the cell. Once you activate Edit mode, you can perform editing directly in the cell or in the Formula Bar.

1 At the lower left corner of your screen, in the Status area, locate the word *Ready*.

Ready indicates that the active cell is ready to accept new data.

2 Point to cell **C4** and double-click to select the cell and simultaneously activate Edit mode. Alternatively, you can select the cell and then press F2 to activate Edit mode.

The blinking vertical insertion point displays somewhere within the cell. The cell is active and ready to be edited (modified).

Note — Performing a Double-Click

Double-clicking may take some practice, but remember that it is not the speed of the two clicks that is important. What is important is that the mouse remain still between the two clicks. Mouse devices with an extra button on the side that functions as a double-click are available.

3 Look at the Status area and notice that *Ready* has been replaced with *Edit*.

This indicates that Edit mode is active. Now you can use the ← and → keys on the keyboard to reposition the insertion point and make changes. See Figure 1.56.

Content visible in Formula Bar

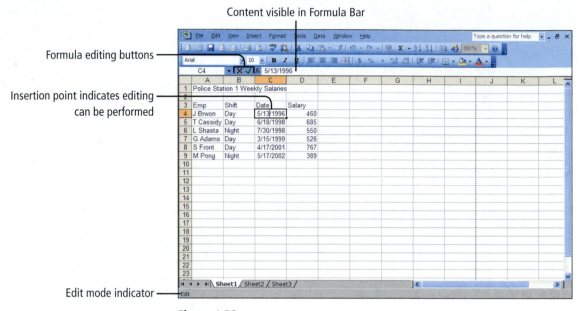

Formula editing buttons

Insertion point indicates editing can be performed

Edit mode indicator

Figure 1.56

4 On the Formula Bar, locate the formula editing buttons. Refer to Figure 1.56.

The Cancel and Enter buttons are visible only when you are entering or editing data in a cell.

5 On the Formula Bar, click the **Cancel** button [X] to exit Edit mode.

The cell remains active, but the insertion point no longer displays.

6 To activate Edit mode using the keyboard, click cell **C5** to make it the active cell, and then press [F2]. Move your mouse pointer away from the cell so you can see the insertion point.

Edit mode is activated, and the insertion point displays at the right edge of the cell. *Ready* is replaced with *Edit* in the Status area.

7 Using either ← or your mouse pointer, position the insertion point to the left of the number *8* in *18*. Press [Delete] to delete the number *8*.

The cell displays *6/1/998*. Recall that [Bksp] removes text to the left of the insertion point one character at a time, and [Delete] removes text to the right of the insertion point one character at a time.

8 Press [Enter] to lock in the entry.

9 Click cell **C5** again to make it the active cell. Pause the mouse pointer in the Formula Bar until the I-beam pointer ⬚ displays. Click to position the pointer ⬚ before the *1* in *6/1* as shown in Figure 1.57.

Sometimes it is easier to perform your editing in the Formula Bar, where you have a better view of the cell contents.

Insertion point in Formula Bar indicates
that editing can be performed

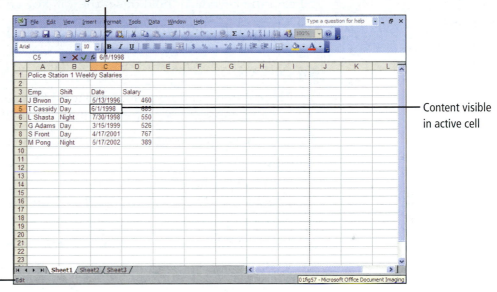

Content visible
in active cell

Edit mode indicator

Figure 1.57

10 Type **1** and then click the **Enter** button ✔ on the Formula Bar.

The date changes to *6/11/1998* and C5 remains the active cell. Recall that clicking the Enter button on the Formula Bar locks in the entry while keeping the current cell active.

More Knowledge — Insert and Overtype Mode

The default for editing data in a worksheet is insert mode. Characters you type are inserted, and the existing characters move to the right to make space for your new typing. You can activate overtype mode, in which your typing replaces any existing characters, by pressing Insert when you are in *Edit* mode. In overtype mode, the letters *OVR* display in the status area, and the insertion point displays as a blinking block. Pressing Insert again turns off overtype mode, removes *OVR*, and reactivates insert mode.

Activity 1.20 Using Undo and Redo

You can reverse an action or a series of actions while entering data into an Excel worksheet by using the Undo command. You can Undo up to your past 16 keyboard actions. If you Undo something by mistake, the Redo command will reverse a previous Undo. Undo an action in any of the following ways:

- On the Standard toolbar, click the Undo button.

- Display the Edit menu, and then click Undo.

- From the keyboard, hold down the Ctrl key and press Z.

- On the Standard toolbar, click the Undo arrow and choose one or more actions to undo.

1 Click cell **A3** to make it the active cell, type **Name** and then press Enter.

The column heading *Emp* is replaced by your new entry, *Name*. Recall that typing a new value into a cell will delete the old value.

2 On the menu bar, click **Edit** to display the Edit menu.

The Undo command line describes the action that the Undo command will replace if you decide to do so. To the left is a reminder that a toolbar button can carry out this command, and to the right is a reminder that a keyboard shortcut can also carry out the command.

3 On the **Edit** menu, click **Undo Typing 'Name' in A3**.

The cell entry *Name* is deleted, and *Emp* displays again in cell A3.

4 Click cell **C3**, type **Hired on** and then press Enter.

Date is replaced with *Hired on*.

5 On the Standard toolbar, click the **Undo** button ⤺▾. Alternatively, you can press Ctrl + Z on the keyboard to reverse the last action.

Date is restored and *Hired on* is deleted—your action was undone. Recall that a toolbar button is a one-click method of performing a command that would otherwise take several clicks to perform from the menu.

6 On the Standard toolbar, click the **Redo** button ↻▾.

Hired on replaces *Date*.

7 Rename the **Sheet1 tab** to **Station 1** and then press Enter.

8 On the Standard toolbar, click the **Save** button 💾 to save the changes you have made to your workbook.

Activity 1.21 Clearing a Cell

You can clear (delete) the contents of a selected cell in one of two ways:

- From the Edit menu, point to the Clear command, and then click Contents.

- Press the Delete key.

Recall that if you type anything into a cell, it is considered to have content—either a value or a formula. Recall also that every cell has some formatting instructions attached to it that determine how the content will display. As you progress in your study of Excel, you will learn to format cells with different looks, such as color or bold text, and to attach comments to a cell. Clearing the contents of a cell deletes the value or formula typed there, but it does *not* clear formatting and comments.

1 Click cell **A4** to make it the active cell. Display the **Edit** menu, point to **Clear**, and then on the displayed submenu, click **Contents**.

2 Click cell **A5,** display the **Edit** menu, and then point to **Clear**.

The displayed submenu indicates *Del* (the Del key) as the keyboard shortcut for the Clear Contents command.

3 Click any empty cell in the worksheet window to close the menu without activating a command.

4 Select cell **A5** again, press Del to clear the contents of the cell.

5 From the keyboard, hold down the Ctrl key and press Z twice to undo the last two actions, which will restore the contents of cells **A5** and then **A4**.

6 On the Standard toolbar, click the **Save** button to save your changes.

Objective 7
Create Formulas

Excel performs calculations on numbers. That is why people use Excel. You can arrange data in a format of columns and rows in other application programs—in a word processing program, for example—and even perform simple calculations. Only a spreadsheet program such as Excel, however, can perform complex calculations on numbers.

Recall that the content of a cell is either a constant value or a formula. Formulas contain instructions for Excel to perform mathematical calculations on values in other cells and then to place the result of the calculations in the cell containing the formula. You can create your own formulas, or you can use one of Excel's prebuilt formulas called a *function*.

When you change values contained in any of the cells referred to by the formula, Excel recalculates and displays the new result immediately. This is one of the most powerful and valuable features of Excel.

Activity 1.22 Typing a Formula in a Cell

In this activity, you will sum the weekly salaries to calculate the total weekly payroll.

1 Click cell **A10** to make it the active cell, type **Total** and then press Enter.

2 Click cell **D10** to make it the active cell, and press ⌷=⌷.

The equal sign (=) displays in the cell with the insertion point blinking, ready to accept more data. All formulas begin with the = sign, which is the signal that directs Excel to begin a calculation. The Formula Bar shows the = sign, and the Formula Bar Cancel and Enter buttons are displayed.

3 At the insertion point, type **d4**

Cell D4 is surrounded by a blue border with small corner boxes, as shown in Figure 1.58. This indicates that the cell is part of an active formula. The color used in the box matches the color of the cell reference in the formula.

Content displayed in Formula Bar

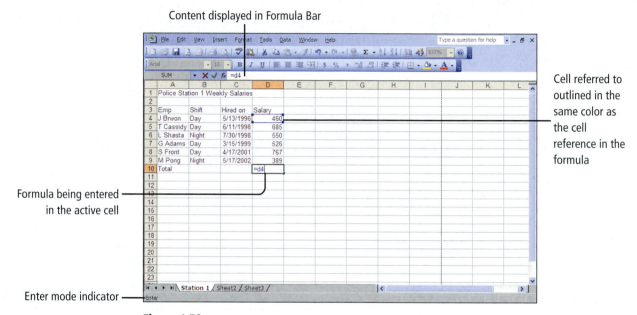

Cell referred to outlined in the same color as the cell reference in the formula

Formula being entered in the active cell

Enter mode indicator

Figure 1.58

4 At the insertion point, press the ⌷+⌷ key (⌷Shift⌷ + ⌷=⌷) and then type **d5**

A border of another color surrounds cell D5, and the color matches the color of the cell address in the active formula. Recall that when typing cell references, it is not necessary to use uppercase letters.

5 At the insertion point, type **+d6+d7+d8+d9** and then press ⌷Enter⌷.

The result of the calculation—*3377*—displays in the cell.

6 Click cell **D10** again to make it the active cell, and look at the Formula Bar, as shown in Figure 1.59.

You created a formula that added the values in cells D4 through D9, and the result of adding the values in those cells displays in cell D10. Although cell D10 displays the result of the formula, the formula itself is displayed in the Formula Bar. This is referred to as the ***underlying formula***. Always view the Formula Bar to be sure of the exact content of a cell—a displayed number might actually be a formula.

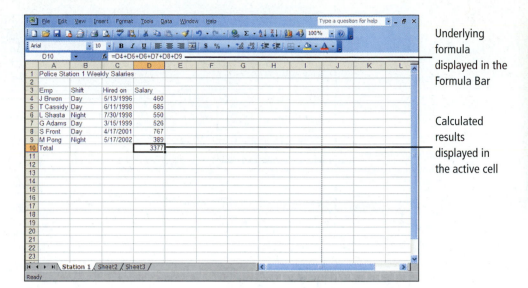

Underlying formula displayed in the Formula Bar

Calculated results displayed in the active cell

Figure 1.59

7 On the Standard toolbar, click the **Save** button ⊞ to save the changes you have made to your workbook.

Activity 1.23 Using Point and Click to Enter Cell References in a Formula

In this activity, you will calculate the annual salary for each officer by multiplying the weekly salary by the number of pay periods in a year. So far, you have entered cell references into a formula by typing them. Another method is to point to the cell you want to refer to and click. The selected cell address is placed in the formula without any typing.

1 Click cell **E3** to make it the active cell, type **Annual** and then press (Enter).

2 In cell **E4**, type **=** to signal the beginning of a formula.

3 With your mouse, point to cell **D4** and click once.

The reference to the cell, D4, is added to the active formula. A moving border surrounds the cell referred to, and the border color and the color of the cell reference in the formula are color coded to match. See Figure 1.60.

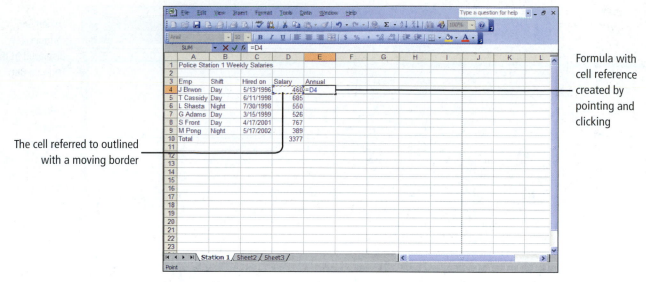

The cell referred to outlined with a moving border

Formula with cell reference created by pointing and clicking

Figure 1.60

4 On your keyboard, locate the ⊗ key (Shift + 8), type ***52** and press Enter.

The calculated annual salary, *23920*, displays in cell E4. The * symbol, called an ***asterisk***, functions in Excel as an ***operator***. Operators are symbols that represent mathematical operations. The mathematical operation of multiplication is represented by the asterisk. Thus, you multiplied the weekly salary (the value in cell D4) by the constant value 52 (the number of weeks in a year) to calculate the annual salary—and placed the result in cell E4.

5 Take a moment to study the symbols you will use to perform mathematical operations in Excel, as shown in the table in Figure 1.61.

Mathematical Symbols Used in Excel

Operator Symbol	Operation
+	Addition
−	Subtraction
*	Multiplication
/	Division
∧	Exponentiation

Figure 1.61

For reading ease, you may include spaces before and after the operators in a formula. Also, when you use more than one operator in a formula, Excel follows a mathematical rule called the ***order of operations***. As you progress in your study of Excel and develop your own formulas, you will practice applying this rule, which has three basic parts:

- Expressions within parentheses are processed first.

- Exponentiation is performed before multiplication and division, which are performed before addition and subtraction.

- Consecutive operators with the same level of precedence are calculated from left to right.

6 In cell **E5**, type **=** to begin a formula.

7 With your mouse, point to cell **D5** and click once.

8 Type ***52** and then press Enter.

The annual salary, *35620*, displays.

9 In cell **E6**, type **=d6*52** and press Enter.

When constructing a formula, you can either type cell references or use the point-and-click method to insert the cell reference. The annual salary, *28600*, displays in cell E6.

10 In cells **E7**, **E8**, and **E9**, use either the point-and-click method or the typing method to construct a formula to multiply each officer's weekly salary by 52. Then compare your screen with Figure 1.62.

11 On the Standard toolbar, click the **Save** button 🖫 to save the changes you have made to your worksheet.

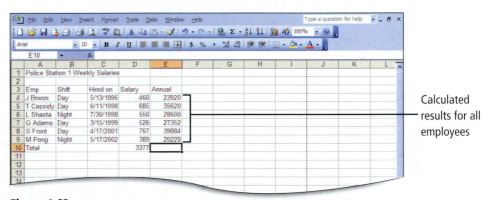

Calculated results for all employees

Figure 1.62

Activity 1.24 Summing a Column of Numbers with AutoSum

Excel has some prebuilt formulas, which are called ***functions***. One function, ***AutoSum***, is frequently used to add columns of numbers. Because it is used so frequently, a toolbar button was created for the AutoSum function. Other functions that are not so frequently used are available through the Insert Function dialog box.

1 Be sure **E10** is the active cell. On the Standard toolbar, click the **AutoSum** button Σ▾.

As shown in Figure 1.63, cells E4:E9 are surrounded by a moving border, and *=SUM(E4:E9)* displays in cell E10. The = sign signals the beginning of a formula, *SUM* indicates the type of calculation that will take place (addition), and *(E4:E9)* indicates the range of cells on which the sum operation will be performed. A ScreenTip provides additional information about the action.

The underlying formula displayed in the Formula Bar

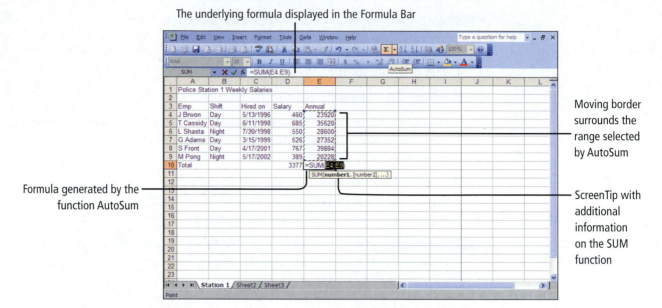

Moving border surrounds the range selected by AutoSum

Formula generated by the function AutoSum

ScreenTip with additional information on the SUM function

Figure 1.63

2 Look at the Formula Bar, and notice that the formula also displays there. Then, look again at the cells surrounded by a moving border.

When the AutoSum function is activated, Excel first looks above the active cell for a range of cells to sum. If no range is above the active cell, Excel will look to the left for a range of cells to sum. Regardless, Excel will propose a range of cells to sum, and if the proposed range is not what you had in mind, simply drag to select a different group of cells.

3 Press Enter. The total annual payroll amount of *175604* displays in cell E10.

4 On the Standard toolbar, click the **Save** button to save the changes you have made to your workbook.

Objective 8
Use Zoom and the Spelling Checker Tool

The Zoom command magnifies or shrinks the columns and rows of a worksheet to increase or decrease the number of cells displayed in the workbook window. Excel's default setting for the magnification size of a worksheet window is 100%, but you can increase the magnification to as much as 400% or decrease it to as little as 10%.

Excel's spelling checker tool checks for misspelled words in your workbook. A word that is not in Excel's dictionary is considered to be misspelled. For example, proper names of cities and people may be correctly spelled, but because Excel's dictionary does not include many of them, they will be flagged as misspelled words. Fortunately, you can add words to the dictionary or have Excel ignore words that are correctly spelled but that are not in Excel's dictionary.

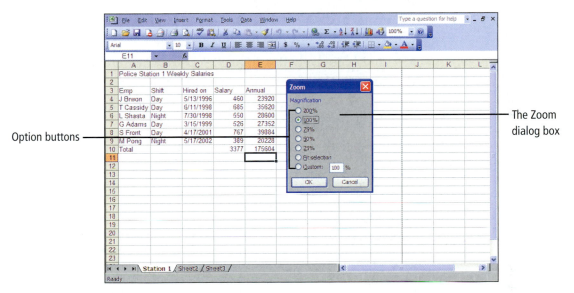

Option buttons

The Zoom dialog box

Figure 1.64

Activity 1.25 Zooming a Worksheet

1 Display the **View** menu, and then click **Zoom**.

The Zoom dialog box displays a list of Magnification options, as shown in Figure 1.64. The round buttons to the left of each option are referred to as *option buttons*.

2 In the **Zoom** dialog box, click the **75%** option button, and then click **OK**.

As shown in Figure 1.65, the sizes of the columns and rows are reduced, and more cells are visible in the worksheet window.

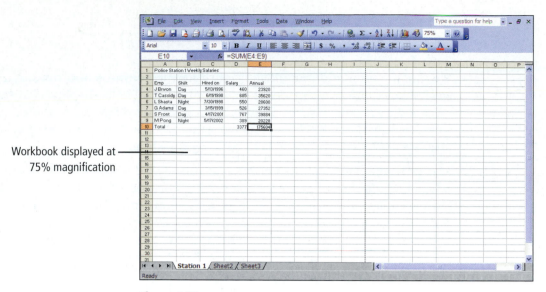

Workbook displayed at 75% magnification

Figure 1.65

3 From the **View** menu, click **Zoom**.

4 In the **Zoom** dialog box, click the **Custom** option button, type **150** in the box to right of *Custom*, and then click **OK**.

The columns and rows are much larger, and fewer cells are visible in the worksheet window.

5 On the Standard toolbar, click the **Zoom button arrow**, as shown in Figure 1.66.

The Zoom button arrow

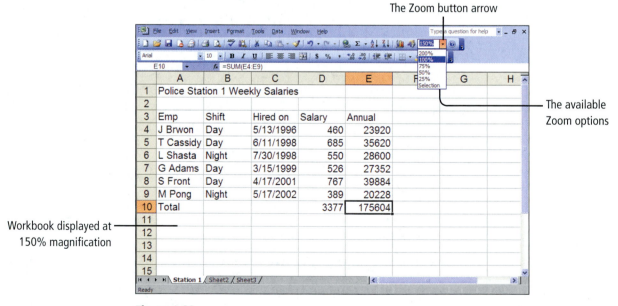

The available Zoom options

Workbook displayed at 150% magnification

Figure 1.66

6 In the displayed list, click **100%**.

The worksheet window returns to its default magnification size of 100%.

Activity 1.26 Checking for Spelling Errors in a Worksheet

1 Hold down `Ctrl` and press `Home` to make **A1** the active cell.

2 On the Standard toolbar, click the **Spelling** button.

The Spelling dialog box displays, as shown in Figure 1.67.

The Spelling dialog box

Word indicated as Not in Dictionary

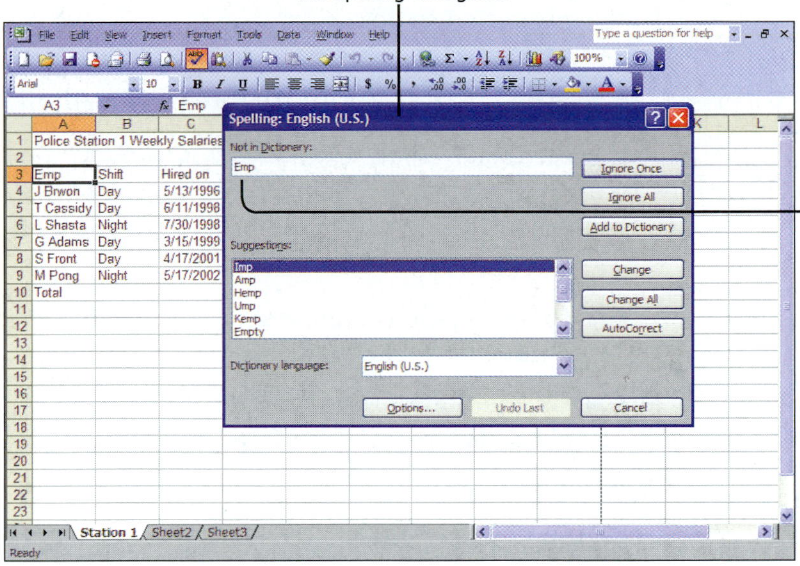

Figure 1.67

Alert!

Does Your Screen Differ?

Your first and last name, which are in the footer, may not be recognized by Excel. If your name displays under Not in Dictionary, click the Ignore Once button until Emp displays as shown in Figure 1.67. If the active cell was not A1, an informational dialog box displays, asking you whether you want to continue checking at the beginning of the sheet. Clicking Yes continues the spelling check from cell A1. Clicking No will end the spelling check command.

---

3 Under **Not in Dictionary**, notice the word *Emp*.

The spelling checker tool does not recognize the abbreviation you used for *Employee*. Under *Suggestions*, Excel provides a list of suggested spellings.

4 Under **Suggestions**, use the scroll bar to scroll through Excel's list of suggested spellings. Because *Emp* is an abbreviation that is useful in this worksheet but does not appear on the **Suggestions** list, click **Ignore All**.

Ignore All instructs Excel to ignore this particular spelling anywhere it is encountered in this worksheet. Excel stops at the next unrecognized word, *Brwon*.

5 Under **Suggestions**, click **Bryon** and then click the **Change** button.

Brwon, which was a typing error, is changed to Bryon. The spelling checker did not find *Brwon* in its dictionary. Although a number of proper names, such as *Brown* and *Bryon* are in the dictionary, many are not. Click Ignore All for those that are not contained in Excel's dictionary. You may want to add proper names that you expect to use often, such as your own last name, to the dictionary if you are permitted to do so.

> **Note — Can't Add Names to the Dictionary?**
>
> Some organizations prevent individuals from adding names to the dictionary to avoid overloading the server or disk drive where the software is located and also to avoid having misspellings inadvertently added to the dictionary.

6 On the displayed message, *The spelling check is complete for the entire sheet*, click **OK**.

7 On the Standard toolbar, click the **Save** button 💾 to save the changes you have made to your workbook.

Objective 9
Print a Worksheet Using the Print Dialog Box

Clicking the Print button on the Standard toolbar prints one complete copy of the active worksheet or all the selected sheets. To choose more options, such as printing additional copies or selecting a different printer, display the Print dialog box.

Activity 1.27 Previewing the Worksheet

1 With the Station 1 worksheet of your workbook **1B_Salary_Analysis** on your screen, display the **File** menu, and then click **Print Preview**.

The active worksheet displays as an image of a piece of paper so that you can see how the worksheet will be placed on the page.

2 On the Print Preview toolbar, click **Zoom**.

The worksheet zooms to 100%—you can read the contents of the page.

3 Click the **Zoom** button again to return to the full-page preview.

4 On the Print Preview toolbar, locate the **Print** button, and notice that the button name includes an ellipsis (…).

Recall that the ellipsis indicates that a dialog box will follow.

5 Click the **Print** button.

6 As shown in Figure 1.68, in the displayed **Print** dialog box, under **Print range** verify that the **All** option button is selected. Under **Print what** verify that **Active sheet(s)** is selected, under **Copies** verify that the Number of copies is **1**, and then click **OK**.

Print dialog box

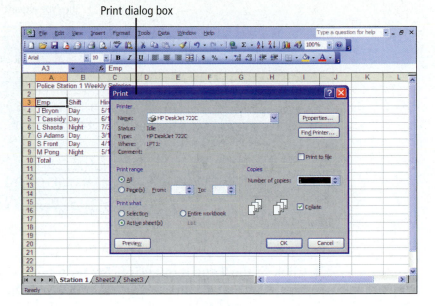

Figure 1.68

Activity 1.28 Closing a Workbook from the File Menu

When you have completed your work, save and close your workbook. Develop the habit of saving your workbook before closing it. If you forget to save it, however, Excel will display a reminder.

1 With your **1B_Salary_Analysis** worksheet still displayed, display the **File** menu, and then click **Close**, saving any changes if prompted to do so.

The workbook closes, leaving the workbook window empty and shaded in gray. Alternatively, close a workbook by clicking its

Close button.

Objective 10
Use Excel Help

Excel's Help feature provides information about all of Excel's features and displays step-by-step instructions for performing many tasks.

Activity 1.29 Using the Type a question for help Box

1 At the right side of the menu bar, locate the box containing the words *Type a question for help*. See Figure 1.69.

The Type a question for help box

Figure 1.69

2 Click in the **Type a question for help** box. At the insertion point, type **How do I create a new workbook?** and then press Enter.

The Search Results task pane displays a list of Help topics with hyperlinks (blue text) listed. Clicking on these hyperlinks will link you to additional information about the topic. See Figure 1.70.

The Search Results task pane

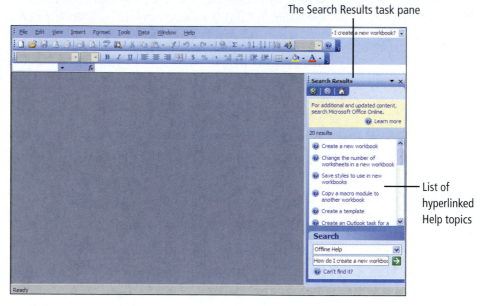

List of hyperlinked Help topics

Figure 1.70

3 On the list of Help topics, click **Create a new workbook**.

4 Click the blue hyperlink **Create a new, blank workbook**.

The topic expands to display additional information.

5 In the upper right corner, click **Show All** to expand the information.

6 Locate and then click the word **task pane** that is displayed in blue.

A definition of the term *task pane* displays in green.

7 Click the word **task pane** again to collapse (hide) the definition.

8 Read the information about creating a new workbook.

9 In the Excel Help window, on the toolbar, click the **Print** button 🖨. See Figure 1.71.

The expanded Microsoft
Excel Help window

Definition hyperlink

Print button

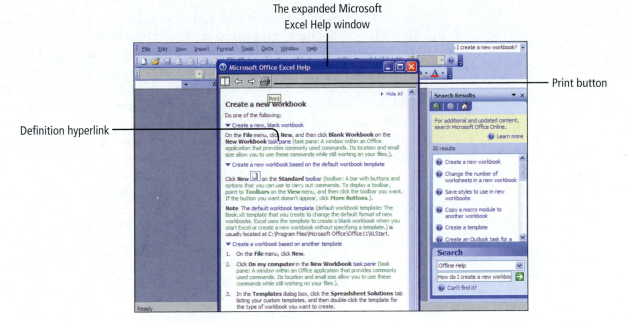

Figure 1.71

10 In the **Print** dialog box, click **Print**.

The Help topic you have displayed is printed. Keep this document for your reference.

11 On the Microsoft Excel Help title bar, click the **Close** button ❌, and then on the task pane, click the **Close** button ❌.

12 On the right side of the title bar, click the **Close** button ❌.

End **You have completed Project 1B**

Summary

Microsoft Excel 2003 is a spreadsheet application that can display and analyze data both numerically and graphically. Excel formulas are both powerful and easy to create.

In this chapter, you opened an existing workbook, added a footer, saved the file with a new name, and previewed and printed the file. The basics of using menus, toolbars and ScreenTips were reviewed. You practiced selecting cells, columns, rows and cell ranges. You navigated within a worksheet using the scroll bars and the name box, and among multiple worksheets in a workbook. You learned how to name a sheet tab so you can clearly label and identify information contained on each worksheet. You also examined an existing chart and saw how changing data also changes the chart.

In Project 6B a new workbook was created. You practiced entering and editing data in a worksheet. You edited text in the formula bar and in a cell, and used the Undo and Redo commands. The power of Excel lies in its ability to perform calculations on numbers. The basic techniques for creating formulas were introduced and then you created simple formulas by typing, by using the point-and-click method, and by using the AutoSum function. You changed the magnification of a worksheet with the Zoom button and used the Spelling Checker tool to ensure that the information was free of spelling mistakes. Finally, you asked a question of the Excel Help feature to explore this tool which is available to assist you as you work with the program.

In This Chapter You Practiced How To

- Start Excel and Navigate a Workbook

- Create Headers and Footers

- Preview and Print a Workbook

- Save and Close a Workbook and Exit Excel

- Create a New Workbook

- Enter and Edit Data in a Worksheet

- Create Formulas

- Use Zoom and the Spelling Checker Tool

- Print a Worksheet Using the Print Dialog Box

- Use Excel Help

Concepts Assessments

Matching   Match each term in the second column with its correct definition in the first column by writing the letter of the term on the blank line in front of the correct definition.

_____ **1.** Located at the lower left of the Excel window, the identifier of individual worksheets within a workbook.

_____ **2.** The basic Excel document, consisting of one or more worksheets.

_____ **3.** The action of moving the workbook window horizontally or vertically to view areas of the worksheet.

_____ **4.** A symbol that represents a mathematical operation.

_____ **5.** A graphical representation of the values in a worksheet.

_____ **6.** A reference to a group of cells, for example, *A1:C18*.

_____ **7.** Data—numbers, text, dates, or times of day—that you type in a cell.

_____ **8.** The intersection of a column and a row.

_____ **9.** Text or graphics that print at the top or bottom of a worksheet.

_____ **10.** The cell bordered in black and ready to receive data or to be modified.

_____ **11.** Highlighting by clicking or dragging with your mouse.

_____ **12.** A window within a Microsoft Office application that displays commonly used commands.

_____ **13.** An instruction in Excel used to perform mathematical operations.

_____ **14.** An Excel feature that assists with your typing by automatically completing data entered in a cell based on similar values in the column.

_____ **15.** The column letter and row number that identify a specific cell.

A Active cell

B AutoComplete

C Cell

D Cell address

E Chart

F Constant value

G Formula

H Headers and footers

I Operator

J Range

K Scrolling

L Selecting

M Sheet tabs

N Task pane

O Workbook

Fill in the Blank Write the correct answers in the space provided.

1. The two most frequently used toolbars are the _____ and the _____ toolbars.

2. To reduce the magnification and thus view more columns and rows on one screen, use the _____ feature.

3. When viewing a menu, an _____ following a command name indicates that a dialog box will display.

4. If a workbook has never been saved, clicking the Save button causes the _____ dialog box to open.

5. To group worksheets for the purpose of applying a header or footer, from the sheet tab shortcut menu click _____.

6. Nonadjacent cells can be selected by holding down the _____ key while clicking the desired cells.

7. The address of the active cell is always displayed in the _____.

8. Switch to another worksheet in the workbook by clicking on the _____.

9. Editing can be performed either in the cell or in the _____.

10. To select all the cells in the worksheet, click the _____ button.

Project 1C—Computer Passwords

Objectives: *Start Excel and Navigate a Workbook, Create Headers and Footers, Preview and Print a Workbook, Save and Close a Workbook and Exit Excel, Enter and Edit Data in a Worksheet, and Use Zoom and the Spelling Checker Tool.*

In the following Skill Assessment, you will complete a workbook for the Desert Park Police Department listing the assigned computer system passwords for the officers. Your completed workbook will look similar to Figure 1.72. You will save the workbook as *1C_Computer_Passwords_ Firstname_Lastname.*

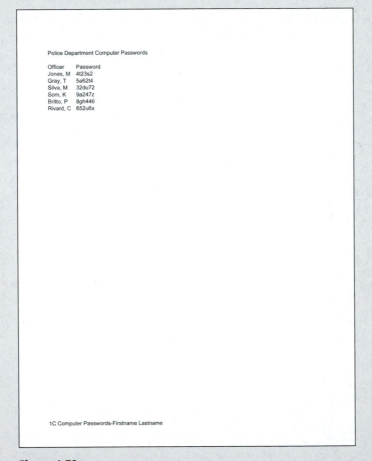

Police Department Computer Passwords

Officer	Password
Jones, M	4t23s2
Gray, T	5a62t4
Silva, M	32du72
Som, K	9a247z
Britto, P	8gh446
Rivard, C	652u6x

1C Computer Passwords-Firstname Lastname

Figure 1.72

1. Start Excel. Display the **File** menu, and then click **Open**.

2. Navigate to the student files that accompany this textbook, and then open the workbook *e01C_Computer_Passwords.*

3. Display the **View** menu, click **Header and Footer**, click the **Custom Footer** button, and in the **Left section**, type **1C Computer Passwords- Firstname Lastname** using your own first and last name. Use the default font and font size.

(Project 1C–Computer Passwords continues on the next page)

(Project 1C–Computer Passwords continued)

4. In the upper right corner of the **Footer** dialog box, click **OK**. In the lower right corner of the **Page Setup** dialog box, click **OK**. Recall that the dotted line indicates the number of columns that will print on the page as the page is currently set up.

5. From the **File** menu, click **Save As**, and then navigate to the location where you are storing your projects for this chapter. In the **File name** box, type **1C_Computer_Passwords_Firstname_Lastname** and then click the **Save** button.

6. In cell **A4**, type **Jones, M** and then press Enter to lock in the entry.

7. Display the **View** menu, and then click **Zoom**. In the **Zoom** dialog box, click the **200%** option button, and then click **OK**. This gives you an enlarged view, which is helpful when you are entering complex statistical data such as passwords.

8. Beginning in cell **A5**, add the following names to column A. Recall that pressing Enter after each entry relocates the active cell to the next row.

   Gray, T
   Silva, M
   Som, K
   Britto, P
   Rivard, C

9. In cell **B4**, type **4t23s2** and then press Enter.

10. Beginning in cell **B5**, add the remaining passwords to column B:

    5a62t4
    32du72
    9a347z
    8gh446
    652u6x

11. Point to cell **B7** and double-click to select the cell and simultaneously activate Edit mode. Using the arrow keys on the keyboard, place the insertion point before the *3*. Press Delete, type **2** and then press Enter to display the corrected password, *9a247z*.

12. On the Standard toolbar, click in the **Zoom** box so that *200%* is highlighted, type **100** and then press Enter. This is another method for changing the Zoom setting.

13. On the Standard toolbar, click the **Save** button to save your changes, and then click the **Print Preview** button.

14. On the Print Preview toolbar, click the **Print** button. In the displayed **Print** dialog box, click **OK** to print one complete copy of your worksheet on the default printer. From the **File** menu, click **Close** to close the workbook. Display the **File** menu again, and click **Exit** to close Excel.

End You have completed Project 1C ──────────

Project 1D — Crossing Guards

Objectives: *Start Excel and Navigate a Workbook, Create Headers and Footers, Preview and Print a Workbook, Save and Close a Workbook and Exit Excel, Enter and Edit Data in a Worksheet, Create Formulas, and Use Zoom and the Spelling Checker Tool.*

In the following Skill Assessment, you will complete a Crossing Guard report for the month of January for the Desert Park Police Department, whose officers volunteer as school crossing guards. Your completed workbook will look similar to the one shown in Figures 1.73a and 1.73b. You will save the workbook as *1D_Crossing_Guards_Firstname_Lastname.*

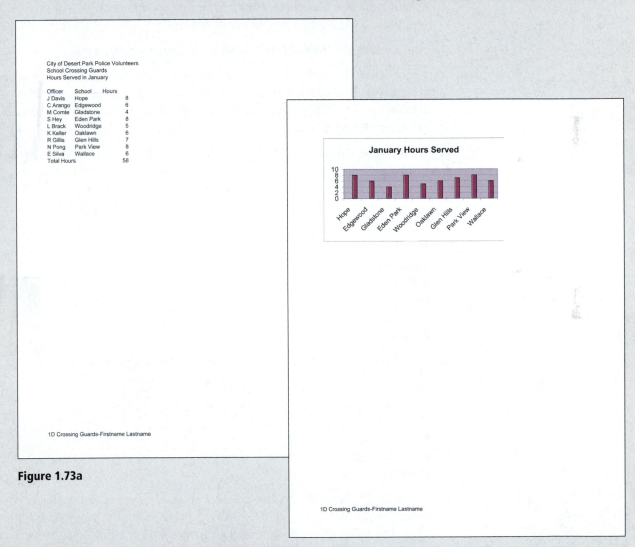

Figure 1.73a

Figure 1.73b

1. Start Excel. On the Standard toolbar, click **Open**.

2. Navigate to the student files that accompany this textbook, and then open the workbook **e01D_Crossing_Guards.**

(Project 1D–Crossing Guards continues on the next page)

(Project 1D–Crossing Guards continued)

3. Right-click the **Sheet1 tab**, and on the displayed shortcut menu, click **Select All Sheets**.

4. Display the **View** menu, click **Header and Footer**, click the **Custom Footer** button, and in the **Left section**, type **1D Crossing Guards-Firstname Lastname** using your own first and last name. Use the default font and font size.

5. In the upper right corner of the **Footer** dialog box, click **OK**. In the lower right corner of the **Page Setup** dialog box, click **OK**. Recall that the dotted line indicates the number of columns that will print on the page as the page is currently set up.

6. Right-click the **Sheet1 tab**, and click **Ungroup Sheets**.

7. From the **File** menu, click **Save As**, and then navigate to the location where you are storing your projects for this chapter. In the **File name** box, type **1D_Crossing_Guards_Firstname_Lastname** and then click the **Save** button.

8. In cells **A6** through **A14**, type the following list of volunteer crossing guards:

J Davis
C Arango
M Comte
S Hey
L Brack
K Keller
R Gillis
N Pong
E Silva

9. In cells **B6** through **B11**, enter the following list of school names:

Hope
Park View
Gladstone
Eden Park
Woodbridge
Oaklawn

10. In cell **B12**, type **G** and notice that as soon as you enter the *G*, the AutoComplete feature of Excel fills in the school name *Gladstone*. Type **len Hills** to enter the school name of *Glen Hills* and to overwrite the AutoComplete entry. Press Enter.

11. In cells **B13** and **B14**, type the remaining two school names, **Edgewood** and **Wallace** overwriting the AutoComplete entries as you type.

12. Click cell **B10** to make it the active cell. Pause the mouse pointer in the Formula Bar until the **I-beam** pointer displays. Click to position

(Project 1D–Crossing Guards continues on the next page)

(Project 1D–Crossing Guards continued)

the pointer before the *b* in *Woodbridge*, press [Delete] to remove the *b* and correct the school name to *Woodridge*. Click the **Enter** button on the Formula toolbar to lock in the change.

13. In cells **C6** through **C14**, enter the following list of hours that each volunteer worked. Because these are numeric values, as you lock them in by pressing [Enter], they are right-aligned in each cell.

8
6
4
6
5
6
7
8
6

14. In cell **A15**, type **Total Hours** and then press the [Tab] key twice to make **C15** the active cell.

15. With **C15** as the active cell, move to the Standard toolbar and click the **AutoSum** button. AutoSum borders the cells above and proposes a formula. Press [Enter] to accept the formula. The total in C15 is *56*.

16. Click cell **C15** again. Compare what is displayed in the cell, *56*, with what is displayed in the Formula Bar, *=SUM(C6:C14)*. Recall that this is called the underlying formula. The formula indicates that the contents of the cells in the range C6:C14 are summed.

17. Right-click the **Sheet1 tab**, click **Rename**, type **Hours** and then press [Enter]. Rename Sheet2 as **Chart** and then be sure that the Chart sheet is displayed.

18. View the graphical chart of the schools and number of hours worked. Notice the height of the Eden Park entry—6 hours. Click the **Hours tab** to return to the previous worksheet.

19. Change the number of hours for Officer *Hey* to **8** and press [Enter]. The calculated result in C15 changes to *58*. Click the **Chart tab** and notice the new height of the Eden Park entry. When you changed the number of hours worked on the Hours worksheet, the entry in the chart was also updated by Excel. Return to the Hours worksheet by clicking the **Hours sheet tab**.

20. On the Hours worksheet, click cell **B13**. Type **P** and notice that the existing value is deleted and that AutoComplete assists with your typing. With *Park View* in the cell, press [Enter] to accept it. Recall that when you type a new value in a cell, the existing value is deleted and replaced by your typing.

(Project 1D–Crossing Guards continues on the next page)

(Project 1D–Crossing Guards continued)

21. Change the school name for Officer *Davis* to **Edgewood** overriding AutoComplete, and then press [Enter]. On the Standard toolbar, click **Undo** to restore the original value of *Hope*. Change the school name for Officer *Arango* to **Edgewood** and press [Enter].

22. Click in the **Name Box**, type **a1** and then press [Enter] to make **A1** the active cell. Recall that you can navigate to a cell address by typing it in the Name Box and that you may type the column reference as either lower- or uppercase.

23. On the Standard toolbar, click the **Spelling** button. If necessary, click the Ignore All button as necessary to ignore the spelling of your name. The first word interpreted by Excel to be misspelled is *Crosing*. Under **Suggestions**, be sure that *Crossing* is selected, and then click the **Change** button. Correct the spelling for *January* and *School*.

24. Click **Ignore All** for the proper names that Excel does not have in its dictionary. Click **OK** when the spelling complete message displays.

25. From the **File** menu, click **Save** to save the changes you have made to your workbook since the last Save operation. Then, display the **File** menu again and click **Print Preview** to view the worksheet page as it will print on paper. Close Print Preview, click the **Chart** worksheet, and then click the **Print Preview** button.

26. On the Print Preview toolbar, click the **Print** button. On the displayed **Print** dialog box, under **Print what**, click the **Entire workbook** option button, and then click **OK** to print one copy of the workbook. Two sheets will print. From the **File** menu, click **Close**, and then exit Excel.

End **You have completed Project 1D** ────────────────

Project 1E — AV Equipment

Objectives: *Start Excel and Navigate a Workbook, Create Headers and Footers, Preview and Print a Workbook, Save and Close a Workbook and Exit Excel, Create a New Workbook, Enter and Edit Data in a Worksheet, and Create Formulas.*

In the following Skill Assessment, you will create a new workbook to generate an inventory report for the audiovisual equipment at the Desert Park Public Library. Your completed workbook will look similar to the one shown in Figure 1.74. You will save the workbook as *1E_AV_Equipment_Firstname_Lastname*.

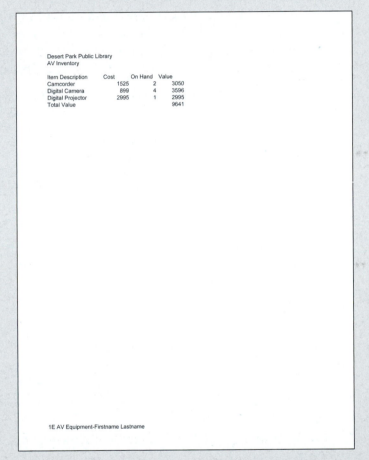

Desert Park Public Library
AV Inventory

Item Description	Cost	On Hand	Value
Camcorder	1525	2	3050
Digital Camera	899	4	3596
Digital Projector	2995	1	2995
Total Value			9641

1E AV Equipment-Firstname Lastname

Figure 1.74

1. Start the Excel program. *Book1* displays in both the title bar and the taskbar, indicating a new, unnamed workbook.

2. Display the **View** menu, click **Header and Footer**, click the **Custom Footer** button, and in the **Left section**, type **1E AV Equipment-Firstname Lastname** using your own first and last name. Use the default font and font size.

(**Project 1E**–AV Equipment continues on the next page)

(Project 1E–AV Equipment continued)

3. In the upper right corner of the **Footer** dialog box, click **OK**. In the lower right corner of the **Page Setup** dialog box, click **OK**. Recall that the dotted line indicates the number of columns that will print on the page as the page is currently set up.

4. If necessary, close the Getting Started task pane by clicking its small black **Close** button. From the **File** menu, click **Save As**, and then navigate to the location where you are storing your projects for this chapter. In the **File name** box, delete the existing text, type **1E_AV_Equipment_Firstname_Lastname** and then click **Save**.

5. In cell **A1**, type **Desert Park Public Library** and press Enter. Because cells B1 and C1 are empty, the content of cell A1 can display into the adjacent cells. Recall, however, that the text is contained entirely within cell A1. In cell A2, type **AV Inventory** and press Enter.

6. Right-click the **Sheet1 tab**, click **Rename**, type **AV Equipment** and notice that the tab expands to accommodate the name. Press Enter.

7. Move to cell **A4**, type **Item Description** and then press Tab twice. In cell **C4**, type **Cost** and then press Tab once. In cell **D4**, type **On Hand** and in cell **E4**, type **Value** and press Enter. Recall that when you use Tab, the cell entry is locked in and the cell to the right becomes the active cell. When Enter is pressed, the active cell becomes the cell below the first cell in which Tab was pressed. A5 is the active cell.

8. Beginning in the active cell, **A5**, enter the following descriptions in cells **A5:A7**:

    Camcorder
    Digital Camera
    Digital Projector

9. Beginning in cell **C5**, enter the following costs in the Cost column:

    1525
    899
    2995

10. Beginning in cell **D5**, enter the following On Hand quantities.

    2
    4
    1

11. Click in cell **E5** and type = to begin a formula. Click cell **C5** to insert it in the formula, type * (the operator for multiplication), and then click cell **D5**. This will multiply the camcorder cost in cell C5 by the number on hand in cell D5. Press Enter to display the result of *3050*.

(Project 1E–AV Equipment continues on the next page)

(Project 1E–AV Equipment continued)

12. Click cell **E5** again, and compare what is displayed in the cell (3050) with what is displayed in the Formula Bar (=C5*D5). Recall that this is called the underlying formula and that to determine the exact content of a cell, check the Formula Bar.

13. In cells **E6** and **E7**, use the point-and-click method to construct similar formulas to multiply the cost of the item by the number on hand. Compare your results with Figure 1.74. Click **Save** to save your changes.

14. In cell **A8**, type **Total Value** and then click cell **E8**. Using the point-and-click method to add the column, type **=** to begin a formula, click cell **E5**, press ⊞, click cell **E6**, press ⊞, and click cell **E7** and press Enter. The result, *9641*, displays in cell E8.

15. On the Standard toolbar, click **Save** to save the changes to your workbook.

16. On the Standard toolbar, click the **Print Preview** button to view the worksheet page. On the Print Preview toolbar, click the **Print** button. In the displayed dialog box, click **OK** to print one copy of your worksheet. Close the workbook, saving any changes if prompted, and then exit Excel.

End **You have completed Project 1E**

Project 1F — Phone Charges

Objectives: *Start Excel and Navigate a Workbook, Create Headers and Footers, Preview and Print a Workbook, Save and Close a Workbook and Exit Excel, Enter and Edit Data in a Worksheet, Create Formulas, Use Zoom and the Spelling Checker Tool, and Use Excel Help.*

In the following Performance Assessment, you will complete a list of phone charges for Desert Park's City Manager, Madison Romero. Your completed workbook will look similar to the one shown in Figure 1.75. You will save the workbook as *1F_Phone_Charges_Firstname_Lastname.*

```
Desert Park City Hall
Phone Charges

First    Last     Dept     Room    Ext      Amount
George   Britto   Finance   105     53       35.18
Mary     Goding   MIS       107     36       42.17
Sam      Motta    Taxes     215     15        7.15
Ann      Aragao   Zoning    216     46       45.84
Total                                        130.34
As of    9/16/2003

1F Phone Charges-Firstname Lastname
```

Figure 1.75

(Project 1F–Phone Charges continues on the next page)

(Project 1F–Phone Charges continued)

1. Start Excel, navigate to the location where the student files for this textbook are stored, and then open workbook **e01F_Phone_Charges**. Display the **View** menu, click **Header and Footer**, click the **Custom Footer** button, and in the **Left section**, type **1F Phone Charges-Firstname Lastname** using your own first and last name. Use the default font and font size. In the upper right corner of the **Footer** dialog box, click **OK**. In the lower right corner of the **Page Setup** dialog box, click **OK**.

2. From the **File** menu, click **Save As**, and then navigate to the location in which you are storing your projects for this chapter. In the **File name** box, type **1F_Phone_Charges_Firstname_Lastname** and then click **Save**.

3. Beginning in cell **A4**, type the following, using the Tab key to move across each row:

First	Last	Dept	Room	Ext	Amount
George	Britto	Finance	105	53	35.18
Mary	Goding	MIS	107	36	16.05
Sam	Motta	Taxes	215	15	7.15
Ann	Aragao	Zoning	216	46	45.84

4. In cell **A9**, type **Total** and then press Enter. In cell **F9**, using the point-and-click method to create a formula to add up the total phone charges, type = to start the formula, click cell **F5**, press +, and then continue in the same manner for the remaining cells. Alternatively, click the **AutoSum** button. The total charges add up to *104.22*.

5. In cell **A10**, type **As of** and then press Tab. In cell **B10**, hold down Ctrl and then press ; to insert today's date.

6. Change the amount for the MIS department to 42.17 and press Enter to recalculate the total—130.34.

7. Press Ctrl + Home to move to cell **A1**, and then on the Standard toolbar, click the **Spelling** button. For proper names, including your own, click Ignore All as necessary. Correct the word *Charges* and then click **Ignore All** for the proper names.

8. Save your changes, and then preview and print the worksheet. Close the file and exit Excel.

End **You have completed Project 1F**

Project 1G — Building Permits

Objectives: *Start Excel and Navigate a Workbook, Create Headers and Footers, Preview and Print a Workbook, Save and Close a Workbook and Exit Excel, Enter and Edit Data in a Worksheet, Create Formulas, and Use Zoom and the Spelling Checker Tool.*

In the following Performance Assessment, you will complete a workbook for the Desert Park Deputy Mayor, Andrew Gore, that summarizes the number of building permits issued for the second quarter. Your completed workbook will look similar to Figure 1.76. You will save the workbook as *1G_Building_Permits_Firstname_Lastname.*

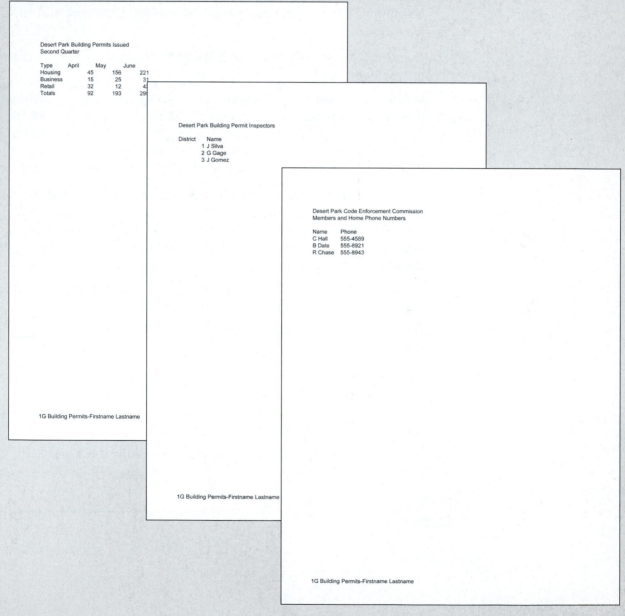

Figure 1.76

(Project 1G–Building Permits continues on the next page)

(Project 1G–Building Permits continued)

1. Start Excel, navigate to your student files, and then open the work-book **e01G_Building_Permits**. Right-click the **Sheet1 tab** and click **Select All Sheets**.

2. From the **View** menu, click **Header and Footer**, click the **Custom Footer** button, and in the **Left section**, type **1G Building Permits-Firstname Lastname** using your own first and last name. Use the default font and font size. In the upper right corner of the **Footer** dialog box, click **OK**. In the lower right corner of the **Page Setup** dialog box, click **OK**. Right-click the **Sheet1 tab**, and click **Ungroup Sheets**.

3. From the **File** menu, click **Save As**, and then navigate to the location where you are storing your projects for this chapter. In the **File name** box, type **1G_Building_Permits_Firstname_Lastname** and then click **Save**.

4. In **Sheet1**, be sure that cell **A1** is the active cell. Click in the **Formula Bar** so that you can edit the text. Click to the left of the *P* in *Permits*, insert the word **Building** followed by a space, and then press Enter.

5. Double-click cell **A2** to display the insertion point within the cell. Alternatively, select the cell and press F2. Edit the text by changing the word *First* to **Second** and then press Enter.

6. In cells **A4:D7**, enter the following data. Use Tab to move across the row and Enter to move down to a new row:

Type	April	May	June
Housing	45	156	221
Business	15	25	31
Retail	32	12	43

7. In cell **A8**, type **Totals** and then, using either the **AutoSum function** button or the point-and-click method, create formulas to sum each month's permits. Your results should be 92, 193, and 295. Rename Sheet1 **2nd Quarter**

8. Select **Sheet2**. Rename the sheet **Inspectors** and then enter the following data in cells **A3:B6**:

District	Name
1	J Silva
2	G Gage
3	J Gomez

(Project 1G–Building Permits continues on the next page)

(Project 1G–Building Permits continued)

9. Select **Sheet3**, rename the sheet **Commission Members** and then in cells **A4:B7**, enter the following data:

Name	Phone
C Hall	555-4589
B Date	555-8921
R Chase	555-8943

10. For each worksheet, make **A1** the active cell and then check the spelling. (Hint: Each worksheet contains one spelling error.) Save your changes. Right-click the **2nd Quarter Sheet** tab, and then click **Select All Sheets** so that all three sheets display in Print Preview.

11. Use Print Preview to review the overall look of your workbook. Display the **Print** dialog box. Because the sheets are still grouped, all are active and will print; thus you need not select the Entire workbook option. Print, close the file, saving any changes, and close Excel.

End You have completed Project 1G

Project 1H — Public Service

Objectives: *Create Headers and Footers, Preview and Print a Workbook, Save and Close a Workbook and Exit Excel, Create a New Workbook, Enter and Edit Data in a Worksheet, Create Formulas, Use Zoom and the Spelling Checker Tool, Print a Worksheet Using the Print Dialog Box, and Use Excel Help.*

In the following Performance Assessment, you will create a new workbook for the Desert Park Deputy Mayor, Andrew Gore, that reports the number of students that attended a public service presentation at their school. Your completed workbook will look similar to the one shown in Figure 1.77. You will save the workbook as *1H_Public_Service_Firstname_Lastname.*

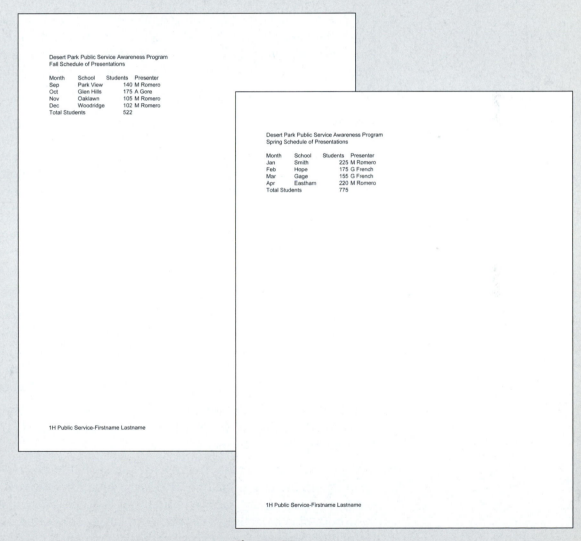

Figure 1.77

(Project 1H–Public Service continues on the next page)

(Project 1H–Public Service continued)

1. Start Excel. On the new blank workbook, right-click the **Sheet1 tab** and click **Select All Sheets**. From the **View** menu, click **Header and Footer**, click the **Custom Footer** button, and in the **Left section**, type **1H Public Service-Firstname Lastname**. Use the default font and font size. In the upper right corner of the **Footer** dialog box, click **OK**. In the lower right corner of the **Page Setup** dialog box, click **OK**. Right-click the **Sheet1 tab**, and click **Ungroup Sheets**.

2. From the **File** menu, click **Save As**, navigate to the location where you are storing your projects for this chapter, and in the **File name** box, type **1H_Public_Service_Firstname_Lastname** and then click **Save**. If necessary, close the task pane.

3. On Sheet1, select cell **A1** and type **Desert Park Public Service Awareness Program** and in cell **A2**, type **Fall Schedule of Presentations** Select **Sheet2**. In cell **A1**, type **Desert Park Public Service Awareness Program** and in cell **A2**, type **Spring Schedule of Presentations**

4. Select **Sheet1**. In cells **A4:D8**, enter the following data:

Month	School	Students	Presenter
Sep	Park View	140	M Romero
Oct	Glen Hills	175	A Gore
Nov	Oaklawn	105	M Romero
Dec	Woodridge	102	M Romero

5. In cell **A9**, type **Total Students** and then, in cell **C9**, use any method (typing, point-and-click, or AutoSum) to construct a formula to sum the total number of students. The total should be 522. Rename the Sheet1 tab to **Fall**

6. Select Sheet2 and enter the following data in cells **A4:D8**:

Month	School	Students	Presenter
Jan	Smith	225	M Romero
Feb	Hope	175	G French
Mar	Gage	155	G French
Apr	Eastham	220	M Romero

7. In cell **A9**, type **Total Students** and then, in cell **C9**, construct a formula to add the total number of students. The total should be *775*. Rename Sheet2 as **Spring**

8. On each worksheet, make cell **A1** the active cell, and then check the spelling by using the Spelling Checker tool; make any necessary corrections. If necessary, ignore proper names. Save your changes. To view both sheets in Print Preview, right-click a **sheet tab**, and click **Select All Sheets**. Click **Print Preview** to review both sheets, and then close Print Preview. From the **File** menu, click **Print**, and in the **Print** dialog box, under **Print what**, click the **Entire workbook** option button. Two sheets will print. Close the workbook, and exit Excel.

End **You have completed Project 1H**

Project 1I—Police Cars

Objectives: *Start Excel and Navigate a Workbook, Create Headers and Footers, Preview and Print a Workbook, Enter and Edit Data in a Worksheet, Create Formulas, and Use Zoom and the Spelling Checker Tool.*

In the following Mastery Assessment, you will create a workbook for the Desert Park Police Department with an inventory of the police cars, including license tag number, date placed in service, and total number of miles driven. Your completed workbook will look similar to the one shown in Figure 1.78. You will save the workbook as *1I_Police_Cars_Firstname_Lastname.*

Figure 1.78

1. Start Excel. In a new workbook, create a custom footer, and in the **Left section**, type **1I Police Cars-Firstname Lastname**

2. Save the file in your storage location for this chapter as **1I_Police_Cars_Firstname_Lastname**

(Project 1I–Police Cars continues on the next page)

(Project 1I–Police Cars continued)

3. On **Sheet1**, in cell **A1**, type **Desert Park Police Department** and, in cell **A2**, type **Police Car Inventory**

4. In cells **A4:C7**, enter the following data:

Tag	Date	Mileage
423-MFG	5-Mar-97	152576
342-QZY	8-May-99	120945
525-KYW	7-Jun-01	65098

5. Type **Total** in column A in the cell below the last car's data. In the appropriate cell, construct a formula to sum the total miles driven. The result should be 338619.

6. Rename the **Sheet1 tab Police Cars**

7. In cell **D4**, type **Expense** and then, using the following rules, create a formula in cells **D5**, **D6**, and **D7** to compute the expenses for each car:

   Rule 1: Cars placed in service before the year 2000 have an expense value of 50 cents per mile.

   Rule 2: Cars placed in service after January of 2000 have an expense value of 30 cents per mile.

8. Change the mileage for **525-KYW** to **165098** and press Enter to recalculate. Create a formula to sum the total expenses. The result should be 186289.9.

9. Click cell **A1**, and then check the spelling. Save your changes. Use Print Preview to review the overall look of your worksheet. Print the worksheet, close the workbook, and exit Excel.

End **You have completed Project 1I**

Project 1J — Cell Phones

Objectives: *Start Excel and Navigate a Workbook, Create Headers and Footers, Preview and Print a Workbook, Enter and Edit Data in a Worksheet, Create Formulas, and Use Zoom and the Spelling Checker Tool.*

The Desert Park Police Department uses cell phones to communicate with the officers. Chief Dennis Johnson wants an analysis of the cell phones that shows the number of minutes per phone used last month and the total cost of each phone. Your completed workbook will look similar to the one shown in Figure 1.79. You will save the workbook as *1J_Cell_Phones_Firstname_Lastname.*

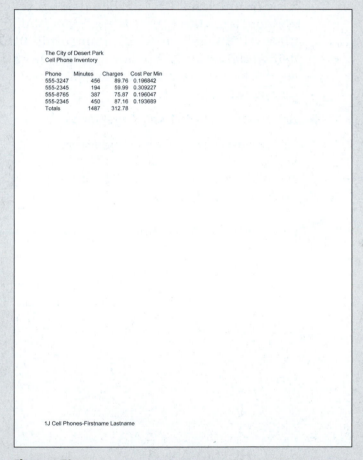

The City of Desert Park
Cell Phone Inventory

Phone	Minutes	Charges	Cost Per Min
555-3247	456	89.76	0.196842
555-2345	194	59.99	0.309227
555-8765	387	75.87	0.196047
555-2345	450	87.16	0.193689
Totals	1487	312.78	

1J Cell Phones-Firstname Lastname

Figure 1.79

1. Start Excel, navigate to your student files, and then open the workbook **e01J_Cell_Phones**. Create a custom footer, and in the **Left section** type **1J_Cell_Phones_Firstname_Lastname**

2. Save the file in your storage location for this chapter as **1J Cell Phones-Firstname Lastname**

(Project 1J–Cell Phones continues on the next page)

(Project 1J–Cell Phones continued)

3. Beginning in cell **A4**, enter the following data:

Phone	Minutes	Charges
555-3247	456	89.76
555-2345	194	59.99
555-8765	387	75.87
555-3356	450	87.16

4. In cell **A9**, enter **Totals** and construct a formula to sum the total Minutes used and the total Charges. Your results should be 1487 and 312.78.

5. In cell **D4**, enter **Cost Per Min** and then, in cell **D5**, type = to begin a formula. Click cell **C5** and then type , which is the operator for division. (This key is next to the Right Shift on most keyboards.) Click cell **B5**, and press Enter. Your result, 0.196842, indicates the *per minute charge* for this phone (charges divided by minutes). Construct similar formulas for the remaining phones, and then compare your results with Figure 1.79.

6. Rename the **Sheet1 tab Cell Phones**

7. Check for and correct spelling errors. (Hint: There are at least three spelling errors.) Save your changes. Use Print Preview to review the overall look of your worksheet. Print the worksheet, close the workbook, and exit Excel.

End You have completed Project 1J

Problem Solving

Project 1K — Permit List

Objectives: *Start Excel and Navigate a Workbook, Create Headers and Footers, Preview and Print a Workbook, Save and Close a Workbook and Exit Excel, Create a New Workbook, Enter and Edit Data in a Worksheet, and Create Formulas.*

The Director of Arts and Parks, Roy Hamilton, wants to compile a list of all community organizations that have requested a summer picnic permit. Additionally, he would like to know the approximate number of people who will be attending each organization's picnic. This will help the department plan for park maintenance and trash collection. Three parks have picnic shelters: North Park, South Park, and Mariposa Park.

Create a workbook that has three worksheets, one for each of the three parks. For each park, create the name of at least three community organizations, the dates of their picnics, and the approximate number of people who will attend each. You might visit your community's Web site to get ideas of various community organizations. Total the number of picnic attendees for each park. Create a footer that includes your name as you have in the past, and save the file as **1K_Permit_List_Firstname_Lastname**.

End **You have completed Project 1K** ——————————————

Project 1L — Museum Visits

Objectives: *Start Excel and Navigate a Workbook, Create Headers and Footers, Preview and Print a Workbook, Enter and Edit Data in a Worksheet, and Create Formulas.*

Gloria French, Public Information Officer for Desert Park, wants to report the number of students who have visited the city's museum over the past year. Create a workbook with one worksheet that lists the names of at least six schools. For each school, list the number of students that visited the museum for both the fall semester and the spring semester. Include totals by school and by semester. For school names, use school names from your local area. Create a footer that includes your name as you have in the past, and save the file as **1L_Museum_Visits_Firstname_Lastname**.

End **You have completed Project 1L** ——————————————

On the Internet

Learning More About Excel 2003

Additional information about using Microsoft Office 2003 Excel is available on the official Microsoft Web site. Take a look at the Top 10 Questions about Excel found at the following URL: **www.microsoft.com/office/excel/using/**

Many additional pages at this site have tips, help, downloads, and more. Plan to visit this site on a regular basis.

GO! with Help

Becoming Familiar with Excel Help

The easiest way to become successful with Microsoft Excel is to get in the habit of using the Help feature. In this exercise, you will access tips from Microsoft Help.

1. If necessary, start Excel to open a new workbook.

2. At the right edge of the menu bar, click in the **Type a question for help** box, type **How do I get Help?** and then press Enter.

   The Search Results task pane displays a list of results.

3. Click **About getting help while you work**.

   A Microsoft Excel Help window displays with a detailed list of various ways to access Help for Excel.

4. Using the **Print** button at the top of the Help window, print the contents of the Help window. Recall that your printed document will not contain any document identifier containing your name.

5. Close the Help window, and close the task pane.

1 chapterone

Getting Started with Access Databases and Tables

In this chapter, you will: complete these projects and practice these skills.

Project 1A
Opening and Viewing a Database

Objectives
- Rename a Database
- Start Access, Open an Existing Database, and View Database Objects

Project 1B
Creating a Database

Objectives
- Create a New Database
- Create a New Table
- Create a Primary Key and Add Records to a Table
- Close and Save a Table
- Open a Table
- Modify the Table Design
- Print a Table
- Edit Records in a Table
- Sort Records
- Navigate to Records in a Table
- Close and Save a Database
- Use the Access Help System

Lake Michigan City College

Lake Michigan City College is located along the lakefront of Chicago—one of the nation's most exciting cities. The college serves its large and diverse student body and makes positive contributions to the community through relevant curricula, partnerships with businesses and nonprofit organizations, and learning experiences that allow students to be full participants in the global community. The college offers three associate degrees in 20 academic areas, adult education programs, and continuing education offerings on campus, at satellite locations, and online.

© Getty Images, Inc.

Getting Started with Access Databases and Tables

Do you have a collection of things that you like, such as a coin collection, stamp collection, recipe collection, or collection of your favorite music CDs? Do you have an address book with the names, addresses, and phone numbers of your friends, business associates, and family members? If you collect something, chances are you have made an attempt to keep track of and organize the items in your collection. If you have an address book, you have probably wished it were better organized. A computer program like Microsoft Access can help you organize and keep track of information.

For example, assume you have a large collection of music CDs. You could organize your CDs into a database because your CDs are a collection of related items. By organizing your CDs in a database, you would be able to find the CDs by various categories that you define. If the information in your address book were placed in a database, you could produce a list of all your friends and family members who have birthdays in the month of April. In this chapter, you will see how useful a database program like Access can be.

Project 1A **Computer Club**

Data refers to facts about people, events, things, or ideas. A ***database*** is a collection of data related to a particular topic or purpose. Data that has been organized in a useful manner is referred to as ***information***. Examples of data that could be in a database include the titles and artists of all the CDs in a collection or the names and addresses of all the students in an organization. Microsoft Office Access 2003 is a database program that you can use to create and work with information in databases. Databases, like the ones you will work with in Access, include not only the data, but also tools for organizing the data in a way that is useful to you.

In Activities 1.1 through 1.8, you will create a new folder where you will store your projects. Then you will copy a database to your folder and rename the database so you can use it to complete the steps in this project. In this project, you will open a database and view information about the Club Events sponsored by the Computer Club at Lake Michigan City College. See Figure 1.1. In addition to the Event Name and the date of the event, the information includes the name of the Event Coordinator and the type of event.

Club Events

Event#	Event Name	Date	Event Type	Coordinator
01	New Member Social	08/15	Social	Jordan Williams
02	Bi-Monthly Meeting	08/15	Meeting	Annette Jacobson
03	Bi-Monthly Meeting	09/1	Meeting	Annette Jacobson
04	Making Access work for	09/10	Training	Mike Franklin
05	Introduction to Outlook	09/16	Training	Mike Franklin
06	Bi-Monthly Meeting	09/15	Meeting	Annette Jacobson
07	Bi-Monthly Meeting	10/1	Meeting	Annette Jacobson
08	Bi-Monthly Meeting	10/15	Meeting	Annette Jacobson
09	Bi-Monthly Meeting	11/1	Meeting	Annette Jacobson
10	Bi-Monthly Meeting	11/15	Meeting	Annette Jacobson
11	Bi-Monthly Meeting	12/1	Meeting	Annette Jacobson
12	Annual Party	12/10	Social	Linda Turpen
13	Project 1A	11/18	Training	Firstname Lastname

Thursday, October 16, 2003   *Page 1 of 1*

Figure 1.1
Project 1A—Computer Club

Objective 1
Rename a Database

To complete the projects in the chapters, you will locate the student files that accompany this textbook and copy them to the drive and folder where you are storing your projects. Databases that you copy to your storage location must be renamed so you can differentiate them from the data files that accompany this book. In this activity, you will learn how to do this.

Activity 1.1 Renaming a Database

1 Using the **My Computer** feature of your Windows operating system, navigate to the drive where you will be storing your projects for this book, for example, Removable Disk (D:) drive.

2 On the menu bar, click **File**, point to **New**, and then click **Folder**.

A new folder is created, the words *New Folder* display highlighted in the folder's name box, and the insertion point is blinking. Recall that within Windows, highlighted text will be replaced by your typing.

3 Type **Chapter 1** and then press Enter.

4 Navigate to the location where the student files that accompany this textbook are located, and then click once to select the file **a01A_ComputerClub**.

Note — Using File Extensions

Access databases use a .mdb extension.

The computer that you are using may be set such that file extensions display. If so, this file name will display as a01A_ComputerClub.mdb. The .mdb extension indicates that this file is a Microsoft database file.

5 Move the mouse pointer over the selected file name and then right-click to display a shortcut menu. On the displayed shortcut menu, click **Copy**.

6 Navigate to and open the **Chapter 1** folder you created in Step 3. Right-click to display a shortcut menu and then click **Paste**.

The database file is copied to your folder and is selected.

7 Move your mouse pointer over the selected file name, right-click to display the shortcut menu, and then on the shortcut menu, click **Rename**. As shown in Figure 1.2, and using your own first and last name, type **1A_ComputerClub_Firstname_Lastname**

Chapter 1 folder

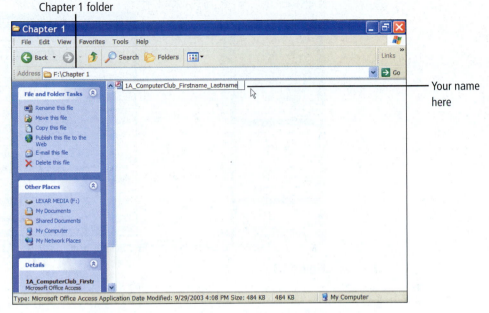

Figure 1.2

8 Press Enter to save the new file name. If the *Confirm File Rename* message displays, click **Yes**. Be sure that the file name is still selected (highlighted), pause your mouse pointer over the selected name, and then right-click to display the shortcut menu.

> ## Note — Naming Files
>
> ### *Use underscores instead of spaces.*
>
> The Microsoft Windows operating system recognizes file names with spaces. However, some Internet file transfer programs do not. To facilitate sending your files over the Internet using a course management system, in this textbook you will be instructed to save files using an underscore rather than a space. On your keyboard, the underscore key is the shift of the hyphen key, to the right of the zero key.

9 On the displayed shortcut menu, click **Properties**.

The Properties dialog box with the database name in the title bar displays. The databases provided with this book have a Read-only attribute that protects them from being altered. To use a database, you must first save the database to the location where you are storing your files, rename the database, and then remove the Read-only attribute so you can make changes to the database.

10 At the bottom of the dialog box, click to clear the check mark next to **Read-only**. See Figure 1.3.

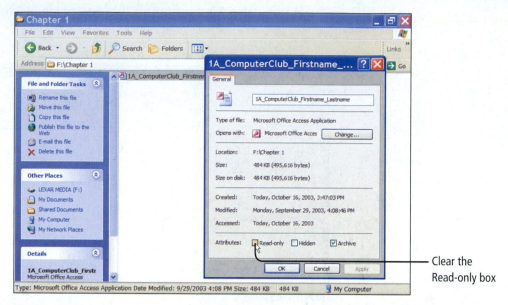

Clear the Read-only box

Figure 1.3

11 Click **OK** to close the dialog box.

12 **Close** the **My Computer** window.

You may want to mark or otherwise make a note of this section for future reference when you need to retrieve, copy, and rename additional databases for use in this textbook.

Objective 2
Start Access, Open an Existing Database, and View Database Objects

Activity 1.2 Starting Access and Opening an Existing Database

Data that is organized in a format of horizontal rows and vertical columns is called a *table*. A table is the foundation on which an Access database is built. In the following activity, you will view a table within a database.

1 On the left side of the Windows taskbar, click the **Start** button ![start].

The Start menu displays.

2 On the computer you are using, determine where the Access program is located and point to **Microsoft Office Access 2003**.

Organizations and individuals store computer programs in a variety of ways. The Access program might be located under All Programs or Microsoft Office or some other arrangement. See Figure 1.4 for an example.

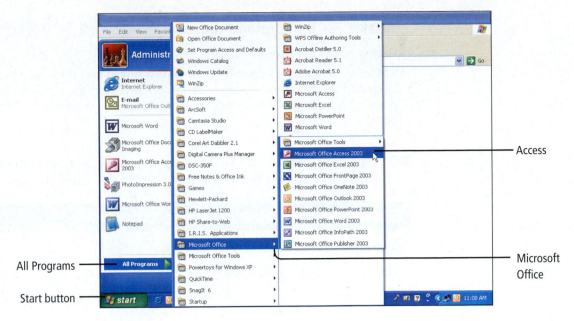

All Programs

Start button

Access

Microsoft Office

Figure 1.4

3 Click once to open the **Access** program.

The Access program opens. Across the upper portion of the Access window is the title bar, a menu bar, and the Database toolbar. The main window is divided into two sections—the *task pane* on the right and a blank gray area on the left. The task pane is a window within a Microsoft Office application that provides commonly used commands. Its location and small size allow you to use these commands while working in your database. A database, when opened, will display in the gray area. See Figure 1.5.

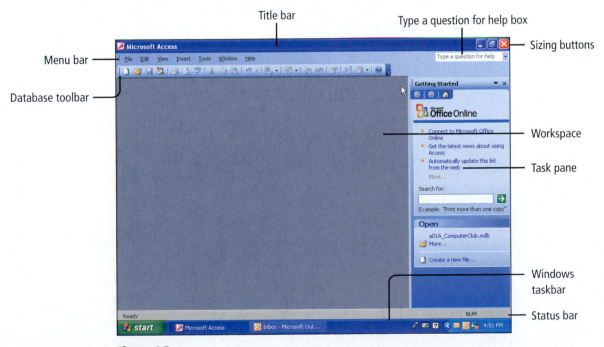

Title bar

Type a question for help box

Menu bar

Database toolbar

Sizing buttons

Workspace

Task pane

Windows taskbar

Status bar

Figure 1.5

Note — Comparing Programs

Access opens the program only.

You may have used Microsoft Word, which opens and displays a blank document, or Microsoft Excel, which opens and displays a blank workbook. Access, however, does not open a blank database—it opens the program only.

4 Take a moment to study the elements of the Access window as shown in Figure 1.5 and as described in the table in Figure 1.6.

Elements of the Access Window

Element	Description
Title bar	Displays the name of the program.
Sizing buttons	Enable you to minimize, maximize, restore, and close the Access window.
Type a question for help box	Allows you to access the Microsoft Access Help feature by typing a question.
Menu bar	Contains the menus of Access commands. Display a menu by clicking on its name in the menu bar.
Database toolbar	Contains a row of buttons that provide a one-click method to perform the most common commands in Access.
Task pane	Displays commonly used commands.
Status bar	Displays information about the task you are working on.
Windows taskbar	Displays the Start button and buttons indicating active windows.
Workspace	Gray area where an open database displays.

Figure 1.6

5 On the Database toolbar, pause your mouse pointer over the **Open** button.

When you position the mouse pointer over a button, Access displays the button's name in a box called a ***ScreenTip***. You should see the ScreenTip *Open*.

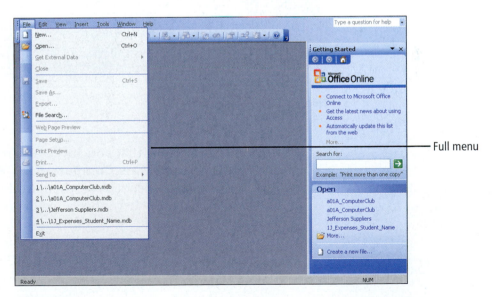 On the menu bar, click **File**.

The File menu displays. When you display a menu in Access, either the short menu, shown in Figure 1.7, or the full menu, shown in Figure 1.8, displays.

Short menu displayed ————

Click to display full ———— menu

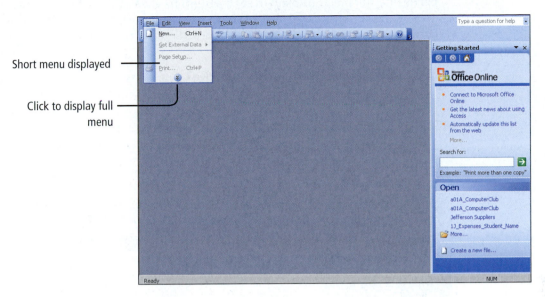

Figure 1.7

The short menu will display fully after a few seconds. Alternatively, you can click the small double arrow at the bottom of the short menu to display the full menu.

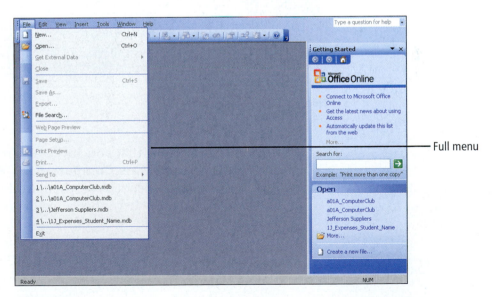

———— Full menu

Figure 1.8

More Knowledge — Displaying the Full Menu

Select the **Always show full menus** *option.*

If you do not see the short version of the File menu as shown in Figure 1.7, your system has been set so that full menus always display. Many individuals prefer the full menu display. To set a system to always display the full menu, display the Tools menu, click Customize, and then click the Options tab. Select (place a check mark in) the Always show full menus check box. Click Close.

7 On the displayed **File** menu, click **Open**.

The Open dialog box displays.

8 Click the **Look in arrow** shown in Figure 1.9 and then navigate to the location where you are storing your projects for this chapter.

Look in arrow

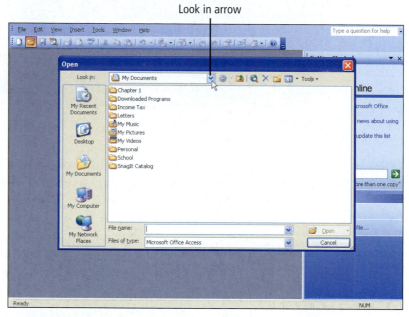

Figure 1.9

9 Locate the database file that you saved and renamed with your name in Activity 1.1. Click the **1A_ComputerClub_Firstname_Lastname** database file once to select it, and then, in the lower right corner, click the **Open** button. Alternatively, you can double-click the name of the database.

10 If the message in Figure 1.10, or similar message, displays on your screen, click **Yes**.

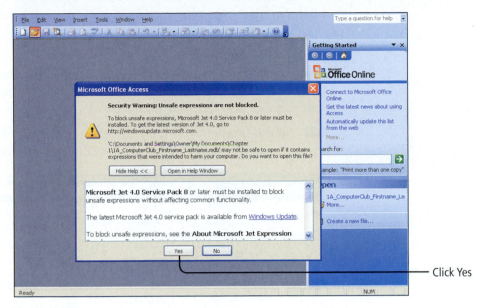

Click Yes

Figure 1.10

11 If another Security Warning message displays, click **Open**.

The ComputerClub Database window opens, as shown in Figure 1.11.

Database window
sizing buttons

Access window
sizing buttons

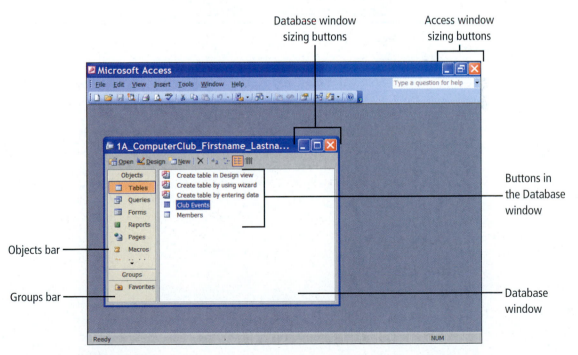

Buttons in
the Database
window

Objects bar

Groups bar

Database
window

Figure 1.11

Activity 1.3 Viewing the Database Window

The **Database window** displays when a database is open. The **Objects bar** on the left side of the Database window has buttons—called **objects**—that you can work with in Access. Objects are the primary components of an Access database.

Just one object—**Tables**—actually *stores* your data; the other objects are used to organize, manage, and manipulate the data. Recall that a table is a collection of data organized in a format of columns and rows. One or more tables can be used to store data in a database.

1 Take a moment to study the elements of the Database window shown in Figure 1.11 and described in the table in Figure 1.12.

Elements of the Database Window

Element	Description
Database window	Displays when a database is open and allows you to access all the database objects.
Objects bar	Contains buttons that activate the objects (tools) of a database.
Groups bar	Contains shortcuts to different types of database objects.
Database window sizing buttons	Enables you to minimize, maximize, and close the Database window.
Buttons in the Database window	Activate commands related to the selected database object.

Figure 1.12

2 In the extreme upper right corner of your screen, locate the **Type a question for help** box. Just above that box, click the Access window's **Minimize** button ▬ . See Figure 1.11.

The Access window is minimized and displays as a button on the Windows taskbar at the lower edge of your screen. See Figure 1.13.

Desktop

Minimized Access button

Figure 1.13

3 On the Windows taskbar, click **Microsoft Access**.

The Access window and Database window are restored. Minimizing windows in this manner enables you to view your Desktop.

4 Look at the Database window (the smaller window) and notice that it also has a set of sizing buttons at the right edge of its title bar. Click its **Maximize** button.

The Database window fills the entire gray workspace within the Access window. The Database window's title bar no longer displays— the name of the database displays instead on the main title bar enclosed in square brackets. See Figure 1.14.

Database name on Access title bar

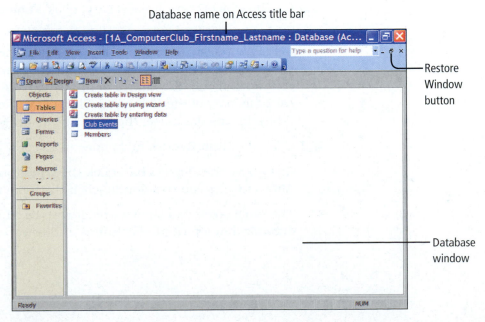

Restore Window button

Database window

Figure 1.14

5 To the right of the **Type a question for help** box, click the small **Restore Window** button ⬚. See Figure 1.14.

The Database window is restored to its original size and position, as shown in Figure 1.11. You can see that the Database window is a separate window that can be manipulated like other windows.

> ## Note — Sizing the Database Window
>
> *Maximize to fill the gray area.*
>
> You have seen that the Database window can be maximized to fill the gray area, or left in its original size, which is smaller and contained within the gray area. Many Access users prefer keeping the Database window smaller than the gray area of the Access window. This visually separates the Objects bar and the other parts of the Database window from features that are part of the larger Access window.

6 On the Objects bar, notice that *Tables* is selected. With the Tables object selected, point to, but do not click, each of the remaining objects one by one.

The Computer Club Database window displays seven objects: Tables, Queries, Forms, Reports, Pages, Macros, and Modules. Each of these objects is used by Access to manage the information stored in the Computer Club database. As you progress in your study of Access, you will learn more about each of these objects.

Activity 1.4 Opening a Table

Recall that tables are the foundation of your Access database because that is where the data is stored. Each table in an Access database stores data about only one subject. For example, in the Computer Club database, the Club Events table stores data about individual club events and the Members table stores data about the Club's members.

1 On the Objects bar, if necessary, click **Tables** to select it.

Notice that to the right of the Objects bar, three command icons display followed by the names of two tables. The command icons provide three different methods for creating a new table. Following the command icons, the names of the tables that have been created and saved as part of the Computer Club database display. There are two tables in this database, the *Club Events* table and the *Members* table.

2 Click the **Club Events** table once to select it if necessary, and then, just above the Objects bar, click the **Open** button ⬚ Open . Alternatively, you can double-click the table name to open it.

The table opens, as shown in Figure 1.15. Here you can see the data organized in a format of columns and rows.

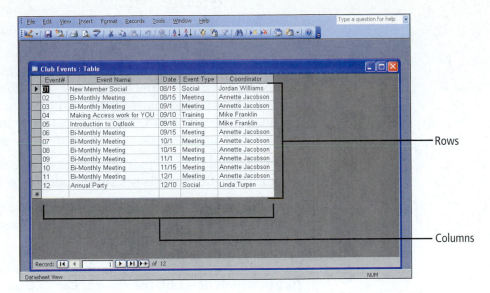

Figure 1.15

3 Along the left side of the open table, move your mouse pointer until it displays as a right-pointing arrow, as shown in Figure 1.16.

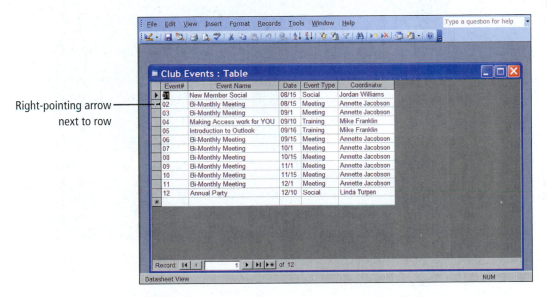

Figure 1.16

4 Pause the arrow pointer at the row containing the event *Annual Party* and click once.

The row containing the information for the Annual Party is highlighted in black. Each horizontal row of a table stores all of the information about one database item. You can see that, in the Club Events table, each event has a separate row in the database table. The information in a row is referred to as a **record**.

5 Use the technique you just used in Step 4 to find and select the record for the training event **Introduction to Outlook**.

6 Across the top of the table, move your mouse pointer over the words *Event Type* until it becomes a down arrow, and then click once to select the column. See Figure 1.17.

Each record contains information located in vertical columns, called **fields**, which describe the record. For example, in the Club Events table, each event (record) has the following fields: Event#, Event Name, Date, Event Type, and Coordinator.

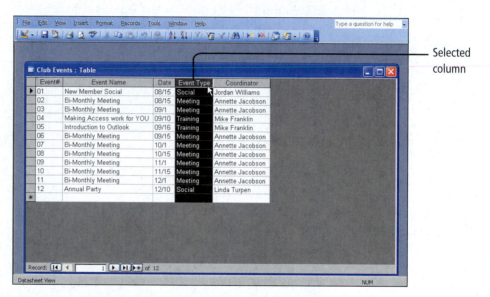

Selected column

Figure 1.17

7 Use your mouse pointer to select the column representing the **Coordinator** field. Take a moment to look at the other column names in the table to familiarize yourself with these *fields*.

8 In the last row of the table, click once in the **Event#** field under the last record in the table. See Figure 1.18.

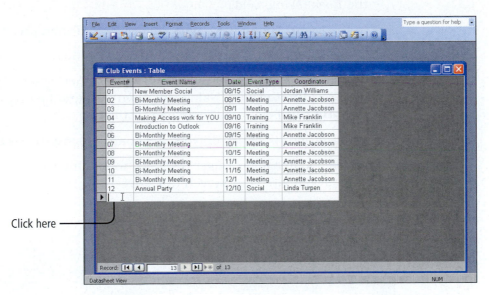

Click here

Figure 1.18

9 In the **Event#** field type **13**

10 Notice the pencil image in the gray box to the left. See Figure 1.19.

In the *row selector*—the small gray box at the left end of a row—a small pencil image displays in the row in which a new record is being entered. The pencil image in the row selector indicates that the information in this record is in the process of being entered and has not yet been saved.

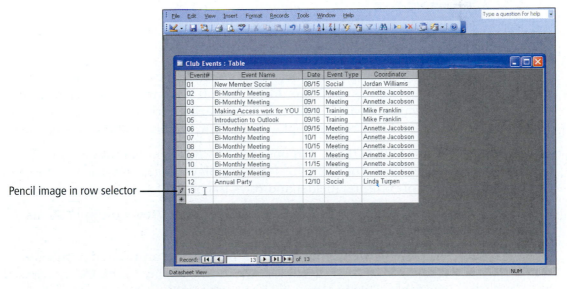

Pencil image in row selector

Figure 1.19

11 Press `Tab` once.

The insertion point is blinking in the next field to the right, which is the *Event Name* field.

12 In the **Event Name** field, type **Project 1A** and then press `Tab`.

13 In the **Date** field, type **11/18** and then press `Tab`.

14 In the **Event Type** field, type **Training** and then press `Tab` to move to the **Coordinator** field. Using your own first and last name, in the **Coordinator** field, type **Firstname Lastname**

15 Press either `Enter` or `Tab` on your keyboard to save the record.

The pencil image no longer displays, indicating that the record is saved. Compare your screen to Figure 1.20.

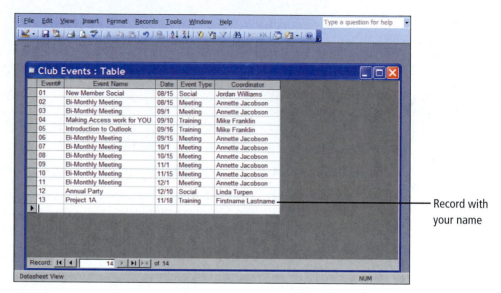

Figure 1.20

Activity 1.5 Viewing a Table

The Tables database object has four *views*. A view is a way of looking at something such as a table or form. As you work with tables of data, there are two ways to look at tables that are particularly useful—the Datasheet view, which is currently displayed on your screen, and the Design view.

In the previous activity, you opened the Club Events table in the Datasheet view. The Datasheet view displays all the records in a table in a format of columns (fields) and rows (records).

1 On the Table Datasheet toolbar, locate the **View** button [icon], as shown in Figure 1.21.

Its picture, displaying a ruler, a pencil, and a protractor, indicates that clicking the button will switch the display to the Design view of the table. This button will change depending on the current view to allow you to switch back and forth between **Design view** and **Datasheet view**.

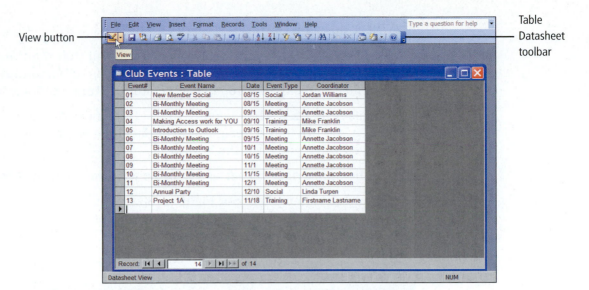

View button ——

Table Datasheet toolbar

Figure 1.21

2 Click the **View** button 📐▾ .

The Design view of the table displays. Notice that in Design view, you do not see the names of the club events—or other information contained in the records. You see only the names of the fields, such as *Event Name* and *Coordinator*. In this view, you can change the design of the table—that is, the way each field displays its associated data.

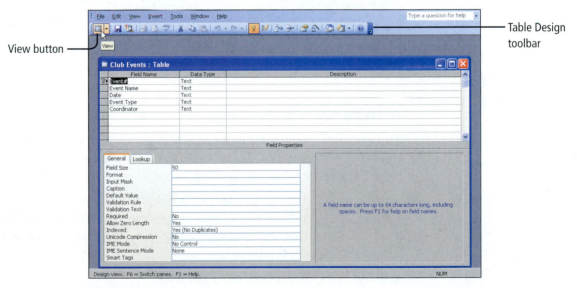

View button ——

Table Design toolbar

Figure 1.22

3 On the Table Design toolbar, locate the **View** button 🔲▾ . See Figure 1.22.

Now the View button displays as a small table—or datasheet. This picture on the View button indicates that clicking the button will return you to the Datasheet (table) view.

4 Click the **View** button 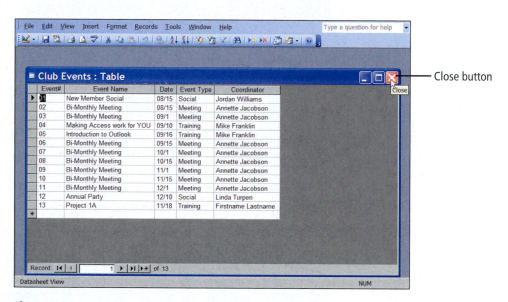.

The table redisplays in Datasheet view. Recall that the Datasheet view of a table displays the individual records in horizontal rows and the field names at the top of each column. Thus, the View button displays as when you are in the Datasheet view and as when you are in the Design view—indicating which view will be displayed when you click the button.

5 In the upper right corner of the Table window, click the **Close** button to close the table. See Figure 1.23.

The Database window displays.

Close button

Figure 1.23

Activity 1.6 Viewing a Query

The second object on the Objects bar is *Queries*. To **query** is to ask a question. The Queries object is a tool with which you can ask questions about the data stored in the Tables objects.

For example, you could use the Queries object to ask how many Club Events are social events. Locating specific information in a database, such as the number of social events, is referred to as **extracting** information from the database.

1 On the Objects bar, click **Queries**.

The Database window displays two command icons that can be used to create a new query. They are followed by one query that has been created and saved as part of the Computer Club database. Later, you will create and save your own queries.

2 Double-click the **Social Events Query**. Alternatively, you can right-click the query name, and then click Open on the displayed shortcut menu, or click once to select the query and then click the Open button ![Open] in the Database window.

When a query is opened, Access *runs*—processes—the query and displays the results. The results of the query will display only selected information from the table.

3 Look at the records that display as a result of this query.

The number of records in the query result is less that the number of records in the original table because certain **criteria**—specifications that determine what records will be displayed—were entered as part of the query. For example, this query was created to locate the names of all the events in the table that are Social Events. Notice that two records display—New Member Social and Annual Party. See Figure 1.24.

Query name in title bar ——

Two records that meet query criteria

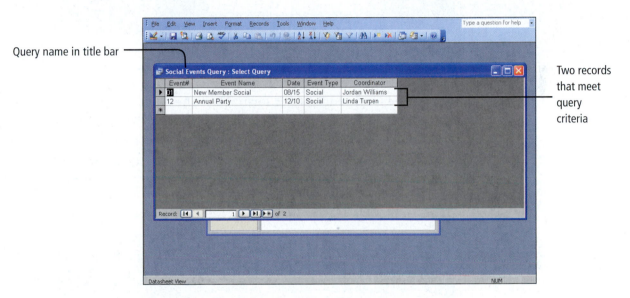

Figure 1.24

4 In the upper right corner of the query window, click the **Close** button ![X] .

The Database window displays.

Activity 1.7 Viewing a Form

Forms, the third object on the Objects bar, provides an alternative method to both enter and display data in the Tables object. The records that display in a form are the same records that are in the table, with one difference: forms can be designed to display only one record at a time.

1 On the Objects bar, click **Forms**.

To the right of the Objects bar, two command icons for creating a new form display, followed by a form that has been created and saved as part of the Computer Club database. Thus far, only one form, the Club Events form, has been created for this database.

2 Double-click the **Club Events** form.

The Club Events form displays with fields filled in with the data representing the first record in the database. See Figure 1.25.

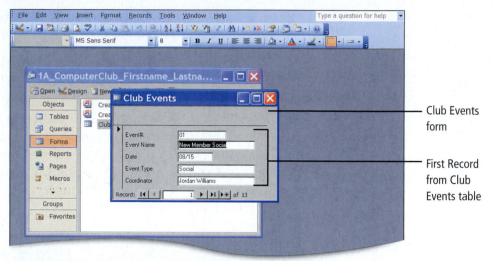

Figure 1.25

3 At the lower edge of the form, click the **Next Record** button until you see the 12th record—the Annual Party event—displayed in the form. See Figure 1.26.

As you click the Next Record button, notice how each individual record in the table of Club Events displays in the window.

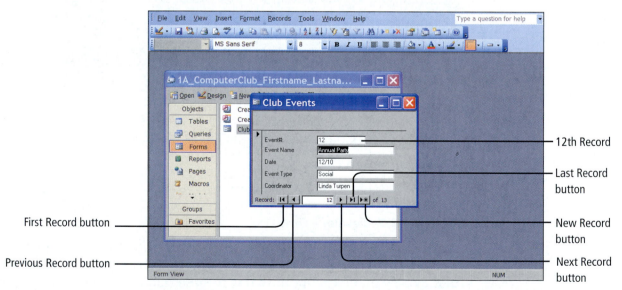

Figure 1.26

4 In the upper right corner of the Club Events form window, click the **Close** button to close the form. The Database window displays.

Activity 1.8 Viewing and Printing a Report

The fourth button on the Objects bar is *Reports*. A **report** is a database object that displays the fields and records from the table (or query) in an easy-to-read format suitable for printing. Reports are created to summarize information in a database in a professional-looking manner.

1 On the Objects bar, click **Reports**. See Figure 1.27.

To the right of the Objects bar, command icons for creating a new report display, followed by a report that has been created and saved as part of the Computer Club database. Thus far, only one report, the Club Events report, has been created for this database.

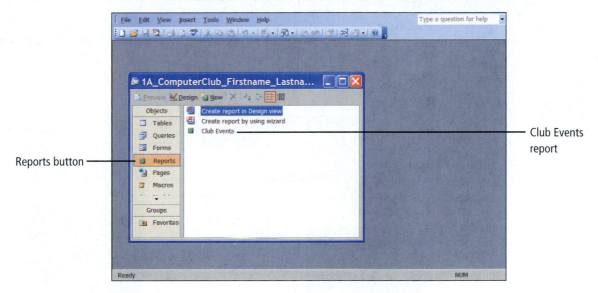

Figure 1.27

2 Double-click the **Club Events** report.

The Club Events report displays, as shown in Figure 1.28.

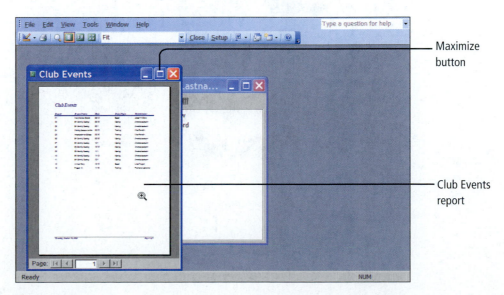

Figure 1.28

3 In the upper right corner of the Club Events report window, click the **Maximize** button ⬜.

The window is maximized on your screen.

4 On the toolbar, pause the mouse pointer over the word *Fit* and see the ScreenTip *Zoom*.

To **zoom** means to make the page view larger or smaller. **Fit** means that an entire page of the report will display on your screen at one time giving you an overall view of what the printed pages will look like.

5 On the toolbar, click the **Zoom arrow** and then, from the displayed list, click **100%**. See Figure 1.29.

Zooming to 100% displays the report in the approximate size it will be when it is printed.

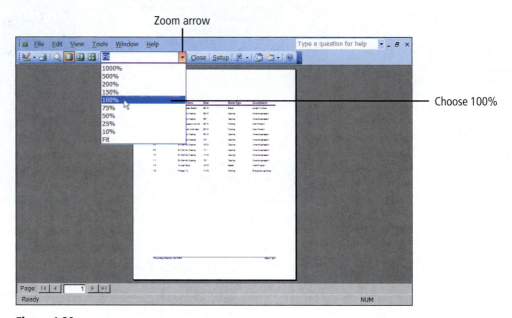

Figure 1.29

6 In the displayed report page, locate the record **Project 1A**. You may need to use the vertical scroll bar in the window to see this record. See Figure 1.30.

Print button

Close Window button

Vertical scrollbar

Record with your name

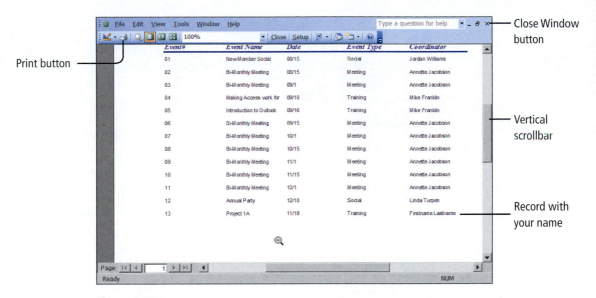

Figure 1.30

Notice that on your screen, the report displays as if it were printed on a piece of paper. A report is designed to be a professional-looking document that you can print.

A report is generated each time you open it and displays up-to-date information. For example, this report was created before you opened the database, but the record you added with your name now displays in the report.

7 On the toolbar, click the **Print** button 🖶. See Figure 1.30.

The Club Events report prints.

8 In the upper right corner of the report window, click the **Close Window** button ⊠ to close the report.

The Database window displays.

9 To the right of the **Type a question for help** box, click the small **Restore Window** button 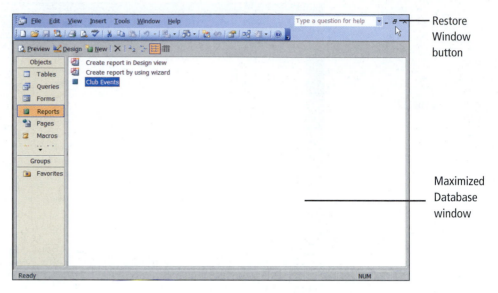 to restore the Database window to its previous size. See Figure 1.31.

Restore Window button

Maximized Database window

Figure 1.31

10 In the Database window, click the **Close** button ✖ to close the Computer Club database. See Figure 1.32.

The Computer Club database closes. The Access program remains open. As you advance in your studies of Access, you will learn about the remaining objects on the Objects bar: Pages, Macros, and Modules.

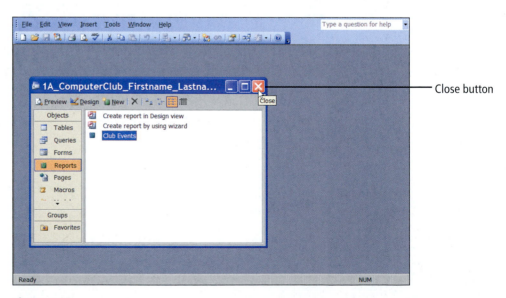

Close button

Figure 1.32

End **You have completed Project 1A** ——————————————————

Project 1B **School**

In the previous project, you opened an existing database. The Tables object and some of the other object tools used for viewing and manipulating the database were already created. In this project, you will begin a new database and create the table yourself.

In Activities 1.9 through 1.27 you will create a new database for the Distance Learning Department at Lake Michigan City College. The database will have one table that will store student records. Your student table object will look like Figure 1.33. You will save the database as *1B_School_Firstname_Lastname.*

1B Students Firstname Lastname   10/16/2003

Student#	Last Name	First Name	Address	City	Postal Code	Balance	First Term Atten
23895	Jackson	Robert	2320 Aldrich Circle	Chicago	60605	$46.00	SP01
45689	Jackson	Laura	1967 Arizona St.	Chicago	60605	$65.00	FA02
54783	Williams	Pat	62 Cockatiel Lane	Chicago	60605	$42.00	SP03
63257	Apodaca	Allen	679 Martinique Pl.	Chicago	60605	$32.00	SU03
64589	Metheny	Elizabeth	10225 Fairview	Chicago	60605	$15.00	FA02
95140	Vaughn	Sydney	2105 Waldo Ave.	Chicago	60605	$56.00	FA03
95874	Van Wegan	Michaela	100 Quantico Ave.	Chicago	60605	$25.00	FA99
96312	Berstein	Krista	136 South Street	Chicago	60605	$12.00	FA00

Page 1

Figure 1.33

Objective 3
Create a New Database

Activity 1.9 Creating a New Database

In this activity you will create a new database. There are two methods to create a new Access database:

- Create a new database using a wizard (an Access tool that walks you step-by-step through a process).

- Create a new blank database—which is more flexible because you can add each object separately.

Regardless of which method you use, you will have to name and save the database before you can create any objects such as tables, queries, forms, or reports. Think of a database file as a container that stores the database objects—tables, queries, forms, reports, and so forth—that you create and add to the database.

1 If necessary, start Access and close any open databases.

2 On the Database toolbar, click the **New** button ⬜ .

The New File task pane displays on the right. See Figure 1.34. Recall that the task pane is a window within a Microsoft Office application that provides commonly used commands related to the current task.

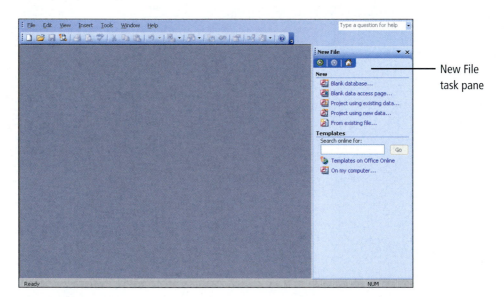

New File task pane

Figure 1.34

3 In the task pane, under **New**, click **Blank database**.

The File New Database dialog box displays.

4 In the **Save in** box, click the **Save in arrow** (the arrow at the right edge of the Save in box) to view a list of the drives available to you.

5 If necessary, navigate to your Chapter 1 folder where you are storing your projects.

6 Clear any text in the **File name** box and then, using your own information, type **1B_School_Firstname_Lastname**

7 In the lower right corner of the dialog box, click **Create**.

The School database is created and the Database window displays with the new database name indicated in the title bar of the Database window.

Objective 4
Create a New Table

When you buy a new address book, it is not very useful until you fill it with names, addresses, and phone numbers. Likewise, a new database is not useful until you **populate**, or fill, a table with data.

In the next activity, you will create a table in Design view and then add the table's fields.

Activity 1.10 Adding Fields to a Table

Recall that fields, located in columns, contain the information that describes each record in your database. The columnar fields describe the records in a table. For example, in the Club Events table you viewed earlier in Project 1A, there were fields for the *Event Name*, *Event Type*, and so forth. These fields provided information about the records in the table.

1 In the Database window, double-click the command icon **Create table in Design view**. See Figure 1.35. Alternatively, right-click the command icon and click Open on the displayed shortcut menu.

The Design view of the new table displays and the title bar indicates *Table1*: Because you have not yet named or saved this table, it has the default name *Table1*. The word *Table* after the colon indicates that this database object is a table. The insertion point is blinking in the first Field Name box, indicating that Access is ready for you to type the first field name. See Figure 1.36.

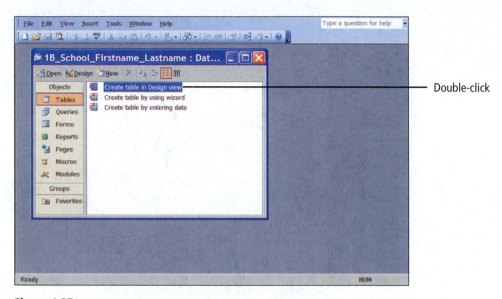

Figure 1.35

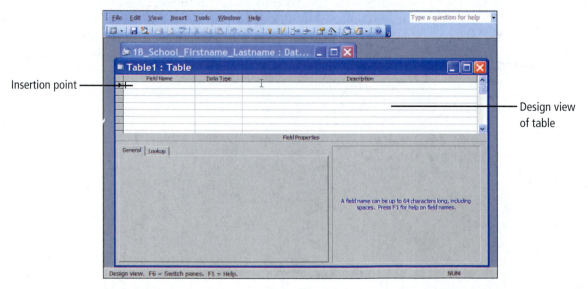

Figure 1.36

2 In the first **Field Name** box, refer to Figure 1.37 and then type **Student#**

Type first field name here

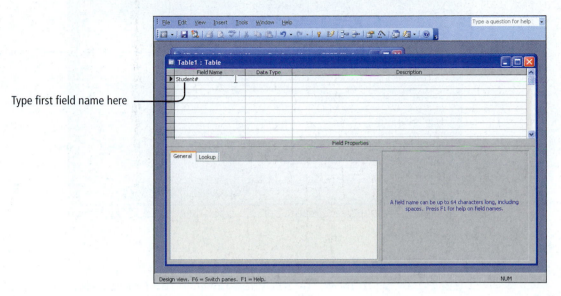

Figure 1.37

3 Press [Tab] to move the insertion point to the **Data Type** column.

The insertion point is blinking in the Data Type column and *Text* displays and is selected. At the right end of the box, an arrow displays. Notice that this arrow does not display until you click in this box. Some Access features become available in this manner—when a specific location is selected.

Data type specifies how Access organizes and stores data in a field. For example, if you define a field's data type as *Text*, any character can be typed as data in the field. If you define a field's data type as *Number*, only numbers can be typed as data in the field.

4 Click the **Data Type arrow** to display a list of data types. From the displayed list, click **Text** to accept the default data type. See Figure 1.38.

This field will contain a student number for each individual record. Although the student number contains only numbers—no letters or characters—it is customary to define such a number as *Text* rather than *Number.* Because the numbers are used only as a way to identify students—and not used for mathematical calculations—they function more like text.

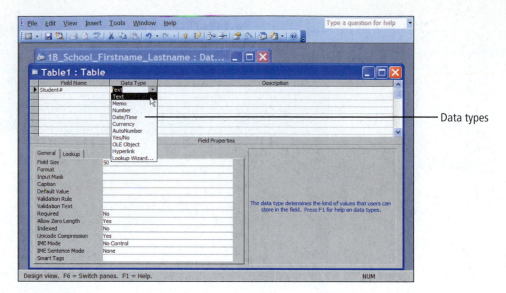

Data types

Figure 1.38

5 Press [Tab] to move the insertion point to the **Description** column.

Descriptions for fields in a table are not required. Include a description if the Field Name does not provide an obvious description of the field. In this instance, the field name *Student#* is self-explanatory, so no additional description is necessary.

6 Press [Tab] again to move the insertion point down and prepare to enter the next field name.

7 Using the technique you just practiced, add the fields shown in the Figure 1.39.

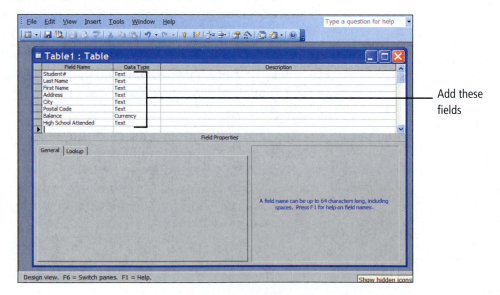

Add these fields

Figure 1.39

Another Way

Creating a New Table in a Database

There are three ways to create a new table in a database:

- Create a table in Design view by creating and naming the fields (columns).
- Create a table using a wizard, a process that helps you, step-by-step, to create the table.
- Create a table by typing data directly into an empty table in the Datasheet view, creating the column (field) names as you do so.

Activity 1.11 Switching Between Views

By naming and defining the data types for the fields, you have determined the number and type of pieces of information that you will have for each student's record in your database. In this activity, you will add the student records to the database. You will use the method of typing records directly into the Datasheet view of the table. You will learn other ways to enter records as your study of Access progresses.

1 On the Table Design toolbar, click the **View** button ▦ ▾ , as shown in Figure 1.40.

A message displays indicating that you must save the table before this action can be completed. See Figure 1.41.

View button —

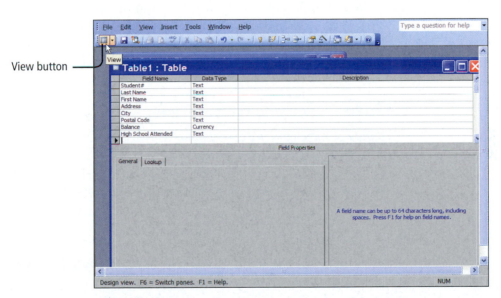

Figure 1.40

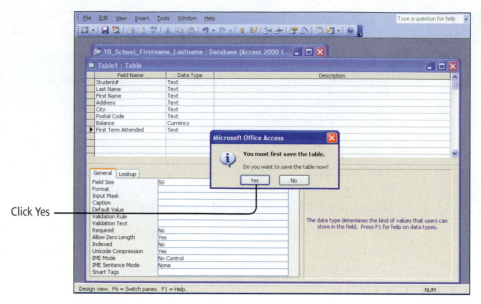

Click Yes ——

Figure 1.41

2 Click **Yes**.

3 In the displayed **Save As** dialog box, in the **Table Name** box, use your own first and last name and type **1B Students Firstname Lastname** and then click **OK**.

The message *There is no primary key defined* displays.

4 Click **No**.

The Datasheet view displays. You will add a primary key to the table in the next activity.

Note — Varying Toolbar Names

Toolbar name changes depending on view.

In Access, the name used to refer to the toolbar changes, depending on the current view of the database object. When a table is displayed in the Design view, the toolbar below the menu bar is referred to as the Table Design toolbar.

Objective 5
Create a Primary Key and Add Records to a Table

A ***primary key*** is a field that uniquely identifies a record in a table. For example, in a college registration system, your student number uniquely identifies you—no other student at the college has your exact student number. Two students at your college could have the exact same name, for example, *David Michaels*, but each would have a different and unique student number. Designating a field as a primary key ensures that you do not enter the same record more than once, because primary keys do not permit duplicate entries within the database.

Activity 1.12 Creating a Primary Key in a Table

If Access creates a primary key for you, as it prompted you to do in the previous activity, Access will add an additional field with a Data Type of

AutoNumber. AutoNumber assigns a number to each record as it is entered into the database. AutoNumber fields are convenient as a primary key for a database where the records have no unique field—such as the CDs in your CD collection. When each record in your table already has a unique number, such as a Student#, you will want to define that as your primary key.

1 On the Table Datasheet toolbar, click the **View** button 🖉▾ to switch to the Design view of your Students table.

When a table is displayed in the Datasheet view, the toolbar is referred to as the *Table Datasheet toolbar*.

2 Click to position the insertion point anywhere in the Field Name for **Student#**.

3 On the toolbar, click the **Primary Key** button 🔑, as shown in Figure 1.42.

The Primary Key image displays to the left of the Student# field.

Primary Key button

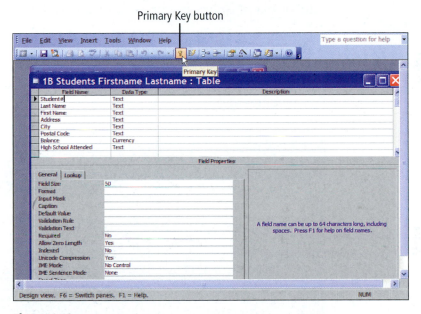

Figure 1.42

Alert!

Does Your Screen Differ?

If you attached the Primary Key to the wrong Field Name, move to the toolbar and then click the Primary Key button again. The Primary Key image will be removed and you can click the correct field name.

4 On the toolbar, click the **View** button 🔲▾ to switch back to the Datasheet view. When prompted, click **Yes** to save the change you have made to the table.

Activity 1.13 Adding Records to a Table

1 With your table in Datasheet view, make sure your insertion point is in the **Student#** column and then type **54783**

2 Press ⟨Tab⟩ to move to the **Last Name** column and then type **Williams**

3 Press ⟨Tab⟩, and then, in the **First Name** column, type **Pat**

4 Continue in this manner until the remainder of the information for Pat Williams is entered as the first record in the Students table shown in Figure 1.43. Press ⟨Tab⟩ after you enter the information for each column.

> ## Note — Entering Currency Data
>
> *Type only the whole number.*
>
> When you enter the information in the Balance column, you only need to type in the whole number, for example, 42, for the Balance in the Pat Williams record. After you press ⟨Tab⟩, Access will add the dollar sign, decimal point, and two decimal places to the entry in that column. The reason for this is that the Balance field has a data type of Currency.

As you type, do not be alarmed if it appears that your entries will not fit into the columns in the table. The widths of the columns in the figure have been adjusted so that you can view the data that is to be entered.

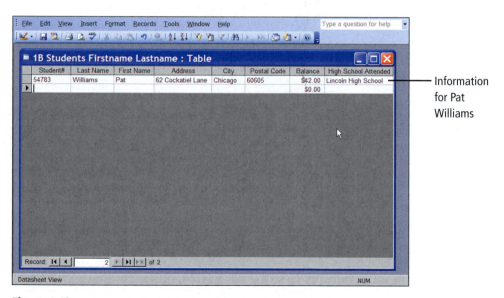

Information for Pat Williams

Figure 1.43

5 Continue entering the remaining seven records shown in Figure 1.44.

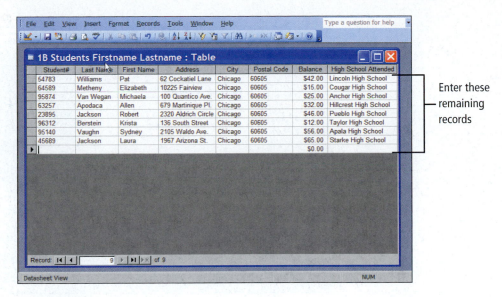

Figure 1.44

Objective 6
Close and Save a Table

When you close a table object, Access saves any additions or changes you made to the records or fields. You do not have to initiate a Save operation.

Activity 1.14 Closing and Saving a Table

1 In the upper right corner of the Table window, click the **Close** button ⊠. See Figure 1.45.

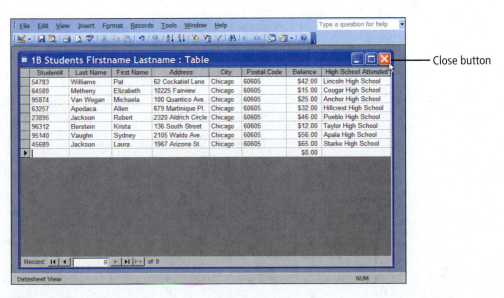

Figure 1.45

The table is closed and the records you entered are saved. Your Students table displays in the Database window. See Figure 1.46.

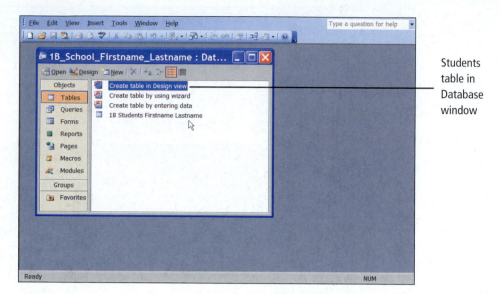

Students table in Database window

Figure 1.46

Objective 7
Open a Table

There are multiple ways to perform tasks in Access. You can open a table in Design view or Datasheet view, depending on what action you want to perform on the table. For example, if you want to view, add, delete, or modify records, use the Datasheet view. If you want to view, add, delete, or modify the field information (such as field name), use the Design view.

Activity 1.15 Opening a Table

1 In the Database window, double-click your **1B Students** table.

The table opens in Datasheet view, but the records do not display in the same order in which you entered them. Rather, Access has placed the records in sequential order according to the Primary key field.

2 Click the **Close** button ⊠ in the upper right corner of the table window to close the table.

The Database window displays.

3 If necessary, click your **1B Students** table once to select it, and then just above the Objects bar, click the **Open** button [Open] in the Database window.

The table opens again in Datasheet view. This is another method to open a table in the Datasheet view.

4 In the upper right corner of the table window, click the **Close** button ⊠ to close the table and display the Database window.

5 Open the table in Design view by clicking your **1B Students** table once (it may already be selected), and then clicking the **Design** button ![Design] in the area above the Objects bar. See Figure 1.47. Alternatively, you can right-click the table name and then click Design View from the displayed shortcut menu.

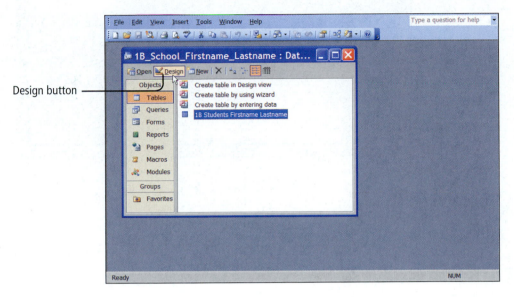

Design button ——

Figure 1.47

6 Leave the table open in Design view for the next activity.

Objective 8
Modify the Table Design

An early consideration when creating a new table is the number and content of the fields in the table. This is referred to as the table's *design*. For example, when setting up an address book database, you will want to have fields for name, address, home phone number, and so forth. After you begin entering records, you might realize that you should have included a field for a cell phone number, too. Fortunately, Access lets you add or delete fields at any time.

Activity 1.16 Deleting Fields

If you decide that a field in your database is no longer useful to you, you can delete that field from the table.

1 In the Design view of your **1B Students** table, position your mouse pointer in the row selector at the far left, next to **High School Attended** field.

The pointer changes to a right-pointing arrow. See Figure 1.48.

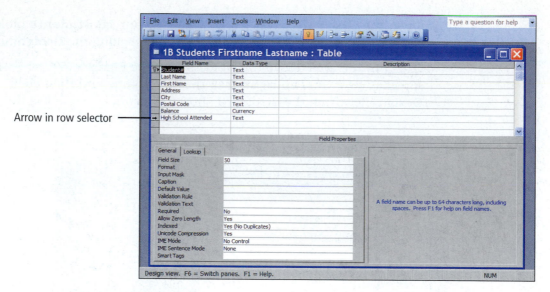

Arrow in row selector

Figure 1.48

2 Click to select the row **High School Attended** and then press Delete.

A message displays asking whether or not you want to permanently delete the field. See Figure 1.49.

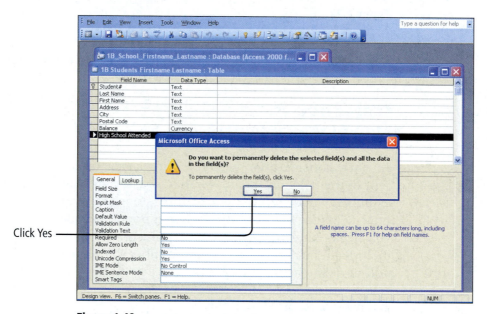

Click Yes

Figure 1.49

3 Click **Yes** to delete the field.

The High School Attended field is deleted. Deleting the field also deletes any data in the field of each record. Later, you could add the field back if you decide to do so, but you would have to re-enter the field's data for each record.

4 Pause your mouse pointer in the title bar area of the table and right-click. On the displayed shortcut menu, click **Datasheet view**, and when prompted, click **Yes** to save the table. This is another way to switch back to Datasheet view.

The High School Attended field no longer displays in the Datasheet view of the table.

5 On the toolbar, click the **View** button 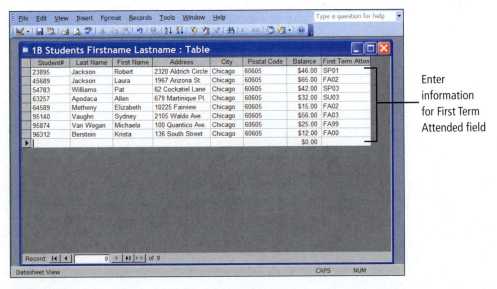 to switch back to Design view.

Activity 1.17 Adding Fields

If you decide to add a field to the table, you can add the field and then, for each record, enter data into the field.

1 At the bottom of the list of fields, click in the next available **Field Name** box, type **First Term Attended** and then press Tab two times.

The default text data type is accepted and the description column is left empty.

2 Use any method to switch back to Datasheet view, and when prompted, click **Yes** to save the table. Notice the new column for the field you just added.

3 For each record, enter the information shown in Figure 1.50 for the **First Term Attended** field.

Note — Using Long Column Headings

Adjust them later.

The column heading for the First Term Attended field may not display entirely. You will adjust this in a later step.

Enter information for First Term Attended field

Figure 1.50

Objective 9
Print a Table

There are multiple ways to print objects in Access. The quickest way to print a database table is to click the Print button on the Database toolbar. This will print one complete copy of the table on the default printer. If you want to print anything other than one complete copy, for example, multiple copies or only selected pages, or to select a different printer, you must initiate the Print command from the File menu.

Activity 1.18 Printing a Table

Although a printed table is not as professional or formal looking as a report, there are times when you may want to print your table in this manner as a quick reference or for proofreading.

1 If necessary, open your **1B Students** table in the Datasheet view.

2 On the toolbar, locate but do not click the **Print** button 🖨.

You could print the table without opening the table by selecting the table from the Database window, and then clicking the Print button on the toolbar. This method does not offer you an opportunity to change anything about the way the table prints.

3 With your **1B Students** table still open, display the **File** menu and then click **Print**.

The Print dialog box displays. Here you can make changes to your print settings. See Figure 1.51.

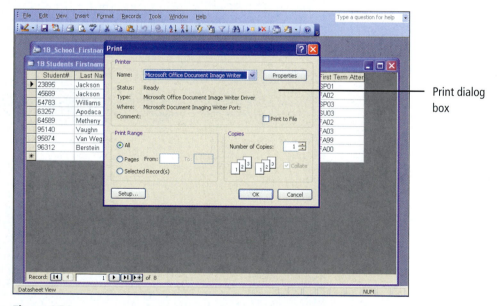

Print dialog box

Figure 1.51

4 In the upper right corner next to the printer name, click the **Properties** button.

The Properties dialog box displays. See Figure 1.52. Because the settings for printer models vary, your Properties box may display differently than that shown in the figure.

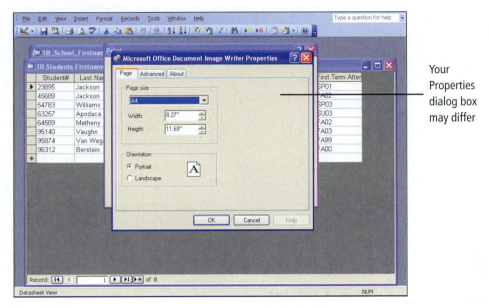

Your Properties dialog box may differ

Figure 1.52

By default, Access prints in ***Portrait orientation***—the printed page is taller than it is high. An alternate orientation is ***Landscape orientation***—the printed page is wider than it is tall.

5 Locate and then click **Landscape**. See Figure 1.53. The properties for printer models vary somewhat. You may have to locate the Landscape orientation on a different tab of your printer Properties dialog box, and thus your screen will differ from the figure shown.

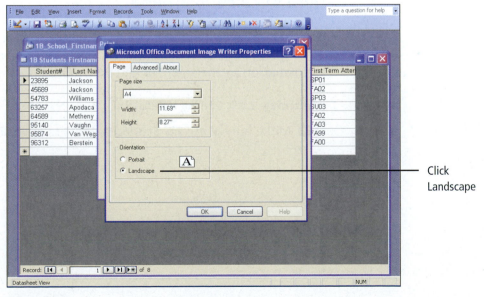

Click Landscape

Figure 1.53

6 Click the **OK** button.

7 In the lower left corner of the **Print** dialog box, click the **Setup** button.

The Page Setup dialog box displays with margins set to 1 inch on the Top, Bottom, Left, and Right of the page. See Figure 1.54.

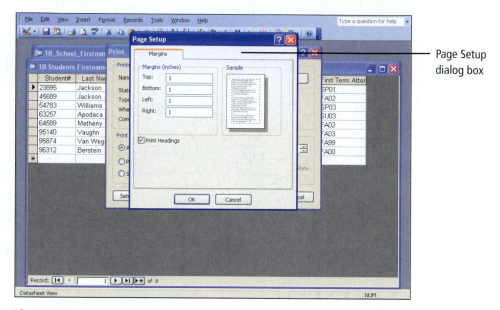

Page Setup dialog box

Figure 1.54

8 Click **OK** to accept the default settings.

9 In the Print dialog box, click **OK**.

Your table prints, and your name is printed at the top of the page in the table name.

Objective 10
Edit Records in a Table

When necessary, you will edit (change) the information in a record. For example, you may realize that you made an error when you entered the information in the table, or the information has changed.

Activity 1.19 Editing a Record

1 Make sure your **1B Students** table is open in Datasheet view.

2 Locate the record for **Pat Williams**. In the **Address** field, click to position the insertion point to the right of *62*. See Figure 1.55.

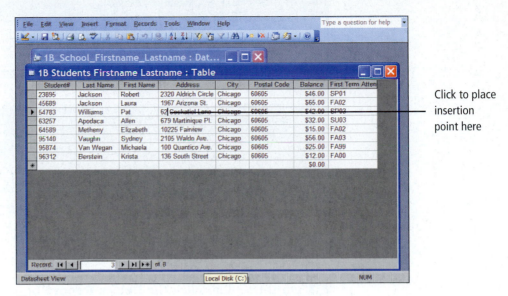

Click to place insertion point here

Figure 1.55

3 Type **5** and then press Tab.

The address for Pat Williams is changed to *625 Cockatiel Lane*. Leave the Students table open.

Activity 1.20 Deleting a Record

Keeping a database up to date means that you may have to delete records when they are no longer needed. In this activity, you will delete the record for Sydney Vaughn, which was mistakenly included in the Students table—she is not a student.

1 Be sure your **1B Students** table is open in Datasheet view.

2 Locate the record for **Sydney Vaughn**, position the mouse pointer in the row selector for Sydney Vaughn's record until it takes the shape of a right-pointing arrow, and then click to select the row.

The entire record is selected. See Figure 1.56.

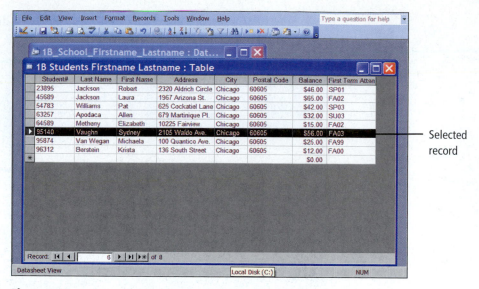

Figure 1.56

3 On the toolbar click the **Delete Record** button [×]. Alternatively, you could press Delete on the keyboard.

A message displays alerting you that you are about to delete a record. If you click Yes and delete the record, you cannot use the Undo button to reverse the action. If you delete a record by mistake, you will have to re-create the record.

4 Click **Yes** to delete the record.

The record is deleted from the 1B Students table.

Activity 1.21 Resizing Columns and Rows

You can adjust the size of columns and rows in a table. Sometimes this is necessary to get a better view of the data. Column widths and row heights are adjusted by dragging the borders between the columns or rows. Reducing the column width allows you to display more fields on your screen at one time. Increasing the width of a column allows you to view data that is too long to display in the column.

Adjusting the size of columns and rows does not change the data contained in the table's records. It changes only your *view* of the data.

1 Be sure your **1B Students** table is open in Datasheet view.

2 In the gray row of column headings, pause your mouse pointer over the vertical line between the **Address** column and the **City** column until it becomes a double-headed arrow, as shown in Figure 1.57.

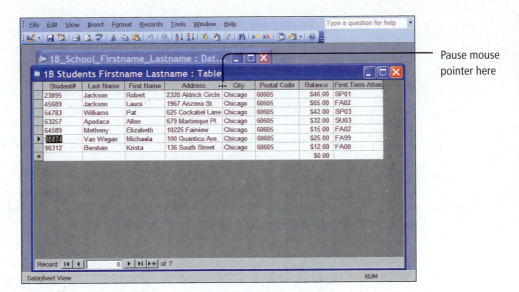

Pause mouse
pointer here

Figure 1.57

3 Press and hold the left mouse button and drag the line in between the columns to the right approximately 0.5 inch. The measurement need not be precise; use your eye to judge this. Release the mouse button.

The column's width is increased.

4 In the gray column headings, point to the vertical bar between the **Address** column heading and the **City** column heading until the double-headed arrow displays, and then double-click.

Access adjusts the width of the Address column to accommodate the widest entry in the column. Use this as a quick method to adjust columns to accommodate the widest entry in a column.

5 In the row of column headings, pause the mouse pointer over the **Student#** column heading until the mouse pointer becomes a downward-pointing black arrow. Then drag to the right until all of the columns are selected. See Figure 1.58.

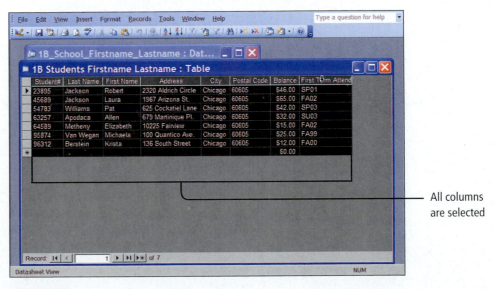

All columns
are selected

Figure 1.58

6 With the columns selected, pause your mouse pointer over the vertical line between any of the column headings until the mouse pointer takes the shape of a double-headed arrow, and then double-click.

All of the columns are resized to accommodate the widest entry in each column. In some instances, the widest entry is the column heading, for example, *First Term Attended*. Use this method as a quick way to adjust the widths of several columns at once.

7 Click anywhere in the table to deselect the table.

8 To adjust row height, point to the horizontal line between the second and third record until the double-headed arrow displays. See Figure 1.59.

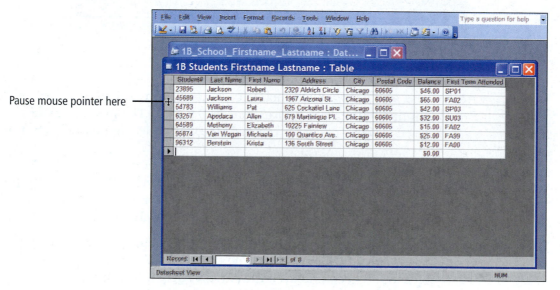

Pause mouse pointer here ————

Figure 1.59

9 Drag the horizontal line down approximately 0.5 inch. The exact measurement is not important. Use your eye to judge the distance. Release the mouse button.

The height of all of the rows is increased by the same amount. Adjusting the row height enables you to see long names that may have wrapped to two lines in a column—and still have many columns visible on the screen.

10 On the menu bar, click **Format** and then click **Row Height**.

The Row Height dialog box displays. Here you can return row heights to their default setting or enter a precise number for the height of the row.

11 Select the **Standard Height** check box and then click **OK**. See Figure 1.60.

The height of all rows is restored to the default setting. Use this dialog box to set the rows to any height.

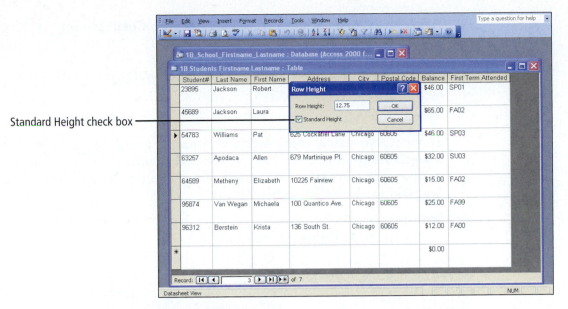

Figure 1.60

Standard Height check box

Activity 1.22 Hiding Columns

When a table contains many fields (columns), you can temporarily hide one or more columns so that you can get a better view of other columns.

1 Click to position your insertion point anywhere in the **City** column, display the **Format** menu, and then click **Hide Columns**.

The City column is hidden from view, and the columns to the right of the City column shift to the left. Hidden columns and the data that they contain are not deleted—they are merely hidden from view.

2 From the **Format** menu, click **Unhide Columns**. See Figure 1.61.

The Unhide Columns dialog box displays. All of the columns except the City column are checked, indicating that they are in view.

Unhide Columns option on Format menu

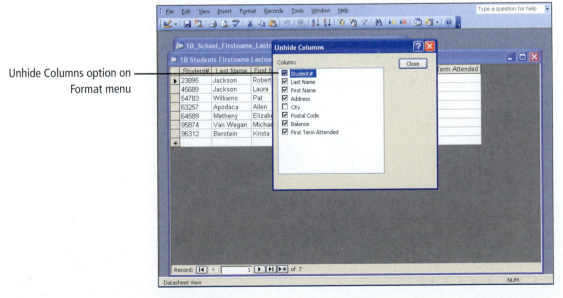

Figure 1.61

3 Select the **City** check box and then click the **Close** button.

The City column returns to view.

4 Click the column heading **City**, press and hold (Shift), and then click the column heading **Balance**.

The City, Postal Code, and Balance columns are selected.

You can hide two or more *adjacent* columns (columns that are next to each other) at one time. If you select a column and then select another column while holding (Shift), those columns are selected in addition to any columns between them.

5 With the three columns selected, display the **Format** menu, and then click **Hide Columns**. See Figure 1.62.

Hide Columns option on Format menu

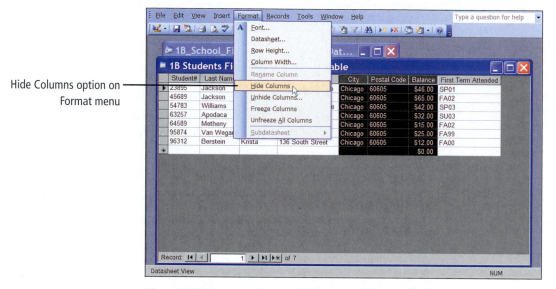

Figure 1.62

The City, Postal Code, and Balance columns are hidden.

6 To unhide the columns, display the **Format** menu, click **Unhide Columns**, and then select the **City**, **Postal Code**, and the **Balance** check boxes. Click the **Close** button.

The three columns are returned to view in your 1B Students table.

Objective 11
Sort Records

Sorting records in a table is the process of rearranging records in a specific order. For example, you could sort the names in your address book database alphabetically by each person's last name, or you could sort your CD collection database by the date of purchase.

Activity 1.23 Sorting Records in a Table

Information stored in an Access table can be sorted in either *ascending order* or *descending order*. Ascending order sorts text alphabetically (A to Z) and sorts numbers from the lowest number to the highest number. Descending order sorts text in reverse alphabetic order (Z to A) and sorts numbers from the highest number to the lowest.

1 Be sure your **1B Students** table is open in the Datasheet view.

2 Click anywhere in the **Last Name** column and then on the toolbar click the **Sort Ascending** button ![Sort Ascending icon]. See Figure 1.63.

The records are sorted in ascending order according to each Student's Last Name.

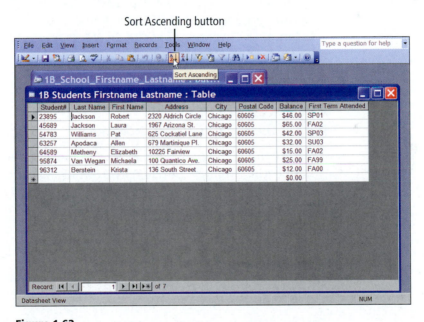

Figure 1.63

3 Click anywhere in the **First Name** column and then on the toolbar click the **Sort Ascending** ⬆️ button.

The records are sorted in ascending order according to each student's First Name.

4 Click the column heading **Last Name**, press and hold ⬚Shift⬚, and then click the column heading **First Name**.

Both the Last Name column and the First Name column are selected.

Information in an Access table can be sorted using more than one field. For example, data can be sorted by the ***primary sort field***—the field that Access sorts by initially—and then, for any records having an identical primary sort field, records are sorted further by the ***secondary sort field***—the field that Access uses to sort records that have matching primary sort fields.

5 On the toolbar, click the **Sort Ascending** button ⬆️.

The records are sorted alphabetically by Last Name. Within records that have identical last names, for example, *Jackson,* the records are sorted alphabetically by First Name.

Access sorts the records consecutively from left to right, meaning any fields that you want to sort *must* be adjacent to each other, and your primary sort field (*Last Name* in this example) must be to the left of the secondary sort field (*First Name* in this example).

6 Look at the two records for which the last name is **Jackson**.

Notice that those two records are also sorted alphabetically by First Name—Laura comes before Robert.

7 On the menu bar, click **Records** and then click **Remove Filter/Sort**.

You can return your records to the original sort order at any time by selecting Remove Filter/Sort from the Records menu. In this instance, the original sort order is by primary key.

8 Leave your **1B Students** table open for the next activity.

Objective 12
Navigate to Records in a Table

The Students table that you created has only seven records, and you can see all of them on the screen. Most Access tables, however, contain many records—more than you can see on the screen at one time. Access provides several tools to help you navigate (move) among records in a table. For example, you can move the insertion point to the last record in a table or to the first record in a table, or move up one record at a time or down one record at a time.

Activity 1.24 Navigating Among Records Using the Navigation Area

Figure 1.64 illustrates the navigation functions in the navigation area of a table.

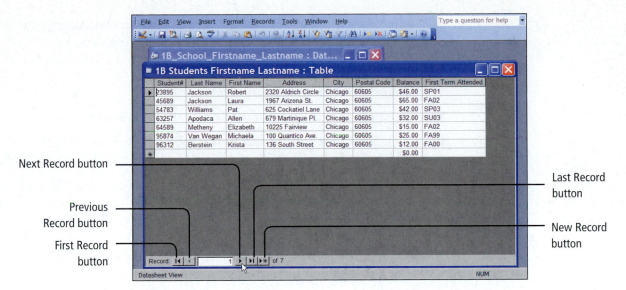

Next Record button

Previous Record button

First Record button

Last Record button

New Record button

Figure 1.64

1 If necessary, open your **1B Students** table in Datasheet view.

2 Click anywhere in the first record of the table.

3 In the navigation area, click the **Next Record** button [▶]. See Figure 1.64.

Depending on the field in which your insertion point was located, the next record in the table is selected, in the same field.

4 In the navigation area, click the **Last Record** button [▶|]. See Figure 1.64.

The last record in the table is selected.

5 Experiment with the different navigation buttons as shown in Figure 1.64.

Activity 1.25 Navigating Among Records Using the Keyboard

You can also navigate among records in a table using the keyboard. Figure 1.65 lists the keystrokes and the resulting movement.

Key Combinations for Navigating a Table

Keystroke	Movement
↑	Moves the selection up one record at a time.
↓	Moves the selection down one record at a time.
Page Up	Moves the selection up one screen at a time.
PageDown	Moves the selection down one screen at a time.
Ctrl + Home	Moves the selection to the first field in the table.
Ctrl + End	Moves the selection to the last field in the table.

Figure 1.65

1 If necessary, open your **1B Students** table in Datasheet view and click anywhere in any record except the last record.

2 Press ↓.

The selection moves down one record.

3 Experiment with the different navigation keystrokes.

4 Click the **Close** button 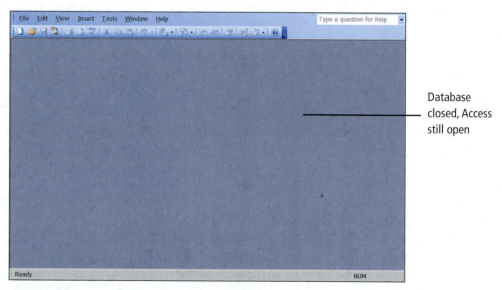 in the table window to close the **1B Students** table. Click **Yes** if you are prompted to save changes to the design of your table.

The Database window displays.

Objective 13
Close and Save a Database

When you close an Access table, any changes are saved automatically. At the end of your Access session, close your database and then close Access.

Activity 1.26 Closing and Saving a Database

1 In the smaller Database window, click the **Close** button ⊠.

The database closes. The Access program remains open. See Figure 1.66.

Database closed, Access still open

Figure 1.66

2 On the title bar of the Access window, click the **Close** button ⊠ to close the Access program.

Objective 14
Use the Access Help System

Access contains a Help feature designed to assist you when performing a task in Access or if you would like more information about a particular topic in Access. There are multiple ways to use the Help feature in Access, including the Office Assistant, and the Type a question for help box.

Activity 1.27 Using the Access Help System

The Office Assistant is an animated figure that displays to assist you with a task.

1 Start Access. On the menu bar, click **Help** and then click **Show the Office Assistant**.

The Office Assistant character displays. The animated character may be a paperclip, or some other character.

2 Double-click the Office Assistant to display the **What would you like to do?** box.

3 With *Type your question here and then click Search* highlighted, type **How do I get help?** and then click **Search**.

4 In the **Search Results** task pane, click **About getting help while you work**. You may have to use the vertical scroll bar to see this topic.

The Microsoft Access Help window displays with hyperlinks (usually in blue text) listed. Clicking on these hyperlinks will link you to additional information about the topic.

5 Click on the links that display and you will see the description of each of these expanded in the area below the link. For example, click **Microsoft Press** to expand the topic and then click it again to collapse it.

6 After viewing the Help topics, click the **Close** button 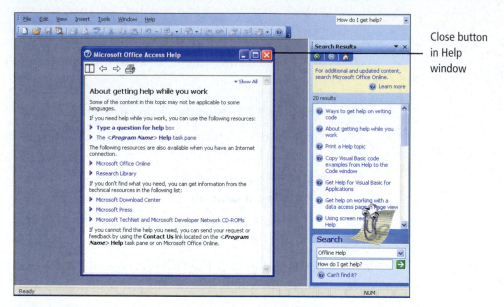 to close the Help window. See Figure 1.67.

Close button in Help window

Figure 1.67

7 In the upper right corner of the Access window, locate the **Type a question for help** box and click it. See Figure 1.68.

The text in the box is selected.

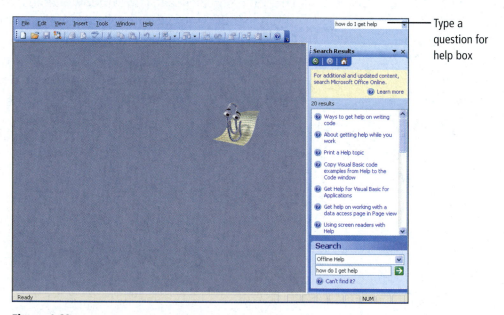

Type a question for help box

Figure 1.68

8 In the **Type a question for help** box, type **table**

9 Press Enter and click **About creating a table (MDB)**.

A window containing information about creating a table displays. See Figure 1.69. Keywords, identified in a different color, display additional information when they are clicked.

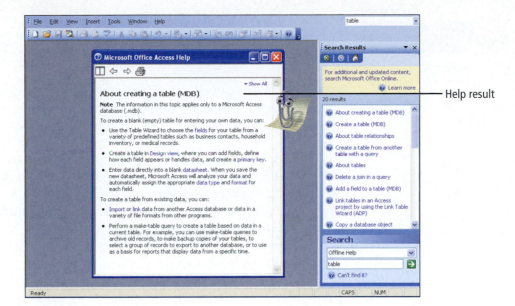

Help result

Figure 1.69

10 In the second bullet, click on the words **Design view**. Scroll down if necessary to view this description.

An explanation of Design View displays in green within the paragraph.

11 In the Microsoft Access Help window, on the toolbar, click the **Print** button 🖨. See Figure 1.70.

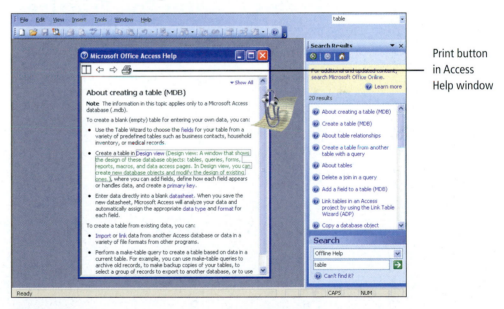

Print button in Access Help window

Figure 1.70

12 In the **Print** dialog box, click **Print** (or **OK**).

The Help topic you have displayed is printed. Keep this document for your reference.

13 Close the Microsoft Access Help window.

14 On the title bar of the Access window, click the **Close** button ☒ to close Access.

End **You have completed Project 1B** ━━━━━━━━━

Summary

Microsoft Access 2003 is a database management system. Databases help you organize information, such as the names and addresses in your address book, a CD collection, or a list of students at a college.

In an existing database, you can either view the information in the database or edit the information. Access contains tools, called objects, which enable you to enter information into a database, and then organize, manipulate, and analyze the information. Information in a database is stored in tables. The data in a table is organized by rows, called records, and columns, called fields. Each record in a table stores information about one database item.

Queries extract information from a table according to the criteria set for the query. Forms are another tool that you can use to either enter or view records—one record at a time. Reports are professional-looking documents that summarize the information in a table.

Information stored in a table can be edited and sorted. Access contains navigation tools to assist you in locating specific records.

In This Chapter You Practiced How To

- Rename a Database
- Start Access, Open an Existing Database, and View Database Objects
- Create a New Database
- Create a New Table
- Create a Primary Key and Add Records to a Table
- Close and Save a Table
- Open a Table
- Modify the Table Design
- Print a Table
- Edit Records in a Table
- Sort Records
- Navigate to Records in a Table
- Close and Save a Database
- Use the Access Help System

Concepts Assessments

Matching   Match each term in the second column with its correct definition in the first column by writing the letter of the term on the blank line in front of the correct definition.

_____ **1.** A printing orientation in which the printed page is taller than it is high.

_____ **2.** The field that serves as a unique identifier for records in a table.

_____ **3.** The Access object that stores the information in a database.

_____ **4.** The process of rearranging items in a specific order.

_____ **5.** The Access object that displays records one at a time.

_____ **6.** A sorting order in which records are sorted alphabetically from A to Z.

_____ **7.** The process of pulling out information from a database according to specified criteria.

_____ **8.** The Access object that displays selected fields and records in an easy-to-read format.

_____ **9.** A printing orientation in which the printed page is wider than it is tall.

_____ **10.** A window within a Microsoft Office application that provides commonly used commands.

_____ **11.** The Access object that assists you in asking a question about the data.

_____ **12.** A sorting order in which records are sorted alphabetically from Z to A.

_____ **13.** Data that has been organized in a useful manner.

_____ **14.** A collection of data related to a particular topic.

_____ **15.** The collection of tools in Access used to enter and manipulate the data in a database.

A Ascending

B Database

C Descending

D Extracting

E Form

F Information

G Landscape

H Objects

I Portrait

J Primary key

K Query

L Report

M Sorting

N Table

O Task pane

Access

chapter one

Concepts Assessments (continued)

Fill in the Blank Write the correct answer in the space provided.

1. Tables are the foundation of an Access database, because that is where the data is _____.

2. Each table in an Access database stores data about only _____ subject.

3. The _____ window displays when a database is open.

4. Each horizontal _____ of a table stores all the information about one database record.

5. Each vertical _____ of a table has a name that describes one category of information contained within each record.

6. The small gray box at the left end of a row in a table is the _____.

7. In the _____ view of a table, only the names of the fields, and not the records, display.

8. Specifications that determine what records will be displayed as a result of a query are called _____.

9. Filling a table with data is referred to as _____ the table.

10. A rule that you define for data within a field is referred to as the _____.

Project 1C — Departments

Objectives: *Rename a Database; Start Access, Open an Existing Database, and View Database Objects; Close and Save a Table; Open a Table; Print a Table; Sort Records; and Close and Save a Database.*

In the following Skill Assessment, you will open an existing database, view the database objects, and add two records to the database table. This database is used by the administration offices at Lake Michigan City College to store information regarding the various departments at the College. Your completed database objects will look like the ones shown in Figures 1.71 and 1.72. You will rename and save the database as *1C_LMccDept_Firstname_Lastname.*

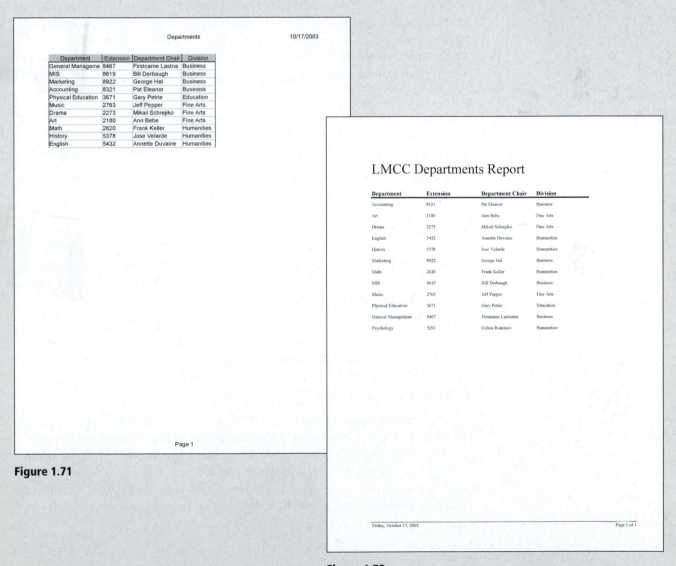

Figure 1.71

Figure 1.72

(Project 1C–Departments continues on the next page)

(Project 1C–Departments continued)

1. On your Windows desktop, open **My Computer** and navigate to the student files that accompany this textbook. Locate and then click once to select the file **a01C_LMccDept**.

2. Move the mouse pointer over the selected file name and then right-click to display a shortcut menu. On the displayed shortcut menu, click **Copy**. Navigate to the drive and folder where you are storing your projects for this chapter. On the menu bar, click **Edit** and then click **Paste**. The database file is copied to your folder and is selected (highlighted).

3. Move your mouse pointer over the selected file name, right-click to display the shortcut menu, and then on the shortcut menu, click **Rename**. In the **File name** box, clear any existing text. Using your own first and last name, type **1C_LMccDept_Firstname_Lastname** and then press Enter to save the new file name. If the **Confirm File Rename** dialog box displays, click **Yes**. Be sure that the file name is still selected (highlighted) and then right-click to display the shortcut menu.

4. On the displayed shortcut menu, click **Properties**. At the lower part of the displayed dialog box, click to clear the check mark next to **Read-only**, and then click **OK** to close the dialog box. Close **My Computer**.

5. Start Access. On the menu bar, click **File** and then click **Open**. Click the **Look in arrow** and then navigate to the location where you are storing your projects for this chapter. Locate the database file that you renamed and saved with your name in Step 3. Click the database file once to select it, and then, in the lower right corner, click the **Open** button. Alternatively, you can double-click the name of the database, and it will open. If the security warning message displays, click **Yes and/or Open**.

6. In the Database window, on the Objects bar, click **Tables** once to display a list of tables in this database. To the right of the Objects bar, double-click the **Departments** table to open the table in Datasheet view. Notice that the table includes fields for Department, Extension, Department Chair, and Division.

7. In the **Department** column, click in the blank record at the bottom of the table and type **General Management** as the department name for the new record. Press Tab once. In the **Extension** field type **8467** and press Tab once. In the **Department Chair** field and using your own information, type your **Firstname Lastname** and press Tab once. In the **Division** field, type **Business** and then press Enter to complete the record.

(Project 1C–Departments continues on the next page)

(Project 1C–Departments continued)

8. On the Table Datasheet toolbar, click the **View** button to switch to the Design view and notice that the **Department** field is the primary key. Recall that one field in a table is designated as the primary key so that each record has a unique identifier. In this case, each department has a different name—no two departments at the college have the same name.

9. On the Table Design toolbar, click the **View** button to return to the Datasheet view. Click anywhere in the **Division** column, and then, on the Table Datasheet toolbar, click the **Sort Ascending** button. Notice that the records are now sorted in alphabetical order by Division.

10. On the Table Datasheet toolbar, click the **Print** button. In the upper right corner of the table window, click the **Close** button to close the table. A copy of the table is printed, and your name is printed as the Chair of the General Management Department. Save any changes if prompted to do so.

11. On the Objects bar, click **Queries** to display a list of available queries in the database. Double-click the **Business Division** query to open the query. Notice that each entry in the *Business Division* query has *Business* in the **Division** field. Recall that a query locates records from a table that meet specific criteria and then displays the result. In this case, the Business Division query was designed to locate all of the records that have *Business* as the Division. You can see that there are four Departments within the Business Division. In the upper right corner of the table window, click the **Close** button to close the query.

12. On the Objects bar, click **Forms** to display a list of available forms in the database. Recall that forms are another database object, in addition to tables, that allow you to view and enter new records into a table—one record at a time. To the right of the Objects bar, double-click the **Departments Form** to open the form. The Departments Form opens and the first record in the table displays.

13. At the bottom of the Department Form, locate the **New Record** button (the button at the bottom of the form with the *) and click it. With the insertion point blinking in the **Department** box, type **Psychology** and then press Tab once. Use the information below to fill in the remaining information for this record.

Department	Extension	Department Chair	Division
Psychology	5291	Celina Rominov	Humanities

14. In the Form window, click the **Close** button to close the form.

(Project 1C–Departments continues on the next page)

(Project 1C–Departments continued)

15. On the Objects bar, click **Reports** to display a list of available reports that have been created for this database. Recall that a report is a professional-looking document that summarizes information from a table in an easy-to-read format. To the right of the Objects bar, double-click the **LMCC Departments Report** to open the report in Print Preview.

16. In the upper right corner of the report title bar, click the **Maximize** button and then on the Print Preview toolbar, click the **Zoom arrow**. Zoom to **100%**. On the Print Preview toolbar, click the **Print** button to print the report. On the Print Preview toolbar, click the **Close** button to close the report. In the Access window, click the **Close** button to close Access.

End You have completed Project 1C

Project 1D — Office Supplies

Objectives: *Create a New Database, Create a New Table, Create a Primary Key and Add Records to a Table, Close and Save a Table, Modify the Table Design, Print a Table, and Close and Save a Database.*

In the following Skill Assessment, you will create a new database to track office supplies for the Distance Learning Department at Lake Michigan City College. The database table will look like the one shown in Figure 1.73. You will save your database as *1D_Office_Supplies_Firstname_Lastname*.

1. Start Access. From the **File** menu, click **New**. In the **New File** task pane, under **New**, click **Blank database**.

2. In the displayed **File New Database** dialog box, click the **Save in arrow**, and then navigate to the folder in which you are storing your projects for this chapter. In the **File name** box, delete any existing text, type **1D_Office_Supplies_Firstname_Lastname** and then in the lower right corner click **Create**. The Office Supplies database is created and the Database window displays with the new database name indicated in the title bar.

3. In the Database window, double-click the command icon **Create table in Design view**. Because you have not yet named or saved this table, the title bar indicates the default name of *Table1*. The insertion point is blinking in the first **Field Name** box.

4. In the first **Field Name** box, type **Inventory #** and then press Tab to move the insertion point to the **Data Type** column. Recall that Data Type refers to the rules that you can define for data within a field.

5. Press Tab to accept the default Data Type of **Text**. Press Tab again to move to the next **Field Name** box.

(Project 1D–Office Supplies continues on the next page)

(Project 1D–Office Supplies continued)

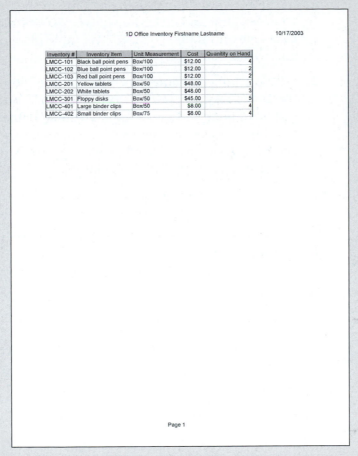

Figure 1.73

6. Use the following information to add the remaining fields to your table. Recall that a description for a field is optional. The descriptions for this table describe the purpose of the corresponding field.

Field Name	Data Type	Description
Inventory Item	Text	
Unit Measurement	Text	Identifies the number of items in a unit
Cost	Currency	Cost per unit
Quantity on Hand	Number	Current number of items available

7. Click in the field name for **Inventory #.** On the toolbar, click the **Primary Key** button to set the **Inventory #** field as the primary key for this table. Within this table, no two items will have the same Inventory number—the Inventory number is a unique identifier. On the Table Design toolbar, click the **View** button to switch to the Datasheet view. When prompted, click **Yes** to save the table.

(Project 1D–Office Supplies continues on the next page)

(Project 1D–Office Supplies continued)

8. In the displayed **Save As** dialog box, in the **Table Name** box, use your own first and last name to type **1D Office Inventory Firstname Lastname** and then click **OK**. The table displays and you can begin to enter records into it.

9. With the table in Datasheet view, be sure your insertion point is in the **Inventory #** column. Type **LMCC-101** and press Tab. Type **Black ball point pens** and press Tab. Type **Box/100** and press Tab. Type **12** in the **Cost** column and press Tab. The dollar sign and the decimal point are inserted for you because a data type of Currency was specified for the Cost field. Type **4** in the Quantity on Hand column and press Enter.

10. Use the following information to add the remaining records to the Inventory table. Press Enter after entering the last record.

Inventory #	Inventory Item	Unit Measurement	Cost	Quantity on Hand
LMCC-102	Blue ball point pens	Box /100	12.00	2
LMCC-103	Red ball point pens	Box/100	12.00	2
LMCC-201	Yellow tablets	Box/50	48.00	1
LMCC-202	White tablets	Box/50	48.00	3
LMCC-301	Floppy disks	Box/50	45.00	5
LMCC-401	Large binder clips	Box/50	8.00	4
LMCC-402	Small binder clips	Box/75	8.00	4

11. Pause the mouse pointer over the gray **Inventory #** column heading, and then click and hold the left mouse button while dragging to the right until all of the columns are selected. With the columns selected, pause your mouse pointer over the vertical line between any of the column headings until the mouse takes the shape of a double-headed arrow, and then double-click. All of the columns are resized to accommodate the widest entry in each column. Recall that you can use this method as a quick way to adjust the widths of several columns at once. Recall also that adjusting the size of columns and rows does not change the data contained in the table's records. It changes only your *view* of the data.

12. Click anywhere in the table to deselect the table. On the Table Datasheet toolbar, click the **Print** button. Because you inserted your name in the table name, it prints in the heading. In the upper right corner of the table window, click the **Close** button to close the table. Click **Yes** to save changes to the layout of the table.

(Project 1D–Office Supplies continues on the next page)

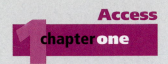

(Project 1D–Office Supplies continued)

13. In the Database window, click the **Close** button to close the Office Supplies database. In the Access window, click the **Close** button to close Access.

End **You have completed Project 1D** ——————————————————————

Project 1E—Recipes

Objectives: *Rename a Database; Start Access, Open an Existing Database, and View Database Objects; Open a Table; Print a Table; Edit Records in a Table; Navigate to Records in a Table; and Close and Save a Database.*

In the following Skill Assessment, you will open and edit an existing database that stores information about the recipes that the Computer Club at Lake Michigan City College prepares for social events. Your completed database objects will look like the ones shown in Figure 1.74. You will save the database as *1E_Recipes_Firstname_Lastname* in the folder designated for this chapter.

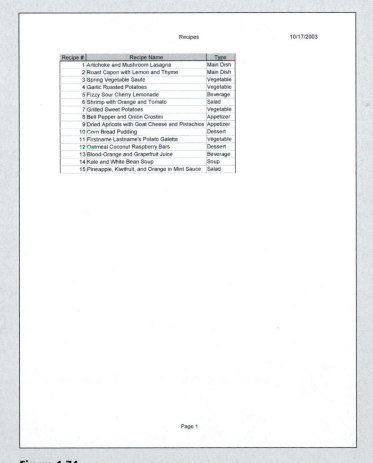

Figure 1.74

(Project 1E–Recipes continues on the next page)

(Project 1E–Recipes continued)

1. Open **My Computer** and navigate to the student files that accompany this textbook. Click once to select the file **a01E_recipes**. Move the mouse pointer over the selected file name, right-click, and on the displayed shortcut menu, click **Copy**.

2. Navigate to the drive and folder where you will be storing your projects for this chapter. On the menu bar, click **Edit** and then click **Paste**. The database file is copied to your folder and is selected. Move your mouse pointer over the selected file name, right-click to display the shortcut menu, and then click **Rename**. Using your own first and last name, type **1E_Recipes_Firstname_Lastname**

3. Press [Enter] to save the new file name. If the Confirm File Rename message displays, click **Yes**. Be sure that the file name is still selected (highlighted), point to the file name, and right-click to display the shortcut menu. On the displayed shortcut menu, click **Properties**.

4. In the lower portion of the displayed dialog box, click to clear the check mark from the **Read-only** check box. Click **OK** to close the dialog box. Close **My Computer** and start Access.

5. On the menu bar, click **File** and then click **Open**. In the displayed dialog box, click the **Look in arrow**, and then navigate to the location where you are storing your projects for this chapter. Locate the database file that you saved and renamed with your name in Step 2. Click the database file once to select it, and then, in the lower right corner, click the **Open** button. Alternatively, you can double-click the name of the database, and it will open.

6. If necessary, in the Database window on the Objects bar, click **Tables** to display a list of tables in this database. To the right of the Objects bar, double-click the **Recipes** table to open the table in Datasheet view.

7. In **record #5**, click in the **Type** field and delete the existing text. Type **Beverage** and then press [Enter]. In **record #11**, click to place the insertion point in front of *Potato*. Use your own information to type **Firstname Lastname's** and then press [Spacebar] once.

8. On the Table Datasheet toolbar, click the **Print** button. In the upper right corner of the table window, click the **Close** button to close the table. On the title bar of the Access window, click the **Close** button to close Access.

End **You have completed Project 1E**

Project 1F — CD Log

Objectives: *Create a New Database, Create a New Table, Create a Primary Key and Add Records to a Table, Close and Save a Table, Sort Records, Print a Table, and Close and Save a Database.*

In the following Performance Assessment, you will create a new database and a new table to store information about the CD collection for the Music Department at Lake Michigan City College. Your completed table will look like the one shown in Figure 1.75. You will save your database as *1F_CDlog_Firstname_Lastname.*

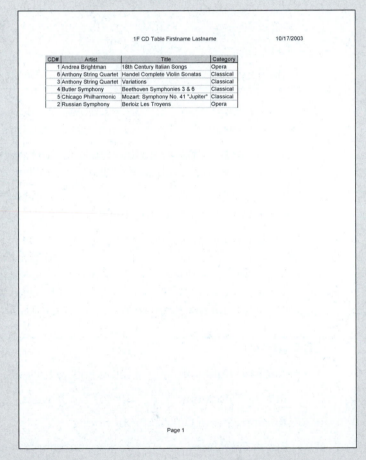

Figure 1.75

(Project 1F–CD Log continues on the next page)

(Project 1F–CD Log continued)

1. Start Access. Display the **New File** task pane and click **Blank database**. In the **File New Database** dialog box, navigate to the drive and folder where you are storing your projects for this chapter. Name the file **1F_CDlog_Firstname_Lastname**

2. In the Database window, double-click the command icon **Create table in Design view**. Use the following information to create the fields for the table.

Field Name	Data Type	Description
CD#	AutoNumber	
Artist	Text	
Title	Text	
Category	Text	Music Classification

3. Because two CDs could have the same title, you will use the **AutoNumber** field that you created as the primary key. Click in the field name for **CD#** and then click the **Primary Key** button. Click the **View** button to switch to the Datasheet view of the table.

4. When prompted, save the table by typing **1F CD Table Firstname Lastname** in the **Save As** dialog box and then click **OK**.

5. With the table open in the Datasheet view, press [Tab] to move to the **Artist** field and type the first artist in the following table. As you type in the **Artist** field, Access fills in the AutoNumber to assign a unique number to each CD. You do not need to type the numbers. Use the following information to create the records.

CD#	Artist	Title	Category
1	Andrea Brightman	18th Century Italian Songs	Opera
2	Russian Symphony	Berlioz Les Troyens	Opera
3	Anthony String Quartet	Variations	Classical
4	Butler Symphony	Beethoven Symphonies 3 & 6	Classical
5	Chicago Philharmonic	Mozart: Symphony No. 41 "Jupiter"	Classical
6	Anthony String Quartet	Handel Complete Violin Sonatas	Classical

(Project 1F–CD Log continues on the next page)

(Project 1F–CD Log continued)

6. Select all of the columns in the table. Display the **Format** menu, click **Column Width**, and in the displayed **Column Width** dialog box, click **Best Fit**. All of the columns are resized to accommodate the widest entry in each column.

7. Click anywhere in the table to deselect it. Click the **Artist** column heading to select the column, press and hold Shift, and then click the **Title** column heading. On the toolbar, click the **Sort Ascending** button. The table is sorted by Artist, and within Artist, it is further sorted by title.

8. On the Table Datasheet toolbar, click the **Print** button. Close the table, save any changes, and then close Access.

End **You have completed Project 1F**

Project 1G — Employees

Objectives: *Rename a Database; Start Access, Open an Existing Database, and View Database Objects; Create a Primary Key and Add Records to a Table; Close and Save a Table; Open a Table; Modify the Table Design; and Print a Table.*

In the following Performance Assessment, you will open an existing database that stores employee information for Lake Michigan City College, add a record, and then work with other objects in the database. The first page of your completed database object will look similar to Figure 1.76. You will rename the database as *1G_Employees_Firstname_Lastname.*

1. Use the Windows My Computer tool to navigate to your student files and then select the file **a01G_Employees**. Copy the file to the drive and folder where you are storing your projects for this chapter. Using your own information, rename the file
1G_Employees_Firstname_Lastname

2. Remove the Read-only attribute from the renamed file so that you can make changes to the database. Start Access.

3. Open your **1G_Employees** database that you renamed in Step 1. Open the **Employees** table and switch to Design view. Set the primary key for this table to **ID**. This is the employee ID number, which uniquely identifies each employee.

(Project 1G–Employees continues on the next page)

(Project 1G–Employees continued)

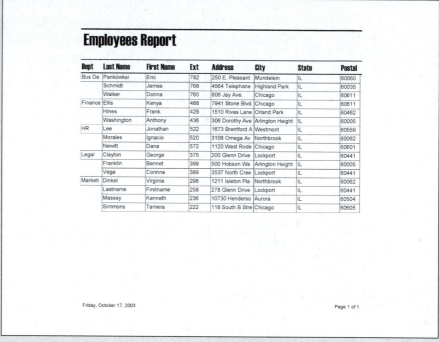

Employees Report

Dept	Last Name	First Name	Ext	Address	City	State	Postal
Bus De	Pankowksi	Eric	782	250 E. Pleasant	Mundelein	IL	60060
	Schmidt	James	768	4564 Telephone	Highland Park	IL	60035
	Walker	Donna	760	806 Jay Ave.	Chicago	IL	60611
Finance	Ellis	Kenya	488	7941 Stone Blvd.	Chicago	IL	60611
	Hines	Frank	429	1510 Rivas Lane	Orland Park	IL	60462
	Washington	Anthony	436	306 Dorothy Ave	Arlington Height	IL	60005
HR	Lee	Jonathan	522	1673 Brentford A	Westmont	IL	60559
	Morales	Ignacio	520	3108 Omega Av	Northbrook	IL	60062
	Newitt	Dana	572	1120 West Rode	Chicago	IL	60601
Legal	Clayton	George	375	200 Glenn Drive	Lockport	IL	60441
	Franklin	Bennet	399	500 Hobson Wa	Arlington Height	IL	60005
	Vega	Corinna	389	3537 North Cree	Lockport	IL	60441
Marketi	Dinkel	Virginia	298	1211 Isleton Pla	Northbrook	IL	60062
	Lastname	Firstname	258	278 Glenn Drive	Lockport	IL	60441
	Massey	Kenneth	236	10730 Henderso	Aurora	IL	60504
	Simmons	Tamera	222	118 South B Stre	Chicago	IL	60605

Friday, October 17, 2003   Page 1 of 1

Figure 1.76

4. Switch to the Datasheet view of the table and save changes to the table when prompted to do so. Add the following record to the table, using your own first and last name.

ID	5588
First Name	Your First Name
Last Name	Your Last Name
Dept	Marketing
Ext	258
Address	278 Glenn Drive
City	Lockport
State	IL
Postal Code	60441
Phone	815-555-0365

5. Use any method to resize all of the columns to accommodate their data and then close the table. On the Objects bar, click **Queries** and open the **Marketing Query**. Because you added your name as a member of the Marketing Department, you should see your record among the other employees in the Marketing Department.

(Project 1G–Employees continues on the next page)

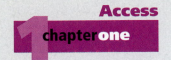

Performance Assessments (continued)

(Project 1G–Employees continued)

6. Close the query. On the Objects bar, click the **Reports** button and open the **Employees Report**. Display the **File** menu, and then click **Page Setup**. In the **Page Setup** dialog box, click the **Page tab**, and then click the **Landscape** option button so that the report prints in Landscape orientation. Print the report. Notice that your name will print as one of the employees in the Marketing Department. Close the report and then close the database. Close Access.

End You have completed Project 1G

Project 1H—DL Courses

Objectives: *Create a New Database, Create a New Table, Create a Primary Key and Add Records to a Table, Modify the Table Design, Close and Save a Table, Print a Table, and Close and Save a Database.*

In the following Performance Assessment, you will create a new database and a new table to store information about Distance Learning courses at Lake Michigan City College. Your completed table will look similar to the one shown in Figure 1.77. You will save your database as *1H_DLcourses_Firstname_Lastname.*

1. Start Access and display the **New File** task pane. Click **Blank database**. Navigate to the drive and folder where you are storing your projects for this chapter. In the **File name** box, type **1H_DLcourses_Firstname_Lastname** as the name for your database, and then click **Create**.

2. Use the following information to create a table in Design view and to add fields to the table.

Field Name	Data Type	Description
Course Number	Text	
Course Name	Text	
Credit Hours	Number	Credit hours for this course

3. Switch to the Datasheet view of the table. Using your own first and last name, save the table as **1H DLcourses Firstname Lastname** and then click **OK**. When prompted if you would like to add a primary key now, click **No**.

(Project 1H–DL Courses continues on the next page)

(Project 1H–DL Courses continued)

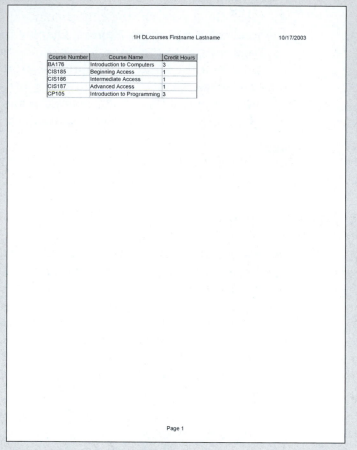

1H DLcourses Firstname Lastname   10/17/2003

Course Number	Course Name	Credit Hours
BA176	Introduction to Computers	3
CIS185	Beginning Access	1
CIS186	Intermediate Access	1
CIS187	Advanced Access	1
CP105	Introduction to Programming	3

Page 1

Figure 1.77

4. Using the following information, fill in the records for the DLcourses table.

Course Number	Course Name	Credit Hours
BA176	Introduction to Computers	3
CP105	Introduction to Programming	3
CIS185	Beginning Access	1
CIS186	Intermediate Access	1
CIS187	Advanced Access	1

5. Switch to the Design view of the table. Set the **Course Number** field as the primary key for this table. Click the **View** button to switch to the Datasheet view of the table. Save the table when prompted. Verify that the records are sorted by the primary key.

6. Use any method to resize the column widths to accommodate their data. Print and then close the table, saving any changes if prompted to do so. Close the database and close Access.

End **You have completed Project 1H**

Project 1I — Suppliers

Objectives: *Create a New Database, Create a New Table, Create a Primary Key and Add Records to a Table, Close and Save a Table, Modify the Table Design, Sort Records, Navigate to Records in a Table, and Close and Save a Database.*

In the following Mastery Assessment, you will create a new database and a new table to store supplier information for Lake Michigan City College. Your completed table will look like the one shown in Figure 1.78. You will save your database as *1I_LMCCsuppliers_Firstname_Lastname*.

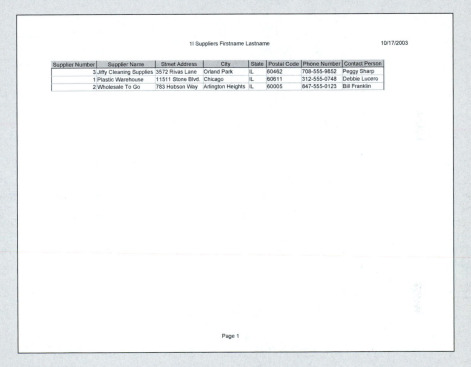

Supplier Number	Supplier Name	Street Address	City	State	Postal Code	Phone Number	Contact Person
3	Jiffy Cleaning Supplies	3572 Rivas Lane	Orland Park	IL	60462	708-555-9852	Peggy Sharp
1	Plastic Warehouse	11511 Stone Blvd.	Chicago	IL	60611	312-555-0748	Debbie Lucero
2	Wholesale To Go	783 Hobson Way	Arlington Heights	IL	60005	847-555-0123	Bill Franklin

1I Suppliers Firstname Lastname   10/17/2003

Page 1

Figure 1.78

(Project 1I–Suppliers continues on the next page)

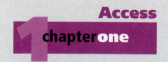

Project 1I–Suppliers continued)

1. Start Access. In your Project folder, create a new database and name it **1I_LMCCsuppliers_Firstname_Lastname**

2. Use the following information to create a new table.

Field Name	Data Type	Description
Supplier Number	AutoNumber	
Supplier Name	Text	
Street Address	Text	
City	Text	
State	Text	
Postal Code	Text	
Phone Number	Text	
Contact Person	Text	Main contact

3. Choose the **Supplier Number** as the primary key for this table. Switch to Datasheet view, and then, using your own information, save the table as **1I Suppliers Firstname Lastname** and then add the following records to the table.

Supplier Number	Supplier Name	Street Address	City	State	Postal Code	Phone Number	Contact Person
1	Plastic Warehouse	11511 Stone Blvd.	Chicago	IL	60611	312-555-0748	Debbie Lucero
2	Wholesale To Go	783 Hobson Way	Arlington Heights	IL	60005	847-555-0123	Bill Franklin
3	Jiffy Cleaning Supplies	3572 Rivas Lane	Orland Park	IL	60462	708-555-9852	Peggy Sharp

4 Resize all of the columns to accommodate their data. Sort the table alphabetically by Supplier Name. Display the **Page Setup** dialog box and change the page orientation to **Landscape**. Print and then close the table. Close the database and then close Access.

End **You have completed Project 1I**

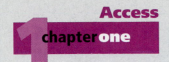

Project 1J—Expenses

Objectives: *Rename a Database; Start Access, Open an Existing Database, and View Database Objects; Modify the Table Design; Print a Table; Edit Records in a Table; Navigate to Records in a Table; and Close and Save a Database.*

In the following Mastery Assessment, you will open an existing database and modify items in the database that stores information about the expenses of the Computer Club at Lake Michigan City College. Your completed database object will look similar to the one shown in Figure 1.79. You will rename the database as *1J_Expenses_Firstname_Lastname*.

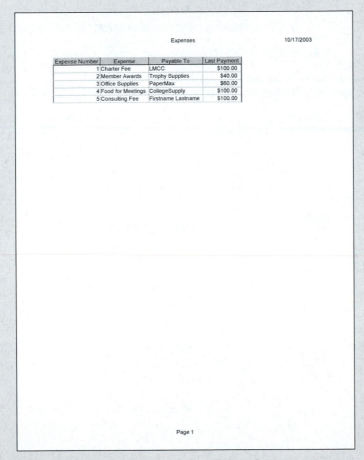

Expense Number	Expense	Payable To	Last Payment
1	Charter Fee	LMCC	$100.00
2	Member Awards	Trophy Supplies	$40.00
3	Office Supplies	PaperMax	$60.00
4	Food for Meetings	CollegeSupply	$100.00
5	Consulting Fee	Firstname Lastname	$100.00

Expenses   10/17/2003

Page 1

Figure 1.79

(Project 1J–Expenses continues on the next page)

Project 1J–Expenses continued)

1. Copy the student file **a01J_Expenses** to the drive and folder where you are storing your projects for this chapter. Rename the database as **1J_Expenses_Firstname_Lastname** and remove the Read-only attribute.

2. Start Access and open the database you renamed in Step 1. Open the **Expenses** table and make the following changes to the table:

   Change the *Expense ID* field to **Expense Number**

   Change the primary key for the table to **Expense Number**

   For the *Member Awards* expense record, change the information in the Payable To column from *LMCC* to **Trophy Supplies**

3. Add the following record using your own name:

Expense Number	Expense	Payable To	Last Payment
AutoNumber	Consulting Fee	Firstname Lastname	100

4. Resize the fields in the table to accommodate their data. Print and then close the table, saving any changes if prompted to do so. Close the database and close Access.

 You have completed Project 1J ————————————————

Access

chapter one

Problem Solving

Project 1K — Video Store

Objectives: *Create a New Database, Create a New Table, Create a Primary Key and Add Records to a Table, Modify the Table Design, Close and Save a Table, Print a Table, and Close and Save a Database.*

Lake Michigan City College has a small video rental shop on campus that rents videos and DVDs to students, staff, and faculty of the college. Create a database that will store information about the movie rentals such as customer names and the names of movies in the inventory. This database should have at least two tables: one for customers and another for the inventory of videos that are available to rent. Create a new database with an appropriate name for the video rental store and add two tables as described above to the database. In each of the tables, add the fields that you think should be included in each of these tables. Designate one field in each table as the primary key. Print your tables.

 End You have completed Project 1K ————————————————

Project 1L — Fix It

Objectives: *Rename a Database; Start Access, Open an Existing Database, and View Database Objects; Create a Primary Key and Add Records to a Table; Open a Table; Modify the Table Design; and Close and Save a Database.*

The Business Division at Lake Michigan City College needs to correct some errors in a student database. Copy the student file a01L_FixIt to your storage location and rename it **1L_FixIt_Firstname_Lastname**. Clear the Read-only property and then open the database. View the FixIt table in this database. Think about the way the data is arranged in the table. Based on the databases you have worked with in this chapter, identify at least four ways this table could be improved. Then make your suggested changes to this database.

 End You have completed Project 1L ————————————————

On the Internet

Databases and Today's Industries

Most of the world's information is stored in some type of database. Databases play a large role in industries today. Their expansive applications have made databases an integral part of business in the current marketplace.

Go online and perform a search to identify the current trends involving databases and the different career paths that include database training as part of their job descriptions.

GO! with Help

Searching Access Help

The Access Help system is extensive and can help you as you work. In this exercise, you will view information about getting help as you work in Access.

1. Start Access. In the **Type a question for help** box, type **Printing a table** and then press Enter.

2. In the displayed **Search Results** task pane, click the result—**Print a record, datasheet, or database object**. Maximize the displayed window, and at the top of the window, click the **Show All** button. Scroll through and read about printing database objects in Access.

3. If you want, print a copy of the information by clicking the printer button at the top of the window.

4. Close the Microsoft Access Help window, then close Access.

chapter**one**

Getting Started with PowerPoint 2003

In this chapter, you will: complete this project and practice these skills.

Project 1A
Editing and Viewing a Presentation

Objectives

- Start and Exit PowerPoint
- Edit a Presentation Using the Outline/Slides Pane
- Format and Edit a Presentation Using the Slide Pane
- View and Edit a Presentation in Slide Sorter View
- View a Slide Show
- Create Headers and Footers
- Print a Presentation
- Use PowerPoint Help

The City of Desert Park

Desert Park, Arizona, is a thriving city with a population of just under 1 million in an ideal location serving major markets in the western United States and Mexico. Desert Park's temperate year-round climate attracts both visitors and businesses, and it is one of the most popular vacation destinations in the world. The city expects and has plenty of space for long-term growth, and most of the undeveloped land already has a modern infrastructure and assured water supply in place.

© Getty Images, Inc.

Getting Started With PowerPoint 2003

Presentation skills are among the most important skills you will ever learn. Good presentation skills enhance all your communications—written, electronic, and interpersonal. In our fast-paced world of e-mail, pagers, and wireless phones, communicating ideas clearly and concisely is a critical personal skill. Microsoft Office PowerPoint 2003 is a *presentation graphics software* program that you can use to effectively present information to your audience. PowerPoint is used to create electronic slide presentations, black and white or color overhead transparencies, and 35mm slides.

In this chapter, you will edit a presentation and become familiar with the parts of the PowerPoint window. You will also practice using the various views available in PowerPoint.

Project 1A **Expansion**

The purpose of any presentation is to influence your audience. Whether you are presenting a new product to coworkers, making a speech at a conference, or expressing your opinion to your city council, you want to make a good impression and give your audience a reason to agree with your point of view. How your audience reacts to your message depends on the information you present and how you present yourself.

In Activities 1.1 through 1.24, you will start Microsoft Office PowerPoint 2003 and open a presentation. You will examine the parts of the PowerPoint window, and then edit, print, and view the presentation as a slide show. The six slides of your completed project will look like Figure 1.1. You will save your presentation as *1A_Expansion_Firstname_Lastname.*

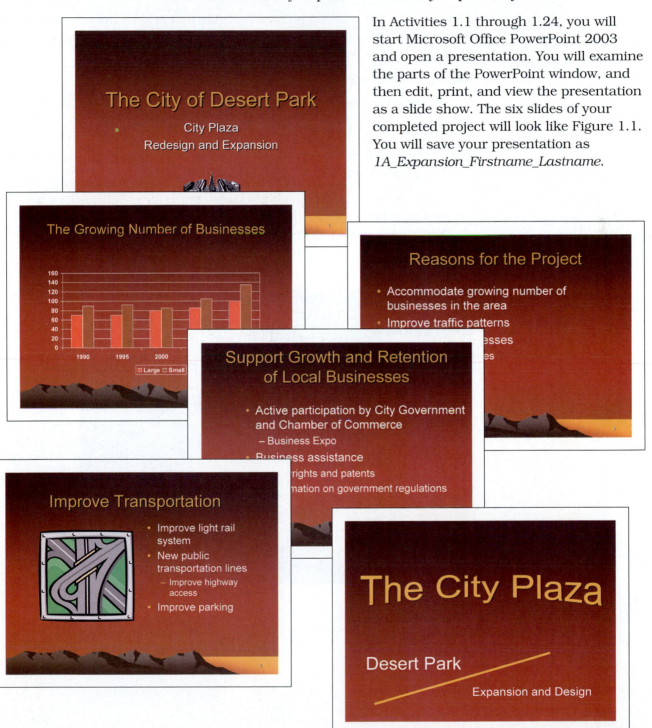

Figure 1.1
Project 1A—Expansion

Objective 1
Start and Exit PowerPoint

In the following activities, you will start PowerPoint, become familiar with the PowerPoint window, open an existing PowerPoint presentation, close a file, and exit PowerPoint.

Activity 1.1 Starting PowerPoint and Opening a Presentation

You can open an existing presentation file by clicking Open from the File menu, by clicking the Open button on the Standard toolbar, or by Clicking Open or More on the Getting Started task pane.

1 On the left side of the Windows taskbar, point to and then click the **Start** button ![start].

The Start menu displays.

2 On the computer you are using, locate the PowerPoint program and then click **Microsoft Office PowerPoint 2003**.

Organizations and individuals store computer programs in a variety of ways. The PowerPoint program might be located under All Programs, or Microsoft Office, or some other arrangement. See Figure 1.2 for an example.

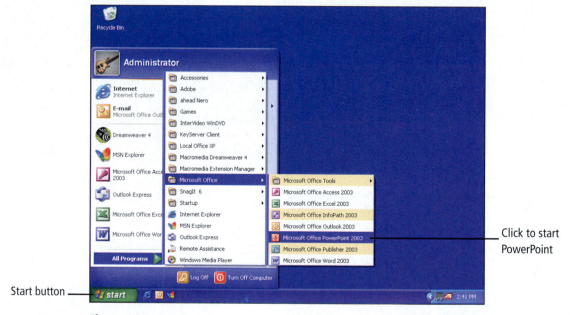

Start button ⎯

Click to start PowerPoint

Figure 1.2

3 Look at the opening PowerPoint screen, and then take a moment to study the main parts of the screen shown in Figure 1.3 and described in the table in Figure 1.4.

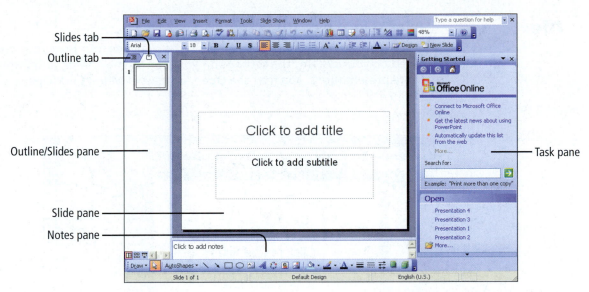

Slides tab

Outline tab

Outline/Slides pane

Slide pane

Notes pane

Task pane

Figure 1.3

Main Parts of the PowerPoint Screen

Screen Element	Description
Outline/Slides pane	Displays either the presentation outline (Outline tab) or all of the slides in the presentation in the form of miniature images called *thumbnails* (Slides tab).
Slide pane	Displays a large image of the active slide.
Notes pane	Displays below the Slide pane and allows you to type notes regarding the active slide.
Task pane	Displays commonly used commands related to the active slide. Its location and small size allow you to use these commands while still working on your presentation.

Figure 1.4

4 In the lower portion of the **Getting Started** task pane, under **Open**, point to **More...** and notice that your pointer displays as a pointing hand. See Figure 1.5.

Alert!

Does Your Screen Differ?

In most instances, the task pane displays the previous four presentations saved on your system. The settings on *your* system may differ, and instead of these presentations, you may see Open, instead of More. Click Open.

Point to More...

Figure 1.5

5 Click **More...**

The Open dialog box displays.

6 In the **Open** dialog box, at the right edge of the **Look in** box, click the **Look in arrow**, to view a list of the drives available on your system. See Figure 1.6.

Click to display a list of drives

Figure 1.6

7 Navigate to the location where the student files for this textbook are stored.

8 Click **p01A_Expansion** and then click the **Open** button.

Slide 1 of the presentation displays in the PowerPoint window, and the task pane on the right is closed.

Activity 1.2 Identifying Parts of the PowerPoint Window

1 Figures 1.7a and 1.7b identify the parts of the PowerPoint window. Take a moment to familiarize yourself with the parts of the window shown, and notice that the *status bar* displays near the bottom of the PowerPoint window.

The status bar indicates that in this presentation, Slide 1 is the active slide and that there are a total of seven slides in the presentation. The first slide of a presentation is the *title slide*. The title slide frequently contains special formatting that is different from the other slides in the presentation so that it is easily distinguishable as the title slide.

Formatting toolbar   Standard toolbar   Menu bar

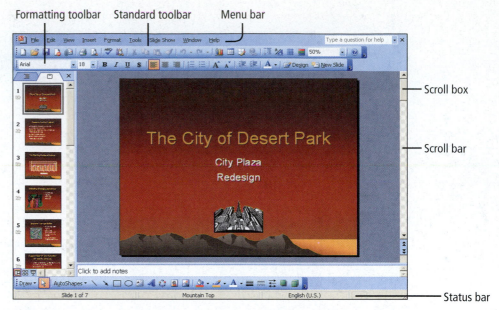

Scroll box

Scroll bar

Status bar

Figure 1.7a

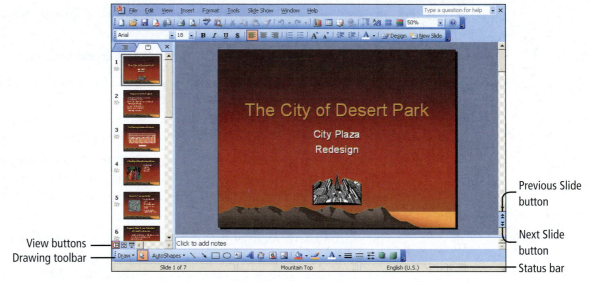

Previous Slide button

Next Slide button

Status bar

View buttons
Drawing toolbar

Figure 1.7b

Alert!

Does Your Screen Differ?

At the left side of your window in the Outline/Slides pane, your window may display the slide miniatures shown in Figure 1.7, or if the Outline tab is selected, it will display the presentation outline.

2 On the right edge of your screen, at the top of the vertical scroll bar, point to the **scroll** box, and then press and hold down the left mouse button.

A *ScreenTip* is a small box that displays the name of a screen element or, in this instance, the current slide number and the title. The ScreenTip indicates *Slide: 1 of 7 The City of Desert Park.*

3 Drag the **scroll** box down slightly until the ScreenTip *Slide: 2 of 7 Reasons for the Project* displays, and then release the left mouse button.

In the Slide pane, Slide 2 displays and becomes the active slide. One word on the slide is underlined with a wavy red line, indicating a misspelling. Later in this chapter, you will use PowerPoint's spelling checker tool to correct spelling errors in the presentation.

4 At the bottom of the vertical scroll bar, locate the double, upward-pointing and downward-pointing arrows. Refer to Figure 1.7b, and then without clicking, point to them to display their ScreenTips— *Previous Slide* and *Next Slide*.

5 Click the **Next Slide** button ⬇ to display **Slide 3** of the presentation, and then click the **Previous Slide** button ⬆ two times to return to **Slide 1**. At the lower left portion of your screen, check to be sure that *Slide 1 of 7* displays in the status bar.

6 Near the lower left corner of the window, locate the **View** buttons, as shown in Figure 1.7b. With your mouse, point to each of the three **View** buttons to display their ScreenTips—*Normal View, Slide Sorter View,* and *Slide Show from current slide (Shift+F5)*.

These buttons provide three different ways to view your presentation, and you will practice each of these views in this chapter.

Activity 1.3 Accessing the Menu Commands

1 On the menu bar, click **File**.

The File menu displays in either the short format shown in Figure 1.8 or the full format shown in Figure 1.9. PowerPoint's commands are organized in *menus*—lists of commands within a category. A short menu will display fully after a few seconds. Alternatively, you can click the small double arrows at the bottom to display the full menu. The File menu lists the last four to nine presentations used on your computer.

Click to expand the menu ——————

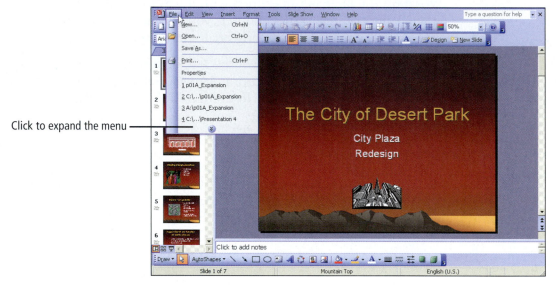

Figure 1.8

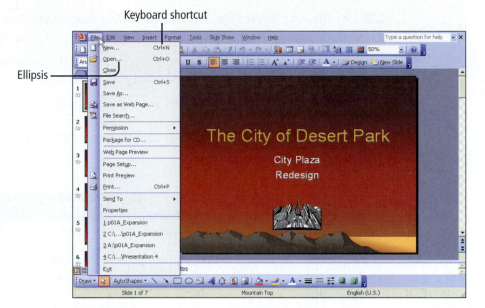

Keyboard shortcut

Ellipsis

Figure 1.9

> **Note** — Displaying the Full Menu
>
> Many individuals prefer the automatic full menu display. To set a system to always display full menus, display the Tools menu, click Customize, and then click the Options tab. Under Personalized Menus and Toolbars, select the Always show full menus check box.

2 Be sure that the full menu is displayed, as shown in Figure 1.9, and notice to the right of some commands there is a keyboard shortcut, for example *Ctrl+N* for the **New** command.

If you press and hold down Ctrl and then press N, the result is the same as clicking File on the menu bar and then clicking New on the File menu. Many commands in PowerPoint can be accomplished in more than one way.

3 On the displayed **File** menu, to the left of some command names, notice that there is an image of the button that represents this command on a toolbar.

This is a reminder that you can initiate the command with one click from a toolbar, rather than from the menu.

4 On the displayed **File** menu, pause the mouse pointer over **Print**, but do not click.

When you point to a command on a menu, the command is shaded and bordered by a rectangular outline.

5 Look at the full **File** menu on your screen and notice the various symbols and characters that are standard across all Microsoft products. Take a moment to study the table in Figure 1.10 for a description of these elements.

Characteristics of Office Menus

Characteristic	Description	Example
… (ellipsis)	Indicates that either a dialog box requesting more information or a task pane will display.	Print…
▶ (triangle)	Indicates that a submenu—another menu of choices—will display.	Send To▶
No symbol	Indicates that the command will perform immediately.	Exit
✔ (check mark)	Indicates that a command is turned on or active.	✔ Standard
Gray option name	Indicates that the command is currently unavailable.	Properties

Figure 1.10

6 With the **File** menu still displayed, move your pointer into the menu bar and point to **Insert**.

The Insert menu displays. After a menu from the menu bar is displayed, you can move your pointer over other menu names and they will display without clicking.

7 Move your mouse pointer anywhere into the slide area of your screen, and then click once to close the menu without accessing a command.

Activity 1.4 Identifying and Displaying Toolbars and ScreenTips

Toolbars are the rows of buttons that display below the menu bar. The buttons on the toolbar provide a one-click method to perform commonly used commands and tasks. The three toolbars that you will use most often in PowerPoint are the Standard toolbar, the Formatting toolbar, and the Drawing toolbar.

Depending on how your system is set, you might see the Standard and Formatting toolbars each occupying separate rows as in Figure 1.11. Or, you might see shortened Standard and Formatting toolbars docked side by side below the menu bar. When the Standard and Formatting toolbars share one row, you can click Toolbar Options to view additional buttons. See Figure 1.12. The instruction in this textbook assumes that your toolbars occupy *separate* rows.

Standard toolbar ──
Formatting toolbar

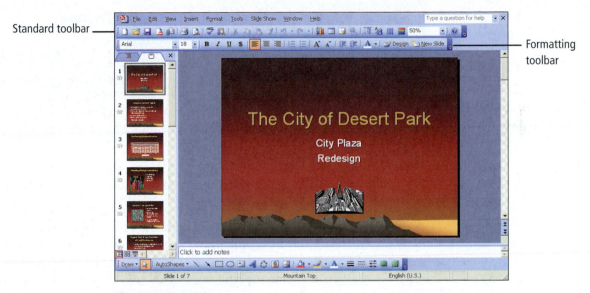

Figure 1.11

Standard toolbar   Formatting toolbar
Toolbar Options button

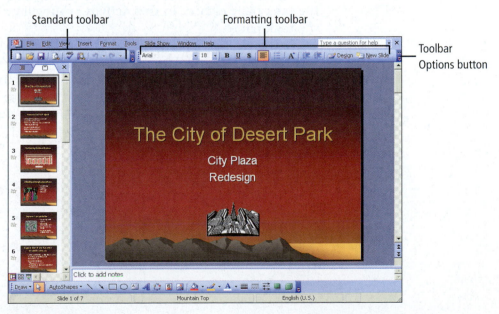

Figure 1.12

1 Look at your screen to determine how toolbars are displayed. On the Standard toolbar, point to, but do not click, any button.

After a few seconds, the ScreenTip for the button displays. Recall that a ScreenTip is a small box that displays the name of a button or part of the PowerPoint window.

2 On the Formatting toolbar, point to, but do not click, any button. The ScreenTip displays.

3 Check your screen to see how your Standard and Formatting toolbars are displayed. If they are *not* displayed on two rows, as

shown in Figure 1.11, click the **Toolbar Options** button ▮, as shown in Figure 1.12, and click **Show Buttons on Two Rows**.

More Knowledge — Displaying a Toolbar

Right-click any toolbar to select another toolbar.

If a toolbar is missing entirely, point to an existing toolbar or to the menu bar and click the right mouse button (also known as *right-clicking*). On the short-cut menu that displays, point to the name of the toolbar you wish to display and click the left mouse button. Alternatively, display the View menu, point to Toolbars, and then click the name of the toolbar you wish to display.

Activity 1.5 Closing and Displaying the Task Pane

Recall that when you opened the PowerPoint program, the **task pane** displayed on the right side of your window. A task pane is a window within a Microsoft Office application that provides commonly used commands. Its location allows you to use these commands while still working on your files. In PowerPoint, the task pane allows you to complete many tasks, including opening and creating files, adding graphic images, and changing the design of your slides. When you opened your presentation, the task pane closed. In this activity, you will redisplay and then close the task pane.

1 On the menu bar, click **View**, and then click **Task Pane**.

The task pane displays at the right side of the window. At the top of the task pane, two buttons display. The Other Task Panes button displays a menu of 16 task panes in PowerPoint. The Close button closes the task pane. See Figure 1.13.

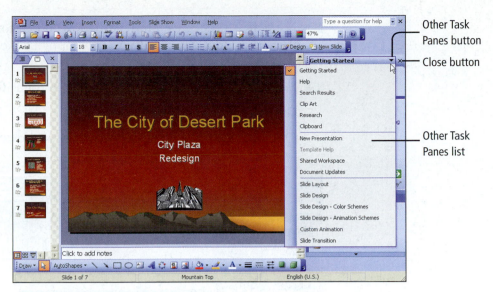

Figure 1.13

2 Click **Other Task Panes** ⬇ to view the list.

3 At the top of the task pane, click **Close** ☒.

Activity 1.6 Creating a New Folder and Saving a File

In the same way that you use file folders to organize your paper documents, Windows uses a hierarchy of electronic folders to keep your electronic files organized. Using Windows' hierarchy of folders, you can group your files in a logical manner. Check with your instructor or lab coordinator to see where you will be storing your presentations (for example, on your own disk or on a network drive) and whether there is any suggested file folder arrangement.

Throughout this textbook, you will be instructed to save your files using the file name followed by your first and last name. Currently, the file p01A_Expansion is displayed in your PowerPoint window. To change the name of the file or its directory or drive location, or to create a new folder in which to store your files, you will use the Save As command on the File menu.

1 On the menu bar, click **File**, and then click **Save As**.

The Save As dialog box displays.

2 In the **Save As** dialog box, at the right edge of the **Save in** box, click the **Save in arrow** to view a list of the drives available to you.

3 Navigate to the drive on which you will be storing your folders and presentations—for example, 3½ Floppy (A:), or the drive designated by your instructor or lab coordinator.

4 To the right of the **Save in** box, notice the row of buttons. Click the **Create New Folder** button 📁.

The New Folder dialog box displays, as shown in Figure 1.14.

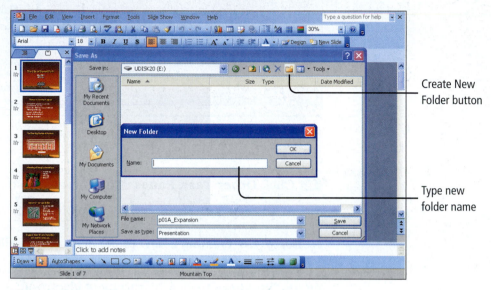

Figure 1.14

5 In the **Name** box, type **Chapter 1** to create a new folder on your disk, and then click **OK.**

6 In the lower portion of the **Save As** dialog box, locate the **File name** box.

The file name *p01A_Expansion* may be highlighted if you selected the default location in the Save in box. If you selected a different location in the Save in box, *p01A_Expansion* may not be highlighted.

7 Click to position your insertion point in the **File name** box and type as necessary to save the file with the name **1A_Expansion_Firstname_Lastname** See Figure 1.15.

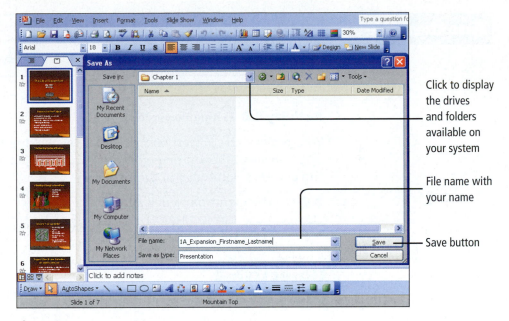

Click to display
the drives
and folders
available on
your system

File name with
your name

Save button

Figure 1.15

8 In the lower right corner, click the **Save** button or press Enter. The new file name displays in the title bar.

Note — Using File Names with Spaces

The Microsoft Windows operating system recognizes file names with spaces. However, some Internet file transfer programs do not. To facilitate sending your files over the Internet using a course management system, in this textbook you will be instructed to save files using an underscore rather than a space.

Activity 1.7 Closing a File

When you are finished working on a presentation, you should save and close it. Closing a file means that you are removing it from your system's random access memory (RAM). You should save a file before closing it, but if you forget to save, PowerPoint will remind you.

1 With your file **1A_Expansion_Firstname_Lastname** still displayed, move your pointer to the menu bar and click **File**.

2 From the **File** menu, click **Close**.

Activity 1.8 Exiting PowerPoint

You can exit the PowerPoint program by clicking Exit from the File menu or by closing all open presentations and then clicking the Close button at the extreme right edge of the title bar.

1 On the menu bar, click **File**.

2 From the displayed menu, click **Exit** to close PowerPoint.

Objective 2
Edit a Presentation Using the Outline/Slides Pane

In Normal View, the PowerPoint window is divided into three areas—the Slide pane, the Outline/Slides pane, and the Notes pane. When you make changes to the presentation in the Outline/Slides pane, the changes are reflected immediately in the Slide pane. Likewise, when you make changes in the Slide pane, the changes are reflected in the Outline/Slides pane.

Activity 1.9 Editing a Presentation Using the Outline

Editing is the process of adding, deleting, or changing the contents of a slide. In this activity, you will change and delete text in the Outline tab.

1 **Start** PowerPoint. On the Standard toolbar, click the **Open** button 📂.

The Open dialog box displays.

2 In the **Open** dialog box, click the **Look in arrow**, and then navigate to the location where you are storing your files. Click to select your file **1A_Expansion_Firstname_Lastname**. Be sure that you click the file that contains your name.

3 In the lower right corner of the **Open** dialog box, click the **Open** button. Alternatively, you can double-click the name of the file to open it.

4 At the lower left corner of the window, locate the **View** buttons, and check to be sure that your presentation is displayed in **Normal View**. If necessary, click the **Normal View** button ▣.

In Normal View, the left side of your window displays the Outline/Slides pane. When the Outline tab is active, you can enter and edit text in your presentation. When the Slides tab is active, thumbnails of your presentation display and you can copy, move, and delete entire slides.

5 In the **Outline/Slides** pane, click the **Slides tab** so that the thumbnail image of each slide is displayed.

6 Click the **Outline tab** to display the text of the presentation in outline format.

The slide numbers in the outline are followed by a small picture called the **slide icon**. See Figure 1.16. The slide number and slide icon indicate the start of a new slide in your presentation. Notice also that the text displays with indents and bullets similar to an outline that you would type in a word processor. PowerPoint uses these indents to determine the outline level in a slide. Misspelled words are flagged with a wavy red line.

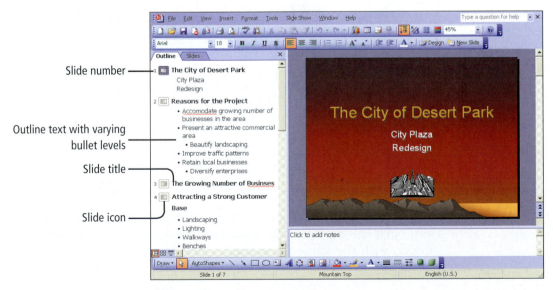

Slide number

Outline text with varying bullet levels

Slide title

Slide icon

Figure 1.16

7 Move your mouse pointer into the text in the **Outline tab** and notice that your pointer displays as an ***I-beam pointer*** ⟦I⟧.

The I-beam pointer indicates that you are pointing to a text area in the Outline/Slides pane or in the Slide pane.

8 In the **Outline tab**, position your **I-beam** pointer in the first slide after the word *Redesign* and then click the left mouse button to position the ***insertion point***—the blinking vertical bar that indicates where text will be inserted when you type—at this location. Press ⟦Space⟧ and then type **and Expansion**

Notice that as you type, the changes are also made in the Slide pane.

9 In the **Outline tab**, locate **Slide 2**, and then pause the mouse pointer over the second bullet symbol so that a four-headed arrow displays, as shown in Figure 1.17. Click the left mouse button.

Notice that the bulleted item and the subordinate (lower-level) bullet below this item are both *selected* (highlighted in black). Clicking on a bullet selects the bulleted item and all subordinate text.

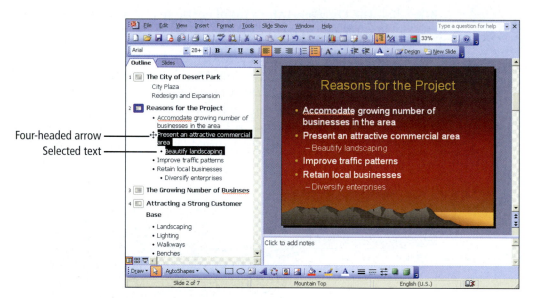

Figure 1.17

10 On your keyboard, press ⟦Delete⟧ to delete the selected text.

11 On the Standard toolbar, click the **Save** button ⟦🖫⟧.

The changes you have made to your presentation are saved. When you click the Save button, your file is stored to the same drive and folder, with the same file name.

Activity 1.10 Promoting and Demoting Outline Text

Text in a PowerPoint presentation is organized according to outline levels, similar to the outline levels you might make for a book report. The highest level on an individual slide is the title. **Bulleted levels** (outline levels identified by a symbol) are identified in the slides by the indentation and the size of the text. Indented text in a smaller size indicates a lower outline level.

It is easy to change the outline level of text to a higher or lower level. For example, you might create a presentation with four bullets on the same level. Then you might decide that one bulleted item relates to one of the other bullets, rather than to the slide title. In this case, a lower outline level should be applied. You can **demote** text to apply a *lower* outline level, or **promote** text and apply a *higher* outline level. Or, you can begin a new slide by promoting bulleted text to a slide title.

1 On the right side of the **Outline tab**, point to the vertical scroll bar, press and hold down the left mouse button, and then drag down until you can view all of the text in **Slide 6**.

2 In the **Slide 6** text, click to position the insertion point anywhere in the second bulleted line—*Business Expo*. On the Formatting toolbar, click the **Increase Indent** button.

The bulleted item is demoted and displays as a lower outline level under the first bullet. See Figure 1.18.

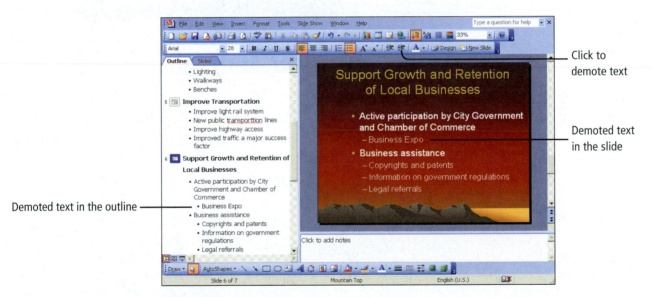

Click to demote text

Demoted text in the slide

Demoted text in the outline

Figure 1.18

3 In the **Outline tab**, locate **Slide 5**, and then click anywhere in the last bulleted item—*Improved traffic a major success factor.*

Slide 5 displays in the Slide pane. Notice that all of the bulleted items are at the highest bullet level, including the last item—*Improved traffic a major success factor.*

4 On the Formatting toolbar, click **Decrease Indent** ![icon] to promote the item one outline level.

The bulleted item is deleted from the slide, and a new Slide 6 is created with the title *Improved traffic a major success factor.* When a bulleted item at the highest level is promoted, it is promoted to a title slide and a new slide is created. See Figure 1.19.

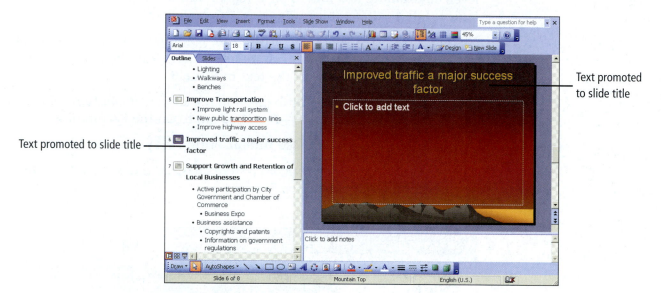

Figure 1.19

5 In the **Outline tab**, on **Slide 7**, click anywhere in the last bulleted line—*Legal referrals.*

Slide 7 displays in the Slide pane.

6 On the Formatting toolbar, click **Decrease Indent** [icon] to apply a higher outline level. Click **Decrease Indent** again [icon] to create a new **Slide 8** with the title *Legal referrals*.

The newly created Slide 8 displays in the Slide pane.

7 On the Standard toolbar, click the **Save** button [icon] to save the changes you have made to your presentation file.

Activity 1.11 Deleting a Slide

In this activity, you will delete Slide 8.

1 In the **Outline/Slides** pane, click the **Slides tab** to display the slide thumbnails.

2 If necessary, click to select **Slide 8**.

Slide 8 is bordered, indicating that it is selected. See Figure 1.20.

Selected slide ——

Figure 1.20

3 Press Delete.

The slide is deleted and the remaining slides are renumbered. In the status bar, *Slide 8 of 8* displays.

Another Way — **Deleting Slides**

When you display a slide that you wish to delete, you can click the Edit menu and then click Delete Slide.

4 On the Standard toolbar, click the **Save** button 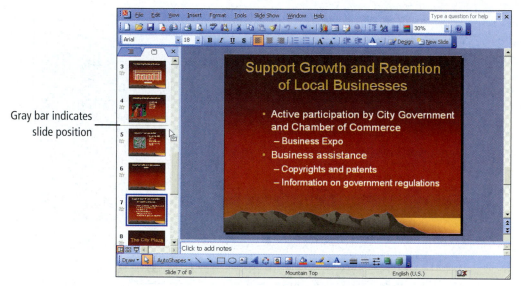 to save the changes you have made to your presentation file.

Activity 1.12 Moving a Slide

It is easy to change the order of the slides in your presentation using the Slides tab.

1 In the **Outline/Slides** pane, if necessary click the **Slides tab** to display the slide thumbnails. Click to select the thumbnail image for **Slide 7**.

2 Point to the selected slide, press and hold down the left mouse button, drag the mouse upward, and notice the horizontal line that displays as you move the mouse. With the horizontal line positioned between **Slides 4** and **5**, release the left mouse button. See Figure 1.21.

Slide 7 is reordered to become Slide 5.

Gray bar indicates slide position

Figure 1.21

3 To close the **Outline/Slides** pane, move your pointer to the right of the **Slides tab**, and then click the **Close** button.

The Outline/Slides pane section of the window closes and the Slide pane fills most of the PowerPoint window.

4 In the lower left corner of your screen, point to the **Normal View** button ▣ and notice that the ScreenTip indicates *Normal View (Restore Panes)*.

You can redisplay the Outline/Slides pane by clicking the Normal View button or by displaying the View menu and clicking Normal (Restore Panes).

5 Make sure the **Outline/Slides** pane is still closed, and then, on the Standard toolbar, click the **Save** button 🖫 to save the changes to your presentation.

Objective 3
Format and Edit a Presentation Using the Slide Pane

You will do most of your *formatting* work in PowerPoint in the Slide pane. Formatting refers to changing the appearance of the text, layout, and design of a slide. You can also edit, promote, and demote text in the Slide pane using the same techniques that you used in the Outline/Slides pane.

Activity 1.13 Editing Text Using the Slide Pane

1 If necessary, **Open** 📂 your file **1A_Expansion_Firstname_Lastname**. Be sure that the **Outline/Slides** pane is closed.

Recall that you can close the Outline/Slides tabs by clicking the Close button to the right of the Slides tab.

2 In the vertical scroll bar at the far right edge of the window, point to the scroll box. Press and hold down the left mouse button so that a ScreenTip displays indicating the number and title of the current slide. Drag up or down as necessary to display **Slide 6**.

3 With **Slide 6** displayed in the **Slide** pane, click to position your insertion point at the end of the last bulleted item on the slide—after the word *access*. Press Enter.

A new bullet, displayed in black, is created.

4 Type **Improve parking**

Notice that as you begin to type, the bullet turns to the color of the other bullets on the slide.

5 Click anywhere in the third bulleted line—*Improve highway access.*

On the Formatting toolbar, click **Increase Indent** to apply a lower level bullet. Compare your slide to Figure 1.22.

Figure 1.22

6 **Save** the file.

Activity 1.14 Changing Slide Layout

Layout refers to the placement and arrangement of the text and graphic elements on a slide. For example, a title slide usually has two elements—a title and a subtitle. Additional slide layouts may include a title and a bulleted list or a title and a chart. PowerPoint includes a number of predefined layouts that you can apply to your slide for the purpose of rearranging the elements. Changing the layout of a slide is accomplished from the Slide Layout task pane. You can display the Slide Layout task pane by clicking the Format menu and then clicking Slide Layout, or by displaying the task pane, clicking the Other Task Panes arrow, and then clicking Slide Layout.

1 Display **Slide 7** either by clicking the **Next Slide** button or by dragging the vertical scroll box to display **Slide 7**.

This slide contains a title and a *placeholder* for bulleted text. A placeholder reserves a portion of a slide and serves as a container for text, graphics, and other slide elements. Recall that this slide was created by promoting a bullet from the previous slide. Promoting a bullet at the highest level results in the creation of a new slide with the bulleted text as the title of the slide.

2 To change the layout of this slide, display the **Format** menu, and then click **Slide Layout**.

The Slide Layout task pane displays all of the predefined layouts available in PowerPoint. See Figure 1.23. The slide layouts are grouped into four categories: *Text Layouts*, *Content Layouts*, *Text and Content Layouts*, and *Other Layouts*.

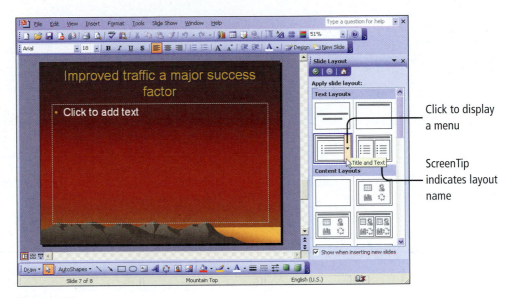

Figure 1.23

3 Take a moment to move the task pane's scroll bar up and down to see the four layout categories and view the layouts. Point to, but do not click, some of the layouts and notice that a ScreenTip displays indicating the name of the layout.

When you point to a slide layout, the right side of the layout displays a bar with an arrow. See Figure 1.23. Clicking the arrow displays a small menu from which you can apply the layout to selected slides or insert a new slide with the layout applied.

4 Scroll to the top to view the four choices under **Text Layouts**, and then click the last layout—**Title and 2-Column Text**.

The slide layout is changed so that there are two side-by-side placeholders on the slide.

5 Click in the **left placeholder**, type **New traffic signals** and then press Enter.

A new bulleted line is created.

6 Type **New street lights** and then press Enter. Type **New crosswalks**

If you inadvertently added an additional bullet by pressing Enter at the end of the bulleted list, press ←Bksp to delete the extra bullet.

7 Click in the **right placeholder**, and then type **Improved parking structures**

8 Press Enter, and then type **Redesigned turn lanes**

9 At the top of the **Slide Layout** task pane, click the **Close** button ☒ to close the **Slide Layout** task pane.

10 Look at the title of this slide and notice that the word *factor* is on the second line of the title by itself.

As a general design rule, you should try to have at least two words on each line of a slide title to create a balanced look.

11 To balance the title, move your pointer into the title placeholder and click after the word *traffic*. Press Enter.

The words *Improved traffic* are on the first line of the slide title and the words *a major success factor* are on the second line of the slide title.

12 Look again at the title of this slide and notice that only the first word of the title—*Improved*—is capitalized.

As a rule, the first letter of each word in a title should be capitalized.

13 Correct the text in the title by clicking in the title placeholder and typing as necessary so that the capitalization matches Figure 1.24. Then, click in a blank area to deselect the placeholder, and compare your slide to Figure 1.24.

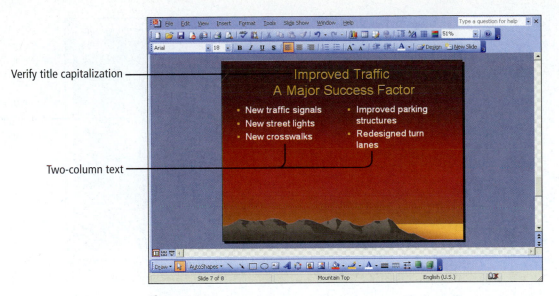

Verify title capitalization

Two-column text

Figure 1.24

14 On the Standard toolbar, click the **Save** button 🖫 to save the changes you have made to your presentation.

Activity 1.15 Checking the Spelling of a Presentation

As you create a presentation, PowerPoint continually checks spelling by comparing the words in your presentation to the PowerPoint dictionary. A word that is incorrectly spelled or that is not in the dictionary is indicated by a red wavy underline. Spelling errors can be corrected in either the Outline/Slides pane or the Slide pane.

1 Display **Slide 2** by dragging the scroll box in the vertical scrollbar up until the appropriate ScreenTip displays. Notice the red wavy underline in the first bullet of this slide.

Alert!

Enabling Spelling Checker

If the red wavy underline does not display under the incorrectly spelled word, the *Check spelling as you type* feature may not be enabled on your system. To enable this feature, click the Tools menu, and then click Options. Click the Spelling and Style tab and click to place a check mark in the Check spelling as you type check box.

2 Pause the mouse the pointer over the incorrectly spelled word, and then right-click (press the right mouse button).

A shortcut menu displays with several suggested spelling corrections. See Figure 1.25.

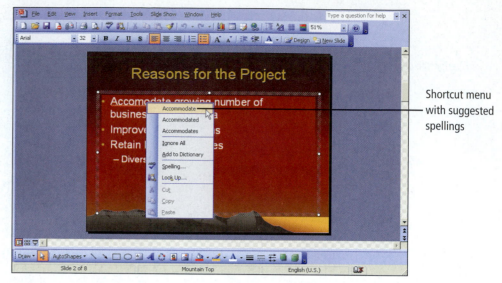

Shortcut menu with suggested spellings

Figure 1.25

3 In the displayed shortcut menu, click **Accommodate**—the correct spelling of the word.

4 On the vertical scrollbar, click the **Next Slide** button ⬇ to display **Slide 3**. Locate the misspelled word in the title, move the pointer over it, and then right-click. From the displayed shortcut menu, click **Businesses** to correct the spelling.

5 Using the same method that you used to correct the spelling errors on **Slides 2** and **3**, scroll through the presentation and correct spelling on the remaining slides (*transportation* on **Slide 6** and any other spelling errors you might have made).

6 **Save** 🖫 the changes you have made to your presentation.

More Knowledge — Checking the Entire Presentation Using the Spelling Command

The Spelling button on the Standard toolbar activates a spelling check of your entire presentation. The spelling checker selects each incorrectly spelled word and displays a dialog box with suggested spellings and the options to ignore the word, change the word, or add the word to the dictionary.

Activity 1.16 Adding Speaker Notes to a Presentation

Recall that when a presentation is displayed in Normal View with the panes displayed, the Notes pane displays below the Slide pane. The Notes pane is used to type speaker's notes that can be printed below a picture of each slide. You can refer to these printouts while making a presentation, thus reminding you of the important points that you wish to make while running an electronic slide show.

1 Drag the scroll box to display **Slide 3**. In the lower left corner of your PowerPoint window, click the **Normal View** button ⊞.

The Outline/Slides pane and the Notes pane are restored on your screen.

2 Look at the PowerPoint window and notice the amount of space that is currently dedicated to each of the three panes—the **Outline/Slides** pane, the **Slide** pane, and the **Notes** pane. Locate the horizontal bar and vertical bar that separate the three panes. See Figure 1.26.

These narrow bars are used to adjust the size of the panes. If you decide to type speaker notes, you will want to make the Notes pane larger.

Separates Slide pane from Outline/Slides pane

Drag this pointer shape to resize the Notes pane

Separates Slide pane from Notes pane

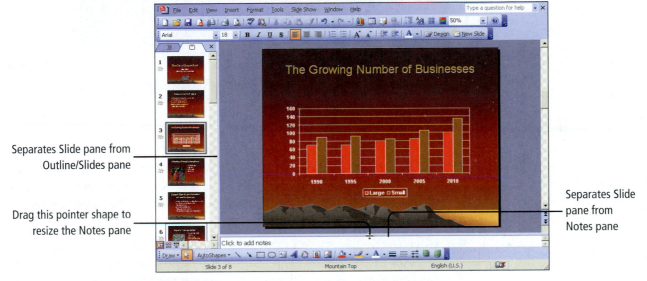

Figure 1.26

3 Point to the small bar that separates the **Slide** pane from the **Notes** pane. The pointer displays as an equal sign with an upward-pointing and a downward-pointing arrow, as shown in Figure 1.26.

4 Press and hold down the left mouse button until a pattern of dots displays in the bar, indicating that you can resize the pane. While still holding down the left mouse button, drag the pointer up approximately one inch and then release the left mouse button to resize the pane.

The displayed slide resizes to fit in the Slide pane and the Notes pane expands.

5 With **Slide 3** displayed, click in the **Notes** pane and type **As the population expands, the number of large and small businesses will continue to grow.** Compare your screen to Figure 1.27.

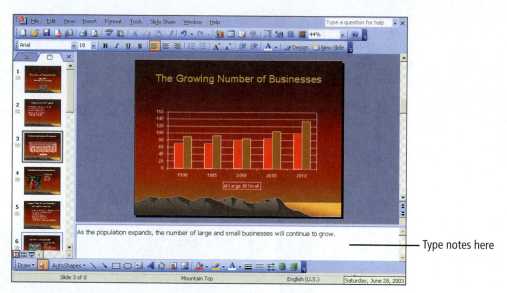

Type notes here

Figure 1.27

6 Display **Slide 7** in the **Slide** pane, and then click in the **Notes** pane. Type **Remember that increased traffic is a major concern for the City. Stress how these changes will improve the traffic flow, not create new problems.**

7 Move to the last slide in the presentation—**Slide 8**. Type the following text in the **Notes** pane: **Stress the importance of the expansion of the City Plaza. Many citizens are working together to create this new space for the benefit of all.**

8 You have finished typing the notes for this presentation. **Save** the presentation.

Objective 4
View and Edit a Presentation in Slide Sorter View

Slide Sorter View displays all of the slides in your presentation in miniature. You can use Slide Sorter View to rearrange and delete slides, apply formatting to multiple slides, and to get an overall impression of your presentation.

Activity 1.17 Selecting Multiple Slides

Selecting more than one slide is accomplished by clicking the first slide that you wish to select, pressing and holding down Shift or Ctrl, and then clicking another slide. Using Shift allows you to select a group of slides that are adjacent (next to each other). Using Ctrl allows you to select a group of slides that are nonadjacent (*not* next to each other). When multiple slides are selected, you can move or delete them as a group. These techniques can also be used when slide miniatures are displayed in the Slides tab.

1 If necessary, **Open** [icon] your file **1A_Expansion_Firstname_Lastname**. At the lower left of your window, click the **Slide Sorter View** button [icon].

The Outline/Slides pane is closed, and the eight slides in your presentation display in order from left to right.

2 Point to **Slide 2**, and then click the left mouse button to select it.

An outline surrounds the slide indicating that it is selected.

3 Press and hold down Ctrl, and then click **Slide 4**.

Slides 2 and 4 are selected.

4 Press and hold down Ctrl, and then click **Slide 6**.

Slides 2, 4, and 6 are selected. See Figure 1.28.

Blue outline surrounding Slides 2, 4, and 6 indicate selected slides

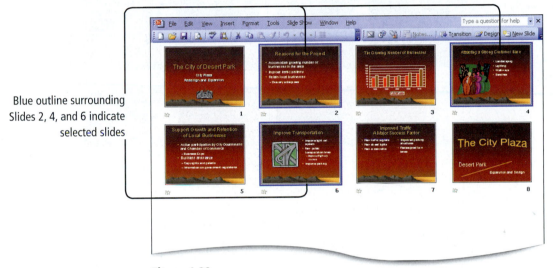

Figure 1.28

5 To deselect **Slide 4** while leaving **Slides 2** and **6** selected, press and hold down Ctrl, and then click **Slide 4**.

Slides 2 and 6 are still selected.

6 Click **Slide 3** *without* holding down Ctrl.

This action deselects Slides 2 and 6, and only Slide 3 is selected.

7 With **Slide 3** still selected, press and hold down Shift, and then click **Slide 6**.

All of the slides between 3 and 6 are selected.

8 Click in the white area below the slides.

The selection is canceled and no slides are selected. Additionally, a large blinking insertion point displays after Slide 8. You can cancel the selection of all slides by clicking anywhere in the white area of the Slide Sorter window.

Activity 1.18 Moving and Deleting Slides in Slide Sorter View

Slide Sorter view is convenient for deleting and moving slides because you can view a large number of slides at one time.

1 If necessary, display your presentation in Slide Sorter View by clicking the **Slide Sorter View** button ▦.

2 Click to select **Slide 3**.

3 While pointing to **Slide 3**, press and hold down the left mouse button, and then drag the slide to the left until the displayed vertical bar is positioned to the left of **Slide 2**. See Figure 1.29. Release the left mouse button.

The slide with the chart becomes Slide 2.

Vertical bar positioned between Slides 1 and 2 to move slide to this position

Figure 1.29

4 Select **Slide 4**, press and hold down Ctrl, and then click **Slide 7**. Make sure that *only* **Slides 4** and **7** are selected, and then press Delete to delete these two slides from the presentation.

5 **Save** 🖫 the presentation file.

Objective 5
View a Slide Show

When a presentation is viewed as an electronic slide show, the entire slide fills the computer screen, and a large audience can view your presentation if your computer is connected to a projection system. An onscreen slide show may include special effects such as slide *transitions*. Transitions refer to the way that a slide appears or disappears during an onscreen slide show. For example, when one slide leaves the screen, it may fade or dissolve into another slide.

Other special effects that you will see as you run the presentation are text and graphic animations. ***Animation effects*** introduce individual slide elements so that the slide can be built (displayed) one element at a time. These effects add interest to your slides and draw attention to important features.

Activity 1.19 Viewing a Slide Show

Transitions and animation effects have been applied to the *1A_Expansion* presentation. Clicking the left mouse button allows you to view each animation effect separately on each individual slide. At the end of the slide, you also click the left mouse button to advance to the next slide. You will learn to add special effects to presentations as you progress in this textbook.

1 Display **Slide 1** of your file **1A_Expansion_Firstname_Lastname** in **Normal View** . Then, take a moment to read Steps 2 through 8 to familiarize yourself with what you will see and do as you view the slide presentation. After you have read the steps, in the lower

left corner of the screen, click the **Slide Show** button and read the steps again as you proceed through the slide show.

2 Watch for the animation effect on the title of the first slide, and then locate the graphic at the bottom center of the slide.

This is a graphic file that includes a blinking light at the top of the tall building. The animation in this graphic is not a part of PowerPoint; rather, it is included in the graphic file itself. Upon opening, the title displays an emphasis animation effect—a colored box displays around the title as it expands, and then the colored box disappears as the text reverts to its original size.

3 Click the left mouse button to advance to the next slide, and notice that only the background is visible. Click the left mouse button again to display the title of the slide.

4 Click the left mouse button to display the chart. Click the left mouse button again to display the chart's first bar element.

5 Continue to click the left mouse button until the chart has finished and the third slide displays. When the third slide transitions onto the screen, only the title displays.

6 Click the left mouse button and notice that the first bullet displays toward the bottom of the slide and then bounces into place. Click the left mouse button again and notice that the first bullet dims to a lighter color as the second bullet bounces into place.

Dimming a previous bullet is a type of text animation that keeps the audience focused on the current bullet.

7 Continue to click the left mouse button until the fourth slide displays—entitled *Support Growth and Retention of Local Businesses*. This slide introduces all the text at once.

8 Click the left mouse button to display the fifth slide, and then click again to drop the title onto the screen. Click again so that the graphic spins onto the screen in a pinwheel effect, and then click the left mouse button three more times to display each line of bulleted text.

9 Click to display the sixth and final slide—entitled *The City Plaza.* The elements on this slide do not require that you click the left mouse button to advance the animations. These elements have been set with automatic slide timings. Click the left mouse button one more time to view the last slide, which is a **black slide** that displays the text *End of slide show, click to exit.* PowerPoint inserts a black slide at the end of every slide show to indicate that the presentation is over. Click the left mouse button to return to Normal View.

More Knowledge — Inserting a Formatted Slide at the End of a Presentation

PowerPoint inserts a black slide to signal the end of a presentation. Some presenters prefer to display a blank slide that contains the same background as the other slides in the presentation. If you prefer this method, you can disable the black slide by clicking the Tools menu, and then clicking Options. Click the View tab, and under Slide Show, click to clear the End with black slide check box.

10 Use any method to display **Slide 3**, and then click the **Slide Show** button 🖳 to start the presentation on **Slide 3**. Click three times, and then after you have viewed the entire third slide, on your keyboard press [Esc] to end the slide show.

You do not have to start a presentation with the first slide. An audience member may ask you a question pertaining to a particular slide. You can begin the slide show on any slide in the presentation by first displaying the slide in Normal View.

11 **Save** 🖫 the presentation.

Objective 6
Create Headers and Footers

A *header* is text that displays at the top of every slide or that prints at the top of a sheet of *slide handouts* or *notes pages*. Slide handouts are printed images of more than one slide on a sheet of paper. Notes pages are printouts that contain the slide image in the top half of the page and notes that you have created in the Notes pane in the lower half of the page.

In addition to headers, you can also create *footers*—text that displays at the bottom of every slide or that prints at the bottom of a sheet of slide handouts or notes pages. In this activity, you will add the slide number to the footer on Slides 1 through 5. You will add to the handouts and notes pages a header that includes the current date and a footer that includes your name and the file name.

Activity 1.20 Creating Headers and Footers on Slides

1 If necessary, **Open** 📂 your file **1A_Expansion_Firstname_Lastname** and verify that **Slide 1** is displayed in **Normal View** 🔲.

2 On the menu bar, click **View**, and then click **Header and Footer** to display the **Header and Footer** dialog box.

At the top of this dialog box, two tabs display—*Slide* and *Notes and Handouts*.

3 Click the **Slide tab**, which contains options to place the header or footer on the actual slide—rather than on the printed handout. Then locate the **Preview** box in the lower right corner of the dialog box and note the pattern of boxes.

As you make changes in the dialog box, the Preview box will change accordingly.

4 Under **Include on slide**, select (click to place a check mark in) the **Slide number** check box, and as you do so, watch the Preview box.

The Preview box in the lower right corner of the dialog box indicates the placeholders on a slide. Recall that a placeholder reserves a location on a slide for text or graphics. The three narrow rectangular boxes at the bottom of the Preview box indicate placeholders for footer text. When you clicked the Slide number check box, the placeholder in the far right corner is filled, indicating the location in which the slide number will display.

5 If necessary, clear the **Date and time** check box so that a check mark does *not* display, and then clear the **Footer** check box.

In the Preview box, the first two small rectangles are no longer solid black.

6 Compare your dialog box to Figure 1.30, and then in the upper right corner of the dialog box, click the **Apply to All** button. This will display the slide number on all the slides in the presentation—not just the selected slides.

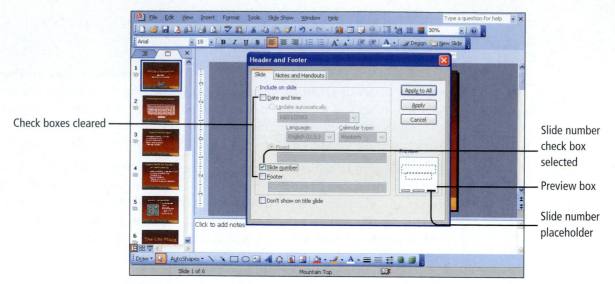

Check boxes cleared

Slide number check box selected

Preview box

Slide number placeholder

Figure 1.30

7 In the **Slide** pane, at the lower end of the vertical scroll bar, click the **Next Slide** button [image] to display each slide and view the slide number in the lower right corner of each slide—with the exception of **Slide 6**.

8 Display **Slide 6**.

The slide number does not display, and the background formatting is different from the other slides in the presentation. Special formatting on this slide suppresses (prevents from displaying) some elements such as headers and footers and the mountain range border that are present on the first five slides of the presentation. You will learn how to suppress these elements in a later chapter.

9 **Save** [image] the presentation.

Activity 1.21 Creating Headers and Footers on Handouts and Notes Pages

1 Display the **View** menu, and then click **Header and Footer** to display the **Header and Footer** dialog box. Click the **Notes and Handouts tab**, which contains options to apply the header and footer that you create to the notes pages and handouts—and not to the actual slides.

2 Under **Include on page**, make sure there is a check mark in the **Date and time** check box (click to add one if necessary), and then click to select the **Update automatically** option button.

The current date and Language display in the appropriate boxes. The Update automatically option will insert the current date on your printed notes and handouts. The date is determined by your computer's internal calendar and clock. Thus, every time the presentation is opened, the current date displays. Conversely, clicking the Fixed option button inserts a date that you type, and which does *not* update.

More Knowledge — Changing the Date Format

You can change the format of the date that displays by clicking the arrow to the right of the date box, and then choosing a date format. You can also change the Language that you wish to display.

3 If necessary, clear the **Header** and **Page number** check boxes to omit these elements from the header and footer.

In the Preview box, corresponding placeholders are no longer selected.

4 If necessary, select the **Footer** check box, and then click to position the insertion point in the **Footer** box. See Figure 1.31, and then using your own first and last name, type **1A Expansion-Firstname Lastname**

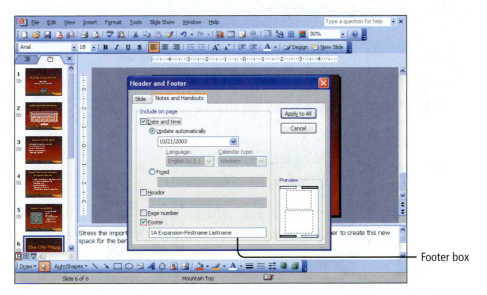

Figure 1.31

5 In the upper right corner of the **Header and Footer** dialog box, click **Apply to All** so that each printed sheet displays the header and footer that you created.

6 Display **Slide 2**. From the **View** menu, click **Notes Pages** to display the current slide in the **Notes Page** view. Notice the date in the upper right corner, and the file name in the lower left corner. See Figure 1.32.

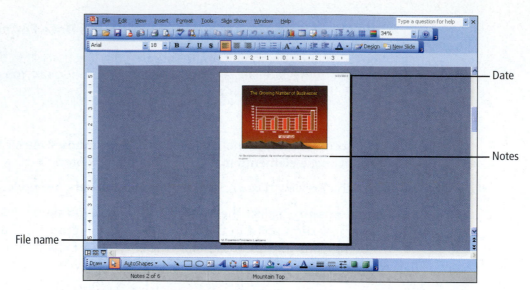

File name ────

Date ────

Notes ────

Figure 1.32

7 To return to **Normal View**, in the lower left corner of the
PowerPoint window, click the **Normal View** button 🔲.

8 **Save** 🔲 the presentation.

Objective 7
Print a Presentation

You can print your presentation as individual slides so that one slide fills
the entire sheet of paper, as slide handouts, or as notes pages. Recall that
slide handouts include *several* slides printed on one sheet of paper. You
can print 1, 2, 3, 4, 6, or 9 slides per page and then distribute the printed
handouts to your audience. The size of the slides on the printout varies,
depending on the number of slides that you choose to print per page.

Activity 1.22 Previewing and Printing Handouts and Slides

Clicking the Print button on the Standard toolbar prints one copy of each
slide in the presentation—filling the entire page with the slide. Printing a
presentation in this manner uses a large amount of ink or toner, depending on the type of printer to which your system is connected. The major-
ity of the projects in this textbook require that you print handouts, *not*
slides. This will conserve paper and printer supplies. To change the print
options, use the Print dialog box.

1 Display the **File** menu and point to **Print**.

Recall that when a menu option is followed by three small dots
(called an ellipsis), it indicates that more information is needed and
either a task pane or a dialog box will display.

2 Click **Print** to open the **Print** dialog box. Take a moment to study the table in Figure 1.33, which describes what you can do in each section of the **Print** dialog box.

The Print Dialog Box

Section	Here you can:
Printer	Change the current printer. Information regarding the printer location and the port that the printer is using is included here.
Print range	Choose the slides that you want to print.
Copies	Specify the number of copies that you want to print.
Print what:	Specify the type of output. You can print slides, handouts, notes pages, or outline view (only the text of the slides, in outline format).
Handouts	Specify the number of slides per page and the order in which the slides are arranged on the page.

Figure 1.33

3 In the lower left portion of the dialog box, click the **Print what arrow**, and then from the displayed list, click **Handouts**.

4 Under **Handouts**, click the **Slides per page arrow**. On the displayed list, click **6** to print all six slides in the presentation on one page.

The preview box to the right indicates six slides.

5 In the same dialog box section, click the **Vertical** option button.

The preview changes its order of how the slides will be printed—slides 1–3 in the first column and then slides 4–6 in the second column.

6 At the bottom of the dialog box, click the **Color/grayscale arrow**. Click **Grayscale**. If necessary, click to select the **Frame slides** check box so that a thin border surrounds each slide on the printout, thus giving the printout a finished and professional look.

Selecting *grayscale* optimizes the look of color slides that are printed on a black and white printer, whereas printing in Pure Black and White hides shadows and patterns applied to text and graphics.

7 Under **Print range**, verify that the **All** option button is selected so that all of the slides in the presentation are included in the handouts printout. Under **Copies**, in the **Number of copies** box, verify that **1** displays so that only one copy of the handouts is printed. Compare your dialog box to Figure 1.34.

Project 1A: Expansion | **PowerPoint** 339

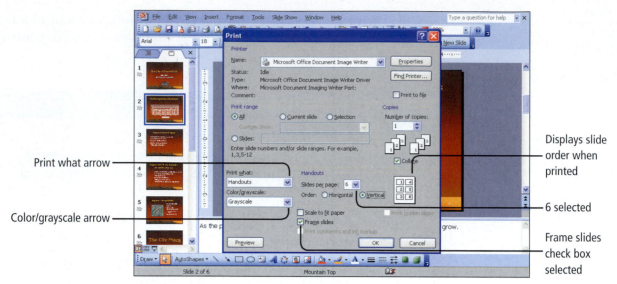

Print what arrow ⎯⎯⎯⎯

Color/grayscale arrow ⎯⎯⎯

Displays slide
order when
printed

6 selected

Frame slides
check box
selected

Figure 1.34

8 In the lower left corner of the **Print** dialog box, click **Preview**.

The Print Preview window opens, displaying your presentation as it will look when printed using the print options that you selected. In this window, you can change the print options and then print your presentation.

Another Way ⎯ **Displaying the Presentation in the Print Preview Window**

You can display the Print Preview window at any time by clicking the Print Preview button on the Standard toolbar.

9 On the Print Preview toolbar, click **Landscape** 🅰.

The presentation displays and will print on paper set up in landscape orientation—11 inches wide by 8½ inches tall.

10 On the Print Preview toolbar, click **Options** Options ▾ , point to **Printing Order**, and then click **Horizontal**.

Slides 1, 2, and 3 display in the top row and slides 4, 5, and 6 display in the bottom row. Compare your Print Preview window to Figure 1.35.

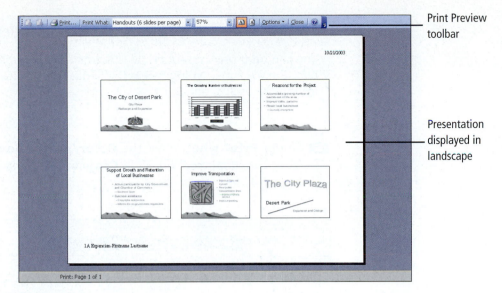

Print Preview toolbar

Presentation displayed in landscape

Figure 1.35

11 On the Print Preview toolbar, click **Portrait** .

The presentation displays and will print on paper set up in portrait orientation—8½ inches wide by 11 inches tall.

12 On the Print Preview toolbar, click **Print** to return to the print dialog box, and then click **OK**.

All six slides in the presentation are printed on one page, and the printout includes a header with the current date on the right and a footer with the file name on the left.

13 On the Print Preview toolbar, click **Close** .

The Print Preview window closes and your presentation is displayed in Normal View.

Activity 1.23 Printing Notes Pages

In this activity, you will print Notes Pages for the slides that contain speaker's notes.

1 Display the **File** menu, and then click **Print**.

2 In the lower left corner of the **Print** dialog box, click the **Print what arrow**, and then from the displayed list, click **Notes Pages**.

3 Under **Print range**, click the **Slides** option button and notice that the insertion point is blinking in the **Slides** box.

In this manner, you can choose to print only specific slides by entering the slide numbers that you want to print.

4 In the **Slides** box, type **2,6**

Note — Printing Several Sequential Slides

You can print several sequential slides by using a hyphen between slide numbers. For example, typing 3–5 in the Slides box results in printouts that include slides 3, 4, and 5.

5 Under **Print what**, click the **Color/grayscale arrow**, and then from the displayed list click **Grayscale**. Compare your dialog box to Figure 1.36.

Notes Pages selected ——

Grayscale selected ——

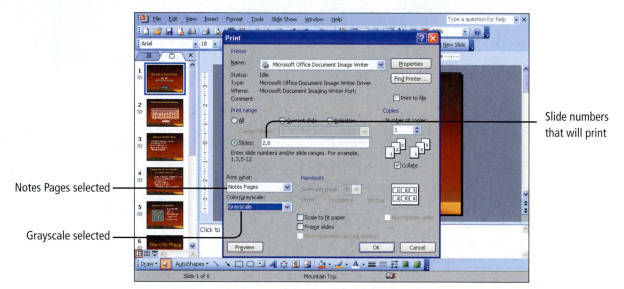

Slide numbers that will print

Figure 1.36

6 In the lower right corner of the **Print** dialog box, click **OK** to print the notes.

Two pages will print.

7 **Save** the presentation.

Objective 8
Use PowerPoint Help

As you work with PowerPoint, you can get assistance by using the Help feature. You can ask questions and PowerPoint Help will provide you with information and step-by-step instructions for performing tasks.

Activity 1.24 Using PowerPoint Help

One way to use Help is to type a question in the *Type a question for help* box, located at the right edge of the menu bar.

1 Move your pointer to the right edge of the menu bar and click in the **Type a question for help** box. With the insertion point blinking in the box, type **How do I open a file?** and then press [Enter].

The Search Results task pane displays with a list of topics that may answer your question.

2 Point to and then click **Open a file**. See Figure 1.37.

The Microsoft Office PowerPoint Help window opens.

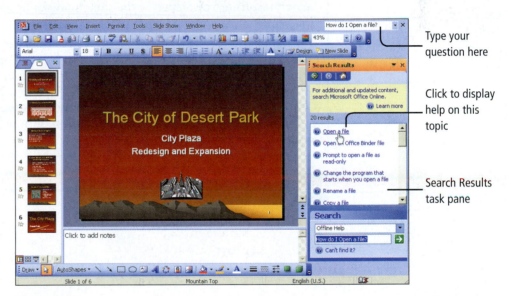

Figure 1.37

3 Read the instructions.

The bulleted items in blue below the Help topic indicate links to related instructions or information.

4 Click the last bullet, **Tips**, to display additional information about opening files.

5 In the second bulleted item, point to and then click the blue words **task pane** to display a green definition of a task pane. Click **task pane** again to close the definition.

6 In the Help window, click the **Close** button ✖, and then **Close** ✖ the **Search Results** task pane.

7 **Save** 🖫 the presentation. In the upper right corner of your screen, to the right of the **Help** box, click the **Close Window** button ✖ to close the presentation. Then, at the far right edge of the title bar, click the **Close** button ✖ to close PowerPoint.

Another Way — **Getting Help Using the Task Pane and the Office Assistant**

You can access Help by clicking the Microsoft Office PowerPoint Help button on the Standard toolbar. This action opens the Help task pane. In the Search box, type a topic that you want to learn more about and then press Enter. Search results are displayed in the same manner as when you used the Type a question for help box.

If installed, the *Office Assistant* provides yet another method for accessing help. This animated character provides tips as you work and when clicked, allows you to ask a question—displaying search results about the topic. You can display the Office Assistant from the Help menu by clicking Show the Office Assistant. When the Office Assistant is displayed, you can hide it by pointing to the Assistant, clicking the right mouse button to display the shortcut menu, and then clicking Hide.

End **You have completed Project 1A** ————————————————————

Summary

In this chapter, you practiced how to start and exit PowerPoint and how to open a presentation. By working with the different views in PowerPoint, you saw that Normal View is useful for editing and formatting presentation text and that Slide Sorter View is useful to get an overall view of your presentation and to rearrange and delete slides. Using Slide Show view, you practiced running an electronic slide show and became familiar with some of the animation effects that are available in PowerPoint. You also learned how to preview and print a presentation.

As you learn more about PowerPoint, take advantage of the resources available in Help. You can explore a wide variety of topics using the Help feature installed on your system, and you can access Microsoft Office online to find out how other people are using PowerPoint. The more that you use Microsoft Office PowerPoint 2003, the more familiar you will become with all of its features.

In This Chapter You Practiced How To

- Start and Exit PowerPoint
- Edit a Presentation Using the Outline/Slides Pane
- Format and Edit a Presentation Using the Slide Pane
- View and Edit a Presentation in Slide Sorter View
- View a Slide Show
- Create Headers and Footers
- Print a Presentation
- Use PowerPoint Help

Concepts Assessments

Matching   Match each term in the second column with its correct definition in the first column by writing the letter of the term on the blank line in front of the correct definition.

_____ **1.** A group of slides printed on one sheet of paper, appropriate for audience distribution.

_____ **2.** The placement of elements on a slide.

_____ **3.** The first slide of a presentation, which often contains distinguishing formatting.

_____ **4.** The name used to refer to slide miniatures that display in the Slides tab and also in the Slide Sorter View.

_____ **5.** Text that displays at the top of every slide or that prints at the top of a sheet of slide handouts or notes pages.

_____ **6.** Effects that are used to introduce individual slide elements so that the slide can be built one element at a time.

_____ **7.** A special effect that occurs when a slide is introduced during an onscreen slide show.

_____ **8.** A small box that displays the name of a button on a toolbar or some other part of a Windows screen when you pause the mouse pointer over it.

_____ **9.** A slide inserted by PowerPoint at the end of every slide show to indicate that the presentation is over.

_____ **10.** A box that reserves a location on a slide and serves as a container for text, graphics, and other slide elements.

_____ **11.** An animated character that displays tips while you work.

_____ **12.** Printed pages that display a picture of the slide at the top of the page and text that the speaker wishes to say during the presentation at the bottom of the page.

_____ **13.** Slides that are not next to each other when displayed in the Slide Sorter View.

_____ **14.** A command that applies a lower outline level to text.

_____ **15.** An option that allows you to choose the slides that you wish to print.

A Animation effects

B Black slide

C Demote

D Handouts

E Headers

F Layout

G Nonadjacent slides

H Notes pages

I Office Assistant

J Placeholder

K Print range

L ScreenTip

M Thumbnails

N Title slide

O Transition

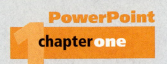
Fill in the Blank Write the correct answer in the space provided.

1. Microsoft PowerPoint 2003 is a _____ program that you can use to effectively present important information to your audience.

2. _____ is the process of making changes to the text in a presentation.

3. A _____ is text that displays at the bottom of every slide or at the bottom of printed notes pages and handouts.

4. An ellipsis following a menu command indicates that a _____ will follow.

5. The _____ displays at the right side of the PowerPoint window and assists you in completing common tasks.

6. When a bulleted item in a slide is _____, a higher outline level is applied.

7. A _____ is a row of buttons that provides a one-click method to perform common commands that would otherwise require multiple clicks to perform from the menu bar.

8. _____ is the process of changing the appearance of the text, layout, and design of a slide.

9. In the PowerPoint window, the point at which text is inserted is called the _____.

10. To display a shortcut menu, click the _____ mouse button.

Project 1B — Safety

Objectives: *Start and Exit PowerPoint, Edit a Presentation Using the Outline/Slides Pane, View and Edit a Presentation in Slide Sorter View, View a Slide Show, Create Headers and Footers, and Print a Presentation.*

In the following Skill Assessment, you will edit a presentation created by the Human Resources Department for a new employee orientation concerning fire safety at City Hall. Your completed presentation will look similar to the one shown in Figure 1.38. You will save your presentation as *1B_Safety_Firstname_Lastname*.

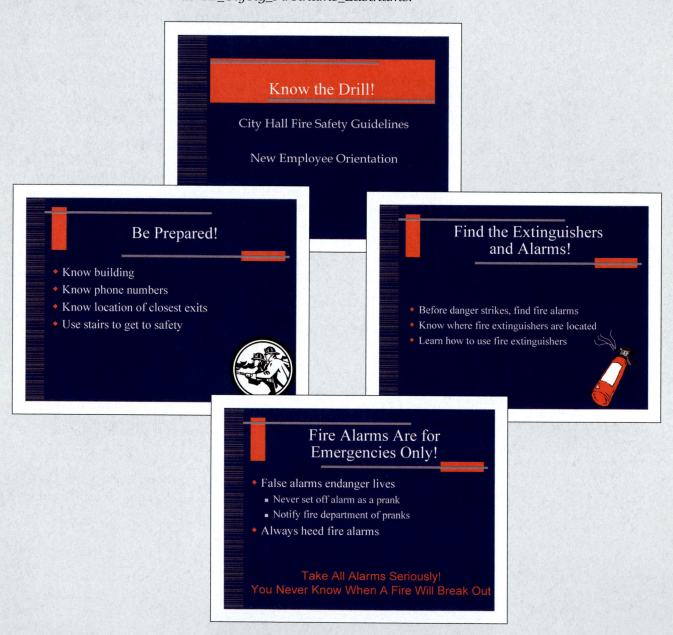

Figure 1.38

(Project 1B–Safety continues on the next page)

(Project 1B–Safety continued)

1. Start PowerPoint. On the Standard toolbar, click the **Open** button. On the displayed **Open** dialog box, click the **Look in arrow** and navigate to the location where the student files for this textbook are stored. Double-click **p01B_Safety**. Alternatively, you can click p01B_Safety once to select it, and then in the lower right corner of the dialog box, click Open.

2. Display the **File** menu, click **Save As**, and then use the **Save in arrow** to navigate to the location where you are storing your projects for this chapter. In the **File name** box, type **1B_Safety_Firstname_Lastname** and then click **Save**.

3. In the **Outline/Slides** pane, click the **Outline tab**. In the **Outline tab**, move your pointer to **Slide 1**. In the subtitle, click to position the insertion point after the word *Hall* and then press Space once. Type **Fire**

4. In the **Outline tab**, click anywhere in **Slide 2**. On the menu bar, click **Edit**, and then click **Delete Slide** to delete the second slide. Recall that this is another way to delete a slide. The remaining slides move up and are renumbered accordingly.

5. In the **Outline tab**, click anywhere in **Slide 3** so that it is displayed in the **Slide** pane. Move your pointer into the slide in the **Slide** pane, and then click to position the insertion point at the end of the last bullet after the word *exits*. The placeholder is selected. Press Enter, and then type **Use stairs to get to safety**

6. Display **Slide 1**. Using the **Outline tab**, the **Next Slide** button, or the scroll bar to the right of the **Slide** pane, scroll through and read the presentation, one slide at a time, and notice the words that are flagged with a red wavy underline indicating incorrect spelling. Point to each misspelled word and click the right mouse button to display the shortcut menu of suggested spellings. Click the correct spelling for each misspelled word. (Hint: You should find two misspelled words—*extinguishers* and *department*.) Alternatively, on the Standard toolbar, click the Spelling button and complete the spelling check.

7. Display **Slide 3**. Point to the small bar between the **Slide** pane and the **Notes** pane until the pointer displays as an upward-pointing and a downward-pointing arrow. If necessary, press and hold down the left mouse button and drag upward slightly to expand the **Notes** pane to approximately one inch high. This should provide adequate space to type notes.

8. Click in the **Notes** pane and type **When a fire alarm is sounded, the elevators stop at the nearest floor. The elevator doors open and remain open so that the elevators cannot be used.**

(Project 1B–Safety continues on the next page)

(Project 1B–Safety continued)

9. In the **View** buttons at the lower left of your window, click the **Slide Sorter View** button to display all four slides. Click **Slide 3** to select it. Press and hold down the left mouse button, and then drag the pointer to the left so that the vertical bar displays to the left of **Slide 2**. Release the left mouse button to drop this slide into position as **Slide 2**.

10. Make sure that **Slide 2**, or any slide, is selected. On the menu bar, click **View**, and then click **Header and Footer**. Click the **Notes and Handouts tab**. If necessary, click to select the **Date and time** check box, and then click the **Update automatically** option button. This will display the current date on printed handouts or notes pages each time the presentation is opened. If necessary, click to select the **Footer** check box, and then in the **Footer** box, using your own first and last name, type **1B Safety-Firstname Lastname**

    If necessary, click to clear (remove the check mark from) the **Header** and **Page number** check boxes, and then click the **Apply to All** button.

11. On the menu bar, click **File**, and then click **Print**. In the displayed **Print** dialog box, click the **Print what arrow**, and then click **Handouts**. Under **Handouts**, click the **Slides per page arrow**, and then click **4**. Under **Handouts**, click the **Horizontal** order option button. Click the **Color/grayscale arrow**, and then click **Grayscale**. Check that the **Frame slides** check box is selected. Click **OK** to print a handout of all four slides on one page.

12. Display the **File** menu again, and then click **Print**. In the displayed **Print** dialog box, click the **Print what arrow**, and then click **Notes Pages**. Click the **Color/grayscale arrow**, and then click **Grayscale**. Under **Print range**, click the **Slides** option button. In the **Slides** box, type **2**

    This action instructs PowerPoint to print only the notes page for Slide 2. Click **OK**.

13. Click **Slide 1** to select it. Move to the **View** buttons at the lower left of your window, and then click the **Slide Show** button to begin viewing the presentation. Click the left mouse button to advance through the slides. Slide transitions (how each new slide displays) and animations (how various slide elements display) have been applied. When the black slide displays, click the left mouse button one more time to close the Slide Show view.

14. On the Standard toolbar, click **Save** to save the changes you have made to your presentation. On the menu bar, click **File**, and then click **Close**.

End You have completed Project 1B ────────────────────

Skill Assessments (continued)

Project 1C—Benefits

Objectives: *Start and Exit PowerPoint, Edit a Presentation Using the Outline/Slides Pane, Create Headers and Footers, and Print a Presentation.*

In the following Skill Assessment, you will edit a presentation concerning a new benefits program for City of Desert Park employees. Your completed presentation will look similar to the one shown in Figure 1.39. You will save your presentation as *1C_Benefits_Firstname_Lastname*.

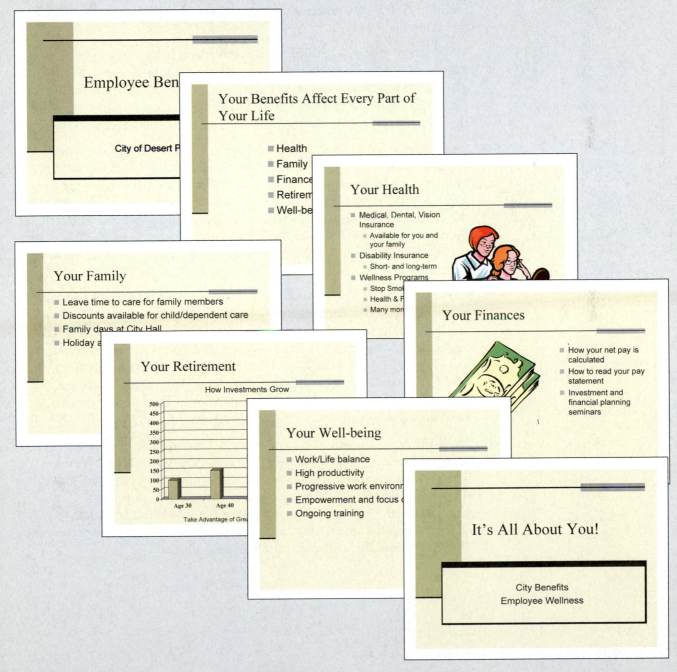

Figure 1.39

(Project 1C–Benefits continues on the next page)

(Project 1C–Benefits continued)

1. Start PowerPoint. On the Standard toolbar, click **Open**, and in the displayed **Open** dialog box, use the **Look in arrow** to navigate to the student files that accompany this textbook. Open the file **p01C_Benefits** by double-clicking it. Alternatively, click once to select the file name, and then click the Open button.

2. Display the **File** menu, click **Save As**, and then use the **Save in arrow** to navigate to the location where you are storing your projects for this chapter. In the **File name** box, type **1C_Benefits_Firstname_Lastname** and then click **Save**.

3. Move to the **Outline/Slides** pane, and then, if necessary, click the **Slides tab**. In the **Slides tab**, click to select **Slide 5**. Point to the selected slide, press and hold down the left mouse button, and then drag upward to position the gray bar between Slides 3 and 4. Release the left mouse button to drop the slide into the new location.

4. With **Slide 4** selected, display the **Format** menu, and click **Slide Layout**. Look at the slide in the **Slide** pane, and notice that the current layout includes a bulleted list on the left, and a placeholder to add a clip art picture on the right. In the **Slide Layout** task pane, point to the vertical scroll box, press and hold down the left mouse button, and then drag up to display the **Text Layouts**. Under **Text Layouts**, use the mouse pointer to display ScreenTips to locate the **Title and Text layout**, and then click to apply this layout to the displayed slide.

5. Close the **Slide Layout** task pane. Move to the **Outline/Slides** pane, and then click the **Outline tab**. On **Slide 3**, click anywhere in the second bullet *Available for you and your family*. On the Formatting toolbar, click **Increase Indent** so that this line is demoted to a lower level bullet under the first bulleted line. Click anywhere in the *Short- and long-term* bullet. On the Formatting toolbar, click **Increase Indent** so that this line is demoted to a lower level bullet under *Disability Insurance*.

6. On **Slide 3**, to the left of *Stop Smoking*, position the mouse pointer over the bullet character until the pointer becomes a four-headed arrow. Click to select the bullet and all of its text. Press and hold down [Shift] and then click the bullet to the left of *Many More!* This action selects the two selected lines and the line between for a total of three bulleted lines. On the Formatting toolbar, click **Increase Indent** to demote all three bullets at one time.

(Project 1C–Benefits continues on the next page)

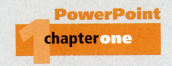

(Project 1C–Benefits continued)

7. Display the last slide—**Slide 7**. In the **Outline tab**, click anywhere in the text of the last bulleted item—*It's All About You!* On the Formatting toolbar, click **Decrease Indent** to promote the bulleted item to a new slide. **Slide 8** is created and the last bulleted item becomes the title of the slide. Press End to move the insertion point to the end of the slide title text, and then press Enter. Notice that a new slide is created. On the Formatting toolbar, click **Increase Indent** to demote by one level, creating the first bullet on **Slide 8**. Type the following two bullets by pressing Enter after the first line. Do *not* press Enter after the last line.

City Benefits

Employee Wellness

8. With **Slide 8** as the active slide, display the **Format** menu, and then click **Slide Layout**. In the **Slide Layout** task pane, under **Text Layouts**, click the first layout in the first row—**Title Slide**. In the **Slide** pane, notice that the text is converted to a title and a subtitle. Close the task pane.

9. From the **View** menu, click **Header and Footer**, and then click the **Notes and Handouts tab**. If necessary, select (click to place a check mark in) the **Date and time** check box, and then click the **Update automatically** option button to insert the current date each time notes pages or handouts are printed. Make sure the **Page number** check box is selected, and then clear the **Header** check box. If necessary, select the **Footer** check box, and then click in the **Footer** box. Type **1C Benefits-Firstname Lastname**

10. In the upper right corner of the **Header and Footer** dialog box, click **Apply to All**. Display the **File** menu, and then click **Print**. Click the **Print what arrow**, and then click **Handouts**. Under **Handouts**, click the **Slides per page arrow**, and then click **4**. Next to **Order**, click the **Horizontal** option button. Click the **Color/grayscale arrow**, and then click **Grayscale**. Make sure that the **Frame slides** check box is selected. Click **OK** to print two pages with four slides on each page.

11. On the Standard toolbar, click **Save** to save the changes to your presentation. On the menu bar, click **File**, and then click **Close**.

End You have completed Project 1C ——————————————

Project 1D — Flyer

Objectives: *Start and Exit PowerPoint, Format and Edit a Presentation Using the Slide Pane, View and Edit a Presentation in Slide Sorter View, Create Headers and Footers, and Print a Presentation.*

In the following Skill Assessment, you will edit a presentation to be used as a flyer concerning the City of Desert Park Employee Credit Union. Your completed presentation will look similar to the one shown in Figure 1.40. You will save your presentation as *1D_Flyer_Firstname_Lastname*.

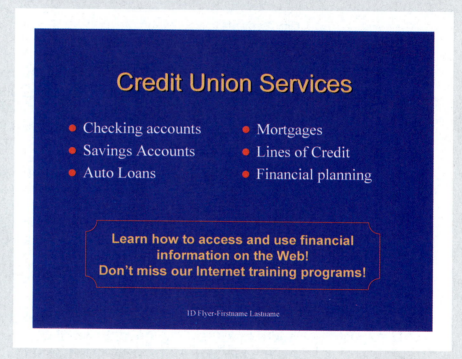

Figure 1.40

(Project 1D–Flyer continues on the next page)

(Project 1D–Flyer continued)

1. Start PowerPoint. From the **File** menu, click **Open**. On the displayed **Open** dialog box, click the **Look in arrow** and navigate to the location where the student files that accompany this textbook are stored. Double-click **p01D_Flyer**, or click once to select the file name and press ⏎.

2. Display the **File** menu, click **Save As**, and then use the **Save in arrow** to navigate to the location where you are storing your projects for this chapter. In the **File name** box, type **1D_Flyer_Firstname_Lastname** and then click **Save**.

3. In the lower left corner of your screen, click the **Slide Sorter View** button to display the three slides in the presentation in Slide Sorter view.

4. Click to select **Slide 1**. Press and hold down Shift and click **Slide 2**. Both Slides 1 and 2 are selected. Press Delete to delete both slides at the same time.

5. In the lower left corner of the screen, click the **Normal View** button. In the **Outline/Slides** pane, click the **Close** button so that only the **Slide** pane displays.

6. In the second column of bulleted items, drag to select the words *and Estate* in the last bulleted line. The placeholder is selected and the background color changes. Press Delete, and then click in the gray area surrounding the slide to deselect the placeholder.

7. On the menu bar, click **View**, and then click **Header and Footer**. In the displayed **Header and Footer** dialog box, click the **Slide tab**. In the **Slide tab**, click to select the **Footer** check box, and then click in the **Footer** box and type **1D Flyer-Firstname Lastname**

8. If necessary, clear any other check boxes in this dialog box. In the upper right corner, click **Apply to All**. Notice that the footer is placed on the slide.

9. This presentation is intended to be used as a flyer and should be printed as a full size slide. From the **File** menu, click **Print**. Click the **Color/grayscale arrow** and then click **Grayscale**. Click **OK**. One full-page copy of the slide prints in grayscale.

10. On the Standard toolbar, click the **Save** button to save your changes to the presentation. On the menu bar, click **File**, and then click **Close**.

End **You have completed Project 1D**

Performance Assessments

Project 1E — Budget

Objectives: *Start and Exit PowerPoint, Edit a Presentation Using the Outline/Slides Pane, Format and Edit a Presentation Using the Slide Pane, View and Edit a Presentation in Slide Sorter View, Create Headers and Footers, and Print a Presentation.*

In the following Performance Assessment, you will edit a presentation to be used by the City of Desert Park Finance Department concerning the City Budget. Your completed presentation will look similar to the one shown in Figure 1.41. You will save your presentation as *1E_Budget_Firstname_Lastname.*

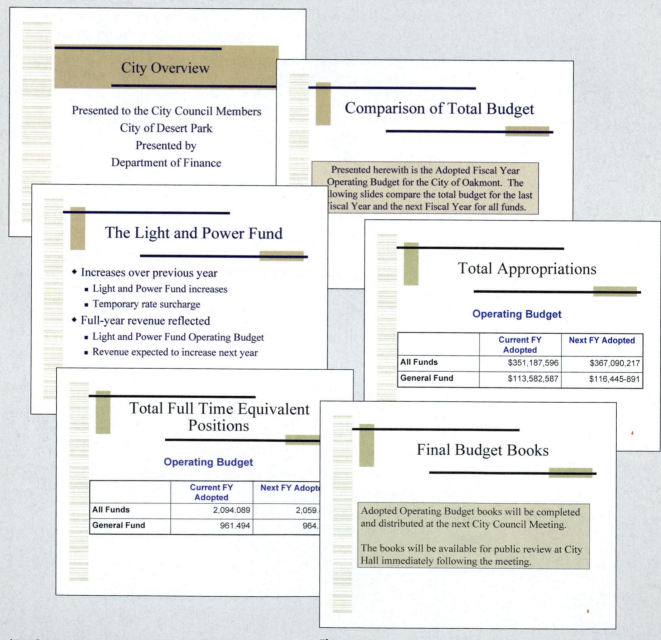

(Project 1E–Budget continues on the next page)

Figure 1.41

(Project 1E–Budget continued)

1. Start PowerPoint, navigate to the location where the student files for this textbook are stored, and open the file **p01E_Budget**. Display the **File** menu, click **Save As**, and then use the **Save in arrow** to navigate to the location where you are storing your projects for this chapter. In the **File name** box, type **1E_Budget_Firstname_Lastname**

2. Scroll through the slides to familiarize yourself with the presentation. As you make the editing changes to this presentation, you may work in either the **Outline/Slides** pane or the **Slide** pane. Choose the method with which you feel most comfortable.

3. On **Slide 1**, click after the words *Desert Park* and press Enter to start a new line. Type **Presented by**

4. Press Enter. Type **Department of Finance** and then display **Slide 4**. Click anywhere in the third bullet, and then click the **Increase Indent** button to demote the third bullet—*Temporary rate surcharge*—to a subordinate level under the first bullet. Click to position the insertion point at the end of the last bullet point in the slide, and press Enter to add a new bullet at the end of the slide. Type **Revenue expected to increase next year**

5. On **Slide 4**, increase the height of the **Notes** pane if necessary, and then type the following note:

   The Light and Power Fund is a temporary surcharge that is expected to continue for the next two fiscal years. The City Council will then vote to determine whether or not the surcharge continues to be in effect.

6. Display **Slide 1**, and then on the Standard toolbar, click **Spelling** to check the spelling of the entire presentation. (Hint: There are two misspelled words.) When the spelling check is complete, click **OK** to close the dialog box.

7. Using either the **Slides tab** or the **Slide Sorter View**, move **Slide 4** so that it becomes **Slide 3**. Then move **Slide 6** so that it becomes **Slide 5**.

8. Display the **Header and Footer** dialog box, and click the **Slide tab**. Add numbers to each slide by selecting the **Slide number** check box, and then clear all the other check boxes on this tab. Click **Apply to All**.

(Project 1E–Budget continues on the next page)

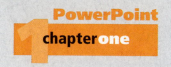

(Project 1E–Budget continued)

9. Display the **Header and Footer** dialog box again, and click the **Notes and Handouts tab**. On the **Notes and Handouts tab**, check that the **Footer** check box is selected, click in the **Footer** box, and then create a footer that will print on all the notes and handouts pages as follows: **1E Budget-Firstname Lastname**

10. Clear all the other check boxes on the **Notes and Handouts tab**, and then click the **Apply to All** button.

11. Display the **Print** dialog box. **Print** the presentation as **handouts**, **6** slides per page in **horizontal** order. Set the **Color/grayscale** to **Grayscale**, and if necessary, select the **Frame slides** check box. After printing the handout page, print in **grayscale** the **notes pages** for **Slide 3** only.

12. On the Standard toolbar, click the **Save** button to save the changes to your presentation. **Close** the presentation.

 End **You have completed Project 1E** ————————————————

Project 1F — Education

Objectives: *Start and Exit PowerPoint, Edit a Presentation Using the Outline/Slides Pane, Format and Edit a Presentation Using the Slide Pane, View a Slide Show, Create Headers and Footers, and Print a Presentation.*

In the following Performance Assessment, you will edit a presentation for a school district board meeting concerning Community Education Programs in the City of Desert Park. Your completed presentation will look similar to the one shown in Figure 1.42. You will save your presentation as *1F_Education_Firstname_Lastname.*

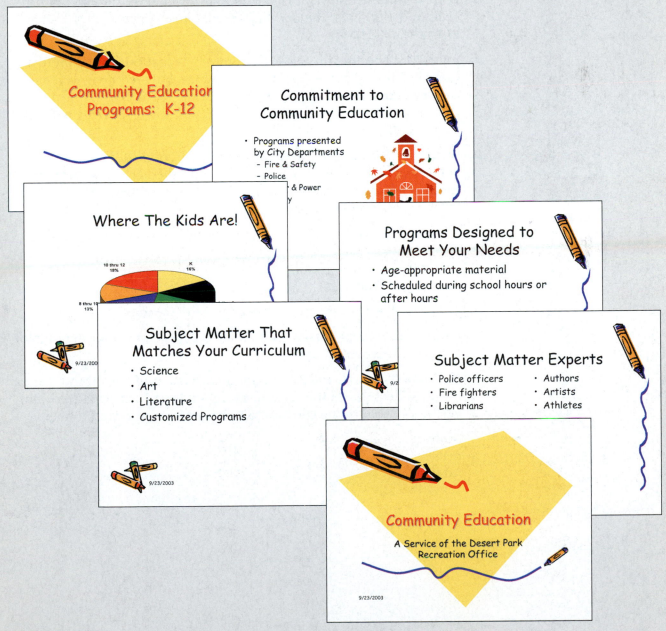

Figure 1.42

(Project 1F–Education continues on the next page)

(Project 1F–Education continued)

1. Start PowerPoint, and from your student files, open the file **p01F_Education**. Display the **File** menu, click **Save As**, and then use the **Save in arrow** to navigate to the location where you are storing your projects for this chapter. In the **File name** box, type **1F_Education_Firstname_Lastname**

2. Use the **Next Page** button to scroll through the slides. In the **Slide** pane, right-click on any misspelled words that are flagged with a wavy red line, and select the proper spelling. In the **Outline/Slides** pane, click to display the **Outline tab**.

3. Display **Slide 3** and notice that there is no title. In the **Slide** pane, click in the title placeholder and add the following title to the slide: **Where The Kids Are!**

4. In the **Outline tab**, on **Slide 4**, promote the last bulleted item to a new slide title. (Hint: Click anywhere in the bulleted item, and click **Decrease Indent**. This must be done in the Outline tab; the Decrease Indent button is not available when the insertion point is in the Slide pane.)

5. In the new **Slide 5**, in the **Outline tab**, click to position the insertion point after *Curriculum.* Press Enter once, and then click the **Increase Indent** button to create the first bulleted item in **Slide 5**. Add the following four bullets to the new slide:

   Science
   Art
   Literature
   Customized Programs

6. Add the following note in the **Notes** pane of **Slide 5**:

   Discuss the activities that the Community Education Outreach program offers in these subject areas.

7. On **Slide 6**, change the **Slide Layout** to **Title and 2–Column Text**. In the **Slide** pane, in the second column, type the following three bullets. Notice that in the **Outline tab**, the two columns are numbered.

   Authors
   Artists
   Athletes

(Project 1F–Education continues on the next page)

(Project 1F–Education continued)

8. In the **Outline tab**, on **Slide 6**, click at the end of the last bullet in the second column, and then press to create a bullet. Then click the **Decrease Indent** button to promote the bullet to a new slide—**Slide 7**. Type the title of the new slide as **Community Education**

9. Change the **Slide Layout** of **Slide 7** to **Title Slide**. Notice that the picture and formatting applied to the **Slide 1** title slide is also applied here. In the **Slide** pane, add the following subtitle: **A Service of the Desert Park Recreation Office**

10. Using the **Header and Footer** command, include on all **slides** the date so that it updates automatically; remove all other header and footer formatting from the slides. On the **Notes and Handouts**, include the **page number** and footer as follows: **1F Education-Firstname Lastname**

11. Clear all other header and footer options on the notes and handouts, and click **Apply to All**. Select **Slide 1**, and then view the presentation as a slide show. Notice that the current date displays on each slide. Slide transitions and animations have been applied.

12. Print the presentation as **handouts**, **4 per page** in **grayscale** and in **horizontal** order. Then, print the **notes page**, in **grayscale**, for **Slide 5** only. Save any changes to your presentation and then close the file.

End **You have completed Project 1F**

Project 1G — Internet

Objectives: *Start and Exit PowerPoint, Edit a Presentation Using the Outline/Slides Pane, Format and Edit a Presentation Using the Slide Pane, View and Edit a Presentation in Slide Sorter View, View a Slide Show, Create Headers and Footers, and Print a Presentation.*

In the following Performance Assessment, you will edit a presentation regarding Internet access at City Hall. Your completed presentation will look similar to the one shown in Figure 1.43. You will save your presentation as *1G_Internet_Firstname_Lastname.*

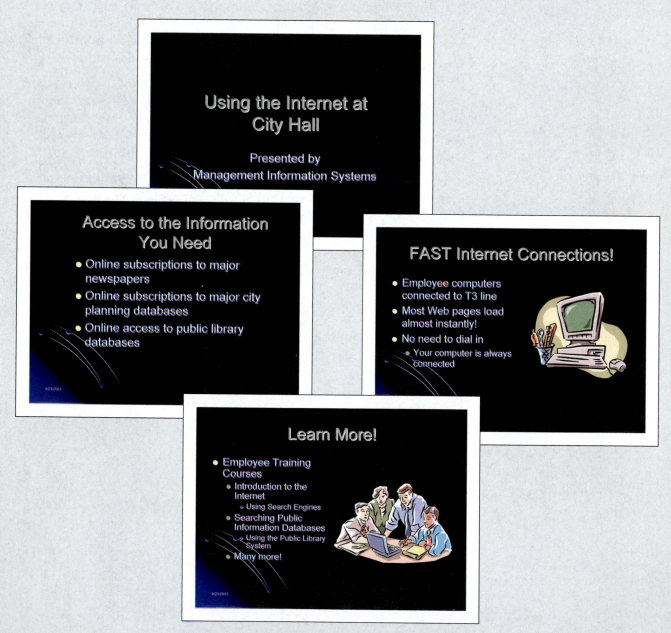

Figure 1.43

(**Project 1G**–Internet continues on the next page)

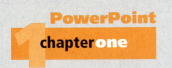

(Project 1G–Internet continued)

1. From your student files, open the file **p01G_Internet**. Display the **File** menu, click **Save As**, and then use the **Save in arrow** to navigate to the location where you are storing your projects for this chapter. In the **File name** box, type **1G_Internet_Firstname_Lastname**

2. Use the **Next Page** button or the vertical scroll bar in the **Slide** pane to scroll through the slides to familiarize yourself with the presentation. As you do so, correct any spelling errors.

3. Change the **Slide Layout** for **Slide 1** to **Title Slide**. Click in the subtitle placeholder and type:

   Presented by
   Management Information Systems

4. Close the **Slide Layout** task pane to maximize your viewing area. Display **Slide 2** and open the **Outline tab**. In the last bulleted item, click after the words *dial in* and then press Enter to create a new bullet. Delete the hyphen (-) and any unnecessary spaces. Capitalize the word *your* and then demote the text by one level.

5. Display **Slide 4**. Demote by one level the two bullets—*Using Search Engines* and *Using the Public Library System*. Promote by one level the last bullet—*Many more!*

6. Create a note for **Slide 4** using the following text: **Employees should call MIS for information regarding workshops.**

7. Switch to **Slide Sorter View**. Delete the last slide in the presentation, and then move **Slide 3** so that it becomes **Slide 2**.

8. Display the **Header and Footer** dialog box. On the **Slide tab**, add the **Date** so that it displays and updates automatically. Clear any other formatting on the slides, and apply to *all* slides. On the **Notes and Handouts**, create the footer **1G Internet-Firstname Lastname** and then *clear* all other header and footer options.

9. Click the **Save** button to save the changes you have made to your presentation.

10. Select **Slide 1** and run the slide show. Then, print the presentation as **handouts**, **4** per page in **horizontal** order. Use **grayscale** and **frame** the slides. Print the **notes page** for **Slide 4**. Close the file.

End You have completed Project 1G

Mastery Assessments

Project 1H — Housing

Objectives: *Start and Exit PowerPoint, Edit a Presentation Using the Outline/Slides Pane, Create Headers and Footers, and Print a Presentation.*

In the following Mastery Assessment, you will edit a presentation regarding access to affordable housing in the City of Desert Park. Your completed presentation will look similar to the one shown in Figure 1.44. You will save your presentation as *1H_Housing_Firstname_Lastname*.

Figure 1.44

(**Project 1H**–Housing continues on the next page)

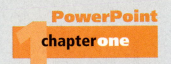
Mastery Assessments (continued)

(Project 1H–Housing continued)

1. From your student files, open the file **p01H_Housing**. Save the file as **1H_Housing_Firstname_Lastname** and then scroll through the slides to familiarize yourself with the presentation. As you do so, correct any spelling errors.

2. On **Slide 1**, apply the **Title Slide** layout. **On Slide 3**, demote the second bullet. In the **Outline tab**, promote the last bullet on **Slide 3** to a new slide, creating **Slide 4**. Using Figure 1.45 as a guide, create **Slide 4** by applying the appropriate slide layout (**Title and 2–Column Text**) and typing the text, demoting text as necessary.

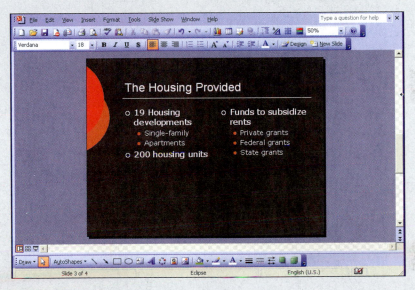

Figure 1.45

3. Move **Slide 2** so that it is the last slide, and then type the following speaker's notes on **Slide 4**:

    Members of the Board of Commissioners serve a three-year term with a maximum of three board members appointed in any given year.

4. Add the slide number to all of the slides, and remove any other slide headers or footers. On the **Notes and Handouts**, include only the date so that it updates automatically, and the footer **1H Housing-Firstname Lastname**

5. Print the presentation as **handouts**, **4** per page in **horizontal** order. Select **Grayscale** and **frame** the slides. Print the notes page for **Slide 4**. Save your changes and close the file.

End **You have completed Project 1H**

Project 1I — Membership

Objectives: *Start and Exit PowerPoint, Edit a Presentation Using the Outline/Slides Pane, Format and Edit a Presentation Using the Slide Pane, View a Slide Show, Create Headers and Footers, and Print a Presentation.*

In the following Mastery Assessment, you will edit a presentation regarding membership in the City of Desert Park Nature Center. Your completed presentation will look similar to the one shown in Figure 1.46. You will save your presentation as *1I_Membership_Firstname_Lastname.*

Figure 1.46

(Project 1I–Membership continues on the next page)

(Project 1I–Membership continued)

1. From your student files, open the file **p01I_Membership**. **Save** the presentation in your storage location as **1I_Membership_Firstname_ Lastname** On **Slide 1**, change the slide layout to **Title Slide**.

2. On **Slide 3**, demote the second bullet—*Parking is included* and then demote the last two bullets.

3. Display **Slide 5**. Change the slide layout to **Title** and **2–Column Text**. In the second column type the following, indenting the addresses so that the second column is formatted similar to the first column:

   Heron Crest Ranch
   4949 Heron Road
   Pine Creek Canyon
   558 Meadow Lane

4. **Delete Slide 4**. **Move Slide 3** so that it becomes **Slide 2**.

5. Add the **Slide number** to all of the slides, and remove any other header or footer formatting on the slides. Create a footer for the notes and handouts pages by typing **1I Membership-Firstname Lastname**. Remove any other header or footer formatting on the notes and handouts pages.

6. Display **Slide 1**, and then view the slide show. Slide transitions and animations have been applied. Print the presentation as **handouts**, **4** per page in **horizontal** order—use **grayscale** and frame the slides. Save your changes and close the file.

End **You have completed Project 1I** ────────────────────

Problem Solving

Project 1J — Park

Objectives: *Start and Exit PowerPoint, Edit a Presentation Using the Outline/Slides Pane, Format and Edit a Presentation Using the Slide Pane, View and Edit a Presentation in Slide Sorter View, Create Headers and Footers, and Print a Presentation.*

Create the content for a presentation regarding a new community park for the City of Desert Park. You will save your presentation as *1J_Park_Firstname_Lastname*.

1. Open the file **p01J_Park**. Save the presentation in your storage location as **1J_Park_Firstname_Lastname** and then notice that this presentation contains two slides—a title slide and a second slide with four bullets.

2. In the **Outline tab**, promote each of the bullets on the second slide to slide titles so that there are a total of six slides. Think about parks in your own community, and then develop at least three bullets for each slide based on the new slide title. The Web site for your local community might be a good source of ideas. Be sure to also develop content for the second slide—*The Westside Community*. Apply an appropriate slide layout to each slide.

3. Create speaker's notes for at least one slide in the presentation. Review the presentation and change the order of the slides if necessary. On the notes and handouts pages, create a footer with the file name and your name in the same manner as the other projects in this chapter.

4. Print notes pages and handouts, 6 slides per page. Save your changes and close the file.

 You have completed Project 1J ————————————————————

Project 1K — Traveling

Objectives: *Start and Exit PowerPoint, Edit a Presentation Using the Outline/Slides Pane, Format and Edit a Presentation Using the Slide Pane, View and Edit a Presentation in Slide Sorter View, View a Slide Show, Create Headers and Footers, and Print a Presentation.*

Create the content for a presentation regarding tips for parents traveling with children to the Grand Canyon. To create this presentation you will need to conduct research on the Grand Canyon to determine the types of activities that children would like. You should also gather information on traveling by car or train with children. You will save your presentation as *1K_Traveling_Firstname_Lastname*.

1. From your student files, open the file **p01K_Traveling**, and save it to your storage location as **1K_Traveling_Firstname_Lastname** This presentation contains a title slide. Create five additional slides based on your research. Your slides may include general information about the Grand Canyon, methods of travel, weather conditions at various times of the year, activities for children, and keeping children safe and occupied while traveling.

2. Change slide layout as necessary, and create notes for at least two slides in your presentation. Create appropriate footers on the slides and handouts, including your name and the filename on the handouts.

3. Save the changes to your presentation, and then print notes pages and handouts, 6 slides per page.

 End **You have completed Project 1K** ────────────────────

On the Internet

Preparing for Microsoft Certification

As you progress through this textbook you will learn the skills necessary to complete the Microsoft certification test for PowerPoint 2003. Access your Internet connection and go to the Microsoft certification Web site at **www.microsoft.com/traincert/mcp/officespecialist/requirements.asp** Navigate to the Microsoft PowerPoint objectives for the certification exam. Print the objectives for the Microsoft PowerPoint user certification and any other information about taking the test.

GO! with Help

Getting Help While You Work

The PowerPoint Help system is extensive and can help you as you work. In this exercise, you will view information about getting help as you work in PowerPoint.

1. Start PowerPoint. In the **Type a question for help** box, type **How can I get help while I work?**

2. In the displayed **Search Results** task pane, click the result—**About getting help while you work**. Maximize the displayed window, and below the Help toolbar, click **Show All**. Scroll through and read all the various ways you can get help while working in PowerPoint.

3. On the Help toolbar, click the **Print** button.

Task Guides

Each book in the *GO! Series* is designed to be kept beside your computer as a handy reference, even after you have completed all the activities. Any time you need to recall a sequence of steps or a shortcut needed to achieve a result, look up the general category in the alphabetized listing that follows and then find your task. To review how to perform a task, turn to the page number listed in the second column to locate the step-by-step exercise or other detailed description. Additional entries without page numbers describe tasks that are closely related to those presented in the chapters.

Word 2003

Word Task	Page	Mouse	Menu Bar	Shortcut Menu	Shortcut Keys
AutoComplete, use	84				Begin typing the first few letters of a month (or other AutoComplete text); when a ScreenTip displays, press Enter
Close, file	98	X on menu bar	File | Close		Ctrl + F4 or Ctrl + W
Close, header or footer	76	Close on Header and Footer toolbar. Double-click in text area of document			
Close, print preview	84	Close or X			
Create, new document	83	Start Word (opens blank document) on Standard toolbar. Click *Create a new document* in Getting Started task pane. Click *Blank document* in New Document task pane	File | New		Ctrl + N
Create, new folder	78	in Open or Save As dialog box			
Delete, text	89		Edit | Clear | Contents		Bksp or Delete
Display, ScreenTip	63	Point to a screen element			
Display, toolbar	54		View | Toolbars	Right-click any toolbar, click toolbar name	

Word Task	Page	Mouse	Menu Bar	Shortcut Menu	Shortcut Keys
Display/hide, task pane	59		View | Task Pane		Ctrl + F1
Document, create new	83	Start Word (opens blank (opens blank document) [icon] on Standard toolbar Click Create a new document in Getting Started task pane Click Blank document in New Document task pane	File | New		Ctrl + N
Document, save	78	[icon]	File | Save		Ctrl + S
Exit Word	81	[icon]	File | Exit		Alt + F4
File, close	98	[icon] on menu bar	File | Close		
Folder, create new	78	[icon] in Open or Save As dialog box			
Font, apply style	97	[B] [I] [U]	Format | Font, Font style	Right-click and then click Font	Ctrl + B or Ctrl + I or Ctrl + U
Font, change	94	Times New Roman [icon] on Formatting toolbar	Format | Font	Right-click and then click Font	
Font, change size	94	12 [icon] on Formatting toolbar	Format | Font, Size	Right-click and then click Font	
Formatting marks, display/hide	67	[¶] on Standard toolbar	Tools | Options | View tab, Formatting marks		
Header or footer, add to document	76	Double-click in a header or footer area on a page (only if header or footer is not empty)	View | Header and Footer; position insertion point in header or footer area and then enter text		
Header or footer, close and return to document	76	[Close] on Header and Footer toolbar Double-click in text area of document			
Header or footer, switch between	76	[icon] on Header and Footer toolbar			
Help, display in Word	101	[icon] on Standard toolbar Click the *Type a question for help* box; type text and press Enter	Help | Microsoft Office Word Help		F1

Word Task	Page	Mouse	Menu Bar	Shortcut Menu	Shortcut Keys
Help, hide Office Assistant	58		Help | Hide the Office Assistant	Right-click Office Assistant and then click Hide	
Help, show Office Assistant	101		Help | Show the Office Assistant		
Insert mode, toggle between overtype/ insert	90	Double-click OVR in status bar			[Ins]
Keyboard shortcut	59				Press and hold down the first key, such as [Ctrl], and then press the second key (if any), such as [F1]
Menu bar, use	59	Click menu name and then click a command			[Alt] + under-lined letter on menu and then underlined letter of command
Menu, display full	59	Double-click menu name in menu bar Wait a few seconds after displaying menu Click expand arrows at bottom of menu	Tools | Customize | Options tab, Always show full menus		
Menu, display full always	59		Tools | Customize | Options tab, Always show full menus	Right-click any toolbar and then click Customize; on Options tab, select Always show full menus	
Menu, use keyboard shortcut shown on menu	59				Press and hold down the first key, such as [Ctrl], and then press the second key (if any), such as [F1]
Navigate, down, a line at a time	63	[v] at the bottom of vertical scroll bar			[↓]
Navigate, up/down, screen at a time	63	Click in gray area above/ below scroll box on vertical scroll bar			[Page Up] [PageDown]
Navigate, to beginning of current line	66	Click at beginning of line			[Home]
Navigate, to beginning of document	66	Drag vertical scroll bar to top, click before first line			[Ctrl] + [Home]

Word Task	Page	Mouse	Menu Bar	Shortcut Menu	Shortcut Keys
Navigate, to beginning of next word	66	Click at beginning of next word			Ctrl + →
Navigate, to beginning of previous word	66	Click at beginning of previous word			Ctrl + ←
Navigate, to end of current line	66	Click at end of line			End
Navigate, to end of document	66	Drag vertical scroll bar to lower end, click after last line			Ctrl + End
Navigate, up a line at a time	63	at the top of the vertical scroll bar			↑
Normal view, display	68	in lower left corner of Word window	View | Normal		Alt + Ctrl + N
Open, existing document	58	on Standard toolbar **More** or document name in Getting Started task pane	File | Open File | document name at bottom of File menu		Ctrl + O
Outline view, display	68	in lower left corner of Word window	View | Outline		Alt + Ctrl + O
Page setup	84	Double-click left or right of ruler	File | Page Setup		
Print Layout view, display	68	in lower left corner of Word window	View | Print Layout		Alt + Ctrl + P
Print, document	81, 98	on Standard toolbar	File | Print		Ctrl + P
Print, preview	84	on Standard toolbar	File | Print Preview		Ctrl + F2
Reading Layout view, close	68	Close on Reading Layout toolbar			
Reading Layout view, display	68	in lower left corner of Word window Read on Standard toolbar	View | Reading Layout		
Save, document	84		File | Save		Ctrl + S
Save, document (new name, location, or type)	78		File | Save As		F12
ScreenTip, display	22	Point to a screen element			
Spelling and Grammar, check entire document	73	on Standard toolbar	Tools | Spelling and Grammar, then choose an action for each suggestion		F7

Word Task	Page	Mouse	Menu Bar	Shortcut Menu	Shortcut Keys
Spelling and Grammar, check individual errors	71			Right-click word or phrase with red or green wavy underline and then choose a suggested correction or other action	
Spelling and Grammar, turn on/off features	71		Tools | Options | Spelling & Grammar tab, then choose Check spelling as you type and/or Check grammar as you type		
Start Word	54	⊞ **start** on Windows task-bar and then locate and click Microsoft Office Word 2003	Start | All Programs | Microsoft Office | Microsoft Office Word 2003		
Task pane, display/hide	59		View | Task Pane		Ctrl + F1
Text, cancel selection	92	Click anywhere in document			
Text, change font	94	Times New Roman ▾ on Formatting toolbar	Format | Font	Right-click and then click Font	
Text, change font size	94	12 ▾ on Formatting toolbar	Format | Font	Right-click and then click Font	
Text, delete	89		Edit | Clear | Contents		Bksp or Delete
Text, enter	84	Click to place insertion point and then type text			
Text, new paragraph or blank line	84				Enter once or twice
Text, overtype/ insert	90	Double-click OVR in status bar, then type			Insert and then type
Text, select	92	Drag over text			Click at beginning, Shift + click at end of selection
Text, select consecutive lines	92				Shift + ↑ or ↓
Text, select consecutive paragraphs	92				Shift + Ctrl ↑ or ↓
Text, select entire document (including objects)	92	Triple-click ⬈ in selection bar	Edit | Select All		Ctrl + A
Text, select line	92	Click ⬈ next to line in selection bar			

Word Task	Page	Mouse	Menu Bar	Shortcut Menu	Shortcut Keys
Text, select one character at a time	92				Shift + → or ←
Text, select one word at a time	92				Shift + Ctrl + → or ←
Text, select paragraph	92	Triple-click in paragraph Double-click ⬚ in selection bar next to paragraph			
Text, select sentence	92				Ctrl + click sentence
Text, select word	92	Double-click word			
Toolbar, display	54		View | Toolbars	Right-click any toolbar, click toolbar name	
Toolbars, show on one or two rows	54	⬚ on Standard or Formatting toolbar, Show Buttons on One Row / Two Rows	Tools | Customize | Options tab, Show Standard and Formatting toolbars on two rows View | ToolbarsCustomize | Options tab, Show Standard and Formatting toolbars on two rows	Right-click any toolbar and then click Customize; on Options tab, select or clear Show Standard and Formatting toolbars on two rows	
View, Normal	68	⬚ in lower left corner of Word window	View | Normal		Alt + Ctrl + N
View, Outline	68	⬚ in lower left corner of Word window	View | Outline		Alt + Ctrl + O
View, Print Layout	68	⬚ in lower left corner of Word window	View | Print Layout		Alt + Ctrl + P
View, Reading Layout	68	⬚ in lower left corner of Word window ⬚ Read on Standard toolbar	View | Reading Layout		
View, Web Layout	68	⬚ in lower left corner of corner of Word window	View | Web Layout		
Web Layout view, display	68	⬚ in lower left corner of Word window	View | Web Layout		
Zoom, magnify or shrink the view of a document	69	100% ▾ arrow on Standard toolbar and then choose a display percentage Click in Zoom box 100% ▾ and then type a percentage	View | Zoom		
Zoom, maximum page width	69	100% ▾ arrow on Standard toolbar and then choose Page Width	View | Zoom, Page Width		

Excel 2003

Excel Task	Page	Mouse	Menu Bar	Shortcut Menu	Shortcut Keys
AutoComplete, use	172				Begin typing the first few letters; when a ScreenTip displays, press Enter
AutoSum, insert	185	Σ ▾ on Standard toolbar	Insert | Function | SUM		Alt + =
Cancel an entry	174, 177	✗ on Formula bar			Esc (entire entry) or Bksp (characters left of insertion point)
Chart, change value(s)	155	Edit value(s) in worksheet			
Clear, cell contents	180		Edit | Clear | Contents	Clear Contents	Del
Close, task pane	134, 166	✗ in task pane	View | Task Pane		Ctrl + F1
Close, workbook	162, 191	✗ on menu bar	File | Close		Ctrl + F4 or Ctrl + W
Create, new folder	162	🗀 in Open or Save As dialog box			
Create, new workbook	166	Start Excel (opens blank workbook) 🗋 on Standard toolbar Click Create a new workbook in Getting Started task pane Click Blank workbook in in New Workbook task pane	File | New		Ctrl + N
Date, enter in cell	175	Type date in allowed format, such as m/d/yy, and click another cell			Type date in allowed format, such as m/d/yy, and press Enter or Tab
Deselect, row or column	144	Click any cell			
Edit, data in cell	177	Double-click cell, type changes, ✓ in Formula bar			F2, type and use ←, →, Bksp, Del as needed, and then Enter

Excel Task	Page	Mouse	Menu Bar	Shortcut Menu	Shortcut Keys
Edit, overtype mode	177				`Ins`
Exit Excel	32	☒	File | Exit		`Alt` + `F4`
File name, view on taskbar	36	Point to taskbar button, view ScreenTip			
Formula, enter in cell	181	Type = followed by formula			
Formula, enter using point-and-click method	183	Type = and then click cells and type operators to enter formula			
Header/footer, create	157		View | Header and Footer, Custom Header or Custom Footer File | Page Setup | Header/Footer tab, Custom Header or Custom Footer		
Help, close window	191	☒ in Help window			
Help, display in Excel	191	⊙ on Standard toolbar Click the *Type a question for help* box; type text and press `Enter`	Help | Microsoft Excel Help		`F1`
Help, print help topic	191	🖨 in Help window		Print	`Ctrl` + `P` in Help window
Menus, display full	138	Double-click menu name in menu bar Wait a few seconds after displaying menu Click double arrows at bottom of menu	Tools | Customize | Options tab, Always show full menus		
Move active cell, down one cell	152	Click cell			`Enter`
Move active cell, down one full screen	152				`PgDn`
Move active cell, left one cell	152	Click cell			`Shift` + `Tab`
Move active cell, left one full screen	152				`Alt` + `Page Up`
Move active cell, left/right/up/down one cell	152	Click cell			`←` or `→` or `↑` or `↓`

Excel Task	Page	Mouse	Menu Bar	Shortcut Menu	Shortcut Keys
Move active cell, right one cell	152	Click cell			Tab
Move active cell, right one full screen	152				Alt + PgDn
Move active cell, to cell A1	152				Ctrl + Home
Move active cell, to column A of current row	152				Home
Move active cell, up one cell	152	Click cell			Shift + Enter
Move active cell, up one full screen	152				PgUp
Move active cell, use Name box	152	Click Name box (left of Formula bar); type cell reference, Enter			
Move to last cell of active area	152				Ctrl + End
Move, to another worksheet	154	Click sheet tab			
Number, enter in cell	174	Type number in cell, click another cell			Type number in cell, press Enter or Tab
Open, workbook	141	[icon] on Standard toolbar More or workbook name in Getting Started task pane	File | Open File | workbook name at bottom of File menu		Ctrl + O
Print, Preview	161	[icon] on Standard toolbar	File | Print Preview File | Print, click Preview button in the dialog box		
Print, worksheet(s)	161	[icon] on Standard toolbar	File | Print, Active sheet(s)		Ctrl + P
Redo	180	[icon] on Standard toolbar	Edit | Redo		Ctrl + Y
Save, new workbook	168	[icon]	File | Save As		Ctrl + S or F12
Save, workbook	168	[icon]	File | Save		Ctrl + S
Save, workbook (new name, location, or type)	162		File | Save As		F12

Excel Task	Page	Mouse	Menu Bar	Shortcut Menu	Shortcut Keys
Scroll, multiple columns to right/left	150	Click between scroll box and scroll arrow on horizontal scroll bar			
Scroll, multiple rows down/up	150	Click between scroll box and scroll arrow on vertical scroll bar			
Scroll, one column to right/left	150	Click right/left scroll arrow on horizontal scroll bar			
Scroll, one row down/up	150	Click down/up scroll arrow on vertical scroll bar			
Select, all cells	144	Click Select All button (where row and column headings intersect)			Ctrl + A
Select, nonadjacent cells	144				Click first cell, Ctrl + click remaining cells
Select, range (adjacent cells)	144	Click first cell, drag to last cell			Click first cell, Shift + click last cell
Select, row or column	144	Click row or column heading in worksheet frame			Shift + Spacebar (row); Ctrl + Spacebar (column)
Spelling check	189	[ABC icon] on Standard toolbar	Tools | Spelling		F7
Start Excel	134	[start icon] on Windows taskbar, and then locate and click Microsoft Office Excel 2003	Start | All Programs | Microsoft Office | Microsoft Office Excel 2003		
Text, enter in cell	169	Type in cell, click another cell			Type in cell, press Enter or Tab
Toolbar buttons, identify	138	Point to button, view ScreenTip			
Toolbars, show on one or two rows	138	[icon] on Standard or Formatting toolbar, Show Buttons on One Row / Two Rows	Tools | Customize | Options tab, Show Standard and Formatting toolbars on two rows View | Toolbars | Customize | Options tab, Show Standard and Formatting toolbars on two rows	Right-click any toolbar, and then click Customize; on Options tab, select or clear Show Standard and Formatting toolbars on two rows	
Undo	180	[undo icon] on Standard toolbar	Edit | Undo		Ctrl + Z
Workbook, close	162, 191	[X icon] on menu bar	File | Close		Ctrl + F4 or Ctrl + W

Excel Task	Page	Mouse	Menu Bar	Shortcut Menu	Shortcut Keys
Workbook, create new	166	Start Excel (opens blank workbook) on Standard toolbar Click Create a new workbook in Getting Started task pane Click Blank workbook in New Workbook task pane	File | New		Ctrl + N
Workbook, open	141	on Standard toolbar More or workbook name in Getting Started task pane	File | Open File | workbook name at bottom of File menu		Ctrl + O
Worksheet, rename	156	Double-click sheet tab, type new name		Right-click sheet tab, click Rename, type new name	
Worksheet, select all (group)	157	Click first sheet, hold down Shift and click last sheet		Right-click sheet tab, click Select All Sheets	
Worksheet, ungroup multiple worksheets	157	Click an inactive sheet tab		Right-click a grouped worksheet tab, click Ungroup Sheets	
Zoom	187	100% on Standard toolbar	View | Zoom		

Access 2003

Access Task	Page	Mouse	Menu Bar	Shortcut Menu	Shortcut Keys
Close, database	272	✖ in the Database window	File | Close		Ctrl + F4 or Ctrl + W
Close, Database window	241	✖ in Database window	File | Close		Ctrl + F4 or Ctrl + W
Close, query	238	✖ in query window	File | Close		Ctrl + F4 or Ctrl + W
Close, table	236	✖ in table window	File | Close		Ctrl + F4 or Ctrl + W
Create, new blank database	246	📄 then click Blank database in New File task pane	File | New		Ctrl + N
Create, table in Design view	247	On Objects bar, click Tables; double-click *Create table in Design view* or click [New], and then click Design View	Insert | Table, Design View	Right-click Create table in Design view command, and then click Open	
Data type, select	247	In Table Design view, click a field's Data Type column, and then select from drop-down list			
Database window, close	241	✖ in Database window			
Database window, restore	241	⬜			
Database, clear Read-only property	222		File | Properties (in My Computer); clear Read-only	In My Computer, right-click database file name, and then click Properties; clear Read-only	
Database, close	272	✖ in the Database window	File | Close		
Database, copy	222		Edit | Copy, and then Edit | Paste in same or other folder (in My Computer)	In My Computer, right-click database file name, and then click Copy; right-click in file name area of destination folder, and then click Paste	Ctrl + C and Ctrl + V
Database, create new (blank)	246	📄 and then click Blank database in New File task pane	File | New		Ctrl + N
Database, open existing	224	📂	File | Open		Ctrl + O

Access Task	Page	Mouse	Menu Bar	Shortcut Menu	Shortcut Keys
Database, rename	222		File | Rename (in My Computer)	In My Computer, right-click database file name, and then click Rename	
Delete, record	263	in Table Datasheet view	Edit | Delete Record, and then click Yes to confirm	Right-click selected record, and then click Delete Record	Delete
Delete, table field	267	In Table Design view, click record selector and then	Edit | Delete Rows Edit | Delete	Right-click a field name, and then click Delete Rows	Delete
Display, next record in form	239		Edit | Go To | Next		PageDown
Edit, record	262	In Table Datasheet view, click in a field, and then type			Delete or Bksp to delete text
Exit, Access	272	in the Access window	File | Exit		Alt + F4
Field, add to table	259	In Table Design view, , and then type field name Click in first field of next available row, and then type field name	Insert | Rows (Design view)	Right-click a field name or blank row, and then click Insert Rows	
Form, close	239	in form window	File | Close		Ctrl + F4 or Ctrl + W
Form, open in Form view	239	Click form name and then Double-click form name		Right-click form name, and then click Open	
Form, switch to Design view	239		View | Design View	Right-click form title bar, and then click Form Design	
Form, switch to Form view	239		View | Form View	Right-click form title bar, and then click Form View	
Go to, first field of first record in datasheet	271	Click in first field			Ctrl + Home
Go to, first record in datasheet	271		Edit | Go To | First		Ctrl + Page Up and then Ctrl + Home
Go to, last field of last record in datasheet	271	Click in last field			Ctrl + End
Go to, last record in datasheet	271		Edit | Go To | Last		Ctrl + PageDown and then Ctrl + End

Access Task	Page	Mouse	Menu Bar	Shortcut Menu	Shortcut Keys
Go to, next record in datasheet	270, 271	▶	Edit | Go To | Next		↓
Go to, previous record in datasheet	270, 271	◀	Edit | Go To | Previous		↑
Open, existing database	224	📂	File | Open		Ctrl + O
Open, form in Design view	239	Click form name and then Design		Right-click form name, and then click Design View	
Open, form in Form view	239	Click form name and then Open Double-click form name		Right-click form name, and then click Open	
Open, query in Datasheet view	238	Click query name and then Open Double-click query name		Right-click query name, and then click Open	
Open, query in Design view	238	Click query name and then Design and then click		Right-click query name, and then click Design View	
Open, report in Design view	241	Click report name and then Design		Right-click report name, and then click Design View	
Open, table in Datasheet view	232, 256	Click table name and then Open Double-click table name		Right-click table name, and then click Open	
Open, table in Design view	232	Click table name and then Design		Right-click table name, and then click Design View	
Page setup, check margins	260	In Print dialog box, click Setup	File | Page Setup		
Primary key, create	252	In Table Design view, click a field name, and then 🔑	Edit | Primary Key	Right-click a field name, and then click Primary Key	
Print, table	260	🖨 in Table Datasheet view	File | Print	Right-click table name, and then click Print	Ctrl + P
Print, landscape/ portrait orientation	260	In Print dialog box, click Properties, Layout tab, and then Landscape or Portrait	File | Properties | Layout tab, Landscape or Portrait		
Print, report	241	🖨 on Print Preview toolbar	File | Print	Right-click on report, and then click Report	Ctrl + P

Access Task	Page	Mouse	Menu Bar	Shortcut Menu	Shortcut Keys
Query, close	238	✖ in query window	File | Close		Ctrl + F4 or Ctrl + W
Query, open in Datasheet view	238	Click query name and then 📁Open Double-click query name		Right-click query name, and then click Open	
Query, open in Design view	238	Click query name and then 📐Design		Right-click query name, and then click Design View	
Query, switch to Datasheet view	238	▦▾ on Query Design toolbar	View | Datasheet View	Right-click query title bar, and then click Datasheet View	
Query, switch to Design view	238	📐▾	View | Design View	Right-click query title bar, and then click Query Design	
Record, add to table	254	In Table Datasheet view, ▶✶, and then type Click in first field of next available record, and then type Click in last field of last record, and then press Tab and type	Insert | New Record (Datasheet view)	Right-click selected record, and then click New Record	Ctrl + +
Record, delete	263	▶✖ in Table Datasheet view	Edit | Delete Record, and then click Yes to confirm	Right-click selected record, and then click Delete Record	Delete
Record, edit	262	In Table Datasheet view, click in a field, and then type			Delete or Bksp to delete text
Report, close	241	✖ in report window	File | Close		Ctrl + F4 or Ctrl + W
Report, maximize window	241	▭ , Double-click title bar			
Report, open in Design view	241	Click report name and then 📐Design		Right-click report name, and then click Design View	
Report, preview	241	Click report name, and then 🔍Preview or 🔍 Double-click report name		Right-click report name, and then click Print Preview	
Report, print	241	🖨 on Print Preview toolbar	File | Print	Right-click on report, and then click	Ctrl + P
Report, switch to Design view	241	📐▾	View | Design View	Right-click report title bar, and then click Report Design	
Report, switch to Print preview	241	🔍▾ or 🔍	View | Print Preview	Right-click report title bar, and then click Print Preview	

Access Task	Page	Mouse	Menu Bar	Shortcut Menu	Shortcut Keys
Report, zoom to size	241	Fit ▾ on Print Preview toolbar	View | Zoom	Right-click on report, and then choose zoom setting	
Resize, column	264	Drag vertical line between column headings left or right	Format | Column Width	Right-click column heading, and then click Column Width	
Resize, column to fit widest entry	264	Double-click vertical line between column headings at right of field	Format | Column Width, Best Fit	Right-click column heading, and then click Column Width; choose Best Fit	
Resize, multiple columns	264	Select multiple columns; drag vertical line between column headings left or right	Format | Column Width	Right-click column heading, and then click Column Width	
Resize, multiple row heights	264	Select multiple rows; drag horizontal line between row headings up or down	Format | Row Height	Right-click row heading, and then click Row Height	
Resize, row height	264	Drag horizontal line between row headings up or down	Format | Row Height	Right-click row heading, and then click Row Height	
Resize, row height to default	264		Format | Row Height, Standard Height	Right-click row heading, and then click Row Height; choose Standard Height	
Sort, records in ascending order	269	Select one or more adjacent columns, and then click [A↓Z]	Records | Sort | Sort Ascending	Right-click anywhere in selected column(s), and then click Sort Ascending	
Sort, records in descending order	269	Select one or more adjacent columns, and then click [Z↓A]	Records | Sort | Sort Descending	Right-click anywhere in selected column(s), and then click Sort Descending	
Start, Access	224	[start] on Windows taskbar, and then locate and click Microsoft Office Access 2003	Start | All Programs | Microsoft Office | Microsoft Office Access 2003		
Table, add field	259	In Table Design view, click [icon], and then type field name Click in first field of next available row, and then type field name	Insert | Rows (Design view)	Right-click a field name or blank row, and then click Insert Rows	
Table, add record	254	In Table Datasheet view, click [icon], and then type Click in first field of next available record, and then type Click in last field of last record, and then press [Tab] and type	Insert | New Record (Data-sheet view)	Right-click selected record, and then click New Record	[Ctrl] + [+]
Table, close	236	[X] in table window	File | Close		[Ctrl] + [F4] or [Ctrl] + [W]

Access Task	Page	Mouse	Menu Bar	Shortcut Menu	Shortcut Keys
Table, create in Design view	247	On Objects bar, click Tables; double-click Create table in Design view or click [New], and then click Design View	Insert | Table, Design View	Right-click Create table in Design view command, and then click Open	
Table, delete field	257	In Table Design view, click record selector and then [icon]	Edit | Delete Rows Edit | Delete (Design view)	Right-click a field name, and then click Delete Rows	[Delete]
Table, deselect	264	Click anywhere in the table			
Table, enter description for field	247	In Table Design view, click a field's Description column, and then type text			
Table, hide columns	267		Format | Hide Columns	Right-click column heading, and then click Hide Columns	
Table, move down one screen	271	Click below scroll box in vertical scroll bar			[PageDown]
Table, move to first field in datasheet	271	Click in first field			[Ctrl] + [Home]
Table, move to first record in datasheet	271	[|◄ icon]	Edit | Go To | First		[Ctrl] + [Page Up] and then [Ctrl] + [Home]
Table, move to last field in datasheet	271	Click in last field			[Ctrl] + [End]
Table, move to last record in datasheet	271	[►| icon]	Edit | Go To | Last		[Ctrl] + [PageDown] and then [Ctrl] + [End]
Table, move to next record in datasheet	270, 271	[► icon]	Edit | Go To | Next		[↓]
Table, move to previous record in datasheet	270, 271	[◄ icon]	Edit | Go To | Previous		[↑]
Table, move up one screen	271	Click above scroll box in vertical scroll bar			[Page Up]
Table, open in Datasheet view	232, 256	Click table name and then [Open] Double-click table name		Right-click table name, and then click Open	
Table, open in Design view	232	Click table name and then [Design]		Right-click table name, and then click Design View	

Access Task	Page	Mouse	Menu Bar	Shortcut Menu	Shortcut Keys
Table, print	260	🖨 in Table Datasheet view	File | Print	Right-click table name, and then click Print	Ctrl + PrtScr
Table, remove sort	269		Records | Remove Filter/Sort	Right-click anywhere in table, and then click Remove Filter/Sort	
Table, save design	251	💾 on Table Design toolbar Switch views, and then click Yes	File | Save		Ctrl + S
Table, select column	232	Click column heading			
Table, select data type	247	In Table Design view, click a field's Data Type column, and then select from drop-down list			
Table, select row	232	Click row selector			
Table, sort records in ascending order	269	Select one or more adjacent columns, and then click ⏏	Records | Sort | Sort Ascending	Right-click anywhere in selected column(s), and then click Sort Ascending	
Table, sort records in descending order	269	Select one or more adjacent columns, and then click ⏏	Records | Sort | Sort Descending	Right-click anywhere in selected column(s), and then click Sort Descending	
Table, switch to Datasheet view	236, 251	▦ ▾	View | Datasheet View	Right-click table title bar, and then click Datasheet View	
Table, switch to Design view	236	📐 ▾	View | Design View	Right-click table title bar, and then click Design View	
Table, unhide columns	267		Format | Unhide Columns, and then select boxes for columns to unhide	Right-click table title bar, and then click Unhide Columns	

PowerPoint 2003

PowerPoint Task	Page	Mouse	Menu Bar	Shortcut Menu	Shortcut Keys
Close, file (presentation)	315	☒	File	Close		Ctrl + F4 or Ctrl + W
Close, Outline/ Slides pane	322	☒ in Outline/ Slides pane			
Close, task pane	312	☒ in task pane	View	Task Pane		Ctrl + F1
Create, new folder	313	📁 in Save As or Open dialog box			
Date and time, add to slide(s)	335		View	Header and Footer	Slide tab, Date and time		
Delete, slide	321		Edit	Delete Slide	Right-click an icon in Outline/ Slides pane, and then click Delete Slide	Select slide, then press Delete
Delete, slide in Slide Sorter view	332		Edit	Delete Slide	Right-click slide icon, and then click Delete Slide	Select slide, then press Delete
Display, full menus	308		Tools	Customize	Options tab, Always show full menus		
Display, next slide (Normal view)	305	⬇ at bottom of Slide pane's vertical scroll bar Drag Slide pane's scroll box down until ScreenTip displays next slide			PageDown
Display, Normal view	316	▣ in lower-left corner of PowerPoint window	View	Normal		
Display, Outline tab	316	Click Outline tab			
Display, previous slide (Normal view)	305	⬆ at bottom of Slide pane's vertical scroll bar Drag Slide pane's scroll box up until ScreenTip displays next slide			Page Up
Display, Slide Sorter view	332	▦ in lower-left corner of PowerPoint window	View	Slide Sorter		
Display, task pane	305		View	Task Pane		
Display, toolbar	311		View	Toolbars	Right-click any toolbar, and then click toolbar name	
Exit PowerPoint	316	☒	File	Exit		Alt + F4

PowerPoint Task	Page	Mouse	Menu Bar	Shortcut Menu	Shortcut Keys
Folder, create new	313	in Save As or Open dialog box			
Footer, add to slide(s)	335		View | Header and Footer | Slide tab; select Footer, and then type text in box		
Handouts, print	338		File | Print, then in Print what list, choose Handouts		
Header or footer, add to notes or handouts	336		View | Header and Footer | Notes and Handouts tab, select Header or Footer, and then type text in box		
Header or footer, change date format	336		View | Header and Footer | choose tab, Date and time, then Update automatically; select a date format		
Help, display in PowerPoint	343	on Standard toolbar Click the *Type a question for help* box; type text and press Enter	Help | Microsoft PowerPoint Help		F1
Help, display Office Assistant	343		Help | Show the Office Assistant		
Menu commands, use	308	Point to menu, click command	Menu name | Command name		Press keys shown next to command on menu
Menu, display full	308	Double-click menu name in menu bar Wait a few seconds after displaying menu Click double arrows at bottom of menu	Tools | Customize | Options tab, Always show full menus		
Move, slide	322	In Slides tab or Slide Sorter view, drag slide to new position			
Normal view, display	316	in lower-left corner of PowerPoint window	View | Normal		
Normal view, display next slide	305	at bottom of Slide pane's vertical scroll bar Drag Slide pane's scroll box down until ScreenTip displays next slide			PageDown

PowerPoint Task	Page	Mouse	Menu Bar	Shortcut Menu	Shortcut Keys
Normal view, display previous slide	305	⬆ at bottom of Slide pane's vertical scroll bar Drag Slide pane's scroll box up until ScreenTip displays next slide			Page Up
Notes pane, resize	328	Drag pane separator bar up toward Slides pane			
Notes, enter speaker notes	328	Click in Notes pane, and then type text	View | Notes Page; type in notes box		
Open, presentation	302	📁 on Standard toolbar Click More or the presentation name in Getting Started task pane	File | Open File | presentation name at bottom of File menu		Ctrl + O
Outline tab, display	316	Click Outline tab			
Outline tab, select slide	316	Click slide icon			
Outline, enter text	316	In Outline tab, click to place insertion point, and then type			
Outline/Slides pane, close	322	✖ in Outline/Slides pane			
Print, grayscale	341		File | Print, then in Color/grayscale list, choose Grayscale		
Print, handouts	338		File | Print, then in Print what list, choose Handouts		
Print, notes pages	341		File | Print, then in Print what list, choose Notes Pages		
Print, presentation with current settings	338	🖨 on Standard toolbar	File | Print		Ctrl + P
Print, slides	338		File | Print, then in Print what list, choose Slides		
Save, file (new name, location, or type)	313		File | Save As		F12
Save, file (presentation)	313	💾 on Standard toolbar	File | Save		Ctrl + S
Slide Layout, apply	324	▼ in task pane, then click Slide Layout	Format | Slide Layout	Right-click in Slide pane or on an icon on the Slides tab; click Slide Layout	

PowerPoint Task	Page	Mouse	Menu Bar	Shortcut Menu	Shortcut Keys
Slide number, add to slide(s)	335		View | Header and Footer | Slide tab, Slide number		
Slide Show, activate starting with current slide	333	▣ in lower-left corner of PowerPoint window			`Shift` + `F5`
Slide Show, activate starting with first slide	333	▣ in lower-left corner of PowerPoint window	Slide Show | View Show View | Slide Show		`F5`
Slide Show, end	333			Right-click, then click End Show	`Esc`
Slide Sorter view, display	332	▦ in lower-left corner of PowerPoint window	View | Slide Sorter		
Slide, delete	321		Edit | Delete Slide	Right-click an icon in Outline/Slides pane, and then click Delete Slide	Select slide, then press `Delete`
Slide, delete in Slide Sorter view	332		Edit | Delete Slide	Right-click slide, and then click Delete Slide	Select slide, then press `Delete`
Slide, move	322	In Slides tab or Slide Sorter view, drag slide to new position			
Slides, print	338		File | Print, then in Print what list, choose Slides		
Slides, select multiple	330	Click slide, then press `Ctrl` and click additional slides			Select slide, then press `Ctrl` and select additional slides
Speaker notes, enter	328	Click in Notes pane, and then type text	View | Notes Page; type in notes box		
Spelling checker, enable feature	327		Tools | Options | Spelling and Style tab, Check spelling as you type		
Spelling, check	327	▣ on Standard toolbar	Tools | Spelling	Right-click word with red wavy line, and then click correct spelling	`F7`
Start PowerPoint	302	▣ start on Windows taskbar, then locate and click Microsoft Office PowerPoint 2003	Start | All Programs | Microsoft Office | Microsoft Office PowerPoint 2003		
Task pane, close	312	✕ in task pane	View | Task Pane		
Task pane, display	312	▾ in task pane	View | Task Pane		
Text, demote (increase indent)	319	▣ on Formatting toolbar			`Tab`

PowerPoint Task	Page	Mouse	Menu Bar	Shortcut Menu	Shortcut Keys
Text, enter	323	Click in placeholder, and then type text			
Text, enter in outline	316	In Outline tab, click to place insertion point, and then type text			
Text, promote (decrease indent)	319	on Formatting toolbar			Shift + Tab
Toolbar and View buttons, identify	305	Point to button, view ScreenTip			
Toolbar, display	311		View | Toolbars	Right-click any toolbar, and then click toolbar name	
Toolbars, show on one or two rows	311	on Standard or Formatting toolbar, Show Buttons on One Row / Two Rows	Tools | Customize | Options tab, Show Standard and Formatting toolbars on two rows View | Toolbars | Customize | Options tab, Show Standard and Formatting toolbars on two rows	Right-click any toolbar, then click Customize; on Options tab, select or clear Show Standard and Formatting toolbars on two rows	

Glossary

Active area The rectangle formed by all the rows and columns in a worksheet that contain or contained entries.

Active cell The cell in which the next keystroke or command will take place. A black border surrounds the cell when it is active.

Animation effects A command that introduces individual slide elements so that the slide can be displayed one element at a time.

Ascending order Sorts text alphabetically (A to Z) and sorts numbers from the lowest number to the highest number.

Asterisk The term used to refer to the * symbol.

AutoComplete An Excel feature that speeds your typing and lessens the likelihood of errors. If the first few characters you type in a cell match an existing entry in the column, Excel fills in the remaining characters for you.

AutoNumber A data type that assigns a number to each record as it is entered into the table.

AutoSum A function (predefined formula) that adds a series of cell values by selecting a range.

Black slide A slide that displays at the end of a slide presentation indicating the end of the slide show.

Bulleted levels Outline levels identified by a symbol.

CD-ROM Compact Disc-Read Only Memory. An optical storage device used to permanently store data and from which you can read and open files. Also referred to as a CD-R.

CD-RW A compact disc that can be used over and over again to read and save files.

Cell The intersection of a column and a row.

Cell address The intersecting column letter and row number of a cell.

Cell content Anything typed into a cell.

Cell reference The intersecting column letter and row number of a cell. Also referred to as a cell address.

Chart A visual representation of your data using graphics.

Column A vertical group of cells in a worksheet.

Column heading The heading that appears above the topmost cell in a column and that is identified by a unique letter.

Column selector In My Computer or Windows Explorer, the headings at the top of the list of files. These headings include Name, Size, Type, and Date Modified.

Constant value Numbers, text, dates, or times of day that are typed into a cell.

Criteria The conditions specified to Access so it can find matching fields and records.

Data Refers to facts about people, events, things, or ideas.

Data type The type of data that can be entered in a field: text, memo, number, date/time, currency, AutoNumber, Yes/No, OLE object, and hyperlink. Specifies how Access organizes and stores data in a field.

Database A collection of data related to a particular topic or purpose.

Database window The window from which all database objects can be manipulated or accessed. The Database window displays when a database is open.

Datasheet view The view in which the information in a table or query can be viewed and manipulated. Datasheet view displays all the records in a table in a format of columns (fields) and rows (records).

Demote A command that applies a lower outline level to text.

Descending order Sorts text in reverse alphabetic order (Z to A) and sorts numbers from the highest number to the lowest.

Deselect To cancel the selection of one or more cells.

Design The number and content of the fields in the table. Good design ensures that a database is easy to maintain.

Design view The view in which the structure of a table or query can be viewed and manipulated.

Desktop The basic screen from which Windows and applications are run. The desktop consists of program icons, a taskbar, a Start button, and a mouse pointer.

Dialog box A box that asks you to make a decision about an individual object or topic. Dialog boxes do not have Minimize buttons.

Double-click The action of clicking the left mouse button twice in rapid succession without moving the position of the mouse pointer

Drag Holding down the left mouse button and moving the mouse pointer over text to select it.

Edit The process of adding, deleting, or changing the contents of a document, worksheet, or slide.

Extracting Pulling out specific information from a database based on the specified criteria.

Field An individual item of information that describes a record and is the same type for all records in the table. In Access, fields are located in vertical columns.

File Work that you save and store on a drive, such as a Word document or a PowerPoint presentation.

File extension The three characters to the right of the period in a file name. Extensions tell the computer the program to use to open the file. File extensions can be displayed or hidden.

Fit An entire page of a report displays onscreen at one time, giving an overall view of what the printed pages will look like.

Floppy disk drive A removable storage device that holds a limited amount of information, usually used to back up or transport files.

Font A set of characters with the same design and shape.

Font styles Bold, italic, and underline used to enhance text.

Footer Area reserved at the bottom of each page for text and graphics that appear at the bottom of each page in a document or section of a document. Displays only in Print Preview or on the page when it is printed.

Form A database object used to enter, edit, and manipulate information in a table.

Format text The process of establishing the overall appearance of text in a document.

Formatting Changing the appearance of the text, layout, and design of a document.

Formatting marks Characters that display on the screen, but do not print, indicating where the Enter key, the Spacebar, and the Tab key were pressed. Also called nonprinting characters.

Formula An equation that you type into a cell and that acts as an instruction to Excel to perform mathematical operations (such as adding and subtracting) on data within a worksheet.

Function A predefined formula that performs calculations by using specific values, called arguments, in a particular order or structure.

Graphical user interface (GUI) A computer environment in which icons with pictures on them are used to issue computer commands rather than written word commands.

Hard disk drive Generally referred to as a hard drive, the main storage device on your computer. It stores the programs that run on your computer, as well as the files that you save.

Header Area reserved at the top of each page for text and graphics that appear at the top of each page in a document or section of a document. Displays only in Print Preview or when the page is printed.

Horizontal scroll bar The bar at the bottom of a window that enables you to move left and right to view information that extends beyond the left and right edges of the screen.

I-beam Pointer A mouse pointer that indicates that you are pointing to a text area in the Outline/Slides pane or in the Slide pane.

Icon A graphic representation; often a small image on a button that enables you to run a program or program function.

Information Data that has been organized in a useful manner.

Insert mode The mode in which text moves to the right to make space for new keystrokes.

Insertion point The blinking vertical bar that indicates where text or graphics will be inserted when you type.

Keyboard shortcut A combination of keys on the keyboard, usually using the [Ctrl] key or the [Alt] key, that provides a quick way to activate a command.

Landscape orientation Refers to the printed page layout when the page is wider than it is high.

Layout The placement and arrangement of the text and graphic elements on a slide.

Maximize To increase the size of a window to fill the screen.

Menu A list of commands within a category.

Menu bar The bar, just under the title bar, that contains command options. These commands are words, not icons.

Minimize To remove the window from the screen without closing it. Minimized windows can be reopened by clicking the associated button in the taskbar.

Mouse pointer The arrow, I-beam, or other symbol that shows the location or position of the mouse on your screen. Also called the pointer.

My Computer A window that gives you access to the files and folders on your computer.

Navigate 1. The act of moving from one point to another in a worksheet or between worksheets in the same workbook. 2. To move within a document.

Nonprinting characters Characters that display on the screen, but do not print, indicating where the Enter key, the Spacebar, and the Tab key were pressed. Also called formatting marks.

Notes pages Printouts that contain the slide image in the top half of the page and speaker's notes in the lower half of the page.

Object The primary component of an Access database, such as a table, form, query, or report.

Objects bar Located on the left side of the Database window and containsed the buttons to access the objects in the database.

Office Assistant An animated character that provides tips and access to Help.

Operating system A set of instructions that coordinates the activities of your computer. Microsoft Windows XP is an operating system.

Operator A symbol that represents a mathematical operation in a formula.

Option buttons The round buttons to the left of each magnification options in the Zoom dialog box.

Order of operations The mathematical rules for performing multiple calculations within a formula.

Overtype mode A mode for entering text in which existing text is replaced as you type.

Placeholder A slide element that reserves a portion of a slide and serves as a container for text, graphics, and other slide elements.

Point A measurement of the size of a font. There are 72 points in an inch, with 10–12 points being the most commonly used font size.

Pointer See mouse pointer.

Populate Fill a table with data.

Portrait orientation Refers to the printed page layout when the printed page is taller than it is high.

Presentation graphics software A program used to effectively present information to an audience.

Primary key One or more fields that uniquely identifies a record in a table.

Primary sort field The field that Access sorts by initially during a sort operation.

Promote A command that applies a higher outline level to selected text.

Pt. Abbreviation for *point* in terms of font size.

Query 1. A database object that locates information based on specified criteria so that the information can be viewed, changed, or analyzed in various ways. 2. A question formed in a manner that Access can interpret.

Quick Launch toolbar An area to the right of the Start button that contains shortcut icons for commonly used programs.

Range A group of adjacent cells.

Recognizer A purple dotted underscore beneath a date or address indicating that the information could be placed into another Microsoft Office application program such as Outlook.

Record All the items of information (fields) that pertain to one particular thing such as a customer, employee, or course. In Access, records are located in horizontal rows.

Recycle bin A storage area for files that have been deleted. Files can be recovered from the Recycle bin or permanently removed.

Report A database object that displays the fields and records from the table (or query) in an easy-to-read format suitable for printing or viewing on the screen.

Restore Return a window to the size it was before it was maximized, using the Restore Down button.

Right-alignment A cell format in which the data aligns with the right boundary of the cell.

Right-click The action of clicking the right mouse button, usually to display a shortcut menu.

Row A horizontal group of cells in a worksheet.

Row heading The heading that appears to the left of the leftmost cell in a row and that is identified by a unique number.

Row selector The small gray box at the left end of a row that, when clicked, selects all the cells in the row.

Sans serif font A font with no lines or extensions on the ends of characters; usually used for titles or headlines.

ScreenTip A small box, activated by holding the pointer over a button or other screen object, that displays its corresponding name and/or function.

Scroll The action of moving the workbook window either vertically (from top to bottom) or horizontally (from left to right) to bring different areas of the worksheet into view on your screen.

Scroll box The box in the vertical and horizontal scroll bars that can be dragged to reposition the document on the screen. The size of the scroll box also indicates the relative size of the document.

Secondary sort field The field that Access uses to sort records that have matching primary sort fields during a sort operation.

Selecting The process of highlighting, by dragging with your mouse, one or more cells so that the highlighted area can be edited, formatted, copied, or moved. Excel treats the selected area as a single unit; thus, you can make the same change or combination of changes to more than one cell at a time.

Selecting text Highlighting text so that it can be formatted, deleted, copied, or moved.

Serif font A font that contains extensions or lines on the ends of the characters; usually the easiest type of font to read for large blocks of text.

Sheet tab A label located at the lower border of the worksheet window. It identifies each worksheet in a workbook and is used to navigate between worksheets.

Shortcut menu A context-sensitive menu that offers a quick way to activate the most commonly used commands for a selected area. The menu is activated by placing the pointer over an object and clicking the right mouse button.

Slide handouts Printed images of more than one slide on a sheet of paper.

Slide icon An icon that displays next to the slide number in the Outline indicating the beginning of a new slide.

Sorting The process of rearranging records in a specific order. Records can be sorted either ascending or descending.

Start button The button on the left side of the taskbar that is used to start programs, change system settings, find Windows help, or shut down the computer.

Status bar The bar at the bottom of a window that gives additional information about the window. In PowerPoint, the status bar indicates the current and total number of slides in the presentation and the applied design template. In Word, the status bar provides information about the current state of what you are viewing in the window, including the page number, and whether overtype or track changes are on or off.

Submenu A second-level menu activated by selecting a menu option.

System tray A notification area on the right side of the taskbar that keeps you informed about processes that are occurring in the background, such as antivirus software, network connections, and other utility programs. It also displays the time.

Table The database object that stores the data in a database. Data is organized in a format of horizontal rows (records) and vertical columns (fields).

Task pane A pane that opens on the side of a window that is used to display commonly used tools.

Taskbar A bar, usually at the bottom of the screen, that contains the Start button, buttons representing open programs, and other buttons that will activate programs.

Thumbnails Miniature images of each slide.

Title bar The line at the top of a window that contains the name of the application and document, along with the Minimize, Maximize/Restore Down, and Close buttons.

Title slide The first slide in a presentation that frequently contains special formatting.

Toolbar A row of buttons that displays below the menu bar and provides a one-click method (using the left mouse button) to perform commonly used commands and tasks. These commands are buttons with icons, not words.

Transitions The way that a slide appears or disappears during an onscreen slide show.

Underlying formula The formula entered in a cell and visible only on the Formula Bar.

Value Numbers, text, dates, or times of day that are typed into a cell. Also referred to as a constant value.

Vertical scroll bar The bar at the right side of a window that enables you to move up and down to view information that extends beyond the top and bottom of the screen.

View A view is a way of looking at something for a specific purpose, such as Design view or Datasheet view.

Wildcard A character, such as an asterisk, that can be used to match any number of characters in a file search.

Window A box that displays information or a program, such as a letter, Excel, or a calculator. Windows usually consist of title bars, toolbars, menu bars, and status bars. A window will always have a Minimize button.

Word wrap Automatically moves text from the right edge of a paragraph to the beginning of the next line as necessary to fit within the margins.

Workbook An Excel file that contains one or more worksheets.

Worksheet A page formatted as a pattern of uniformly spaced horizontal and vertical lines.

Zoom An option to make the page view larger or smaller.

Index

selecting (Excel), 144
width, Access, 264–266
command characteristics, 62, 140, 310
command icons, Create table in Design view (Access), 248
commands
    Access
        File menu. See File menu commands
        Format menu. See Format menu commands
        Records menu, Remove Filter/Sort, 270
        accessing in menus, 59–63, 309–310
        displayed in task pane, 303
    Excel
        Edit menu. See Edit menu commands
        File menu. See File menu commands
        Tools menu. See Tools menu commands
    keyboard shortcuts. *See* keyboard shortcuts
    PowerPoint
        File menu. See File menu commands
        Format menu. See Format menu commands
        Insert menu. See Insert menu commands
        View menu. See View menu commands
    toolbar buttons. *See* toolbars
    unavailable menu
        commands, 310
    Windows XP
        All Programs, 12
        Compressed (zipped) Folder, 43
        New, 23
    Word
        current task, 57
        File menu. See File menu commands
        Tools menu. See Tools menu commands
        View menu. See View menu commands
compressing files, 4, 41–47
consecutive lines/paragraphs
    selecting, 94
constant value, cell content, 169
Contents pane, 22–23
    sorting files, 27
context-sensitive menus, 9, 24
Control Panel, Regional and Language Options, 176
copying. *See also* **moving**
    between applications, 22
    databases, 222
    files, 27–34
Create New Folder button
    Excel, 163
    PowerPoint, 314
    Word, 79

Create table in Design view command icon, 248
criteria, for record query, 239
Currency, data type, 254
Custom Footer button (Excel), 158, 170
Customize button (Windows XP), 11
Customize command (Tools menu)
    Access, 228
    Excel, 139
    Word, 60
Customize dialog box
    PowerPoint, 309
    Word, 60
customizing toolbars, 140
cut and paste
    moving files, 33–34
    text/data between applications, 22

D

data, 221
    locking in cells, 170–172
Data Type column, 249
data types (Access), 250
    AutoNumber, 253
    Currency, 254
    Number, 249
    Text, 249
Database toolbar (Access)
    in Access window, 225–226
    New button, 246
    Open button, 226
database wizard, 246
databases, 221
    closing, 272
    copying, 222
    creating, 245–247
    file extension, 222
    opening, 224–226, 228–229
    renaming, 222–223
    saving, 272
    viewing the window, 230–232
Datasheet view (Access)
    adding records, 251
    opening tables, 256
    viewing tables, 236–237
dates
    changing date format, 337
    typing into, worksheets, 175–176
Decrease Indent button (Formatting toolbar, PowerPoint), 320
defaults
    alignment, 170
    date format, 176
    PowerPoint, 317
Delete key, 89–90
Delete Record button (Access), 264
Delete Slide command (Edit menu, PowerPoint), 321
deleting
    fields, 257–259
    files, 27–34
        recovering deleted files, 34
        Recycle bin, 6
    records from tables, 264

slides
    Slide Sorter view, 332
    Slides tab, 321
    text, 89–90
demoting outline text, 319–321
descending order, 269
Description column, 250
deselecting
    columns, 148
    slides, 331
Design button (Access), 257
Design view (Access)
    creating a new table, 247–248
    opening a table, 256
    viewing a table, 236–237
desktop, 6–7
    viewing from Access, 230–231
diagonal sizing box, 143
dialog boxes, 62
    Access
        File New Database, 247
        Open, 228
        Page Setup, 262
        Print, 260, 275
        Properties, 223, 261
        Unhide Columns, 267
    Excel
        Font, 159
        Footer, 158–160
        Function, 137
        Insert Function, 185
        New Folder, 163
        Open, 141
        Options, 138, 172–173
        Page Setup, 158, 160, 170
        Print, 190
        Row Height, 266
        Save As, 162–164, 168–169
        Spelling, 189
        Zoom, 187–188
    PowerPoint
        Customize, Options tab, 309
        Header and Footer, 335–337
        New Folder, 314
        Open, 304, 316
        Options, Spelling and Style tab, 327
        Print, 339, 342
        Save As, 313
    Windows XP
        Compressed (zipped) Folder command, 43
        Extraction Wizard, 46–47
        password requests, 7
    Word
        Customize, 60
        Font, 97
        New Folder, 79
        Open, 58
        Options, 74
        Page Setup, 87–88
        Print, 81, 101
        Save As, 78–79, 88
        Spelling and Grammar, 73–74
dictionary
    adding names to, 190
    suggestions list, 74, 189